SOCIAL PROBLEMS 95/96

Twenty-Third Edition

Editor

Harold A. Widdison
Northern Arizona University

Harold A. Widdison, professor of sociology at Northern Arizona University in Flagstaff, holds degrees in Sociology and Business Administration from Brigham Young University and Case-Western Reserve University. Employed as an education specialist with the U.S. Atomic Energy Commission, he was awarded a Sustained Superior Performance Award. As a medical sociologist, Dr. Widdison is actively involved in his community with the local medical center's neonatal committee, a founding member of Compassionate Friends, a member of the board of directors of the Hozhoni Foundation for the mentally handicapped, and a consultant on death, dying, and bereavement.

Annual Editions
A Library of Information from the Public Press

Cover illustration by Mike Eagle

Dushkin Publishing Group/
Brown & Benchmark Publishers
Sluice Dock, Guilford, Connecticut 06437

The Annual Editions Series

Annual Editions is a series of over 65 volumes designed to provide the reader with convenient, low-cost access to a wide range of current, carefully selected articles from some of the most important magazines, newspapers, and journals published today. Annual Editions are updated on an annual basis through a continuous monitoring of over 300 periodical sources. All Annual Editions have a number of features designed to make them particularly useful, including topic guides, annotated tables of contents, unit overviews, and indexes. For the teacher using Annual Editions in the classroom, an Instructor's Resource Guide with test questions is available for each volume.

Printed on Recycled Paper

VOLUMES AVAILABLE

Africa
Aging
American Foreign Policy
American Government
American History, Pre-Civil War
American History, Post-Civil War
Anthropology
Archaeology
Biology
Biopsychology
Business Ethics
Canadian Politics
Child Growth and Development
China
Comparative Politics
Computers in Education
Computers in Business
Computers in Society
Criminal Justice
Developing World
Drugs, Society, and Behavior
Dying, Death, and Bereavement
Early Childhood Education
Economics
Educating Exceptional Children
Education
Educational Psychology
Environment
Geography
Global Issues
Health
Human Development
Human Resources
Human Sexuality
India and South Asia
International Business
Japan and the Pacific Rim
Latin America
Life Management
Macroeconomics
Management
Marketing
Marriage and Family
Mass Media
Microeconomics
Middle East and the Islamic World
Money and Banking
Multicultural Education
Nutrition
Personal Growth and Behavior
Physical Anthropology
Psychology
Public Administration
Race and Ethnic Relations
Russia, the Eurasian Republics, and Central/Eastern Europe
Social Problems
Sociology
State and Local Government
Urban Society
Violence and Terrorism
Western Civilization, Pre-Reformation
Western Civilization, Post-Reformation
Western Europe
World History, Pre-Modern
World History, Modern
World Politics

Cataloging in Publication Data
Main entry under title: Annual Editions: Social problems. 1995/96.
   1. United States—Social conditions—1960.—Periodicals. I. Widdison, Harold A., *comp.*
II. Title: Social problems.
309′.1′73′092′05   73–78577   ISBN 1–56134–370–6
HN51.A78

Twenty-Third Edition

Printed in the United States of America

o the Reader

In publishing ANNUAL EDITIONS we recognize the enormous role played by the magazines, newspapers, and journals of the *public press* in providing current, first-rate educational information in a broad spectrum of interest areas. Within the articles, the best scientists, practitioners, researchers, and commentators draw issues into new perspective as accepted theories and viewpoints are called into account by new events, recent discoveries change old facts, and fresh debate breaks out over important controversies.

Many of the articles resulting from this enormous editorial effort are appropriate for students, researchers, and professionals seeking accurate, current material to help bridge the gap between principles and theories and the real world. These articles, however, become more useful for study when those of lasting value are carefully *collected, organized, indexed,* and *reproduced* in a *low-cost format,* which provides easy and permanent access when the material is needed. That is the role played by *Annual Editions.* Under the direction of each volume's *Editor,* who is an expert in the subject area, and with the guidance of an *Advisory Board,* we seek each year to provide in each *ANNUAL EDITION* a current, well-balanced, carefully selected collection of the best of the public press for your study and enjoyment. We think you'll find this volume useful, and we hope you'll take a moment to let us know what you think.

Welcome to *Annual Editions: Social Problems 95/96.* When Democrat Bill Clinton was elected president in 1992 he expressed great optimism for social reform, based on what appeared to be an end to political deadlock. His campaign promises to eliminate welfare as we know it, to reinvent government, and to provide health care for every American has been much more difficult to achieve than he had envisioned. During the first two years of Clinton's presidency, both houses of Congress composed a Democratic majority, which, many believed, should have enabled him to make major changes in the way things had been done in the past. However, significant numbers of his own party apparently did not share his vision of what the future could and should be. At the conclusion of 1994, Congress shifted to a Republican majority, all but dashing the president's original hopes for an executive-legislative alliance. President Clinton, to achieve at least some of his campaign objectives, has been forced to reevaluate his strategies and goals. This edition of *Annual Editions: Social Problems* has been revised to reflect what has been occurring throughout the Clinton presidency.

The editor reviewed hundreds of articles for this edition. Due in part to a preoccupation of many authors with the political struggles going on between President Clinton and Congress over welfare and health care reform, current, informative, well-written articles on all areas included in the last edition were difficult to find for this edition. As a result some sections are shorter than desired, other sections were combined, and a new section on cities was created. The editor was faced with a dearth of information in some areas and a superabundance of high-quality information in others. To make room for new materials, some excellent articles that had become dated had to be deleted.

This edition begins with two articles examining various theories of social problems. Following this introductory section are eight units. Unit 1 clusters articles concerning the basic unit of society—the family—including the changes it is experiencing and the implications of these changes for society. Articles in the second unit examine the causes and impact of crime, delinquency, and violence in American society and what, if anything, can be done to control them. Unit 3 is a combination of articles dealing with the problems of the aged and health care. Unit 4 examines issues, trends, and public policies impacting on poverty and inequality. Unit 5 looks at the implications of existing immigration policies and the utility of or dysfunctions of cultural pluralism. Unit 6 is new and explores the problems facing cities and those who must live in them. Unit 7 examines sex and gender issues and the growing problems associated with drug abuse. The final unit examines global issues that transcend national geographic boundaries.

To assist the reader in identifying specific topics or issues covered in the various articles, we have created a *topic guide.* This guide lists various topics in alphabetical order and the articles in which they are discussed. A reader doing research on a specific topic is advised to check this guide first.

Most of the authors of the articles express serious concern about the troubled state of America's cities, families, economy, and deteriorating position as a world power, as well as concern about the conditions of Earth's environment, but they have not given up. Most suggest strategies to save the family, reduce crime, make cities safer, and improve the environment.

If you have suggestions for articles or topics to be included in future editions of this series, please write and share them. You are also invited to use the form provided on the last page of this book for rating the articles.

Harold A. Widdison
Editor

Introduction

Two introductory articles summarize the three major theoretical approaches to studying social problems: symbolic interactionism, functionalism, and conflict.

Unit 1

Parenting and Family Issues

Five selections examine how the socially stabilizing force of the family has been assaulted by the dynamics of economic pressure, unemployment, and homelessness.

The concepts in bold italics are developed in the article. For further expansion please refer to the Topic Guide and the Index.

Unit 2

Crime, Delinquency, and Violence

Seven articles discuss the extent and significance of crime and delinquency in today's society.

The concepts in bold italics are developed in the article. For further expansion please refer to the Topic Guide and the Index.

Unit 3

Aging, Health, and Health Care Issues

Seven articles discuss aging, health, and health care issues.

The concepts in bold italics are developed in the article. For further expansion please refer to the Topic Guide and the Index.

The concepts in bold italics are developed in the article. For further expansion please refer to the Topic Guide and the Index.

Unit 5

Cultural Pluralism: Race and Ethnic Relations

Three selections discuss various aspects of cultural pluralism: that it has been minimized, that diverse differences promote unity, and that diversity is the sign of social maturity.

Unit 6

Cities, Urban Growth, and the Quality of Life

Four articles examine the current state of cities in the United States and various other countries.

The concepts in bold italics are developed in the article. For further expansion please refer to the Topic Guide and the Index.

Unit 7

Drug and Sexual Issues

Four selections examine the dynamics of social control of the private lives of a society's citizens.

Unit 8

Global Issues

Five articles discuss common human social problems faced by people worldwide. Topics include the environment, inflation, and cultural misunderstanding.

The concepts in bold italics are developed in the article. For further expansion please refer to the Topic Guide and the Index.

Ch. 9 · 17, 18, 19, 21

Ch 10   20

Ch. 11   15, 16

Ch. 12   3, 4, 5, 6

Ch 15   38, 41, 42

The concepts in bold italics are developed in the article. For further expansion please refer to the Topic Guide and the Index.

opic Guide

This topic guide suggests how the selections in this book relate to topics of traditional concern to students and professionals involved with the study of social problems. It is useful for locating articles that relate to each other for reading and research. The guide is arranged alphabetically according to topic. Articles may, of course, treat topics that do not appear in the topic guide. In turn, entries in the topic guide do not necessarily constitute a comprehensive listing of all the contents of each selection.

TOPIC AREA	TREATED IN:	TOPIC AREA	TREATED IN:
Abortion	35. Truth and Consequences: Teen Sex	Drinking	2. How Social Problems Are Born
Abuse	6. Why Leave Children with Bad Parents?	Drugs	2. How Social Problems Are Born 5. Disease Is Adolescence 9. Ethics, Neurochemistry, and Violence Control 36. Society of Suspects
Adolescence	5. Disease Is Adolescence		
African Americans	4. Endangered Family 27. American Melting Plot 29. Is White Racism the Problem?	Economy	4. Endangered Family 19. Confronting the AIDS Pandemic 26. When Problems Outrun Policy 33. Terminal Decline of a Nation 39. Mirage of Sustainable Development
Aging/Elderly	15. Old Money 16. New Face of Aging		
Aid to Families with Dependent Children (AFDC)	23. Does Welfare Bring More Babies?	Education	27. American Melting Plot 28. America: Still a Melting Pot? 33. Terminal Decline of a Nation 34. Off Course
AIDS	29. Confronting the AIDS Pandemic 35. Truth and Consequences: Teen Sex	Employment	33. Terminal Decline of a Nation 37. Separating the Sisters
Alienation	40. West's Deepening Cultural Crisis	Energy	41. Decade of Discontinuity
American Medical Association	21. Who's Protecting Bad Doctors?	Environment	18. Deadly Migration 38. Rape of the Oceans 39. Mirage of Sustainable Development 41. Decade of Discontinuity
Asians	27. American Melting Plot		
Business/Industry	15. Old Money 17. Risky Business 18. Deadly Migration 38. Rape of the Oceans	Ethics	9. Ethics, Neurochemistry, and Violence Control
		Family	3. Fount of Virtue, Spring of Wealth 4. Endangered Family 5. Disease Is Adolescence 6. Why Leave Children with Bad Parents? 9. Ethics, Neurochemistry, and Violence Control 22. Old Traps, New Twists 24. Going Private
Children	5. Disease Is Adolescence 6. Why Leave Children with Bad Parents? 11. Danger in the Safety Zone 12. Honey, I Warped the Kids 14. Global Crime Wave 22. Old Traps, New Twists 23. Does Welfare Bring More Babies?		
Cities	30. Can We Stop the Decline of Our Cities? 32. Cities of Violence	Fathering	4. Endangered Family
		Feminism	34. Off Course 37. Separating the Sisters 42. Crowded Out
Civil Liberties	36. Society of Suspects		
Conservation	18. Deadly Migration 38. Rape of the Oceans	Foreign Policy	19. Confronting the AIDS Pandemic 28. America: Still a Melting Pot? 38. Rape of the Oceans
Crime and Delinquency	7. New Outlaws 8. Getting Serious about Crime 10. Crime Takes on a Feminine Face 11. Danger in the Safety Zone 13. Economics of Crime 14. Global Crime Wave 25. No Exit 32. Cities of Violence 36. Society of Suspects	Future	16. New Face of Aging 27. American Melting Plot 39. Mirage of Sustainable Development 40. West's Deepening Cultural Crisis 41. Decade of Discontinuity
		Guns	1. Social Problems 2. How Social Problems Are Born
Democracy	32. Cities of Violence		

Introduction

Before initiating any analysis of social problems, it is always useful to agree on what it is that is being talked about. Things that are symbolic or seem to represent a serious social problem to one group might be seen by others as a symptom of a much larger problem, or even as no problem at all.

Two articles are included in this section that explore the complexities of social problems. While some individuals take a very simplistic black-and-white approach in defining social problems and, in turn, what must be done to eliminate them, sociologists realize how complex and intertwined social problems are in all aspects of social life. But even sociologists do not agree as to the best approach to take in the study of social issues.

The authors in the first article introduce the reader to sociology's three dominant theoretical positions and give examples of how those espousing each theory would look at specific issues. The three theories—symbolic interactionism, functionalism, and conflict—represent three radically different approaches to the study of social problems and their implications for individuals and societies. The perceived etiology of problems and their possible resolutions reflect the specific orientations of those studying them. As you peruse the subsequent articles, try to determine which of the three theoretical positions the various authors seem to be utilizing. The authors conclude this article by suggesting several approaches students may wish to consider in defining conditions as "social" problems and how they can and should be analyzed.

The second article in this section explores how social problems are born, that is, why some issues, actions, or behaviors become defined as significant social problems while others do not. This author believes that the logic underlying symbolic language is the critical factor in determining if an individual concern will eventually evolve into a societal-level social problem.

The editor felt it desirable to introduce this book of readings with a discussion of this type in order to help readers understand the social and sociological aspects of problems and issues plaguing modern society. The other 40 articles included in this edition range from what it is like to survive on the inhospitable streets of a large city to the pending destruction of the world's environment. The reader should ask why the issue addressed in each article is a social problem. Is it a case of rights in conflict, a case of conflicting values, or a consequence of conflicting harms? To find out, the reader might first skim over each article to get a general idea of where the author is coming from—that is, the author's theoretical position—and then reread the article to see just what the author indicates as the cause of the problem and what can or should be done to resolve or eliminate it.

SOCIAL PROBLEMS:

Definitions, Theories, and Analysis

Harold A. Widdison and H. Richard Delaney

INTRODUCTION AND OVERVIEW

When asked, "What are the major social problems facing humanity today?" college students' responses tend to mirror those highlighted by the mass media—particularly AIDS, child abuse, poverty, war, famine, racism, sexism, crime, riots, the state of the economy, the environment, abortion, euthanasia, homosexuality, and affirmative action. These are all valid subjects for study in a social problems class, but some give rise to very great differences of opinion and even controversy. Dr. Jack Kevorkian in Michigan and his killing machine is one example that comes to mind. To some he evokes images of Nazi Germany with its policy of murdering the infirm and helpless. Others see Kevorkian's work as a merciful alternative to the slow and agonizing death of individuals with terminal illnesses. In the latter light, Kevorkian is not symbolic of a potentially devastating social issue, but of a solution to an escalating social problem.

The same controversy exists at the other end of life—specifically, what obligations do pregnant women have to themselves as opposed to the unborn? Some individuals see abortion as a solution to the problems of population, child abuse, disruption of careers, dangers to the physical and emotional health of women, as well as the prevention of the birth of damaged fetuses, and they regard it as a right to self-determination. Others look at abortion as attacking the sanctity of life, abrogating the rights of a whole category of people, and violating every sense of moral and ethical responsibility.

Affirmative action is another issue that can be viewed as both a problem and a solution. As a solution, affirmative action attempts to reverse the effects of hundreds of years of discrimination. Doors that have been closed to specific categories of people for many generations are, it is hoped, forced open; individuals, regardless of race, ethnicity, and gender, are able to get into professional schools, and secure good jobs, with the assurance of promotion. On the other hand, affirmative action forces employers, recruiting officers, and housing officials to give certain categories of individuals a preferred status. While affirmative action is promoted by some as a necessary policy to compensate for centuries of exclusion and discrimination, others claim that it is discrimination simply disguised under a new label but with different groups being discriminated against. If race, sex, age, ethnicity, or any other characteristic other than merit is used as the primary criterion for selection or promotion, then discrimination is occurring. Discrimination hurts both sides. William Wilson, an African American social scientist, argues that it is very damaging to the self-esteem of black individuals to know that the primary reason they were hired was to fill quotas.

Both sides to the debate of whether these issues themselves reflect a social problem or are solutions to a larger societal problem have valid facts and use societal-level values to support their claims. Robin William Jr. in 1970 identified a list of 15 dominant value orientations that represent the concept of the good life to many Americans:

1. Achievement and success as major personal goals.
2. Activity and work favored above leisure and laziness.
3. Moral orientation—that is, absolute judgments of good/bad, right/wrong.
4. Humanitarian motives as shown in charity and crisis aid.
5. Efficiency and practicality: a preference for the quickest and shortest way to achieve a goal at the least cost.
6. Process and progress: a belief that technology can solve all problems and that the future will be better than the past.
7. Material comfort as the "American dream."
8. Equality as an abstract ideal.
9. Freedom as a person's right against the state.
10. External conformity: the ideal of going along, joining, and not rocking the boat.
11. Science and rationality as the means of mastering the environment and securing more material comforts.
12. Nationalism: a belief that American values and institutions represent the best on earth.
13. Democracy based on personal equality and freedom.
14. Individualism, emphasizing personal rights and responsibilities.

15. Racism and group-superiority themes that periodically lead to prejudice and discrimination against those who are racially, religiously, and culturally different from the white northern Europeans who first settled the continent.

This list combines some political, economic, and personal traits that actually conflict with one another. This coexistence of opposing values helps explain why individuals hold contradictory views of the same behavior and why some issues generate such intensity of feelings. It is the intent of this article and the readings included in this book to attempt to help students see the complex nature of a social problem and the impact that various values, beliefs, and actions can have on them.

In the next segment of this article, the authors will look at specific examples of values in conflict and the problems created by this conflict. Subsequently the authors will look at the three major theoretical positions that sociologists use to study social problems. The article will conclude with an examination of various strategies and techniques used to identify, understand, and resolve various types of social problems and their implications for those involved.

As noted above, contemporary American society is typified by values that both complement and contradict each other. For example, the capitalistic free enterprise system of the United States stresses rugged individualism, self-actualization, individual rights, and self expression. This economic philosophy meshes well with Christian theology, particularly that typified by many Protestant denominations. This fact was the basis of German sociologist Max Weber's "The Protestant Ethic and The Spirit of Capitalism" (1864). He showed that the concepts of grace (salvation is a gift—not something you can earn), predestination (the fact that some people have this gift while others do not), and a desire to know if the individual has grace gave rise to a new idea of what constitutes success. Whereas, with the communitarian emphasis of Catholicism where material success was seen as leading to selfishness and spiritual condemnation, Protestantism viewed material success as a sign of grace. In addition, it was each individual's efforts that resulted in both the economic success and the spiritual salvation of the individual. This religious philosophy also implied that the poor are poor because they lack the proper motivation, values, and beliefs (what is known as the "culture of poverty") and are therefore reaping the results of their own inadequacies. Attempts to reduce poverty have frequently included taking children from "impoverished" cultural environments and placing them in "enriched" environments to minimize the potentially negative effects parents and a bad environment could have on their children. These enrichment programs attempt to produce attitudes and behaviors that assure success in the world but, in the process, cut children off from their parents. Children are forced to abandon the culture of their parents if they are to "succeed." Examples of this practice include the nurseries of the kibbutz in Israel and the Head Start programs in America. This practice is seen by some social scientists as a type of "cultural genocide." Entire cultures were targeted (sometimes explicitly, although often not intentionally) for extinction in this way.

This fact upsets a number of social scientists. They feel it is desirable to establish a pluralistic society where ethnic, racial, and cultural diversity exist and flourish. To them attempts to "Americanize" everyone are indicative of racism, bigotry, and prejudice. Others point to the lack of strong ethnic or racial identities as the unifying strength of the American system. When immigrants came to America, they put ethnic differences behind them, they learned the English language and democratic values, and they were assimilated into American life. In nations where immigrants have maintained their ethnic identities and held to unique cultural beliefs, their first loyalty is to their ethnic group. Examples of the destructive impact of strong ethnic loyalties can be seen in the conflict and fragmentation now occurring in the former Soviet Union, Czechoslovakia, and Yugoslavia.

James Q. Wilson (1994:54–55) noted in this regard:

> We have always been a nation of immigrants, but now the level of immigration has reached the point where we have become acutely conscious, to a degree not seen, I think, since the turn of the century, that we are a nation of many cultures. I believe that the vast majority of those who have come to this country came because they, too, want to share in the American Dream. But their presence here, and the unavoidable tensions that attend upon even well-intentioned efforts at mutual coexistence, makes some people—and alas, especially some intellectuals in our universities—question the American Dream, challenge the legitimacy of Western standards of life and politics, and demand that everybody be defined in terms of his or her group membership. The motto of this nation—*E pluribus unum,* out of the many, one—is in danger of being rewritten to read, *Ex uno plures*—out of the one, many."

THEORETICAL EXPLANATIONS: SYMBOLIC INTERACTION, FUNCTIONALISM, CONFLICT

In their attempts to understand social phenomena, researchers look for recurring patterns, relationships between observable acts, and unifying themes. The particular way in which researchers look at the world reflects not only their personal views and experiences, but their professional perspective as well. Sociologists focus on interactions between individuals, between individuals and groups, between groups, and between groups and the larger society in which they are located. They try to identify those things that facilitate or hinder interaction, and the consequences of each. But not all sociologists agree as to the most effective/appropriate approach to take, and they tend to divide into three major theoretical camps: symbolic interactionism, functionalism, and conflict theory. These three approaches are not mutually exclusive, but they do represent radically different perspectives of the nature of social reality and how it should be studied.

Symbolic Interaction

This theoretical perspective argues that no social condition, however unbearable it may seem to some, is inherently or objectively a social problem until a significant number of politically powerful people agree that it is contrary to the public good. Scientists, social philosophers, religious leaders, and medical people may "know" that a specific action or condition has or will eventually have a devastating effect on society or a specific group in society, but until they can convince those who are in a position to control and perhaps correct the condition, it is not considered a social problem. Therefore it is not the social condition, but how the condition is defined and by whom, that determines if it is or will become a social problem. The social process whereby a specific condition moves from the level of an individual concern to a societal-level issue can be long and arduous or very short. An example of the latter occurred in the 1960s when some physicians noticed a significant increase in infants born with severe physical deformities. Medical researchers looking into the cause made a connection between the deformities and the drug thalidomide. Pregnant women suffering from severe nausea and health-threatening dehydration were prescribed this drug, which dramatically eliminated the nausea and appeared to have no bad side effects. But their babies were born with terrible deformities. Once the medical researchers discovered the connection, they presented their findings to their colleagues. When the data were reviewed and found to be scientifically valid, the drug was banned immediately. Thus a small group's assessment of an issue as a serious problem quickly was legitimized by those in power as a societal-level social problem and measures were taken to eliminate it.

Most situations are not this clear-cut. In the mid-1960s various individuals began to question the real reason(s) why the United States was involved in the war in Southeast Asia. They discovered data indicating that the war was not about protecting the democratic rights of the Vietnamese. Those in power either ignored or rejected such claims as politically motivated and as militarily naive. Reports from the Vietcong about purported U.S. military atrocities were collected and used as supportive evidence. These claims were summarily dismissed by American authorities as Communistic propaganda. Convinced of the validity and importance of their cause, the protesters regrouped and collected still more evidence including data collected by the French government. This new information was difficult for the U.S. government to ignore. Nevertheless, these new claims were rejected as being somewhat self-serving since the Vietcong had defeated the French in Indochina and presumably the French government could justify its own failure if the United States also failed.

Over the years the amount of data continued to accumulate augmented by new information collected from disenchanted veterans. This growing pool of evidence began to bother legislators who demanded an accounting from the U.S. government and the Department of Defense, but none was forthcoming. More and more students joined the antiwar movement, but their protests were seen as unpatriotic and self-serving—that is, an attempt to avoid military service. The increasing numbers of protesters caused some legislators to look more closely at the claims of the antiwar faction. As the magnitude of the war and the numbers of American servicemen involved grew, the numbers of people affected by the war grew as well. Returning veterans' reports of the state of the war, questionable military practices (such as the wholesale destruction of entire villages),

complaints of incompetent leadership in the military, and corrupt Vietnamese politicians gave greater credibility to the antiwar movement's earlier claims and convinced additional senators and representatives to support the stop-the-war movement, even though those in power still refused to acknowledge the legitimacy of the movement.

Unable to work within the system and convinced of the legitimacy of their cause, protesters resorted to unconventional and often illegal actions, such as burning their draft cards, refusing to register for the draft, seeking refuge in other countries, attacking ROTC (Reserve Officers' Training Corps) buildings on college campuses, and even bombing military research facilities. These actions were initially interpreted by government officials as criminal activities of self-serving individuals or activities inspired by those sympathetic with the Communist cause. The government engaged in increasingly repressive efforts to contain the movement. But public disaffection with the war was fueled by rising American casualties; this, coupled with the discontent within the ranks of the military, eventually forced those in power to acquiesce and accept the claims that the war was the problem and not the solution to the problem. Reaching this point took nearly 15 years.

For the symbolic interactionist, the fact that socially harmful conditions are thought to exist is not the criterion for what constitutes a social problem. Rather the real issue is to understand what goes into the assessment of a specific condition as being a social problem. To the symbolic interactionist, the appropriate questions are, (a) How is it that some conditions become defined as a social problem while others do not? (b) Who, in any society, can legitimate the designation of a condition as a social problem? (c) What solutions evolve and how do they evolve for specific social problems? (d) What factors exist in any specific society that inhibit or facilitate resolution of social problems?

In summary, symbolic interactionists stress that social problems do not exist independently of how people define their world. Social problems are socially constructed as people debate whether or not some social condition is a social problem and decide what to do about it. The focus is on the meanings the problem has for those who are affected by it and not on the impact it is having on them.

Functionalism

A second major theory sociologists use to study social problems is functionalism. Functionalists argue that society is a social system consisting of various integrated parts. Each of these parts fulfills a specific role that contributes to the overall functioning of society. In well-integrated systems, each part contributes to the stability of the whole. Functionalists examine each part in an attempt to determine the role it plays in the operation of the system as a whole. When any part fails, this creates a problem for the whole. These failures (dysfunctions) upset the equilibrium of the system and become social problems. To functionalists, anything that impedes the system's ability to achieve its goals is, by definition, a social problem. Unlike the symbolic interactionists, the functionalists argue that a social problem is not contingent on someone's assessment that it is a problem. Serious social problems may exist without anyone being aware of the detrimental effects they are having on various members of society or on society itself. Functionalists examine the stated objectives, values, and goals of a group; observe the behaviors of the members of the group; and assess how their behaviors impact on the abilities of the group to achieve its goals.

Many times the stated objectives (what sociologists call the "manifest functions") produce results that were not desired nor intended (what sociologists call "latent functions") and are in fact working against the group's abilities to accomplish its goals. Sociologists attempt to make the members of the group aware of the consequences of specific behaviors. For example, in an attempt to help single mothers of infants to provide for their children adequately, the American government created Aid to Families with Dependent Children (AFDC), a program designed to provide single women with enough money to feed, clothe, and house their children. This program was motivated by the Judeo-Christian philosophy that society is obligated to care for those who cannot care for themselves. In this regard the program has been a success. But it also has had a dark side in that it has discouraged the establishment of stable households with a father present, since two-parent families do not qualify for aid. If a woman marries or is known to be living with a man, she loses her eligibility and her benefits. As a result, males have been pushed to the periphery of the family. Many lower-class, unskilled males cannot earn as much as a single mother under AFDC. It does not mean that men are not around, only that they are discouraged from becoming permanent fixtures in these families. As a result, a program designed to help families ended up altering the structures of families and in the process created a whole new social problem.

Functionalists also argue that if a behavior or social institution persists, it must be meeting some need within the society. Merely defining a behavior as a problem does not assure its demise. To eliminate any behavior researchers/society must first find out what functions it is serving and then make the behavior dysfunctional, which in turn will cause the behavior to disappear. As poverty, crime, and inequality exist and persist in all societies, the task of the social scientist is to discover how and why. In this regard most individuals would argue that poverty is not desirable and should, if possible, be eliminated. Yet, as discussed by Herbert J. Gans in his article "The Uses of Poverty: The Poor Pay All," poverty benefits a significant portion of society. The incentive to eradicate poverty is neutralized by specific benefits to the nonpoor. Five of the 13 functions Gans identified are as follows:

1. Poverty ensures that society's "dirty work" will be done. Poverty functions to provide a low-wage labor pool that is willing, or rather unable to be unwilling, to perform dirty work at low cost.
2. Because the poor are required to work at low wages, they subsidize a variety of economic activities that benefit the affluent.
3. Poverty creates jobs for a number of occupations and professions that serve or "service" the poor, or protect the rest of society from them, such as social workers, police, and prison staff.
4. The poor buy goods others do not want, thus prolonging the economic usefulness of such goods—that is, day-old bread, fruit, and vegetables that would otherwise have to be thrown out, secondhand clothes, and deteriorating automobiles and buildings.
5. The poor, being powerless, can be made to absorb the costs of change and growth in American society. Urban renewal and expressways, for example, have typically been located in poor neighborhoods.

Although not explicitly stated by Gans, the poor cannot afford the ever-spiraling costs of health care and become those upon which the fledgling physician can practice his or her profession. As part of the learning process, mistakes are common and the poor are thus likely to have a lower level of medical expertise. Many medical, dental, and nursing schools are located within the inner city. In exchange for free or greatly reduced fees, poor people become guinea pigs to help student nurses, doctors, and dentists become experienced enough to practice on the more affluent.

The functionalists examine conditions, behaviors, and institutions in an attempt to try to understand the functions being met by these specific phenomena. To eliminate any of these problems the associated behaviors have to become dysfunctional. But because many of the functional alternatives to each problem would be dysfunctional for the affluent and powerful members of society, there is an incentive for the behavior to persist.

In summary, functionalists emphasize the interrelationship of the various parts of a system and believe that changes in one part will have significant implications for other parts. Any particular social problem is only a part of a larger whole. This means that in order to understand a social problem, one must place it in a broader context. A social problem is a consequence of the way a social system is put together.

Conflict Theory

Those social philosophers adhering to the conflict perspective view life and all social interaction as a struggle for power and privilege. They see every person and every group as being in competition for scarce and valued resources. They believe that even though people occasionally may have to cooperate with each other or even form alliances, they are still essentially in conflict. As soon as the alliance is no longer beneficial, conflict will often ensue. Unlike the functionalists who see the elements of a society as harmoniously working together and contributing to the whole, conflict theorists view all the parts as being in competition with each other. They see the guiding principle of social life as disequilibrium and change, not equilibrium and harmony. But, like the functionalists, they argue that social problems can and do exist independently of people's assessments of them. They argue that whether people are aware of it or not, they are enmeshed in a basic struggle for power and survival. Each group in society is attempting to achieve gains for itself that must necessarily be at the expense of other groups. It is this consistent conflict over limited resources that threatens societal peace and order.

Whereas the functionalists try to understand how different positions of power came into existence (Davis & Moore 1945), the conflictists show how those in power attempt to stay in power (Mills 1956). The conflict theorists see social problems as the natural and inevitable consequences of groups in society struggling to survive and gain control over those things that can affect their ability to survive. Those groups that are successful then attempt to use whatever means they must to control their environment and consolidate their position, thus increasing their chances of surviving. According to conflict theorists, those in power exploit their position and create poverty, discrimination, oppression, and crime in the process. The impact of these conditions on the exploited produces other pathological conditions such as alienation, alcoholism, drug abuse, mental illness, stress, health problems, and suicide. On occasions, such as that which occurred in Los Angeles in the summer of 1991 when policemen were found innocent of the use of excessive force in the beating of Rodney King, the feelings of helplessness and hopelessness can erupt as rage against the system in the form of violence and riots or as in Eastern Europe as rebellion and revolution against repressive governments.

The conflict theorists argue that drug abuse, mental illness, various criminal behaviors, and suicide are symptoms of a much larger societal malaise. To understand and eliminate these problems, society needs to understand the basic conflicts that are producing them. The real problems stem from the implications of being exploited. Being manipulated by the powerful and denied a sense of control tends (a) to produce a loss of control over one's life (powerlessness), (b) to lead to an inability to place one's productive efforts into some meaningful context (meaninglessness), (c) not to being involved in the process of change but only in experiencing the impact resulting from the changes (normlessness), and (d) to cause one to find oneself isolated from one's colleagues on the job (self-isolation). Conflictists see all of these problems as the product of a capitalistic system that alienates the worker from himself and from his or her fellow workers (Seeman 1959).

To protect their positions of power, privilege, prestige, and possessions, those in power use their wealth and influence to control organizations. For example, they manipulate the system to get key individuals into positions where they can influence legislation and decisions that are designed to protect their power and possessions. They might serve on or appoint others to school boards to assure that the skills and values needed by the economy are taught. They also assure that the laws are enforced internally (the police) or externally (the military) to protect their holdings. The war in the Persian Gulf is seen by many conflict theorists as having been fought for oil rather than for Kuwait's liberation.

When the exploited attempt to do something about their condition by organizing, protesting, and rebelling, they threaten those in power. For example, they may go on a strike that might disrupt the entire nation. Under the pretext that it is for the best good of society, the government may step in and stop the strike. Examples are the air-traffic-controllers strike of 1987 and the railroad strike in 1991. In retaliation the workers may engage in work slow-down, stoppage, and even sabotage. They may stage protests and public demonstrations and cast protest votes at the ballot boxes. If these do not work, rebellions and revolutions may result. Those in power can respond very repressively as was the case in Tiananmen Square in China in 1989, threaten military force as the Soviet Union did with the Baltic countries in 1990, or back down completely as when the Berlin Wall came down. Thus reactions to exploitation may produce change but inevitably lead to other social problems. In Eastern Europe and the former Soviet Union, democracy has resulted in massive unemployment, spiraling inflation, hunger, crime, and homelessness.

Sometimes those in power make concessions to maintain power. Conflict theorists look for concessions and how they placate the poor while still protecting the privileged and powerful. The rich are viewed as sharing power only if forced to do so and only to the extent absolutely necessary.

Robert Michels (1949), a French social philosopher, looked at the inevitable process whereby the members of any group voluntarily give their rights, prerogatives, and power to a select few who then dominate the group. It may not be the conscious decision of those who end up in positions of power to dominate the group, but, in time, conscious decisions may be made to do whatever is necessary to stay in control of the group. The power, privilege, and wealth they acquire as part of the position alters their self-images. To give up the position would necessitate a complete revision of who they are, what they can do, and with whom they associate. Their "selves" have become fused/confused with the position they occupy, and in an attempt to protect their "selves," they resist efforts designed to undermine their control. They consider threats to themselves as threats to the organization and therefore feel justified in their vigorous resistance. According to Michels, no matter how democratic an organization starts out to be it will always become dominated and controlled by a few. The process whereby this occurs he labeled the "Iron Law of Oligarchy." For example, hospitals that were created to save lives, cure the sick, and provide for the chronically ill, now use the threat of closure to justify rate increases. The hospital gets its rate increase, the cost of health goes up, and the number of individuals able to afford health care declines, with the ultimate result being an increase in health problems for the community. Although not explicitly stated, the survival of the organization (and its administrators) becomes more important than the health of the community.

In summary, the conflict theoretical model stresses the fact that key resources such as power and privilege are limited and distributed unequally among the members/groups in a society. Conflict is therefore a natural and inevitable result of various groups pursuing their interests and values. To study the basis of social problems, researchers must look at the distribution of power and privilege because these two factors are always at the center of conflicting interests and values. Moreover, whenever social change occurs, social problems inevitably follow.

Conflict and Functionalism: A Synthesis

While conflict theorists' and functionalists' explanations of what constitutes the roots of social problems appear to be completely contradictory, Dahrendorf (1959) sees them as complementary. "Functionalism explains how highly talented people are motivated to spend twenty-five years of study to become surgeons; conflict theory explains how surgeons utilize their monopoly on their vital skills to obtain rewards that greatly exceed that necessary to ensure an adequate supply of talent." (See also Ossowski 1963; van de Berghe 1963; Williams 1966; Horowitz 1962; and Lenski 1966 for other attempts at a synthesis between these two theoretical models.)

SOCIAL PROBLEMS: DEFINITION AND ANALYSIS

Value Conflicts

It is convenient to characterize a social problem as a conflict of values, a conflict of values and duties, a conflict of rights (Hook, 1974), or a social condition that leads to or is thought to lead to harmful consequences. Harm may be defined as (a) the loss to a group, community, or society of something to which it is thought to be entitled, (b) an offense perceived to be an affront to our moral sensibilities, or (c) an impoverishment of the collective good or welfare. It is also convenient to define values as individual or collective desires that become attached to social objects. Private property, for example, is a valued social object for some while others disavow or reject its desirability; because of the public disagreement over its value, it presents a conflict of values. A conflict of values is also found in the current controversy surrounding abortion. Where pro-life supporters tend to see life itself as the ultimate value, supporters of pro-choice may, as some have, invoke the Fourteenth Amendment's right-to-privacy clause as the compelling value.

Values-versus-Duties Conflicts

A second format that students should be aware of in the analysis of social problems is the conflict between values and obligations or duties. This approach calls our attention to those situations in which a person, group, or community must pursue or realize a certain duty even though those participating may be convinced that doing so will not achieve the greater good. For example, educators, policemen, bureaucrats, and environmentalists may occupy organizational or social roles in which they are required to formulate policies and follow rules that, according to their understanding, will not contribute to the greater good of students, citizens, or the likelihood of a clean environment. On the other hand, there are situations in which, we, as a individuals, groups, or communities, do things that would not seem to be right in our pursuit of what we consider to be the higher value. Here students of social problems are faced with the familiar problem of using questionable, illogical, or immoral means to achieve what is perhaps generally recognized as a value of a higher order. Police officers, for example, are sometimes accused of employing questionable, immoral, or deceptive means (stings, scams, undercover operations) to achieve what are thought to be socially helpful ends and values such as

removing a drug pusher from the streets. Familiar questions for this particular format are, Do the ends justify the means? Should ends be chosen according to the means available for their realization? What are the social processes by which means themselves become ends? These are questions to which students of social problems and social policy analysis should give attention since immoral, illegal, or deceptive means can themselves lead to harmful social consequences.

Max Weber anticipated and was quite skeptical of those modern bureaucratic processes whereby means are transformed into organizational ends and members of the bureaucracy become self-serving and lose sight of their original and earlier mission. The efforts of the Central Intelligence Agency (CIA) to maintain U.S. interests in Third World countries led to tolerance of various nations' involvement in illicit drugs. Thus the CIA actually contributed to the drug problem the police struggle to control. A second example is that of the American Association of Retired Persons (AARP). To help the elderly obtain affordable health care, life insurance, drugs, and so forth, the AARP established various organizations to provide or contract for services. But now the AARP seems to be more concerned about its corporate holdings than it is about the welfare of its elderly members.

RIGHTS IN CONFLICT

Finally, students of social problems should become aware of right-versus-right moral conflicts. With this particular format, one's attention is directed to the conflict of moral duties and obligations, the conflict of rights and, not least, the serious moral issue of divided loyalties. In divorce proceedings, for example, spouses must try to balance their personal lives and careers against the obligations and duties to each other and their children. Even those who sincerely want to meet their full obligations to both family and career often find this is not possible because of the real limits of time and means.

Wilson (1994:39,54) observes that from the era of "Enlightenment" and its associated freedoms arose the potential for significant social problems. We are seeing all about us in the entire Western world the working out of the defining experience of the West, the Enlightenment. The Age of Enlightenment was the extraordinary period in the eighteenth century when individuals were emancipated from old tyrannies—from dead custom, hereditary monarchs, religious persecution, and ancient superstition. It is the period that gave us science and human rights, that attacked human slavery and political absolutism, that made possible capitalism and progress. The principal figures of the Enlightenment remain icons of social reform: Adam Smith, David Hume, Thomas Jefferson, Immanuel Kant, Isaac Newton, James Madison.

The Enlightenment defined the West and set it apart from all of the other great cultures of the world. But in culture as in economics, there is no such thing as a free lunch. If you liberate a person from ancient tyrannies, you may also liberate him or her from familiar controls. If you enhance his or her freedom to create, you will enhance his or her freedom to destroy. If you cast out the dead hand of useless custom, you may also cast out the living hand of essential tradition. If you give an individual freedom of expression, he or she may write *The Marriage of Figaro* or he or she may sing "gangsta rap." If you enlarge the number of rights one has, you may shrink the number of responsibilities one feels.

There is a complex interaction between the rights an individual has and the consequences of exercising specific rights. For example, if an individual elects to exercise his or her right to consume alcoholic beverages, this act then nullifies many subsequent rights because of the potential harm that can occur. The right to drive, to engage in athletic events, or to work, is jeopardized by the debilitating effects of alcohol. Every citizen has rights assured him or her by membership in society. At the same time, rights can only be exercised to the degree to which they do not trample on the rights of other members of the group. If a woman elects to have a baby, must she abrogate her right to consume alcohol, smoke, consume caffeine, or take drugs? Because the effects of these substances on the developing fetus are potentially devastating, is it not reasonable to conclude that the rights of the child to a healthy body and mind are being threatened if the mother refuses to abstain during pregnancy? Fetal alcohol effect/syndrome, for instance, is the number-one cause of preventable mental retardation in the United States, and it could be completely eliminated if pregnant women never took an alcoholic drink. Caring for individuals with fetal alcohol effect/syndrome is taking increasingly greater resources that could well be directed toward other pressing issues.

Rights cannot be responsibly exercised without individuals' weighing their potential consequences. Thus a hierarchy of rights, consequences, and harms exists and the personal benefits resulting from any act must be weighed against the personal and social harms that could follow. The decision to use tobacco should be weighed against the possible consequences of a wide variety of harms such as personal health problems and the stress it places on society's resources to care for tobacco-related diseases. Tobacco-related diseases often have catastrophic consequences for their users that cannot be paid for by the individual, so the burden of payment is placed on society. Millions of dollars and countless health care personnel must be diverted away from other patients to care for these individuals with self-inflicted tobacco-related diseases. In addition to the costs in money, personnel, and medical resources, these diseases take tremendous emotional tolls on those closest to the diseased individuals. To focus only on one's rights without consideration of the consequences associated with those rights often deprives other individuals from exercising their rights.

The Constitution of the United States guarantees individuals rights without clearly specifying what the rights really entail. Logically one cannot have rights without others having corresponding obligations. But what obligations does each right assure and what limitations do these obligations and/or rights require? Rights for the collectivity are protected by limitations placed on each individual, but limits of collective rights are also mandated by laws assuring that individual rights are not infringed upon. Therefore, we have rights as a whole that often differ from those we have as individual members of that whole.

For example, the right to free speech may impinge in a number of ways on a specific community. To the members of a small Catholic community, having non-Catholic missionaries preaching on street corners and proselytizing door-to-door could be viewed as a social problem. Attempts to control their actions such as the enactment and enforcements of "Green River" ordnances (laws against active solicitation), could eliminate the community's problem but in so doing would trample on the individual's constitutional rights of religious expression. To protect individual rights, the community may have to put up with individuals pushing their personal theological ideas in public places. From the perspective of the Catholic community, aggressive non-Catholic missionaries are not only a nuisance but a social problem that should be banned. To the proselytizing churches, restrictions on their actions are violations of their civil rights and hence a serious social problem.

Currently another conflict of interests/rights is dividing many communities, and that is cigarette smoking. Smokers argue that their rights are being seriously threatened by aggressive legislation restricting smoking. They argue that society should not and cannot legislate morality. Smokers point out how attempts to legislate alcohol consumption during the Prohibition of the 1920s and 1930s was an abject failure and, in fact, created more problems than it eliminated. They believe that the exact same process is being attempted today and will prove to be just as unsuccessful. Those who smoke then go on to say that smoking is protected by the Constitution's freedom of expression and that no one has the right to force others to adhere his or her personal health policies, which are individual choices. They assert that if the "radicals" get away with imposing smoking restrictions, they can and will move on to other health-related behaviors such as overeating. Therefore, by protecting the constitutional rights of smokers, society is protecting the constitutional rights of everyone.

On the other hand, nonsmokers argue that their rights are being violated by smokers. They point to an increasing body of research data that shows that secondhand smoke leads to numerous health problems such as emphysema, heart disease, and throat and lung cancer. Not only do nonsmokers have a right not to have to breathe smoke-contaminated air, but society has an obligation to protect the health and well-being of its members from the known dangers of breathing smoke.

These are only a few examples of areas where rights come into conflict. Others include environmental issues, endangered species, forest management, enforcement of specific laws, homosexuality, mental illness, national health insurance, taxes, balance of trade, food labeling and packaging, genetic engineering, rape, sexual deviation, political corruption, riots, public protests, zero population growth, the state of the economy, and on and on.

It is notable that the degree to which any of these issues achieves widespread concern varies over time. Often, specific problems are given much fanfare by politicians and special interests groups for a time, and the media try to convince us that specific activities or behaviors have the greatest urgency and demand a total national commitment for a solution. However, after being in the limelight for a while, the importance of the problem seems to fade and new problems move into prominence. If you look back over previous editions of this book, you can see this trend. It would be useful to speculate why, in American society, some problems remain a national concern while others come and go.

The Consequences of Harm

To this point it had been argued that social problems can be defined and analyzed as (a) conflicts between values, (b) conflicts between values and duties, and (c) conflicts between rights. Consistent with the aims of this article, social problems can be further characterized and interpreted as social conditions that lead, or are generally thought to lead, to harmful consequences for the person, group, community, or society.

Harm—and here we follow Hyman Gross's (1979) conceptualization of the term—can be classified as (a) a loss, usually permanent, that deprives the person or group of a valued object or condition it is entitled to have, (b) offenses to sensibility—that is, harm that contributes to unpleasant experiences in the form of repugnance, embarrassment, disgust, alarm, or fear, and (c) impairment of the collective welfare—that is, violations of those values possessed by the group or society.

Harm can also be ranked as to the potential for good. Physicians, to help their patients, often have to harm them. The question they must ask is, "Will this specific procedure, drug, or operation, produce more good than the pain and suffering it causes?" For instance, will the additional time it affords the cancer patient be worth all the suffering associated with the chemotherapy? In Somalia, health care personnel are forced to make much harder decisions. They are surrounded by starvation, sickness, and death. If they treat one person, another cannot be treated and will die. They find themselves forced to allocate their time and resources, not according to who needs it the most, but according to who has the greatest chance of survival.

Judges must also balance the harms they are about to inflict on those they must sentence against the public good and the extent to which the sentence might help the individual reform. Justice must be served in that people must pay for their crimes, yet most judges also realize that prison time often does more harm than good. In times of recession employers must weigh harm when they are forced to cut back their workforce: Where should the cuts occur? Should they keep employees of long standing and cut those most recently hired (many of which are nonwhites hired through affirmative action programs)? Should they keep those with the most productive records, or those with the greatest need for employment? No matter what employers elect to do, harm will result to some. The harm produced by the need to reduce the workforce must be balanced by the potential good of the company's surviving and sustaining employment for the rest of the employees.

The notion of harm also figures into the public and social dialogue between those who are pro-choice and those who are pro-life. Most pro-lifers are inclined to see the greatest harm of abortion to be loss of life, while most pro-choicers argue that the compelling personal and social harm is the taking away of a value (the right to privacy) that everyone is entitled to. Further harmful consequences of abortion for most pro-lifers are that the value of life will be cheapened, the moral fabric of society will be weakened, and the taking of life could be extended to the elderly and disabled, for example. Most of those who are pro-choice, on the other hand, are inclined to argue that the necessary consequence of their position is that of keeping government out of their private lives and bedrooms. In a similar way this "conflict of values" format can be used to analyze, clarify, and enlarge our understanding of the competing values, harms, and consequences surrounding other social problems. We can, and should, search for the competing values underlying such social problems as, for example, income distribution, homelessness, divorce, education, and the environment.

Loss, then, as a societal harm consists in a rejection or violation of what a person or group feels entitled to have. American citizens, for example, tend to view life, freedom, equality, property, and physical security as ultimate values. Any rejection or violation of these values is thought to constitute a serious social problem since such a loss diminishes one's sense of personhood. Murder, violence, AIDS, homelessness, environmental degradation, the failure to provide adequate health care, and abortion can be conveniently classified as social problems within this class of harms.

Offenses to our sensibilities constitute a class of harm that, when serious enough, becomes a problem affecting moral issues and the common good of the members of a society. Issues surrounding pornography, prostitution, and the so-called victimless crimes are examples of behaviors that belong to this class of harm. Moreover some would argue that environmental degradation, the widening gap between the very rich and the very poor, and the condition of the homeless also should be considered within this class of harm.

A third class of harms—namely impairments to the collective welfare—is explained, in part, by Gross (1979:120) as follows:

> Social life, particularly in the complex forms of civilized societies, creates many dependencies among members of a community. The welfare of each member depends upon the exercise of restraint and precaution by others in the pursuit of their legitimate activities, as well as upon cooperation toward certain common objectives. These matters of collective welfare involve many kinds of interests that may be said to be possessed by the community.

In a pluralistic society, such as American society, matters of collective welfare are sometimes problematic in that there can be considerable conflict of values and rights between various segments of the society. There is likely to remain, however, a great deal of agreement that those social problems whose harmful consequences would involve impairments to the collective welfare would include poverty, poor education, mistreatment of the young and elderly, excessive disparities in income distribution, discrimination against ethnic and other minorities, drug abuse, health and medical care, the state of the economy, and environmental concerns.

BIBLIOGRAPHY

Dahrendorf, R. (1959). *Class and class conflict in industrial society.* Stanford, CA: Stanford University Press.

Davis, Kingsley, & Moore, Wilbert E. (1945). Some principles of stratification. *American Sociological Review, 10,* 242–249.

Gans, Herbert J. (1971). The uses of poverty: The poor pay all. *Social Policy.* New York: Social Policy Corporation.

Gross, Hyman. (1979). *A theory of criminal justice.* New York: Oxford University Press.

Hook, Sidney. (1974). *Pragmatism and the tragic sense of life.* New York: Basic Books.

Horowitz, M. A. (1962). Consensus, conflict, and cooperation. *Social Forces, 41,* 177–188.

Lenski, G. (1966). *Power and privilege.* New York: McGraw-Hill.

Michels, Robert. (1949). *Political parties: A sociological study of the oligarchical tendencies of modern democracy.* New York: Free Press.

Mills, C. Wright. (1956). *The power elite.* New York: Oxford University Press.

Ossowski, S. (1963). *Class structure in the social consciousness.* Translated by Sheila Patterson. New York: The Free Press.

Seeman, Melvin. (1959). On the meaning of alienation. *American Sociological Review, 24,* 783–791.

Van den Berghe, P. (1963). Dialectic and functionalism: Toward a theoretical synthesis. *American Sociological Review, 28,* 695–705.

Weber, Max. (1964). *The protestant ethic and the spirit of capitalism.* Translated by Talcott Parsons. New York: Scribner's.

William, Robin Jr. (1970). *American society: A sociological interpretation,* 3rd. ed. New York: Alfred A. Knopf.

Williams, Robin. (1966). Some further comments on chronic controversies. *American Journal of Sociology, 71,* 717–721.

Wilson, James Q. (1994, August). The moral life." *Brigham Young Magazine,* pp. 37–55.

Wilson, William. (1978). *The declining significance of race.* Chicago: University of Chicago Press.

CHALLENGE TO THE READER

As you read the articles that follow, try to determine which of the three major theoretical positions each of the authors seems to be using. Whatever approach the writer uses in his or her discussion suggests what he or she thinks is the primary cause of the social problem/issue under consideration.

Also ask yourself as you read each article, (1) What values are at stake or in conflict? (2) What rights are at issue or in conflict? (3) What is the nature of the harm in each case, and who is being hurt? (4) What do the authors suggest as possible resolutions for each social problem?

How Social Problems Are Born

Nathan Glazer

Nathan Glazer is co-editor of The Public Interest.

How do we get more attention, more public action, for a problem we consider important? More important, how do we get the right kind of public attention and action, right in scale, and right in the kinds of solutions the public is willing to accept and fund?

Contemporary social scientists are skeptical about the possibilities of achieving such a rational ordering of things. Consider the following from the sociologist Joseph Gusfield:

Human problems do not spring up, full-blown and announced, into the consciousness of bystanders. Even to recognize a situation as painful requires a system for categorizing and defining events. . . . "Objective" conditions are seldom so compelling and so clear in their form that they spontaneously generate a "true" consciousness. Those committed to one or another solution to a public problem see its genesis in the necessary consequences of events and processes; those in opposition often point to "agitators" who impose one or another definition of reality.

This passage is taken from Gusfield's *The Culture of Public Problems: Drinking-Driving and the Symbolic Order* (University of Chicago Press, 1981) and he exhibits in it a common approach in today's social sciences to the issue of how we make social problems out of social conditions, which may be crudely summarized as: It's all in the head. We need a system of defining and categorizing events before we know we have a problem. When most of us agree we do have a problem—when a social condition has been changed into a problem—we interpret this as a case of the problem having become worse, or a case of increasing empathy and sympathy on the part of the public for those suffering. Paradoxically, we often recognize that we have a problem when the condition we are responding to has improved. Recall how the problem of "poverty" burst upon us in the early days of the Kennedy administration. John Kenneth Galbraith had just published *The Affluent Society,* and Michael Harrington had published *The Other America,* but as we now know poverty had been declining all through the forties and fifties.

So our first explanation of how a condition has become a problem may not hold—the problem may not have become worse. Our second, that we have become wiser or more understanding or more sympathetic to the plight of others, is flattering to us, but Gusfield does not give us that credit. It is our categories, rather than reality, that have changed. As we look further into his study of drinking-driving in the book from which I have quoted, we find it is rife with discussions of symbolism, dramaturgy, rhetoric, metaphor, and the like. "The Fiction and Drama of Public Consciousness," one chapter title announces. "The Literary Art of Science: Drama and Pathos in Drinking-Driver Research," another reads.

This is not a case of individual idiosyncrasy. Much of the writing by leading social scientists on how we fix upon social problems, on how they get on the agenda of public attention, is skeptical as to the kind of simple and direct relation

Reprinted with permission of the author and *The Public Interest,* No. 115, Spring 1994, pp. 31-44. © 1994 by National Affairs, Inc.

we might imagine: the problem gets worse, or we become more sensitive to it. More likely, an interest group of some sort, an advocacy group, has taken it up and made it a matter of public concern. The arts of publicity are more relevant than the findings of science.

Thus, in Gusfield's *The Culture of Public Problems,* devoted to the problem of the drinking driver—one would think a serious enough issue to deserve direct attention—we will find rather more references to the literary critic Kenneth Burke than to any scientist or social scientist.

The issue for Gusfield is not only the social construction of public problems, which do indeed have many dimensions, among which the determination of fact, of the existing situation, is only one, but the social construction of science itself, a rather popular theme among social scientists and advanced literary critics these days.

THE ROLE OF RHETORIC

There is undoubtedly a degree of overkill in Gusfield's approach but there is something to learn from it too, as we consider how we get the right kind of public attention for an issue of importance. One problem to which Gusfield points is that we move very rapidly from the problem itself, which may be both undeniable and important, to the arts of publicity and attention-getting, and, as he argues, these arts also affect almost immediately the very facts that we use to get attention and that are the bedrock of our initial concern. Thus, if we examine the facts which we use as the basis to claim attention, public money, funds for research, we see that the facts themselves become shaped by the need to compete with other claims, other problems, for which the arts of publicity are also employed.

Half of the 50,000 deaths a year from automobile accidents are attributed regularly, we are told, to drink on the part of the driver. When we examine this oft-repeated statistic, according to Gusfield—and he goes into the source of the figure in detail—it turns out that it is hardly solidly based, that many questions can be raised about it. Similarly with the statistic on how many Americans have serious drinking problems—a common figure of 9 or 10 million was used when Gusfield was writing his book in the early

1980s; its sources are murky and uncertain, and of course depend on what we mean by drinking problems.

It is not only in the case of drinking-driving and alcoholism that the first necessary step in defining a problem—finding out just what the scale of the problem is—immediately gets mixed up with the necessary requirements of the next steps in getting attention for it, bringing it to the notice of necessary publics. And so we are familiar with disputes right now about the scale of date rape on campus, as well as with the prior question of just what date rape is. Similarly with child abuse, and many other public issues.

Is Gusfield only playing games when he asks just how do the authorities decide that an accident was based on drinking, and other questions which undermine the statistic that half of all automobile accident fatalities are owing to drinking? Of course drinking-driving is a serious problem, so why does he bother us with the figures used in making a case to congressional committees or attracting publicity or funds? But his approach does alert us to a number of things of importance. First, that rhetoric, drama, the arts of gaining access to the mass media or congressmen, are implicated at the very beginning in all our efforts to gain attention to social problems. Second, that there is no easy way of scaling social problems from the point of view of how "important" they are. In the passage I reprinted from his *The Culture of Public Problems,* he placed the words "objective" and "true" in quotation marks. Third, that because this is so there is the constant danger of overkill, over-dramatization, the constant possibility that those most gifted in the arts of publicity and drama will engross a larger share of funds and attention than *their* problem warrants. (I leave aside for the moment the question of whether we can decide on any objective basis how much money or attention one problem deserves as against another, or the methods by which we might decide. Whatever our answer, we would probably all agree that some problems seem to have gained an inordinate amount of attention compared to others of apparently similar or greater scale. This has been argued in the case of AIDS. Very likely the attention AIDS gets is in part related to the number of people in the arts and fashion and publicity who are affected.)

It is revealing that Gusfield titled an earlier book, on the temperance move-

ment, *Symbolic Crusade,* and it is clear that the use of the term "crusade" is meant to suggest to us that a movement that tried to deal with a problem that was serious enough at the time, and that may be as serious today, was overdone, excessive, shrill, in some ways more than the problem called for. (After all, it led, astonishingly, to the passage of a constitutional amendment banning alcoholic drinks.) The use of the word "crusade" today implies that we are confronted with something that is rather too grand, too much, for its object, and the word tends to evoke skepticism of the cause to which it is attached, rather than inspiring greater commitment to the cause. What, after all, in our laid-back contemporary world, used to horrors of all sorts, deserves a "crusade," with its religious implications? (We seem happier with the word "war," as in war against poverty, and war against drugs, headed by a czar rather than a pope.)

THE KNOWLEDGE PROBLEM

Gusfield does I believe emphasize too much the social construction of problems rather than their objective realities (and I am not using quotation marks, as he did around "objective"), but his work draws our attention to a surprising fact about social scientists' examination of the question of how a social condition becomes a social problem: There is a considerable degree of skepticism of how we go about it, or indeed how we can go about it in a democracy in which the mass media inevitably shape public perception and knowledge.

One finds the same in another social scientist, the late Aaron Wildavsky, who devoted a considerable part of his enormous energy and great talents to the study of how society deals with risk. Wildavsky gave more credit to the objective realities than Gusfield does, but he doubted they could play a major role in determining how we allocate our resources in dealing with risk. While he dealt primarily with environmental risks, he would have said the same thing about social risks and social problems. But despite his much greater respect for science and scientists and their ability to determine the degree of danger from various environmental risks (had he been speaking about social problems he might well have approached Gusfield in skepticism), he also believed that any hope of matching our resources to our problems by taking account of the scale of the danger they posed was probably a vain one. The problems were primarily political, and when Wildavsky said political he meant also cultural, tied up with our interests, our values, our perceptions, which brings him not far from Gusfield.

"What would be needed," he and Mary Douglas asked in their book *Risk and Culture,*

> to make us able to understand the risks that face us?—Nothing short of total knowledge (a mad answer to an impossible question). The hundreds of thousands of chemicals about whose dangers so much is said are matched easily by the diversity of the causes of war or the afflictions of poverty or the horrors of religious and racial strife. Just trying to think of what categories of objects a person might be concerned about is alarming. Indeed, it might be better for mental health to limit rather than expand sources of concern. Since no one can attend to everything, some sort of priority must be established among dangers. . . . Ranking dangers . . . so as to know which ones to address and in what order, demands prior agreement on criteria. There is no mechanical way to produce a ranking.

Scientists may come together on this (less likely social scientists) but there is no way of making their agreement public policy: We are not a nation of philosophers and kings. The issue then becomes political, with everything involved in that term. Douglas and Wildavsky quote some other authorities on risk:

> Values and uncertainties are an integral part of every acceptable-risk problem. As a result, there are no value-free processes for choosing between risky alternatives. The search for an "objective method" [again, in quotation marks] is doomed to failure and may blind the searchers to the value-laden assumptions they are making.

Another quotation from a different source:

> Not only does each approach fail to give a definitive answer, but it is predisposed to representing particular interests and recommending particular decisions. Hence, choice of a method is a political decision with a distinct message about who should rule and what should matter.

Scientists may agree on what risks should be addressed, in what order, with what resources, but even that is not assured, and when it comes to social problems and social scientists agreement is even less likely. Popular passions will be aroused, they will affect what politicians and administrators do, and one can only hope that knowledge—authentic knowledge, solidly based, scientifically established, something I still believe in despite the assault on its possibility we have seen in the newer trends in the humanities and social sciences—will play some role in determining what legislators and administrators do.

So in almost all transitions from social condition to social problem we are in the grip of passions, interests, perceptions, values that are not going to be affected much by what the scientists tell us. Gusfield called the fight for temperance a "crusade," Aaron Wildavsky uses the term "sectarian," with its religious connotations, to describe those who devote themselves to getting the public and government to pay attention to what they conceive of as major risks, and he uses the term not as an epithet but as a carefully constructed concept which for him describes the character of the people and groups who have done so much to alert us to environmental risks.

Despite the fact that there is a great deal that we can learn from the work of Gusfield and Wildavsky on how social conditions become social problems, I will separate myself from the full scope of their arguments. I believe that there are objective ways of determining the scale of a problem, even if all our efforts are somewhat corrupted by our political attitudes, by human failings that affect even scientists, and other factors; and that while we have undoubtedly seen cases in which the attention to a problem and the resources devoted to it can properly arouse skepticism, there are indeed conditions which hardly need to be "socially constructed," which spring to our eyes and appeal to our human sympathies and simply demand attention, and for which there would appear to be only one central question to consider: What to do about it. Yet we must be alerted to the issues the social scientists raise when we consider pragmatically how to make a social condition a social problem.

THE CASE OF PROHIBITION

Our two authors have tended to concentrate on issues which have in some way been misconstrued owing to interests and passions, perceptions and values, they do not share. Thus, temperance was initially raised as a moral problem, a problem of making people better. This was in time joined by other considerations: temperance would fight poverty among workingmen, making them better workers, fathers, husbands. Eventually the method chosen to make them better was that of depriving them of the means for bad behavior. We consider Prohibition a great failure, but it did (according to the best authority) reduce the consumption of alcohol by half.

It is not clear how the problem of excessive alcohol consumption might have been better construed at the time; it could not easily have been construed differently from what it was in a largely rural and small-town, Protestant and evangelical America, fearful of the rising numbers of immigrants and Catholics, of the growth of the big cities with their wider range of acceptable behavior, their greater tolerance. We now see the crusade as mistaken, because we see the problem of alcohol consumption, when it becomes a problem, as one of mental health, and its incidence and impact have declined, at least in public perception, perhaps in reality. That decline has much to do with our viewing alcohol—as so much else—in the context of health rather than sin, as we have seen the decline of the theological ethic, and the rise of the therapeutic ethic. (The decline in alcoholism may also be connected with changes in taste and fashion, from hard liquor to wine, from wine to water.)

Just as Gusfield's temperance crusaders are seen as motivated by the fight against sin, evil, bad behavior, when they might have chosen (and in time their successors did) a more effective way of viewing the problem, Wildavsky's environmental crusaders are viewed as sectarians, impassioned, moving from one topic that arouses their indignation to another, incapable of placing in the balance the goods the technologies they oppose have brought, or comprehending the impact on lives and economies of the measures they demand. Religion has now been replaced by a suspicion of science and technology, a suspicion of big organizations, whether industrial firms or government, even though government is called upon to restore the ecological balance (but the distrust of government is such that it is primarily the courts and judges who are depended on to keep government in line in enforcing the rules and regulations).

TOBACCO, A SUCCESS STORY

Despite the rather sour tone adopted by many of our best social scientists toward crusaders and sectarians and indeed toward the passion for reform in general (a tone we may trace, perhaps, to Richard Hofstadter's *The Age of Reform*), we live in a society afflicted with problems that are hardly imaginary, hardly the result of misperceptions inspired by the passions of crusaders and sectarians. And we have seen successes in transforming conditions into problems in which we do not sense that crusaders and sectarians are driving forces, but rather scientific understanding and pragmatic policymakers. Perhaps the largest success (partial it is true), is the decline in tobacco consumption, and the decline in its social acceptance. While the battle against smoking is not without its sectarians, the costs of smoking to health are undeniable and ever more solidly documented, and the efforts that have been devoted to reducing its incidence have been balanced and, in time, effective.

Interestingly enough, the effort to reduce the consumption of tobacco has not been conducted, as so many others have, by means of major federal legislation, giving responsibility to a major federal agency, new or old, operating under law and issuing detailed regulations. Nor do we have a single major reform organization devoted to the cause of eradicating smoking—there is no equivalent to the Women's Christian Temperance Union, the Anti-Saloon League, the major environmental organizations. There are anti-tobacco crusaders, but they are local rather than national, hardly organized, and their effectiveness has been in getting local restrictive legislation, and in getting large organizations to set rules limiting the areas where smoking is permitted. At the national level, there have been warnings rather than prohibitions, the voluntary—though under pressure—banning of advertising on TV, the local pressure against billboards.

The campaign for the reduction of smoking has thus been characterized first by the fact that it was initiated by almost unambiguous scientific findings, announced by high medical authority, rather than by mass pressure from a mass organization; second that it has been conducted more on the local level than on the national; third that it has been characterized more by voluntary concessions, as in the case of advertising, than by national prohibition.

I have been trying to understand just why the campaign against smoking has been successful to the degree it has, so much more successful than the campaign against drugs for example, and why its characteristics have been so instinctive, but it has not been easy to get light on this matter. Seeking for some understanding on the shelves of the Widener Library at Harvard, I discover to my surprise that there is very little on the subject. "Smoking" comes in the Library of Congress cataloguing system between "drink" and "drugs," and while one finds shelf upon shelf of material on these two subjects, on smoking, there is almost nothing, a few disparate volumes. I wonder whether this is because we prefer studying failure rather than success; or because the limited degree of national coercive action means there is less to study; or because tobacco is inherently less glamorous than drink and drugs. But it kills as many people and if we have an example of success, even partial success, it should be worthy of study.

I am sure that to the smoker my assessment of the moderate nature of the campaign against smoking, compared to the crusade against drink, or the war against drugs, is too benign. Yet it is my impression there is something to be learned from the smoking story as we try to understand the more effective ways in which we convert social conditions into social problems. One thing to be learned, for example, is that moderation in the campaign, the willingness to accept slow but steady progress, may prevent a major backlash. In the case of drinking, the backlash was the repeal of the Eighteenth Amendment. Much had been learned from Prohibition and one important thing that had been learned was that it was better to leave the matter to the states and the localities. As a result, drink disappeared from the national agenda, and an issue that had troubled American political life for generations was domesticated. Excessive drinking became a medical and health problem, not a moral or legal problem.

BACKLASHES

The war against drugs has not yet met such a backlash, but it may in the campaign for legalization. There are incredible problems around legalization, but there are incredible problems around our efforts to eradicate drug use, too, and we may well find in time that questions will be raised about why we spend billions ineffectively in trying to eliminate the sources of drugs and in trying to eradicate dealing in drugs, why so large a proportion of our criminal justice resources—in police, judges, prosecutors, courts, jails, prisons—is devoted to the attempt to wipe out drug use.

We may shortly find another case of backlash in the case of child abuse. The story of child abuse is also one of a case, as in smoking, in which reform starts from the top, rather than as a result of mass pressure from crusaders or sectarians, and in which doctors rather than movement people play the central role, at least at the beginning. The story is an interesting one. It begins with interest in sponsoring research on the issue of child abuse in the Children's Bureau in the then-Department of Health, Education, and Welfare. They funded the work on this subject of Dr. C. Henry Kempe, a pediatrician who specialized in immunology, and who noted that the interns and residents he supervised were more interested in diagnosing rare blood diseases in the children under their care than in noting physical injuries to the children. Dr. Kempe wanted to draw attention to this problem. In one of his first efforts to report on the physical abuse of children, he organized a seminar at an academic meeting on the physical abuse of children. We are told by Barbara J. Nelson, who has researched this story, that

> fellow members of the program committee suggested that a title such as physical abuse which emphasized legally liable and socially deviant behavior might make some members wary of attending the seminar. Kempe agreed, renaming the seminar the "Battered Child Syndrome." In one stroke he labeled the problem in a manner which downplayed the deviant aspects while highlighting the medical aspects. From an agenda-setting perspective the effect of the label cannot be overestimated.

In 1962 Kempe published an article under that title in the *Journal of the American Medical Association*. The rest is history. The mass media took up the phrase and the issue (scarcely a case of a situation that had become observably worse, but rather one for which the right label had been found) became a national one, a classic case of how a social condition becomes a social problem. The Children's Bureau proposed a model child abuse reporting statute in 1963, and by 1967 every state had passed a reporting law. Laws were revised over time to become ever stronger. To the physical abuse of children, attractive enough to the mass media, was added concern for their sexual abuse, and we may well have now reached a stage where considerably more is reported and even prosecuted than exists, and we may be on the verge of a backlash against the attention and resources devoted to the problem, a common stage in the history of such "victories."

Of course it is inevitable, what with changing cycles of attention and fashion, that at one point there will be great attention to a social problem, at a subsequent point much less, with very little change in the problem itself. But what most impresses when one considers the range of problems with which the mass media, scientists, social scientists, legislators, voluntary organizations, all deal, is that no problem is fully neglected. This is not surprising in a democracy where everything is open, every issue has its advocates, and the mass media are ever ready to exploit a problem which has been lying fallow and relatively neglected. There are entrepreneurs of problem-making, problem-enhancing, at all levels: professionals in given areas, who see a problem others do not, such as battered children; bureaucrats seeking to maintain old missions, expand into new missions, as in the case of the Children's Bureau; legislators who leap into an area in which there is no or little legislation and try to make it their own, as Congressman Mario Biaggi did in the case of child abuse; scientists, natural and social, who see opportunities for research; editors and journalists, seeking new and interesting topics; advocacy organizations, some single-mindedly dealing with one clientele, one issue, others seeking to expand into new issues as old ones lose interest and salience. We see the change in perception starting in some cases through some administrative or bureaucratic action at the top, in others being initiated by an outside advocacy group, in others seemingly launched on the public stage by a single book, e.g., Rachel Carson's *Silent Spring,* Ralph Nader's *Unsafe at Any Speed.* The number of enterprises of this sort that have failed (including I am sure many books as good as Nader's and Carson's and trying to draw attention to a

problem as serious as the effect of pesticides on the environment or automobile safety) are far more numerous than the few that have achieved remarkable success.

There is one factor in the potential success of such enterprises that has not been much noted. I think the scale and steadiness of public response to the entrepreneurs of problem-making depends not only on the seriousness of the problem, on the degree to which it impinges directly on public perception, the degree to which it agitates and concerns the public, but on whether any effective action to deal with it is visible. Consider what is called the "urban crisis," the problem of the inner cities. One may argue with the term, it is not well-defined, and contains within itself a host of other problems. It was once high on the public agenda, in the 1960s and 1970s, and then declined, despite steady study, publications, popular books, advocacy groups, special academic programs, and I would conclude this was for one reason: There was nothing to be done, or at least nothing much to be done. Other problems present clear targets, things to be done, even if they will fail: prohibit drink, ban smoking in enclosed spaces, interdict drugs. We learn from the experience, even if slowly and poorly, and eventually we learn there is not much to be done: people will drink and take drugs, there will be cycles of greater or lesser use, and moderate impact is all we can hope for.

We are now at a moment in which great attention is being given in the mass media to a specific problem that can be considered part of the "urban crisis," gun violence, the use of guns in situations, whether of fights among youths or of robbery, in which they were until recently less available or less used, with an accompanying high rate of homicide particularly affecting young black males (who are also those who are using the guns), bystanders, shopkeepers, taxicab drivers. We are now seeing efforts by those in the field of public health to try to recast the problem as a public health one. Thus, it is likened to an "epidemic," which it certainly is, as the word is popularly used, but public health people wonder whether equating it to epidemics such as tuberculosis or AIDS will give us more insight into what is happening, or direct more attention and more effective attention to it, or suggest more tools with which to deal with it.

The model for the campaign against

gun violence that is now developing is the successful reduction of smoking, or of driving under the influence of drink. The public health model calls for such actions as proper tracing of the incidence of the condition, relating it to other social conditions, developing campaigns of information and modes of treatment, devising techniques of education or publicity which change habits—which, for example, would make the possession and use of guns reprehensible. Undoubtedly we will be hearing and seeing a good deal more about this in the coming months, perhaps years. Any such effort, if we take as a model the case of driving under the influence of drink, or smoking, must be long-range. The campaign will take forms we cannot imagine now, and we cannot know whether we will achieve the relative success of our efforts to reduce smoking and drinking-driving, or the relative failure of our efforts to reduce the use of drugs.

But one contrast comes to mind and suggests a caution: smoking and drinking-driving were not matters in which incidence was concentrated in one social class, one ethnic or racial group. One could argue the same with gun violence, if one concentrates on the possession of guns, and the overall incidence of deaths from guns, and if one places in the same statistical category suicides from the use of an available gun, hunting accidents, domestic violence which climaxes with shooting. These kinds of deaths from guns are old matters, and there has not been, I think, any marked change in recent years. The gun violence that is now the subject of so many newspaper and TV stories is a different matter, concentrated in the inner city, affecting largely one major minority group—young blacks—even though it is also present generally and affects almost everybody.

Is anything gained by lumping this phenomenon into a general category of "gun violence," and considering it under the category of public health? I think not. It is one thing to change behavior, through publicity appeals, through campaigns that change popular attitudes toward a behavior from acceptance to disapproval, when that behavior is found throughout the society, and when those to whom one is appealing are representative of the society in general. It must be a different matter when one deals with behavior that is encapsulated in a specific social group. Consider one consequence of creating a general category of "gun violence." One possible approach, the one most popular today in the mass media and among political leaders, is: Make it harder to get guns. This is likely to work among the middle classes and among groups who presently hold guns legally. It is likely to be completely ineffective among the groups whose very behavior has raised the issue to the high pitch of current concern, the young people who are killing each other in the urban ghettoes, and more occasionally (but often enough) killing others. It suggests to us that it is still important to consider just what the problem is, and we move in rather ineffective directions if we frame it improperly. Is the problem "gun violence," or is it rather the larger one of the complex of social problems in the inner cities that we still have no effective means of attacking? Can the problem of gun violence be effectively isolated from this larger complex and reduced? It seems to me doubtful, but many efforts are under way, from Jesse Jackson's exhortations to the attempt to reframe the issue as one of public health to the campaign of Jay Winston of the Harvard School of Public Health to get anti-gun messages into TV programs. And we will learn from these efforts whether gun violence is more like smoking or more like drugs.

Parenting and Family Issues

- **The Family (Articles 3–6)**
- **Homelessness (Article 7)**

Throughout history, the family has been the most effective and primary transmitter (for good or ill) of values, beliefs, and behaviors. But the American family has been under increasing assault since the 1960s. Some individuals argue that it is not so much an assault as it is a restructuring of an antiquated social institution. Single parents, couples with no children, single individuals, unmarried people living together, homosexual couples—almost any and all combinations of persons living under a common roof is now classified by some as a "family."

Questions raised by the articles included in this section include: (a) Just what is a family? (b) What impact is the "new" family structure having on its members, especially the children? (c) What impact are other social institutions having on the family? (d) How does what is happening in the family impact on other institutions? (e) What can and should be done to strengthen the family?

"Fount of Virtue, Spring of Wealth: How the Strong Family Sustains a Prosperous Society" examines the role that strong families play in a prosperous society. Cross-cultural anthropological studies reveal that there are links between violence, poverty, drug abuse, health (both physical and mental), educational accomplishments, and family stability.

"Endangered Family" looks at the unique problems facing black families. This article is not an indictment of blacks, but an attempt to understand why a black child has only one chance in five of growing up with two parents. The economy is a significant culprit. While opportunities for work declined for black men, many opportunities for employment opened for black women, making it possible for them to survive without men. At the same time, governmental programs were created that inadvertently pushed black men out of the family. Increasingly, black leaders are realizing that if the black family is to be saved, it is up to the black community.

"The Disease Is Adolescence" argues that the biggest problem associated with growing into adulthood is the lack of viable, caring role models. The author notes that every child who makes it "successfully" through the teen years has had at least one adult in his or her life who cared, who became involved in his or her life, and who listened.

"Why Leave Children with Bad Parents?" focuses on the implications of programs that stress parental rights and/or family preservation over the welfare of children. In attempting to keep families intact, social welfare agencies aggressively encourage the return of abused children to their abusive parents even when no evidence exists that the parents will not abuse them again.

"The New Outlaws: Cities Make Homelessness a Crime" addresses the human consequences of city officials' attempts to eliminate aggressive begging, shanty-towns, and loitering in public parks. The public pressure to implement such elimination measures has resulted in the creation of new laws (or the enforcement of existing laws) that turn the homeless into criminals.

Looking Ahead: Challenge Questions

What personal experiences have you had with problems in your family?

Is the current high divorce rate good or bad for society?

How do the problems facing children of single parents differ from those who have two parents?

Is it possible to preserve families, especially abusive families, and still protect the health and well-being of children?

In what ways are the lives of American children, particularly minority children, in peril?

What are the primary causes for homelessness? To what extent is homelessness an individual or a societal problem? How can we solve the problem without criminalizing the homeless?

What are the real personal implications of being forced to survive on welfare?

In what key ways would the approaches of symbolic interactionists, functionalists, or conflict theorists differ in the study of family issues?

What conflicts in rights, values, and duties seem to underlie each issue?

Unit 1

FOUNT OF VIRTUE, SPRING OF WEALTH

How the Strong Family Sustains a Prosperous Society

Charmaine Crouse Yoest

Charmaine Crouse Yoest is a Bradley fellow at the University of Virginia and a public policy consultant. She is former deputy director of policy at the Family Research Council, a Washington-based study institute.

"Daddy," I asked, "will you have to go to war?"

At that point, the Vietnam War, for me, consisted primarily of television footage of helicopters and soldiers in the jungle. I was terrified that my father would be called to go to war and die at any moment.

"No, honey," he replied, "the military doesn't draft men who are in school."

Still not understanding why men had to fight and die in wars, I pressed on. "But what if you did have to go? Would you really go?"

"Yes, I would. Sometimes men have to fight to protect the people they love," he explained. "If a burglar wanted to break into our house, I would fight to keep your mom and you and your brother safe."

As he talked, I understood: There are things that are worth dying for. For my dad, like many other people, the list begins with family.

That night my father taught me the integral connection between family and country—that there are times when the burglar is another country and the house our families live in is our country.

And so it is with most of the lessons children need to learn as they grow and mature—they are best taught and modeled in the context of family. Children are the future citizens of any nation. For this reason, societies have a stake in whether children are raised to become good citizens rather than bad ones.

President Theodore Roosevelt wrote: "Sins against pure and healthy family life are those which of all others are sure in the end to be visited most heavily upon the nation." Sociologist Urie Bronfenbrenner, in outlining the needs of children, provides a compelling rationale for the state's interest in preserving the family as the primary context for cultivating healthy children and seeing them develop into productive citizens.

> The informal education that takes place in the family is not merely a pleasant prelude, but rather a powerful prerequisite for success in formal education from the primary grades onward. This empowering experience reaches further still. As evidenced in longitudinal studies, it appears to provide a basis, while offering no guarantee, for the subsequent development of the capacity to function responsively and creatively as an adult in the realms of work, family life, and citizenship.[1]

Quite simply, the family lays the foundation. As increasing bodies of research attest, our families are the fertile ground from which children acquire the patterns, habits, lessons, and values that, in our increasingly interdependent society, affect us all.

From a societal viewpoint, the family is important because of its role in shaping good citizens. Fundamentally, the state

---

1. Urie Bronfenbrenner, "What Do Families Do?" *Family Affairs* (New York: Institute for American Values, Winter/Spring 1991), 4.

President Theodore Roosevelt wrote: "Sins against pure and healthy family life are those which of all others are sure in the end to be visited most heavily upon the nation."

needs stability, achievement, and loyalty from its citizens, and families foster these three qualities.

THE STATE'S NEED FOR STABILITY IN ITS CITIZENRY

There can be no more graphic testimony to a society's need for law and order than the smoldering images of riot-torn Los Angeles. Events like the L.A. riots, New York City's "wilding" episode, and the depredations of Jeffrey Dahmer overshadow the complex policy discussions over the merit of various government spending programs and actions, and they are a keen reminder that, above all else, society is meant to protect its citizens. Although we rarely do it consciously, each of us gives up a measure of individual rights and autonomy in order to live within the bounds of community. We do so with the expectation of greater stability and security than we would have on our own. Thus, while we chafe at the delay in stopping at intersections when the light is red, few of us begrudge that infringement on our personal freedom because of the safety and order it brings to our daily travels.

Some do, however; there are more and more individuals claiming their right to become a law unto themselves. While running red lights is a relatively minor breach of the community contract, the daily escalation of violence in our country attests to increasing instability and weakening of the social order.

Respect for authority and willingness to accept personal limits are character traits upon which social order is built. The lessons that build that kind of private discipline, so important to public stability, are best taught in the home. Kay James,

former assistant secretary at the U.S. Department of Health and Human Services (HHS), tells a true story about two young boys growing up in a poverty-stricken neighborhood.

One day while roaming the neighborhood, the two boys broke into the local school and stole several chickens from the cafeteria refrigerator. Both boys then proudly took their bounty home to their mothers for dinner that night.

The first mother cried out in delight: "Boy, I don't know where you got this, but we sure are going to eat good tonight!"

The second boy came home to a different response. "Son," his mother asked, "I know you don't have a job, and you don't have money. Where did you get those chickens?"

When she heard the details, she took the chickens by the feet and started pummeling her son with them. She backed him into a corner, and with one hand still holding the birds and the other pointed right in his face, she said, "Boy, I will starve before I let one of my children bring stolen food into this house!"

That was all she said before she turned and opened the back door and flung those chickens into the backyard. "If you want to help out around here," she declared, "you can get a job."[2]

Kay recounts that several years later the first mother was left grieving beside the casket of her son, shot to death in a drug deal. The second woman was Kay's own mother. Both she and her brother learned

---

2. Kay James, *Never Forget* (Grand Rapids, Mich.: Zondervan Publishing House, 1993), 46.

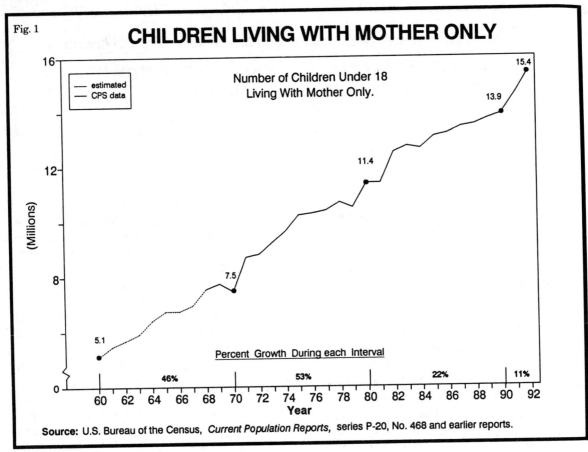

Fig. 1

CHILDREN LIVING WITH MOTHER ONLY

Number of Children Under 18 Living With Mother Only.

Percent Growth During each Interval

Source: U.S. Bureau of the Census, *Current Population Reports*, series P-20, No. 468 and earlier reports.

an enduring and valuable lesson in honesty and respect for authority that night.

Many children today are not being taught respect for any authority—in part because of the increase in father absence. The active involvement of fathers in the raising and disciplining of children, particularly young boys, is crucial. Myriam Miedzian, author of *Boys Will Be Boys: Breaking the Link Between Masculinity and Violence*, stated in testimony before the U.S. House of Representatives that "raising a son without a nurturant father in the home significantly increases the likelihood of the boy becoming violent."[3] She added that this is true even in other cultures:

Cross-cultural anthropological studies indicate that violent behavior is often characteristic of male adolescents and

adults whose fathers were absent or played a small role in their son's early rearing. For example, anthropologists Beatrice Whiting's and John Whiting's study of children in six cultures revealed that those tribes in which the father was most loosely connected with the family and had least to do with the rearing of children, were the most violent. These findings are corroborated by other studies.[4]

Is it any wonder, then, that violence is increasing in our society when the number of children in single-parent, female-headed homes has increased 202 percent since 1960? Today, nearly one-third—28 percent—of all children are born into single-parent homes (see figure 1). In the black community, it has reached as high as 68 percent.

Unfortunately, because of the disparity between the white and black communities in the percentages of single-parent

3. Myriam Miedzian, testimony to the Select Committee on Children, Youth, and Families, U.S. House of Representatives, "Babies and Briefcases: Creating a Family-Friendly Workplace for Fathers," June 11, 1991, 1.

4. Miedzian, "Babies and Briefcases," 3.

"Cross-cultural anthropological studies indicate that violent behavior is often characteristic of male adolescents and adults whose fathers were absent or played a small role in their son's early rearing."

homes, there has developed a mistaken perception that increased levels of crime in some communities is a racial issue rather than one of family structure. A study by Douglas A. Smith and G. Roger Jarjoura, published in 1988, disproved this fallacy:

> Many studies that find a significant association between racial composition and crime rates have failed to control for community family structure and may mistakenly attribute to racial composition an effect that is actually due to the association between race and family structure.[5]

The research points to a strong correlation between the increasing numbers of children growing up in single-parent homes and the rising levels of violence and crime in our country. One reason is the appalling number of adolescent boys who live on the streets and whose need for belonging, identity, camaraderie, and security that should come from family is filled by gangs. Leon Bing, author of *Do or Die*, talked with two fourteen-year-old gang members, "Sidewinder" and "Bopete," in a youth detention center:

> Bopete: "Sometimes I think about not goin' back to banging' when I get outta here. I play in sports a lot here, and I . . ."
>
> Sidewinder's laugh interrupts. "Sound like a regular ol' teenager, don't he? I sound like that, too, after the drive-by. I got shot twice in the leg . . . and when that happen I didn't want to bang no more, either. Makin' promises to God, all

like that. But when it heal up . . ." He is silent for a moment; then, "I tell you somethin'—*I don't feel connected to any other kids in this city or in this country or in this world. I only feel comfortable in my 'hood. That's the only thing I'm connected to, that's my family. One big family—that's about it.*" (emphasis mine)

> "In my 'hood, in the Jungle, it ain't like a gang. It's more like a nation, everybody all together as one. Other kids, as long as they ain't my enemies, I can be cool with 'em." Bopete lapses into silence. "I'll tell you, though—if I didn't have no worst enemy to fight with, I'd probably find somebody."
>
> Sidewinder picks it up. "I'd find somebody. 'Cause if they ain't nobody to fight, it ain't no gangs. It ain't no life. I don't know . . . it ain't no . . ."
>
> "It ain't no fun."
>
> "Yeah! Ain't no fun just sittin' there. Anybody can just sit around, just drink, smoke a little Thai. But that ain't fun like shootin' guns and stabbin' people. *That's* fun."[6]

The family also promotes societal stability by providing men with a proper channel for their sexuality and providing appropriate role models for adolescent boys of a stable, healthy masculinity. Without the nuclear family of husbands and wives, mothers and fathers, to provide these crucial social functions, a vacuum of enormous and devastating proportions is developing. Miedzian quoted the classic work of sociologist Walter Miller:

> Miller pointed out that the extreme concern with toughness and the frequent

---

5. Douglas Smith and G. Roger Jarjoura, "Social Structure and Criminal Victimization," *Journal of Research in Crime and Delinquency* 25 (February 1986), 27–52.

6. Leon Bing, *Do or Die*, as quoted by William Tucker, "Is Police Brutality the Problem?" *Commentary* 95 (January 1993), 26.

"Anybody can just sit around, just drink, smoke a little Thai,"
a gang member said. "But that ain't fun like shootin'
guns and stabbin' people. That's fun."

violence in lower-class culture probably originates in the fact that for a significant percentage of these boys there is no consistently present male figure whom they can identify with and model themselves on. Because of this they develop an "almost obsessive . . . concern with 'masculinity'" which Miller refers to as "hypermasculinity."[7]

Little boys, as they grow toward manhood, must make a break from the feminine role modeled for them by their mothers and establish their own masculine identity. With a father in the home, they can do this relatively painlessly by imitating their dads; when they become men, they can find masculine roles in becoming husbands and fathers themselves. But in our society today, far too many boys are growing up without that male role model and entering an adult society that has ceased to value and support marriage.

In his book *Men and Marriage*, George Gilder champions marriage as an indispensable social construct for the appropriate channeling of male sexual aggression into creativity. "Without a durable relationship with a woman," explains Gilder, "a man's sexual life is a series of brief and temporary exchanges, impelled by a desire to affirm his most rudimentary masculinity."[8]

He goes on to make the case that this male impulse, biologically based though it is, results in a destabilizing influence on society. And, ultimately, it is not fulfilling for men themselves. In the end, looking for meaning in life and given impetus through societal constructs, a man will marry: "The man's love . . .

offers a promise of dignity and purpose. For he then has to create, by dint of his own effort . . . a life that a woman could choose. Thus are released and formed the energies of civilized society. He provides, and he does it for a lifetime, for a life."[9]

A civilized society, a stable society—the antithesis of the mayhem engendered by the new "evolving" family forms—is precisely the objective. Family, based on the fundamental marital union, is the foundation for a strong nation.

As society experiments and individuals reject the responsibilities of family, we all pay a price. Sen. Daniel Patrick Moynihan sounded this alarm in a 1965 article that was greeted with widespread approbation. Three decades later, daily headlines confirm his prescience:

From the wild Irish slums of the nineteenth century eastern seaboard, to the riot-torn suburbs of Los Angeles, there is one unmistakable lesson in American history: a community that allows a large number of young men to grow up in broken families, dominated by women, never acquiring any stable relationship to male authority, never acquiring any set of rational expectations about the future—that community asks for and gets chaos. Crime, violence, unrest, disorder—most particularly the furious, unrestrained lashing out at the whole social structure—that is not only to be expected; it is very near to inevitable. And it is richly deserved.[10]

---

7. Miedzian, "Babies and Briefcases," 2.
8. George Gilder, *Men and Marriage* (Gretna, La.: Pelican Books, 1992), 14.

9. Gilder, *Men and Marriage*, 290.
10. Daniel Patrick Moynihan, *Family and Nation: The Godkin Lectures, Harvard University* (San Diego, New York, London: Harcourt, Brace, Jovanovich, 1986), 9.
11. Alan Carlson, *Family Questions: Reflections on the American Social Crisis* (New Brunswick and Oxford: Transaction Books, 1988), 7.

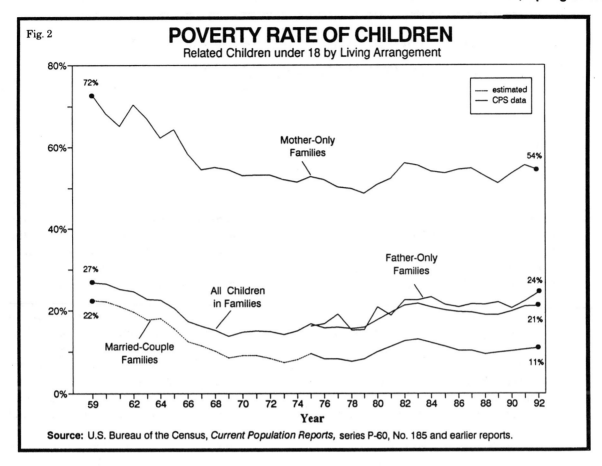

Fig. 2

POVERTY RATE OF CHILDREN
Related Children under 18 by Living Arrangement

Mother-Only Families

Father-Only Families

All Children in Families

Married-Couple Families

estimated
CPS data

72%   54%

27%   24%

22%   21%

        11%

Year

Source: U.S. Bureau of the Census, *Current Population Reports,* series P-60, No. 185 and earlier reports.

THE FAMILY AND ECONOMIC STABILITY

The family fosters stability through its role in character formation. Stability has other facets, however. Among these is economic stability.

The White House Conference on Children in 1970 came to the conclusion that "society has the ultimate responsibility for the well-being and optimum development of all children."[11] Like many ideas that at first glance pass muster, this one contains a kernel of truth: When a child has been abandoned or abused, someone must step in to care for that child. But it is essential to recognize that this is merely a remedial action; the family is the first line of defense and provision of our children. Nevertheless, it has become increasingly common to hear terminology that reflects the philosophy inherent in the White House Conference statement. Some refer to "society's children," but even more often we hear, "America's children." In many

cases, this is an innocent turn of phrase; in others, it reflects a lack of recognition of the primacy of the parental responsibility for children.

But what relevance do parental rights and responsibilities have in the context of economic stability? Headlines scream, "Numbers of American Children in Poverty Rising," and some public opinion brokers draw the erroneous conclusion that economics is the major factor in producing poverty.

The truth is that not all American children have shared equally in the rising poverty rates. Children in single-parent homes are five times more likely to live in poverty than children in two-parent homes (see figure 2). Additionally, children in two-parent homes move more easily out of poverty through fluctuations in the economy; children in single-parent homes live in more persistent poverty despite improvements in economic conditions.

The strong correlation between family structure and poverty among children is consistently overlooked or downplayed

Children in single-parent homes are five times more likely to live in poverty than children in two-parent homes.

by policymakers. Of course, some children in two-parent homes live in poverty. However, with a differential of this magnitude—*five times*—the importance of the nuclear family in providing basic economic essentials for children should be unquestioned.

The inescapable difficulty of raising children alone is even more clear if we look at the poverty levels of children living with only their fathers: These children are less likely than children living with only their mothers to live in poverty, but they are *still twice as likely* to live in poverty as children in two-parent homes.

There is a striking contrast between the changes in the poverty levels of children living with only their mothers and children in two-parent homes. With improvements in the economy in the past, the poverty level of children in two-parent families has dramatically dropped; at the same time, the poverty level of children in single-parent homes has steadily increased with very few fluctuations. During the 1975 and 1982 recessions, more children became impoverished, with a subsequent drop occurring during the recovery in families with married parents.

By meeting children's and other family members' most basic economic needs so effectively and efficiently, the family functions as a stabilizing bulwark. Its absence leaves gaping holes. Just look at the last three decades in our country— welfare dependency has increased dramatically in the wake of unprecedented family breakdown. The majority of women receiving Aid to Families with Dependent Children (AFDC) are not married to the fathers of their children. Fifty-three percent of all AFDC recipients have "no marriage tie." The second most prevalent reason for AFDC payments, 38.5 percent, is divorce or separation. The group

most likely to become long-term (ten years or more) AFDC recipients are women who are single mothers. Marriage remains the No. 1 escape route from the welfare rolls.

When parents shirk their responsibility to provide financially for their own children, everyone suffers. Even though the government has stepped into the breach to provide subsistence for children abandoned by their fathers, a bureaucratic safety net has proved a poor substitute for paternal provision. The fact remains, the family is society's best vehicle for the self-reliance of individuals and the care of children. Even the centrist-Democrat Progressive Policy Institute, in its *Mandate for Change* document, states: "It is no exaggeration to say that a stable, two-parent family is an American child's best protection against poverty."[12] Research clearly demonstrates this truth. The U.S. Department of Health and Human Services found that in 1985–86 "the poverty rate for married teens living with husband and children was 28% compared with 81% for unmarried teen mothers living alone with their children."[13]

THE ROLE OF THE FAMILY IN PHYSICAL AND MENTAL HEALTH

Another facet of societal stability is the general level of health of its population. In an era of high-tech medical care, health is an area where the family has a significant, but little recognized, effect. Yet research

---

12. Elaine Ciulla Kamarck and William Galston, "A Progressive Family Policy for the 1990s," *Mandate for Change* (New York: Berkley Books, 1993), 157.
13. Gilbert Crouse and David Larson, "Cost of Teenage Childbearing: Current Trends," *ASPE Research Notes: Information for Decision Makers*, U.S. Department of Health and Human Services (August 1992).

demonstrates another, slightly surprising, contribution the family makes to its members: Children in stable, two-parent homes are healthier than other children, and adults who are married are healthier than those who are not.

The National Commission on America's Urban Families released its *Families First* report in January 1993, saying that: "In sum, problems of psychological distress and poor mental health, which carry profound social as well as personal consequences, are among the most pervasive and most damaging consequences of current family fragmentation in the United States."[14]

There is increasing recognition that divorce is a prime contributor to health problems for both adults and children. However, skeptics have claimed that the ill effects of divorce on children can actually be attributed to the negative predivorce environment of the home and that divorce is an improvement for those children. While it is certainly true that the nature of the marital relationship has a profound effect on children, one study cited by the Urban Commission indicates that divorce may not be the best solution for a contentious home. A 1991 study compared two sets of troubled boys, the first from divorced homes and the second from intact homes. After a five-year follow-up, the researchers found that the former group of boys had higher rates of both substance abuse and mental health problems than the latter.[15]

One of the most influential studies to be done in recent years was the 1991 report by Deborah Dawson of the National Center for Health Statistics based on the 1988 National Health Interview Survey on Child Health, which was a survey of seventeen thousand children nationwide. On the positive side, Dawson found "overall good health of the child population." However, she found that after controlling for social and demographic characteristics, "children who had experienced the separation of their natural parents . . . were more likely than other children to

have had an accident, injury, or poisoning in the preceding year."[16]

But the most startling results came when Dawson turned to the emotional and psychological health of children: "Children living with formerly married mothers were more than three times as likely as those living with both biological parents to have received treatment for emotional or behavioral problems in the preceding twelve months."[17]

She found an elevated score for children living with stepparents and never-married mothers, as well. Finally, in looking at the "overall behavioral problem score," she found that children living with their biological parents once again scored better. "This pattern was repeated in the scores for antisocial behavior, anxiety or depression, headstrong behavior, hyperactivity, dependency, and peer conflict or social withdrawal," reported Dawson.

Adults as well as children are affected. Researchers at Yale and the University of California at Los Angeles have found that marriage is a significant buffer against the stresses of life for adults. Among both blacks and whites, men and women, being married correlates with a lower rate of psychiatric illness. They concluded, "The loss of a spouse through death, divorce, or separation is especially predictive of ill health."[18]

HOW THE FAMILY PROMOTES INDIVIDUAL ACHIEVEMENT

The greatest wealth a society has is its citizens. To thrive, a country needs the productivity of motivated citizens who press forward to achieve. The mystique of the "American work ethic" springs out of the innumerable individual accomplishments and innovations that have, collectively, made the United States the great nation that it is.

14. *Families First*, Report of the National Commission on America's Urban Families (Washington, D.C.: January 1993), 29.

15. William Doherty and Richard Needle, "Psychological Adjustment and Substance Use among Adolescents before and after a Parental Divorce," *Child Development* 61 (April 1991), 332–35; as cited in *Families First*.

16. Deborah Dawson, "Family Structure and Children's Health: United States, 1988," U.S. Department of Health and Human Services, Public Health Service, Centers for Disease Control, National Center for Health Statistics (June 1991), 7.

17. Dawson, "Family Structure," 3.

18. David Williams, David Takeuchi, and Russell Adair, "Marital Status and Psychiatric Disorders among Blacks and Whites," *Journal of Health and Social Behavior* 33 (1992), 140–57; as cited in *The Family in America* (Rockford, Ill.: The Rockford Institute, October 1992).

Children in stable, two-parent homes are physically and mentally healthier than other children, and adults who are married are healthier than those who are not.

This, too, begins in the family. One very accomplished professional woman remembers hearing her father, Mr. Stone, say to his family on many occasions, "We Stones are hard workers!" The repetition left an indelible impression. It is this unique ability of the family to encourage the development of character in its members that makes it invaluable in preparing young people to be positive contributors to society. Values that are essential in the work force—discipline, respect for authority, perseverance—most often are forged in the family crucible.

Family also provides motivation. The historian and family expert, Alan Carlson, has said, "The family contains within its bounds the necessary positive incentives which make human beings behave in economically useful ways."[19] In echoes of Gilder, the point is that both men and women will strive harder to achieve and provide for those they love than they will for themselves.

And, as any teacher in any school across our nation will attest, the family is an irreplaceable foundation for education. The data underscore a family's integral role in preparing children for learning. More specifically, just as crime, health, and poverty are affected by family structure, the research leaves no doubt that children in two-parent families have a significant advantage in formal education. According to a U.S. Department of Education study of twenty-five thousand students, after controlling for socioeconomic status, race, and sex:

[Students] from single-parent families were still more likely to fail to perform at the basic proficiency levels. They were about one-quarter to one-third more likely to perform below the basic reading and math levels and were more than two and a half times as likely to drop out of school as were students from two-parent families.[20]

(Additionally, Deborah Dawson found that children in single-parent homes were 40–75 percent more likely to repeat a grade and 70 percent more likely to be expelled from school.)

Although there are several factors contributing to the worsening state of American education, we cannot afford to turn a blind eye to the effect single parenthood is having on the readiness to learn, and the ability to learn, of millions of young children. If our country is to stay competitive, it cannot afford to have poorly educated citizens and workers. In particular, as we move into an increasingly sophisticated, highly technical economy, we will need equally sophisticated workers.

THE FAMILY'S PART IN FOSTERING LOYALTY

My brother and I as kids used to belt out the *Battle Hymn of the Republic* with childish enthusiasm . . . "Mine eyes have seen the glory of the coming of the Lord," building to a crescendo on the "Glory, Glory Hallelujahs." We loved that part, drawing out the emphasis on the high note with questionable musical effect. The song is indelibly linked in my mind with the laughter of my grandfather,

---

19. Carlson, *Family Questions*, xvi.

20. "Characteristics of At-Risk Students in NELS: 88," U.S. Department of Education, National Center for Education Statistics, 13–14; as cited in *Families First*.

Gloria Steinem stated that "family is content, not form." This rationalization accompanied the sixties' changes in individual behavior—changes that gave rise to skyrocketing rates of divorce and out-of-wedlock births.

a proud Marine and World War II veteran, who took great joy in teaching us patriotic songs. Now, many years after his death, the song tends to evoke for me, not laughter, but a wistfulness mixed with a deep and abiding pride in the heritage of courage and patriotism he gave us.

Like many veterans, my grandfather did not talk much about his war experiences. He did not have to. The mere fact of his service gave testimony to his devotion to his country. Semper Fi! No school civics lesson could compare with the example of patriotism set by my grandfather.

Years later, the last notes of Taps sounded over Arlington National Cemetery as the chaplain stepped over to hand my mother-in-law the folded flag. My father-in-law had died after a full life, surviving service in two wars. Beyond our circle of friends and family, up the hill as far as the eye could see, were row after row of rounded white tombstones, standing in mute testimony to the men and women who were dedicated to the defense of our country.

One last, essential need a country has of its citizens is devotion. Our Constitution says our Founding Fathers had come together to "provide for the common defense." The gravestones in Arlington Cemetery represent devotion to country. Where does that kind of sacrifice, that bravery, come from? What made so many willing to die?

Why were they willing? For love of country, surely. But that love and devotion is most often predicated upon the fact that the country hosts what we hold most dear: our families.

'LOVE THE ONE YOU'RE WITH . . .'

What kind of social construct produces a good citizen? Many view the sweeping changes occurring in families as a benign social progression. In the last few decades, more and more people have joined the chorus of voices saying, "All you need is love." According to this viewpoint, family structure simply does not matter very much. Gloria Steinem, for instance, has stated that "family is content, not form." This rationalization accompanied the sixties' and seventies' changes in individual behavior—changes that gave rise to the skyrocketing rates of divorce and out-of-wedlock births. Partly causal factor and partly retrospective rationale, the cries of "family is what you make it" provide both a blazing path for those seeking individual self-actualization and an explanation for those seeking a context for their own bewildering circumstances. Unfortunately, the theory does not match up too closely with reality.

One man, now a successful professional in his midtwenties with a beautiful wife and a well-adjusted life, still vividly remembers the effect the loss of his father in a car crash had on him as a young teenager. He hears the public debate over family structure with strident voices claiming that single-parent families are "just as good" as two-parent homes and compares those claims to his own experience.

"Do they mean," he asks, "that my dad's death just didn't matter? How can

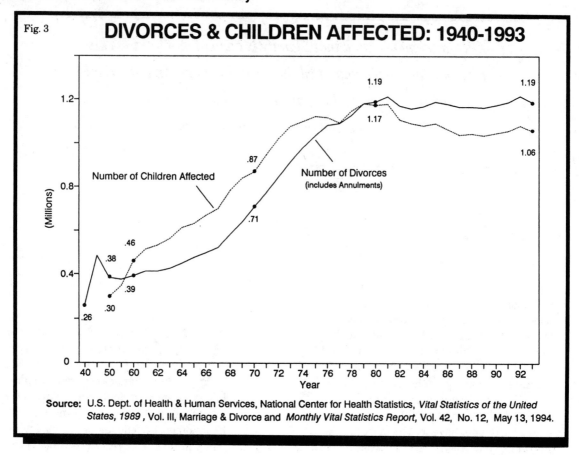

Fig. 3

DIVORCES & CHILDREN AFFECTED: 1940-1993

Source: U.S. Dept. of Health & Human Services, National Center for Health Statistics, *Vital Statistics of the United States, 1989* , Vol. III, Marriage & Divorce and *Monthly Vital Statistics Report*, Vol. 42, No. 12, May 13, 1994.

they imply that growing up without my father was irrelevant?"

Another woman struggled through her parents' divorce as a teenager. As an adult, she built her own successful life—until she began contemplating marriage herself. Then, her parents' experience became a barrier, as it does for many children of divorce. Today, even with an adoring, devoted fiancé, she says she struggles with feelings of insecurity. "How do I know," she wonders, "that he won't leave me like my father left my mom?"

Even though the personal anecdotes are piling up and are supported by an ever-increasing body of social science research, many authorities in our society deny the intrinsic importance of the family. *Time* magazine, in a special issue devoted to "Beyond the Year 2000," claimed that "the very term nuclear family gives off a musty smell." Leslie Wolfe, executive director of the Center for Women Policy Studies, said in that issue in an article entitled: "The Nuclear Fam-

ily Goes Boom": "The isolated nuclear family of the 1950s was a small blip in the radar. We've been looking at it as normal, but in fact it was a fascinating anomaly."

The real surprise in Wolfe's statement is that she did not come right out and use the overworked sobriquet of "Ozzie and Harriet" as a target in her sneer at the 1950's. Typically, those attacking the nuclear family exercise no such self-restraint. In a 1989 report, Daniel Seligman of *Fortune* reported that:

we sidled up to Nexis the other day and nonchalantly asked how many news stories in 1989 included the phrase "Ozzie and Harriet." Startling answer: 88 stories. Usual context . . . A politician was onstage reciting the news that the traditional nuclear family—the kind symbolized by the Nelsons during their marathon stint on black-and-white TV—was dead or dying.[21]

21. Daniel Seligman, *Fortune*, July 17, 1989; as cited in "Catching the Reruns: Ozzie, Harriet, and the Media," *Family Affairs* 2 (New York: Institute for American Values, Summer/Fall 1989), 13.

Almost one hundred years after Nietzsche declared that "God is dead," his intellectual descendants, in perhaps a natural succession of thought, are crying, "The family is dead."

Almost exactly one hundred years after Friedrich Nietzsche declared that "God is dead," his intellectual descendants, in perhaps a natural succession of thought, are crying, "The family is dead."

Stephanie Coontz, who has written a book titled *The Way We Never Were: American Families and the Nostalgia Trap*, is one such pessimist. Perhaps her entire thesis—and that of the ideological movement she represents—can be summed up by this statement:

Although there are many things to draw on in our past, there is no one family form that has ever protected people from poverty or social disruption, and no traditional arrangement that provides a workable model for how we might organize family relations in the modern world.[22]

Predictably, she joins the chorus attacking sitcom straw men: "1950's family strategies and values offer no solution to the discontents that underlie contemporary romanticization of the 'good old days.' Contrary to popular opinion, 'Leave it to Beaver' was not a documentary."[23]

The depth of the philosophical disagreement on the family can be seen in a further look at Senator Moynihan's statements on family. Despite his early and courageous recognition of the consequences of family breakdown, he, too, denies the existence of a specific "form" that is recognizable as *family*:

It would be enough for a national family policy to declare that the American government sought to promote the stability and well-being of the American family;

. . . and that the President, or some person designated by him, would report to the Congress on the condition of the American family in all its many facets—not of THE American family, for there is as yet no such thing, but rather of the great range of American family modes in terms of regions, national origins, and economic status.[24]

This debate over the value of the family and its place in society is nothing new. Nevertheless, at times, we retread ground that has proven sterile in the past, unwisely failing to learn from history.

Sociologists tell us that an almost inescapable component of the growth of modernity is a corollary rise in individualism. This has certainly been true in our own society. And individualism has had a marked effect on family life. Problems arise when "the sacredness of the family" is replaced by "the sacredness of the individual."[25] Harvard sociologist Carle Zimmerman has identified cycles of two or three generations where individualism has replaced an emphasis on family,[26] including eight major periods in Western history in which the family was viewed as old-fashioned. In each of these times, society began valuing the individual over the concerns of the family as a unit. The results in each instance led to societal decay.

Examples of the failure of individualism include the Greek and Roman societies in the third century B.C. and the fourth century A.D., respectively. Greek society in the third century B.C. engendered the collapse of the patriarchal family, leading to an emphasis on the indi-

22. Stephanie Coontz, *The Way We Never Were* (New York: Basic Books, 1992), 5.
23. Coontz, *The Way We Never Were*, 29.
24. Moynihan, *Family and Nation*, 11.
25. Don McNally, "The Family in History," *Vanguard* (September/October 1980), 13.
26. McNally, "The Family in History," 13–14; citing Carle Zimmerman, *The Family of Tomorrow* (1949) and Christopher Dawson, *The Dynamics of World History*.

Judith Stacey, author of Brave New Families, *says: "The 'family' is not here to stay. All democratic people, whatever their kinship preferences, should work to hasten its demise."*

vidual and devotion to public life that resulted in late marriages and small families. The final cultural breakdown led to Roman conquest. The Roman Empire in the fourth century A.D. made the same mistake, resulting in its fall.[27]

GOVERNMENT'S INFLUENCE ON THE FAMILY

As we approach the twenty-first century, the family and the government are in an uneasy alliance in America. Forward movement, however, has become a wobble rather than a smooth progression as the balance between family and government has been shaken askew. A battle rages—sometimes quietly, sometimes with guns blazing—as those who would increase the power of government jockey for position with those who resist in favor of family autonomy. David Blankenhorn, in looking at these combatants, gives this analysis:

There is a particularly sterile argument about the role of government. The traditional argument between left and right has been over the size of government. The conservatives want less, the liberals want more, and that's the perennial argument. The debate regarding families is not really, should government be smaller or larger. What matters is the relationship of public policy to family well-being. What is the distribution of costs and benefits to families and what is the message of public policy about what

we value and what we devalue about the importance of family in this society.[28]

The central question remains: Do we value families? While their role in strengthening society should be undisputed, it is not. The family is indispensable in the formation and continuity of a strong and stable society. Even in the face of those who view the family as irrelevant, the family stands on its own, with its own intrinsic strength. So much so, in fact, that some recognize the superiority of family over government in accomplishing societal goals.

The real battle is with those who see the family as competition and threat. Witness Judith Stacey, author of *Brave New Families*: "The 'family' is not here to stay. Nor should we wish it were. On the contrary, I believe that all democratic people, whatever their kinship preferences, should work to hasten its demise."[29]

Although Stacey's sentiments are based on the overarching philosophy of individualism, her conclusions fall in line with those who have, throughout history, seen the interests of family as diametrically opposed to those of society—and come down on the side of an omniscient, paternalistic government. Plato, Marx, Hitler, Stalin—all in their own way recognized the strength of the family. But rather than viewing that strength as a basis upon which to build a thriving, vital society, they sought to control and dampen its vibrancy.

History has proven the bankruptcy of opposition to the family. The way forward for individuals and for the nation is in rebuilding and reemphasizing the family. The society that does so will, in the doing, become stronger.

27. McNally, "The Family in History," 13–14; citing Carle Zimmerman, *The Family of Tomorrow* (1949) and Christopher Dawson, *The Dynamics of World History*.

28. David Blankenhorn, "The Relationship of Public Policy to Family Well-Being," *American Family* (August 1988), 3.

29. As cited by David Popenoe, "The Controversial Truth: Two-Parent Families Are Better," *New York Times*, 16 Dec. 1992, 21.

ENDANGERED FAMILY

*For many African-Americans, marriage and childbearing do not go together.
After decades of denial and blame, a new candor is emerging as
blacks struggle to save their families.*

L ate on a sultry summer morning, Dianne Caballero settles onto her porch in the New York suburb of Roosevelt, bemused by the scene playing out across the street. Behind electric clippers, a muscular black man is trimming hedges with the intensity of a barber sculpting a fade; nearby, his wife empties groceries from the car. In most quarters, they might elicit barely a nod. But in this largely black, working-class community, the couple is one of the few intact families on the block. All too common are the five young women who suddenly turn into view, every one of them pushing a baby stroller, not one of them married. Resigned, Caballero says with a sigh, "Where are the men?"

It's a lament she knows too well. Like her mother before her and her daughter after, Caballero, who is black, had a child out of wedlock at 16. Twenty-three years later, even she is astounded at the gulf between motherhood and marriage. When her mother got pregnant in the

This article was reported by Farai Chideya, Michele Ingrassia, Vern E. Smith and Pat Wingert. It was written by Michele Ingrassia.

'50s, she says, she was considered unique. When Caballero had a baby in 1970, no one ostracized her, though it still wasn't something "nice" girls did. But by the time her daughter had a baby seven years ago, it was regarded as "normal." Now, Caballero says regretfully, it's commonplace. "And there doesn't

---

A black child has only one chance in five of growing up with two parents

---

seem to be anything happening to reverse it."

That prospect troubles black leaders and parents alike, those like Caballero, who worries that her granddaughter is destined to be the fourth generation in her family to raise a child without a man. The odds are perilously high:

- For blacks, the institution of marriage has been devastated in the last generation: 2 out of 3 first births to black women under 35 are now out of wedlock. In 1960, the number was 2 out of 5. And it's not likely to improve any time soon. A black child born today

has only a 1-in-5 chance of growing up with two parents until the age of 16, according to University of Wisconsin demographer Larry L. Bumpass. The impact, of course, is not only on black families but on all of society. Fatherless homes boost crime rates, lower educational attainment and add dramatically to the welfare rolls.

- Many black leaders rush to portray out-of-wedlock births as solely a problem of an entrenched underclass. It's not. It cuts across economic lines. Among the poor, a staggering 65 percent of never-married black women have children, double the number for whites. But even among the well-to-do, the differences are striking: 22 percent of never-married black women with incomes above $75,000 have children, almost 10 times as many as whites.

Nearly 30 years ago, Daniel Patrick Moynihan, then an assistant secretary of labor, caused a firestorm by declaring that fatherless homes were "the fundamental source of the weakness of the Negro Community." At the time, one quarter of black families were headed by women. Today the situation has only grown worse. A majority of black families with children—62 percent—are now headed by one parent. The result is what Johns Hopkins University sociologist Andrew Cherlin calls "an almost complete separation of marriage and child-bearing among African-Americans."

It was not always so. Before 1950, black and white marriage patterns looked remarkably similar. And while black marriage rates have precipitously dipped since then, the desire to marry remains potent: a NEWSWEEK Poll of single African-American adults showed that 88 percent said that they wanted to get married. But the dream of marriage has been hammered in the last 25 years. The economic dislocations that began in the '70s, when the nation shifted from an industrial to a service base, were particularly devastating to black men, who had migrated north in vast numbers to manufacturing jobs. The civil-rights movement may have ended legal segregation, but it hasn't erased discrimination in the work force and in everyday life. "When men lose their ability to earn bread, their sense of self declines dramatically. They lose rapport with their children," says University of Oklahoma historian Robert Griswold, author of "Fatherhood in America."

Some whites overlooked jobs and discrimination as factors in the breakdown of the black family. Back in the '60s, at the peak of the battle over civil rights, Moynihan infuriated blacks by describing a pattern of "pathology." Understandably, blacks were not willing to tolerate a public discussion that implied they were different—less deserving—than whites. The debate quickly turned bitter and polarized between black and white, liberal and conservative. Emboldened by a cultural sea change during the Reagan-Bush era, conservatives scolded, "It's all your fault." Dismissively, this camp insisted that what blacks need are mainstream American values—read: *white* values. Go to school, get a job, get married, they exhorted, and the family will be just fine. Not so, liberals fired back. As neoliberal University of Chicago sociologist William Julius Wilson argued in "The Declining Significance of Race," the breakdown of the African-American family resulted from rising unemployment, not falling values. Liberals have regarded the conservative posture as "blaming the victim," a phrase that, not coincidentally, white psychologist William Ryan coined in a 1965 assessment of Moynihan's study. To

this camp, any family structure is good, as long as it's nurturing. "Marriage is important in the black community, just not the most important thing," says Andrew Billingsley, the University of Maryland sociologist who wrote the pioneering "Black Families in White America." "It is not an imperative for black people who can afford it."

Who's right? Both sides are too busy pointing fingers to find out. "We're never going to get to where we need to be if we first have to settle whose fault it is," says writer Nicholas Lemann, whose 1991 book, "The Promised Land," chronicles the great migration of blacks from the rural south to the industrialized North. But if there is any optimism, it is that now, after more than two decades on the defensive and with a Democratic president in the White House for the first time in 12 years, the African-American community is beginning to talk a little more openly about its problems. "Because of all the debate about morality, social programs, individual responsibility, it became very difficult to have an honest discussion," says Angela Glover Blackwell, who heads the Children's Defense Fund's Black Community Crusade for Children. "I'd like to think we've entered an era where we're willing to accept that there is a dual responsibility" between government and ordinary citizens.

Without question, government must do more to help. But increasingly, African-Americans are unwilling to wait for White America to step in. "During inte-

gration," says Virginia Walden, who owns a day-care center in Washington, D.C., "we kept saying that the white people did us wrong, and that they owed us. Well, white people did us wrong, but I tell my children, "Don't nobody owe you anything. You've got to work for what you get'." In response, many African-American men and women have thrown themselves into a range of grass-roots efforts from volunteer work in their communities to adopting children—stopgap efforts, perhaps, but to many, also

Steep Rise in Out-of-Wedlock Births

Since the sexual revolution, the rate has shot up for both races. But the numbers are much higher for black women than white women.

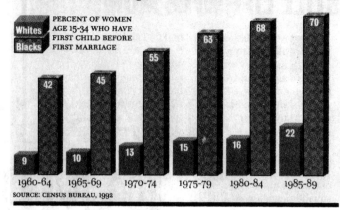

SOURCE: CENSUS BUREAU, 1992

NEWSWEEK

POLL

WHAT BLACK ADULTS THINK

How important are the following reasons young, unmarried black people today are having children?

(Percent saying very important)

53% They don't understand sex or birth control

48% They won't use birth control or have abortions for personal or religious reasons

38% They want something all their own

37% They want to prove they are adults

35% They are following the examples of older people they know

THE NEWSWEEK POLL, AUGUST 12-15, 1993

cathartic and energizing. In many neighborhoods, the black church has led the awakening. Ministers began chastising themselves for sidestepping some basic moral issues. "We don't use 'family values' as an ax," says Wallace Smith, pastor of Shiloh Baptist Church in Washington. "But if someone is shacked up, we encourage them to get married." Smith is remarkably blunt about his own belief in the importance of a stable marriage. "Dan Quayle," he says, "was right."

At their kitchen tables and in their church basements every day, black families talk to each other, as they always have, about their fears. And part of what worries them is the growing tension between black men and black women, who are quick to blame each other for the massive retreat from marriage. "Black men say black women are 'Sapphires,' trying to dominate," explains Harvard psychologist Alvin Poussaint, referring to the wife of Kingfish in "Amos 'n' Andy," who epitomized the bitchy, bossy black woman. But Boston anchorwoman Liz Walker believes that many black men mistake self-reliance for highhandedness. "I don't think black women have thrown black men out," says Walker, who sparked a controversy when she became pregnant out of wedlock six years ago, long before TV's Murphy Brown knew what a home pregnancy test was. "I think black women have been abandoned."

More commonly, though, black women feel the fallout of the economic and psychological battering the African-Ameri-

can male has taken in the last generation. Of course black women want love and commitment. But not with a man whose chief qualification for marriage is that he's, well, a man. The remarkable success of Terry McMillan's 1991 novel, "Waiting to Exhale," underscores that passion. The book's main characters are four strong-minded black women who can't seem to find men who measure up. They clearly struck a nerve. "When Terry McMillan wrote that book, the reason it was so popular was because it was *us*," says Walker, 42. Giddy one night from too much birthday champagne and pepperoni pizza, McMillan's quartet—Robin, Gloria, Bernadine and Savannah—get to the essential question: what's happened to all the men, they ask. Where are they hiding?

They're ugly.
Stupid.
In prison.
Unemployed.
Crackheads.
Short.
Liars.
Unreliable.
Irresponsible.
Too possessive . . .
Childish.
Too goddam old and set in their ways.

The litany drives the women to tears. But does marriage really matter? Or is a family headed by a single mother just as good as the nuclear unit? The evidence come down solidly on the side of marriage. By every measure—economic, social, educational—the statistics conclude that two parents living together are better than one. Children of single mothers are significantly more likely to live in poverty than children living with both parents. In 1990, Census figures show, 65 percent of children of black single mothers were poor, compared with only 18 percent of children of black married couples. Educationally, children in one-parent homes are at greater risk across the board—for learning problems, for being left back, for dropping out. Psychiatrist James P. Comer, who teaches at Yale University's Child Study Center, says that the exploding population of African-American children from single-parent homes represents "the education crisis that is going to kill us. The crisis that we're concerned about—that American kids don't achieve as well as European kids and some Asian kids—won't

kill us because [American students are] scoring high enough to compete. The one that will kill us is the large number of bright kids who fall out of the mainstream because their families are not functioning."

Statistics tell only part of the story. Equally important are the intangibles of belonging to an intact family. "Growing up in a married family is where you learn the value of the commitments you make to each other, rather than seeing broken promises," says Roderick Harrison, chief of the Census Bureau's race division. "It deals with the very question of what kind of personal commitments people can take seriously."

Boys in particular need male role models. Without a father, who will help them define what it means to be a man? Fathers do things for their children that mothers often don't. Though there are obviously exceptions, fathers typically encourage independence and a sense of adventure, while mothers are more nurturing and protective. It is men who teach boys how to be fathers. "A woman can only nourish the black male child to a certain point," says Bob Crowder, an Atlanta lawyer and father of four, who helped organize an informal support group for African-American fathers. "And then it takes a man to raise a boy into a man. I mean a real man." Mothers often win the job by default, and struggle to meet the challenge. But sometimes, even a well-intentioned single mother can be smothering, especially if her son is the only man in her life. Down the road a few years, she hears erstwhile daughters-in-law lament how she "ruined" him for every other woman. Like the street-smart New Yorker she is, Bisi Ruckett, who is Dianne Caballero's daughter, says flat out that she can't "rule" her boyfriend. And just as quickly, she concedes she can't compete with his mom. "If he tells her he needs a zillion dollars, she'll get it," says Ruckett, 23.

Without a father for a role model, many boys learn about relationships from their peers on the street. In the inner city in particular, that often means gangs; and the message they're selling is that women are whores and handmaidens, not equals. Having a father does not, of course, guarantee that the lessons a young male learns will be wholesome. But research shows that, with no father, no minister, no boss to help define responsibility, there's nothing to prevent a boy from treating relationships perversely. University of Pennsylvania professor Elijah Anderson, who authored a 1990 study on street life, says that, among the poor, boys view courting as a "game" in which the object is to perfect a rap that seduces girls. The goal: to add up one's sexual conquests, since that's the measure of "respect."

Often, for a girl, Anderson says, life revolves around the "dream," a variation of the TV soaps in which a man will whisk her away to a life of middle-class

---

Wallace Smith, pastor of Washington's Shiloh Church, puts it bluntly: 'Dan Quayle was right.'

---

bliss—even though everywhere she looks there are only single mothers abandoned by their boyfriends. Not surprisingly, the two sexes often collide. The girl dreams because she must. "It has to do with one's conception of oneself: 'I will prevail'," Anderson says. But the boy tramples that dream because he must—his game is central to his vision of respect. "One of the reasons why, when a woman agrees to have a baby, these men think it's such a victory is that you have to get her to go against all the stuff that says he won't stick around."

For teenage mothers not mature enough to cope, single parenthood is not the route to the dream, but entrapment. They have too many frustrations: the job, the lack of a job, the absence of a man, the feeling of being dependent on others for help, the urge to go out and dance instead of pacing with a crying child. Taken to its extreme, says Poussaint, the results can be abuse or neglect. "They'll see a child as a piece of property or compete with the child—calling them dumb or stupid, damaging their growth and education to maintain superiority," he says. The middle class is not exempt from such pain. Even with all the cushions money could buy—doctors and backup doctors, nannies and backup nannies—Liz Walker says that trying to raise her son, Nicholas, alone was draining. "Certainly, the best situation is to have as many people in charge of a family as possible," says Walker, who is now married to Harry Graham, a 41-year-old corporate-tax lawyer; together, they're raising her son and his two children from a previous marriage. "I can see that now," she adds. "Physically, you *need* it."

More and more, black men aren't there to build marriages or to stick around through the hard years of parenting. The question we're too afraid to confront is why. The biggest culprit is an economy that has locked them out of the mainstream through a pattern of bias and a history of glass ceilings. "The economic state of the African-American community is worse in 1993 than it was in 1963," says NAACP head Benjamin

Chavis Jr. He could be speaking, just as easily, about the black family, since the two fell in tandem.

A man can't commit to a family without economic security, but for many African-American men, there is none. The seeds of modern economic instability date back to the 1940s, when the first of 6½ million blacks began migrating from the rural South to the urban North as farm mechanization replaced the need for their backs and hands. At first, black men built a solid economic niche by getting factory jobs. But just as the great migration ended in the '70s, the once limitless industrial base began to cave in. And as steel mills and factories swept offshore, the "last hired, first fired" seniority rules disproportionately pushed black men out. During that time, says Billingsley, unemployment for blacks became twice as high as it was for whites, "and it has rarely dropped below that [ratio] since." Unarguably, economic restructuring hit whites as well as blacks, but the new service sector favored those with education—and there were many more educated white men than blacks in the '70s as vast numbers of baby boomers streamed out of the nation's colleges looking for jobs.

Ironically, just as the job market collapsed for black men, it opened for black women, who went to college while black men went to war. Armed with the college degrees that black males didn't have and pushed by the burgeoning women's movement, growing numbers of black women found spots in corporate America. As with white women in the '80s, that bought them greater independence. But the jobs of black women came at the expense of black men. Throughout the workplace, says Yale's Comer, "there was a trade-off. The one black woman was a two-fer: you got a black and a woman." Since then, the gap between white women's income and black women's has disappeared—black women's salaries are the same as whites'.

But the chasm between black and white men has barely moved. In 1969, black men earned 61 cents for every dollar white men earned; by 1989, the number had increased to only 69 cents. And that's for black men who were working; more and more, they found themselves without jobs. During the same time, the number of black men with less than a high-school education who found jobs dropped from two thirds to barely half. And it's likely to worsen: in

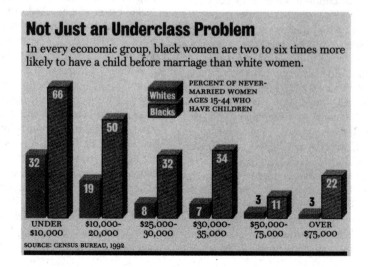

Not Just an Underclass Problem

In every economic group, black women are two to six times more likely to have a child before marriage than white women.

PERCENT OF NEVER-MARRIED WOMEN AGES 15-44 WHO HAVE CHILDREN

Whites / Blacks

	UNDER $10,000	$10,000-20,000	$25,000-30,000	$30,000-35,000	$50,000-75,000	OVER $75,000
Whites	32	19	8	7	3	3
Blacks	66	50	32	34	11	22

SOURCE: CENSUS BUREAU, 1992

the last 25 years, the proportion of black men in college has steadily eroded. "America has less use for black men today than it did during slavery," says Eugene Rivers, who helps run computer-training programs as pastor of Boston's Azusa Christian Community.

Though he is scarcely 11, Lugman Kolade dreams of becoming an electrical engineer. But he already wears the grievous pain of a man who feels left out. Lugman is a small, studious, Roman Catholic schooler from Washington, D.C., who will enter the sixth grade this fall, a superb student who won the archdiocese science fair with a homemade electric meter. Unlike most boys in the Male Youth Project he attended at Shiloh Baptist Church, his parents are married. His mother works for the Department of Public Works; describing what his father does doesn't come easy. "My father used to be a [construction] engineer. He left his job because they weren't treating him right; they would give white men better jobs who did less work. Now he drives an ice-cream truck."

Black men were hurt, too, by the illegal economy. As the legitimate marketplace case them aside, the drug trade took off, enlisting anyone lured by the promise of fast money. Ironically, says Comer, "you had to make a supreme and extra effort to get into the legal system and no effort to get into the illegal system." For many on the fringes, there was no contest. "It overwhelmed the constructive forces in the black mainstream," he says. Disproportionately, too, black men are in prison or dead. While African-Americans represent only 12 percent of the population, they composed 44 percent of the inmates in state prisons and local jails in 1991; and, in 1990, homicide was the leading cause of death for young black men.

The economy explains only one part of what happened. The sexual revolution in the '70s was the second great shift that changed the black family. Although the social tide that erased taboos against unwed motherhood affected all women, whites and blacks took different paths. White women delayed both marriage and childbearing, confident that, down the road, there would be a pool of marriageable men. Not so for black women, who delayed marriage but not children because they were less certain there would be men for them. In what they called a "striking shift," Census officials reported earlier this year that less than 75 percent of black

women are likely to ever marry, compared with 90 percent of whites.

More dramatic is the childbearing picture. Between 1960 and 1989, the proportion of young white women giving birth out of wedlock rose from 9 to 22 percent, markedly faster than it did for blacks. The slower rate of increase for blacks was small comfort. Their rate—42 percent—was already so high by 1960 that if it had kept pace with the white race, ti would have topped 100 percent by now. As things stand, it's 70 percent.

Traditionally, the extended family has served as a safety net. But the terrible irony of history is that it has also hurt the black family. While intended as a cushion, the network, in effect, enabled more single women to have children. And that helps explain why not only poor black women, but middle- and upper-class blacks as well, have had children out of wedlock at higher rates than white women. Historically, white women have had only themselves to rely on for child rearing, and so marriage became more of an imperative. For blacks, the network of extended kin is a tradition rooted in African customs that emphasize community over marriage. Although historians say that most black children grew up in two-parent households during slavery, as well as in the 19th and early 20th centuries, high rates of poverty, widowhood and urban migration reinforced the need for interdependence that continues today. The oft-repeated African proverb "It takes a whole village to raise a child" echoes back to that.

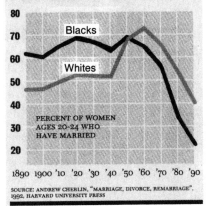

Rejecting Marriage

Before 1950, young black women were actually more likely to get married than white women.

PERCENT OF WOMEN AGES 20-24 WHO HAVE MARRIED

SOURCE: ANDREW CHERLIN, "MARRIAGE, DIVORCE, REMARRIAGE", 1992, HARVARD UNIVERSITY PRESS

Now the extended family is breaking down. Yet the black family's expectations for it haven't diminished. Both sides feel the strains. With the soaring number of teenage mothers, grandparents today are getting younger and more likely to be working themselves. A 32-year-old grandmother isn't necessarily eager, or able, to raise a grandchild, especially when that child becomes a teenager and the problems multiply. And, after generations of no fathers, there are no grandfathers, either. What's more, the tradition of a real neighborhood is disappearing. "It used to be that everyone looked out for everyone else," said community activist Claudette Burroughs-White of Greensboro, N.C. "Now I think people are kind of estranged. They don't get involved. It's safer not to." Many families left in the inner city—the ones most in need of support—are increasingly isolated from relatives able to flee to the suburbs. "Not every poor black mother is in a strong kinship network," says Cherlin. "Many are living alone, hiding behind double-locked doors in housing projects."

What's the solution? Nearly 30 years after Lyndon Johnson launched the War on Poverty, experts on the black family return again and again to the same ideas—better education, more jobs, discouraging teen pregnancy, more mentoring programs. But now the question is, who should deliver—government or blacks themselves? Ever since the government started abandoning social programs in the '70s and early '80s, black families have been left on their own to find a way out. Those who would argue against funneling in more government dollars say we tried that, but "nothing works." Lemann, who believes that most of the positive social changes in Black America were sparked by government intervention, dismisses the conceit that spending on social welfare failed. The War on Poverty, he says "threw out some untested ideas, some of which worked"—like Head Start, the Job Corps and Foster Grandparents—"and some of which didn't." Beyond the all-or-nothing extremes, there is room for solutions. Moynihan believes the nation has been in a collective "denial phase" about the black family for the last 25 years. But he says he's encouraged. "We're beginning to get a useful debate on this."

Will self-help do it? Though few African-American leaders expect what they call "White America" to come to the rescue, they're equally skeptical that the thousands of programs filling church rec rooms and town-hall meeting rooms can, on their own, turn things around. "People who are trying to salvage a lot of the children are burnt out, they think it's like spitting into the ocean," says Poussaint, who doesn't dispute the pessimism. "The problems are overwhelming. It's like treating lung cancer and knowing that people are still smoking."

There aren't many places left to look for answers. When black leaders peak with one voice, it is about the deep crisis of faith and purpose that came with integration: the very promise that African-Americans would be brought into the American mainstream has left many by the wayside. What's the penalty for doing nothing? "We could revert to a caste society," says Moynihan. Others are just as bleak. There are sparks of hope, says Comer, but he warns: "It's getting late, very late." The problems of the black family have been apparent for decades. And so has our collective understanding that we must take them on. What we need to find now is a voice to start the dialogue.

The disease is adolescence

*...and the symptoms are violence, suicide, drugs,
alcohol, car wrecks, and poverty*

DOUGLAS FOSTER · ROLLING STONE

This ankle is most assuredly broken," Dr. Barbara Staggers says, sounding almost gleeful.

Staggers is tall, 39 years old, African-American, a physician. She smiles broadly and turns. Her 16-year-old Latino patient, laid out on a few chairs, narrows his eyes, perhaps startled by the pleasure he can hear in her voice. Staggers pats the boy's hand, surveys his pale face. Her eyes follow his long, muscled leg, stopping to study the spot where his foot draws down to the south. There, the bone takes a sharp detour east, its trajectory sketched by a plum-colored bruise, the fruit of basketball played too hard. Staggers raises her arms in a V of triumph and grins. "Yep. Broken. Yes!"

After following Staggers on rounds—here in a clinic at Fremont High School and at the Teen Clinic of Children's Hospital in north Oakland, California—even a casual observer might understand her glee. This is the first clean break of the day. The patient, suffering from the kind of injury doctors are trained to handle, will be treated and sent on his way. Within a few months, he will be playing ball too aggressively again.

Many of Staggers' other patients suffer far murkier ailments. So far today she has seen teenagers who are suicidal and homicidal; victims of sexual abuse; sufferers of serious diseases from asthma to AIDS; and kids who are addicted to everything from alcohol to crack and junk. She has also seen teenagers who are pregnant or love starved and too many who have given up all hope.

The crisis among patients like Staggers' has been widely reported as a tale of inner-city poverty and youth crime, but her weekly schedule is a rebuke to that simple notion. Many of her patients are poor, minority teenagers, but she also draws patients from more privileged neighborhoods. One kind of patient comes to her after taking a bullet in the belly during a downtown shootout. Another kind arrives bruised and broken, having drunk himself sick before wrecking his parents' luxury car in a high-speed crash.

"As a physician, I'm dealing with people who are incredibly resilient physically," Staggers says in her cramped office at the school clinic, just before the injured athlete arrives. "Yet they still see their most positive option as being dead." In conversation, Staggers rolls her shoulders forward for emphasis and explains things in well-crafted bursts. "Guns and cars are different kinds of weapons, but they can be weapons all the same. Different presenting symptoms. The same disease."

While black teenagers are far more likely to be shot to death, white teens are more likely to be injured or killed in an automobile crash—or to kill themselves. But both groups share this underlying condition: Three-quarters of the deaths of young people from 10 to 24—a total of 30,000 each year—occur not from disease but from preventable causes.

For most other age groups in the country, the risk of a violent death or injury from these causes has leveled off or declined. Not so for adolescents, or for young people in their 20s, whose escalating risk of violent injury and death begins in their teens. Among youths age 15 to 19, the risk of being shot to death more than doubled in the past decade.

Consider this toll: Among youths 10 to 19, 3,398 were murdered and 2,237 killed themselves in 1990. During the 1980s, 19,346 teenagers were murdered and 18,365 killed themselves. That added up to 37,711 for the decade. Today's teenager runs roughly twice the risk of being murdered or becoming a victim of suicide compared with teens during most years of the turbulent 1960s. As if the old dangers were not threatening enough, HIV infection has begun to cut a wider swath.

Across lines of race and class, adolescence has become a high-risk activity.

As the athlete with the broken ankle hobbles off to have his bone set, Staggers surveys a waiting room full of difficult cases. Few of her patients readily reveal the underlying reasons for their visits. The receptionist's sign-in sheet contains a litany of mundane complaints—aching ears, persistent coughs, upset stomachs. Inside the examining room, the more serious business will tumble out if Staggers can find a way to get the kids to talk. On this morning, it turns out that the earache was caused by a beating, the cough by parental neglect, and the stomachache by a suicide attempt.

Staggers sees several patients who are exploring their sexuality. "This school has a fair number of kids who openly identify [themselves] as gay or bisexual," she says. Staggers has double-barreled concerns about one boy: Does he know everything he needs to know about safer sex? Are the older men he has been staying with overnight—perhaps trading sex for shelter—taking advantage of his youth and naïveté?

The boy is handsome, soft-spoken, painfully shy. He has had several near-fatal bouts of asthma, but his

Across lines of race and class, the number of preventable teenage deaths is rising at an alarming rate.

family is scattered and nobody seems to be in charge of his care. Treating teens like this boy seems to require a kind of double vision: Staggers is treating the asthma but also trying to anticipate an underlying danger, counseling him to avoid exploitation, drug abuse, AIDS.

Next door, three young women have arrived—a few days after their junior prom—for pregnancy tests. As she reads their names, Staggers raises her eyebrows in disappointment. These three girls know better. They've been taught how to protect themselves from sexually transmitted diseases and pregnancy.

Like these young women, teenagers all over the country, most of whom are sexually active, increasingly risk serious illness and death through sex. A recent report by the Centers for Disease Control (CDC) found

that among teens, new HIV infections are occurring at a startlingly high rate.

Preparing to meet with the girls individually, Staggers suppresses an exasperated scowl and replaces it with a stoic, neutral expression. This part of her practice—inspiring teens to make use of what they already know—is by far her biggest challenge. It demands the ability to hector and persuade without seeming to nag or lecture.

"It's hard when you're angry, but you have to take time with these kids if you expect to make a difference," Staggers says. "To make an impact, you have to push past the facts. You have to press the girls for more information and look for the underlying causes. I ask them, 'Is an orgasm worth dying for?' and 'Why do you want to be pregnant?' They'll tell you they want to get

---

"They get right in your face"

Are girls turning meaner?

SINCE HALF THE PEOPLE IN THE WORLD ARE WOMEN, I USED TO THINK that half the world was safe. Now I don't think that way. It seems to me that women are getting meaner and meaner, and that the youngest ones—the girls my age—are the worst.

In California, the proportion of teenage girls behind bars for violent crimes has increased by 11 percent over the last five years. "Girls pick more fights, they get right in your face," a girl in junior high tells me.

The San Francisco high school I attended was constructed to hold about a thousand students, but now holds three times that number. Simple overcrowding means fights. There were times during my senior year when the freshman girls seemed to be looking for trouble, shoving their way through the packed hallways, cussing and fussing for the right to their own space.

In my last year of high school, I saw two tiny freshmen beat down a senior like she was a kindergartner. While the senior lay on the hallway floor trying to shield her head, the freshmen were busy stomping on her long black hair and kicking her in the head. The senior tried to mask her humiliation, but I could see her tears.

Popular culture also has decided it's "in" for girls to be rough. The hottest fashion for girls is the thuggish look, prison blues. The hip-hop hard-core group Apache raps about wanting a "gangsta bitch" for a girlfriend. In the video "Latin Lingo" by Cypress Hill, two Latinas are depicted having a catfight. The camera seems to swoop around the chest level, just in case a breast flops out.

At school, girls who fight may get suspended, but they also get plenty of respect and attention from

an education first. But then they'll go and have unprotected sex. Many of them don't think they have any control. The boys tell them they don't like the feel of a condom. The boys say, 'Trust me.' And the girls desperately want to trust somebody."

Staggers believes there's an "influential connection" between the 1 million teenagers who get pregnant each year and the violence that pervades their lives. "Even though, in many ways, they don't want to get pregnant, they do it to replace some of the people they've lost," she says. At first blush, this sweeping statement seems hyperbolic, a shade New Age. To blame teenage pregnancies on violence in the streets seems a bit of a stretch. But during her examination, one of the three prom revelers, a striking and articulate high school senior, proves a spot-on example. This young

their friends. At 13, middle school student Allison Sandoval is already a veteran fighter who has been suspended from school twice. Her first fight wasn't intentional. She had confronted a girl she heard was talking about her, and the next thing she knew a crowd had formed around them. The crowd began pushing the two girls closer together, and suddenly Sandoval found herself swinging.

After that, says Sandoval, her friends pressured her to keep fighting. "If you don't fight this girl for them they think you're not down for your friends." Now, she says, she has a pretty good idea why so many girls fight. "They want to say 'Don't mess with me.' They want to be seen as troublemakers. They want to be just like the guys and stand out too." Even her parents pay more attention to her when she's getting into trouble for fighting, Sandoval says.

But now Sandoval is thinking of retiring. Even when she wins a fight, she doesn't often feel proud. "I feel bad, like I've made a mistake. Sometimes I don't even know the girl."

Are girls becoming tougher than guys? That's the question one has to ask these days. Petite Tony, 16, was expelled for fighting a boy twice her size. "This guy was picking on my little friend," she recalls, "and I told him to hit me if he wanted to pick on someone. He slapped me. After that, I punched him, and we got into it."

Andrea N. Jones
YO! (Youth Outlook)

Excerpted with permission from the Bay Area journal of youth life YO! *(Spring 1993). Subscriptions: $24/yr. (6 issues) from Pacific News Service, 450 Mission St., Room 506, San Francisco, CA 94105. Back issues free of charge from same address.*

woman can rattle off safe-sex guidelines so expertly that she could work for the CDC. Still, here she is waiting for the results of her pregnancy test, having picked up a bad case of herpes after the big dance.

I ask if there's anything else bothering her. At that, the forthright teenager becomes querulous. She hems and dodges. Finally, her hands flapping back and forth, she admits to having a hard time keeping a clear head ever since the recent murder of her 25-year-old cousin. The killing has left her feeling betrayed. Her cousin was called out of his home by his friends—among them people she knows from the neighborhood. Clearly, the young man was set up. She puffs big clouds of air through her cheeks. You learn not to trust anybody, she says.

Boy! Oh, my! Don't tell me!" Staggers hunches over the telephone, as if the sheer weight of her concerns can be brought to bear on her umpteenth case of life or death.

Now at the hospital clinic, she's packed into her chair, surrounded by papers and correspondence and piles of telephone messages. Boxes of research files, speech materials, and papers spill out of crates.

This is the first time I've heard Staggers stopped cold. A patient is nearing physical collapse from starving herself.

"Uh, oh! Anorexia and psychosis, too. She's hearing voices. Ah, man," Staggers says, frowning. "Do we know how much she weighs?"

"Excuse me. She weighs how much? Boy, oh, boy. Is she pale and blue-looking? When anorectics need hospital care, we're talking cardiovascular trouble. And so we're talking risk of instant death."

Staggers quickly refers the doctor to Lucile Salter Packard Children's Hospital at Stanford, across the bay. Packard has an eating-disorders clinic and inpatient psychiatric care. Swiveling in her chair, Staggers looks glum. "That was a tough one. You know, among anorectics, the odds aren't terrific. One-third of those who get treated get better, one-third or more stay the same—and up to a fifth die."

She's up and out before finishing the sentence, clearly discomfited by the notion that there are cases even she can't get traction on. We've been talking about some of the others troubling her sleep. There's a 14-year-old female patient who lives with a 28-year-old pimp and drug dealer. So far, he's not sexually involved with the girl, and he doesn't show any signs of trying to pressure her into prostitution. "I've been watching to see if he would try to pimp her out," Staggers says. "He seems to genuinely care for and protect her."

Staggers could turn the girl over to Child Protective Services, but the public agency is overwhelmed with urgent cases and the best they could offer is foster care. Staggers still remembers, with a shiver of disgust, an 11-year-old girl with chronic illness turned over to the agency a few years ago. The girl's parents were homeless, and officials believed she could not be adequately cared for on the street. So they separated the girl from her parents.

"She ended up getting hospitalized as a psychiatric case," Staggers remembers. "Her parents were good to her, and she missed them. What we did initially, by referring the case, was take a tragedy and make it worse. In the end, we got the parents jobs and a house. The kid is doing wonderfully now." With that experience as a backdrop, Staggers calculates that her current 14-year-old patient may be better off staying with the one person who has cared for her, even if he's a pimp.

Staggers hurries off to meet with a middle-class teenage girl, a runaway from her suburban home. "I can't tell you how many middle-class girls I have who get involved with the gangs at this age," she says. "This girl was an A student. Now she's failing." Staggers sends in two peer counselors, young women who have graduated from gang-involvement and drug-treatment programs themselves, for some straight talk with the teen. Then the doctor follows up, both with the girl and with her parents, getting her to agree to go to family therapy and advising them to lighten up once they get their daughter home.

As the parents and daughter file out, reunited, Staggers allows herself a moment of relief. Her eyebrows bobble, and she grins. About her advice to the parents, she explains, "We don't get very far by just telling teenagers not to take risks because it scares us. When we demand to know why they've screwed up, the kid says, 'I had to. Everybody else was doing it.' The adult replies, 'If everybody else jumped off the cliff, would you, too?'

"The honest answer to that question," continues Staggers, "is *yes*. It's really, really important that we understand this. For the teen at that moment, being

---

Teenagers are less likely to get medical care than any other age group in the country.

---

down at the bottom together feels better than being on the edge of a cliff alone. What we need to engage our teens in discussing is this question: What else can you do to be part of a group and still survive, while taking reasonable risks? If you've got to jump off the cliff, can't you choose one that's not 50 feet high? Can you jump off the cliff that's 2 feet high instead?"

Staggers' approach involves more engaged listening than most doctors or parents ever muster. Her method uncovers underlying symptoms. She mentions a boy who was in the hospital recovering from injuries suffered in an automobile accident. Since his breath smelled as if he'd been drinking at the time of the accident, alcohol treatment was recommended. But nobody asked him why he'd crashed into the wall in the first place. Staggers did ask. "He told me, 'I've done this before. Several times,'" Staggers recalls. "And so we knew he needed suicide-prevention counseling, too.

The experience left me wondering: How many suicides are really homicides? And how many homicides are really suicides?"

From experiences like this, Staggers developed her theory about the common problems of teenagers. She believes a festering generational grievance cuts across differences of income, ethnic background, and particular trauma.

But if adolescence itself has become a high-risk activity—a disease to be treated with preventive therapy, as Staggers believes—what is the most effective treatment? Collecting her belongings at the end of a day, Staggers considers this question carefully and answers a bit haltingly. "With all the kids I know who make it, there's one thing in common: an individual contact with an adult who cared and who kept hanging in with the teen through his hardest moments," Staggers says. "People talk programs, and that's important. But when it comes down to it, individual, person-to-person connections make the difference....Every kid I know who made it through the teenage years had at least one adult in his life who made that effort."

When Staggers leaves work in downtown Oakland, she beats a retreat to the suburbs where she was brought up, and where she presently lives with her second husband, 8-year-old son, and 9-year-old stepson. Zipping along at 75 mph, it's a short drive but a world away. The freeway slices around inner-city Oakland like a melon spoon, cutting southeast past a string of suburban villages, to Castro Valley.

"Notice anything?" Staggers laughs as we emerge from the car outside Castro Valley High School. At Fremont High, most of the school gates were chained shut, and security guards roamed the halls, two-way radios at the ready. The average grade point average is 1.7, and only a small fraction of the students will go to college. At Castro Valley High, students wander freely. Most students come from two-parent families, and incomes are high. Almost all of them will go on to college.

"You're about to find out that problems for teens are similar even in very different settings," Staggers says.

Just last spring, one Castro Valley teenager was killed with a baseball bat in a brawl after a Little League game. Although not reported at the time, tensions at the school had been fierce in the weeks before the brawl. The school's wrestling coach had been charged with making sexual advances to a boy on his team. That had led to gay-baiting teasing aimed at the wrestlers, some of whom were also baseball players. Then ongoing racial skirmishes between Anglo and Latino students resulted in a series of confrontations.

Natalie Van Tassel, an ebullient white woman who has worked in Castro Valley schools for 25 years, was Staggers' counselor during high school. She still works with Castro Valley's troubled teens.

The women compare notes about sexual activity among teenagers. "I don't think I'm misrepresenting the past," Van Tassel says. "I mean, I came from a small Midwestern town where most of the girls got married the day after graduation because they were all pregnant. But what has happened is that the explosion of sexual activity moved down in the age groups—12, 13, 14..."

Staggers interrupts. "Among mine: 10, 11, 12..."

"And the big difference is," Van Tassel continues, "if you wanted to be sexually active in your high school years, you could do it without running the risk of dying because of it."

Van Tassel finds it toughest to deal with teenagers who have no meaningful relationship with any adult. Suburban teenagers are set loose to fend for themselves far too early, Van Tassel says. "The parents here have a great capacity to give their kids things. Giving them so many material things masks what they're failing to give—time. What I see are kids without real parents."

Staggers is pounding the table. "See, it's the same disease, different symptoms. Here the kids have economic opportunity, but no real family life." She's worked up now. "I'm tired of hearing people say, 'I'm too busy.' If you have kids—or you're related to kids—and they don't have adults in their lives, it's your job to either take care of them yourself or find some other grown-up who can do it for you. Either do it or find someone who can. But just throwing up your hands and saying, 'Time, time, there's no time'—that just doesn't cut it with me. How can we get that message through to adults?"

Staggers doesn't wear a watch. Sometimes her schedule seems chaotic, full of what appears—to some of her superiors, at any rate—to be overly generous amounts of time for her patients. There have been rumblings about her supposed failings as an administrator and turf fights with the hospital administration. Staggers' department has been hit with a series of cutbacks in staff and resources in a hospital restructuring.

In the midst of the cutbacks, even Staggers' clinic at Fremont High may be in jeopardy. "That's where services should be—in the schools, in the community," Staggers says firmly. "Can you imagine those kids turning up at a hospital clinic? With no insurance, no parent support, no information? Yet they're the kids who need treatment most."

But Staggers knows that her real beef is not with the budget-cutting administrators at her hospital. She's at odds, fundamentally, with the way medicine is currently organized. Staggers is trying to practice public health medicine in a fee-for-service world. No matter what kind of proposal is eventually adopted to reform the nation's health care system, the underlying problem for doctors like Staggers will remain. Her focus on prevention, no matter how socially important, simply does not generate the fees that would fund such a practice.

When she gets agitated on this subject, Staggers sets her jaw and waves her arms. Teenagers are less likely to receive medical care than any other age group in the country, she insists, and rarely do they get the kind of care they need, even when they are treated. For all the hazy rhetoric floating around in Washington about the domestic agenda, Staggers can't understand how anyone expects to make headway without taking into account the special problems of teens.

Staggers often gives speeches around the country. She's a doctor of publicity, too, turning out between appointments on one day, for example, to support the efforts of community groups in Oakland trying to shut down alcohol outlets. ("You put alcohol and firearms together, and you account for 50 to 75 percent of all adolescent deaths," she says.) She also regularly testifies before state legislative committees.

The uphill nature of her cause was evident at an afternoon hearing in May 1993 in Sacramento, the state capital. With teens and their advocates from all over the state waiting to testify about their problems, a special hearing about teenage health was abruptly canceled because legislators were busy downstairs grappling with a state budget that was $9 billion from balancing. In times of such stark shortage, it's harder than ever to get teenagers the attention they desperately need.

When Staggers was honored with the Lewis Hine Award in New York this year for her service to young people, Hillary Rodham Clinton, a fellow honoree, asked for her advice. The first lady got an impassioned briefing about adolescent medicine.

"She listened carefully, and I hope it made a difference in her thinking," Staggers says. "If only the federal government could restructure health care so there's community-based operations and more school-based clinics, we might get a grip on some of these problems."

Why Leave Children With Bad Parents?

Family: Last year, 1,300 abused kids died—though authorities knew that almost half were in danger. Is it time to stop patching up dead-end families?

MICHELE INGRASSIA AND JOHN MCCORMICK

THE REPORT OF DRUG PEDdling was already stale, but the four Chicago police officers decided to follow up anyway. As they knocked on the door at 219 North Keystone Avenue near midnight on Feb. 1, it was snowing, and they held out little hope of finding the pusher they were after. They didn't. What they discovered, instead, were 19 children living in horrifying squalor. Overnight, the Dickensian images of life inside the apartment filled front pages and clogged network airwaves.

For the cops that night, it seemed like a scavenger hunt gone mad, each discovery yielding a new, more stunning, find. In the dining room, police said, a half-dozen children lay asleep on a bed, their tiny bodies intertwined like kittens. On the floor beside them, two toddlers tussled with a mutt over a bone they had grabbed from the dog's dish. In the living room, four others huddled on a hardwood floor, crowded beneath a single blanket. "We've got eight or nine kids here," Officer John Labiak announced.

Officer Patricia Warner corrected him: "I count 12." The cops found the last of 19 asleep under a mound of dirty clothes; one 4-year-old, gnarled by cerebral palsy, bore welts and bruises.

As the police awaited reinforcements, they could take full measure of the filth that engulfed this brigade of 1- to 14-year-olds. Above, ceiling plaster crumbled. Beneath their feet, roaches scurried around clumps of rat droppings. But nothing was more emblematic than the kitchen. The stove was inoperable, its oven door yawning wide. The sink held fetid dishes that one cop said "were not from that day, not from that week, maybe not from this year." And though the six mothers living there collected a total of $4,500 a month in welfare and food stamps, there was barely any food in the house. Twice last year, a caseworker from the Illinois Department of Children and Family Services (DCFS) had come to the apartment to follow up reports of serious child neglect, but when no one would let her in, the worker left. Now, it took hours to sort through the mess. Finally, the

police scooped up the children and set out for a state-run shelter. As they left, one little girl looked up at Warner and pleaded, "Will you be my mommy?"

Don't bet on it. Next month the children's mothers—Diane Melton, 31; Maxine Melton, 27; May Fay Melton, 25; Denise Melton, 24; Casandra Melton, 21, and Denise Turner, 20—will appear in Cook County juvenile court for a hearing to determine if temporary custody of the children should remain with the state or be returned to the parents. Yet, for all the public furor, confidential files show that the DCFS is privately viewing the 19 children in the same way it does most others—"Goal: Return Home."

Why won't we take kids from bad parents? For more than a decade, the idea that parents should lose neglected or abused kids has been blindsided by a national policy to keep families together at almost any cost. As a result, even in the worst cases, states regularly opt for reunification. Even in last year's budget-cutting frenzy, Congress earmarked nearly $1 billion for family-preservation programs over the next five years. Yet there is mounting evidence that such efforts make little difference—and may make things worse. "We've oversold the fact that all families can be saved," says Marcia Robinson Lowry, head of the Children's Rights Project of the American Civil Liberties Union. "All families *can't* be saved."

Last year there were 1 million confirmed

cases of abuse and neglect. And, according to the American Public Welfare Association, an estimated 462,000 children were in substitute care, nearly twice as many as a decade ago. The majority of families can be repaired if parents clean up their acts, but experts are troubled by what happens when they don't: 42 percent of the 1,300 kids who died as a result of abuse last year had previously been reported to child-protection agencies. "The child-welfare system stands over the bodies, shows you pictures of the caskets and still does things to keep kids at risk," says Richard Gelles, director of the University of Rhode Island's Family Violence Research Program.

Nowhere has the debate over when to break up families been more sharply focused than in Illinois, which, in the last two years, has had some of the most horrific cases in the nation. Of course, it's not alone. But unlike many states, Illinois hasn't been able to hide its failures behind the cloak of confidentiality laws, largely because of Patrick Murphy, Cook County's outspoken public guardian, who regularly butts heads with the state over its aggressive reunification plans. The cases have turned Illinois into a sounding board for what to do about troubled families.

The Chicago 19 lived in what most people would consider a troubled home. But to veterans of the city's juvenile courts, it's just another "dirty house" case. In fact, Martin Shapiro, the court-appointed attorney for Diane Melton, plans to say that conditions could have been worse. He can argue that Melton's children weren't malnourished, weren't physically or sexually abused and weren't left without adult supervision. He's blunt: "Returning children to a parent who used cocaine—as horrific as that might seem—isn't all that unusual in this building." If only all the cases were so benign.

What Went Wrong?

ON THE LAST NIGHT OF JOSEPH Wallace's life, no one could calm his mother's demons. Police say that Amanda Wallace was visiting relatives on April 18, 1993, with 3-year-old Joseph and his 1-year-old brother, Joshua, when she began raving that Joseph was nothing but trouble. "I'm gonna kill this bitch with a knife tonight," Bonnie Wallace later told police her daughter threatened. Bonnie offered to keep the boy overnight, but Amanda refused, so Bonnie drove them to their apartment on Chicago's impoverished West Side. It's unclear what forced Amanda's hand, but authorities tell a harrowing tale: at about 1:30 a.m., she stuffed a sock into Joseph's mouth and secured it with medical tape. Then she went to the kitchen, retrieved a brown extension cord and wrapped it around Joseph's neck several times. She carried her

son to the living room, stood him on a chair, then looped the cord around the metal crank arm over the door. In the last act of his life, Joseph waved goodbye.

Amanda Wallace, 28, has pleaded not guilty to charges of first-degree murder. No one ever doubted that Amanda was deeply troubled. When Joseph was born, she was a resident at the Elgin Mental Health Center in suburban Chicago, and a psychiatrist there warned that Amanda "should never have custody of this or any other baby." Three times, the DCFS removed Joseph from his mother. Yet three times, judges returned him to Amanda's dark world. Six months after the murder—which led to the firing of three DCFS employees—a blue-ribbon report blasted the Illinois child-welfare system, concluding that it had "surely consigned Joseph to his death."

Even in the most egregious instances of abuse, children go back to their parents time and again. In Cook County, the public guardian now represents 31,000 children. Only 963 kids were freed for adoption last year. But William Maddux, the new supervising judge of the county's abuse and neglect section, believes the number should have been as high as 6,000. Nationwide, experts say, perhaps a quarter of the children in substitute care should be taken permanently from their parents.

But it's not simply social custom that keeps families together, it's the law. The Adoption Assistance and Child Welfare Act of 1980 is a federal law with a simple goal—to keep families intact. The leverage: parents who don't make a "reasonable effort" to get their lives on track within 18 months risk losing their kids forever. The law itself was a reaction to the excesses of the '60s and '70s, when children were often taken away simply because their parents were poor or black. But the act was also one of those rare measures that conservatives and liberals embraced with equal passion—conservatives because it was cheap, liberals because it took blame away from the poor.

By the mid-'80s, though, the system began to collapse. A system built for a simpler time couldn't handle an exploding underclass populated by crack addicts, the homeless and the chronically unemployed. At the same time, orphanages began shutting their doors and foster families began quitting in droves. The system begged to know where to put so many kids. It opted for what was then a radical solution: keeping them in their own homes while offering their parents intensive, short-term support—child rearing, housekeeping and budgeting. But as family-preservation programs took off, the threat of severing the rights of abusive parents all but disappeared. What emerged, Gelles argues, was the naive philosophy that a mother who'd hurt her child is not much different from one who can't keep house—and that with enough supervi-

JOSEPH WALLACE

"Mother has a history of impulsive behavior, inappropriate anger, difficulty in getting along with others and recurrent suicidal attempts," the caseworker wrote. Nonetheless, her written recommendation was: "Goal, return home." Police have since charged that Amanda, Joseph's mother, hanged her son with an electrical cord.

FROM CASEWORKER REPORT
ON JOSEPH WALLACE

COURTESY FAYE AND MICHAEL CALLAHAN

sion, both can be turned into good parents.

In hindsight, everyone in Chicago agrees that Joseph Wallace's death was preventable, that he died because the system placed a parent's rights above a child's. Amanda could never have been a "normal" parent. She had been a ward of the state since the age of 8, the victim of physical and sexual abuse. Between 1976 and Joseph's birth in 1989, her psychiatrist told the DCFS, she swallowed broken glass and batteries; she disemboweled herself, and when she was pregnant with Joseph, she repeatedly stuck soda bottles into her vagina, denying the baby was hers. Yet 11 months after Joseph was born, a DCFS caseworker and an assistant public defender persuaded a Cook County juvenile-court judge to give him back to Amanda, returning him from the one of the six foster homes he would live in. The judge dispatched Amanda with a blessing: "Good luck to you, Mother."

Over the next two years, caseworkers twice removed Joseph after Amanda attempted suicide. But a DCFS report, dated Oct. 31, 1992, said she had gotten an apartment in Chicago, entered counseling and worked as a volunteer for a community organization. And though the report noted her turbulent history, it recommended she and Joseph be reunited. Joseph Wallace was sent home for the last time 62 days before his death, by a judge who had no measure of Amanda's past. "Would somebody simply summarize what this case is about for me and give me an idea why you're all agreeing?" the judge asked. Amanda's lawyer sidestepped her mental history. Nevertheless, the DCFS and the public guardian's office signed on. When Amanda thanked the judge, he said, "It sounds like you're doing OK. Good luck."

Murphy says that deciding when to sever parents' rights should be obvious: "You remove kids if they're in a dangerous situation. No one should be taken from a cold house. But it's another thing when there are drugs to the ceiling and someone's screwing the kids." Ambiguous cases? "There haven't been gray cases in years."

No one knows that better than Faye and Michael Callahan, one of the foster families who cared for Joseph. When Joseph first came to them he was a happy, husky baby. When he returned after his first stretch with Amanda, "he had bald spots because he was pulling his hair out," Faye says. By the third time, she says, Joseph was "a zombie. He rocked for hours, groaning, 'Uh, uh, uh, uh'." The fact that he was repeatedly sent home still infuriates them. Says Michael: "I'd scream at those caseworkers, 'You're making a martyr of this little boy!'"

See No Evil, Hear No Evil

EARLY LAST THANKSGIVING, ARETHA McKinney brought her young son to the emergency room. Clifford Triplett was semiconscious, and his body was pocked with burns, bruises and other signs of abuse, police say. The severely malnourished boy weighed 17 pounds—15 percent less than the average 1-year-old. Except Clifford was 5.

This wasn't a secret. In a confidential DCFS file obtained by NEWSWEEK, a state caseworker who visited the family last June gave a graphic account of Clifford's life: "Child's room (porch) clothing piled in corner, slanted floor. Child appears isolated from family—every one else has a well furnished room. Child very small for age appears to be 2 years old. Many old scars on back and buttocks have many recent scratches." In April, another caseworker had confronted McKinney's live-in boyfriend, Eddie Robinson Sr., who claimed that Cliff was a "dwarf" and was suicidal—neither of which doctors later found to be true. Robinson added that Cliff got "whipped" because he got into mischief. "I told him that he shouldn't be beat on his back," the caseworker wrote. "Robinson promised to go easy on the discipline."

It's one thing to blame an anonymous "system" for ignoring abuse and neglect. But the real question is a human one: how can caseworkers walk into homes like Clifford's, document physical injury or psychological harm and still walk away? A Cook County juvenile-court judge ruled last month that both McKinney and Robinson had tortured Clifford (all but erasing the possibility that he'll ever be returned to his mother). But caseworkers are rarely so bold. In Clifford's case, the April worker concluded that abuse apparently had occurred, but nine days later another found the home "satisfactory." Says Gelles: "Caseworkers are programmed by everything around them to be deaf, dumb and blind because the system tells them, 'Your job is to work to reunification'."

Murphy charges that for the past two

SAONNIA BOLDEN

"The amount of stress and frustration has been reduced. Sadie appears to have a lot more patience with her children and she continues to improve her disciplinary techniques." The same day the worker wrote this, Sadie's daughter Saonnia died after boiling water was poured on her. An autopsy uncovered 62 injuries, many recent.

FROM CASEWORKER REPORT
ON SAONNIA BOLDEN

years, Illinois has made it policy to keep new kids out of an already-clogged system. "The message went out that you don't aggressively investigate," he says. "Nobody said, 'Keep the ----ing cases out of the system'." But that, he says, is the net effect. "That's just not true," says Sterling Mac Ryder, who took over the DCFS late in 1992. But he doesn't dispute that the state and its caseworkers may have put too much emphasis on reunification—in part because of strong messages from Washington.

The problems may be even more basic. By all accounts, caseworkers and supervisors are less prepared today than they were 20 years ago, and only a fraction are actually social workers. Few on the front lines are willing, or able, to make tough calls or buck the party line. In the end, says Deborah Daro, research director of the National Committee to Prevent Child Abuse, "the worker may say, 'Yeah, it's bad, but what's the alternative? I'll let this one go and pray to God they don't kill him'."

In most cases, they don't. Nevertheless, children who grow up in violent homes beyond the age of 8 or 10 risk becoming so emotionally and psychologically damaged that they can never be repaired. "The danger," says Robert Halpern, a professor of child development at the Erikson Institute in Chicago, "is not just the enormous dam-

age to the kid himself, but producing the next generation of monsters."

Clifford Triplett is an all-too-pointed reminder of how severe the injuries can be. He has gained eight pounds, and his physical prognosis is good. But there are many other concerns. "When he came, he didn't know the difference between a car and a truck, the difference between pizza and a hot dog," says his hospital social worker, Kathleen Egan. "People were not introducing these things to him." Robinson and McKinney are awaiting trial on charges of aggravated battery and felony cruelty. McKinney's attorney blames Robinson for the alleged abuse; Robinson's attorney declined to comment. Clifford is waiting for a foster home. A few weeks ago he had his first conversation with his mother in months. His first words: "Are you sorry for whipping me?"

Band–Aids Don't Work

ACCORDING TO THE CASEWORKER'S report, 2½-year-old Saonnia Bolden's family was the model of success. Over 100 days, a homemaker from an Illinois family-preservation program called Family First worked with Sadie Williams and her boyfriend Clifford Baker. A second helper—a caseworker—shopped with Sadie for shoes and some furniture for her apartment; she evaluated Sadie's cooking, housekeeping and budgeting. She even took her to dinner to celebrate her progress. On March 17, 1992, the caseworker wrote a report recommending that Sadie's case be closed: "Due to the presence of homemaker, the amount of stress and frustration has been reduced. Sadie appears to have a lot more patience with her children and she continues to improve her disciplinary techniques."

What the Family First caseworker evidently didn't know was that, just hours before she filed her report, Saonnia had been beaten and scalded to death. Prosecutors claim that Williams, angered because her young daughter had wet herself, laid the child in the bathtub and poured scalding water over her genitals and her buttocks. Williams and Baker were charged with first-degree murder; lawyers for Baker and Williams blame each other's client. Regardless of who was responsible, this wasn't

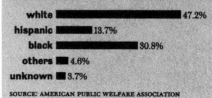

Race of Foster Children

Contrary to public opinion, foster care is not dominated by minorites. Nearly half the kids there are white.

white	47.2%
hispanic	13.7%
black	30.8%
others	4.6%
unknown	3.7%

SOURCE: AMERICAN PUBLIC WELFARE ASSOCIATION

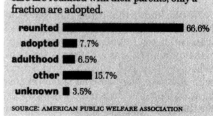

Where Do Children Go?

Two thirds of children who leave foster care are reunited with their parents; only a fraction are adopted.

reunited	66.6%
adopted	7.7%
adulthood	6.5%
other	15.7%
unknown	3.5%

SOURCE: AMERICAN PUBLIC WELFARE ASSOCIATION

A One-Man Children's Crusade

Twenty years ago, an angry young lawyer named Patrick Murphy wrote a book that exposed an injustice: state social workers too often seized children from parents whose worst crime was poverty. Today Murphy is the scourge of a child-welfare system that too often leaves kids with their abusive, drugged-out parents. He has not made the about-face quietly. In many cities, confidentiality laws protect caseworkers and judges from public outcries when their bad decisions lead to a parent's murder of a child. In Chicago, Murphy calls blistering press conferences to parcel out the blame. To those who say he picks on parents who are poor, black and victimized, he hotly retorts: "So are their kids."

Murphy is the Cook County (Ill.) public guardian, the court-appointed lawyer for 31,000 abused and neglected children. He's also a self-righteous crusader. last year, campaigning to rein in one "family preservation" program, Murphy sent every Illinois legislator color autopsy photos of a little girl scalded and beaten to death after caseworkers taught her family new disciplinary skills. It's a loner's life, poring over murder files and railing at fellow liberals who think the poor can do no wrong. "A lot of people hate my guts," Murphy shrugs. "I can't blame them."

His views on family reunification changed because child abuse changed. Drugs now suffuse 80 percent of the caseload; sexual and physical assaults that once taxed the imagination are now common. Murphy believes that most families should be reunited—but the child-welfare agencies waste years trying to patch up dead-end families when they should be hurrying to free children for early adoption. Murphy, 55, blames such folly on bleeding hearts like himself, who once lobbied for generous social programs without working to curb welfare dependency and other ills.

Now children of troubled families must pay the price—sometimes with their lives. "We inadvertently pushed a theory of irresponsibility," he says. "And we created a monster—kids having kids."

To Murphy's critics, that smacks of scorn for the less fortunate. "He's a classic bully," says Diane Redleaf of the Legal Assistance Foundation of Chicago, who represents parents trying to win back their kids. "Thousands of poor families are *not* torturing their children." Redleaf has drafted legislation that would force Murphy to get a judge's order each time he wants to speak about a case. That would protect children's privacy—and give the system a convenient hiding place. Murphy will fight to keep things as they are. His is the only job, he says, in which a lawyer knows that his clients are truly innocents.

J.M.

---

the first assault. The autopsy on Saonnia's visibly malnourished body found 62 cuts, bruises, burns, abrasions and wrist scars, among other injuries. Eleven were still healing—meaning they probably happened during the time the homemaker was working with the family.

Since Illinois's Family First program began in 1988, at least six children have died violently during or after their families received help. In many other instances, children were injured, or simply kept in questionable conditions. Such numbers may look small compared with the 17,000 children in Illinois who've been in the program. But to critics, the deaths and injuries underscore the danger of using reunification efforts for deeply troubled families. Gelles, once an ardent supporter of family preservation, is adamant about its failures. "We've learned in health psychology that you don't waste intervention on those with no intention of changing," he argues.

A University of Chicago report card issued last year gave the Illinois Family First program barely passing grades. Among the findings: Family First led to a slight *increase* in the overall number of children later placed outside their homes; it had no effect on subsequent reports of maltreatment; it had only mixed results in such areas as improving housing, economics and parenting, and it had no effect on getting families out of the DCFS system. John R. Schuerman, who helped write the report, says it's too simplistic to call Family First a

failure. Still, he concedes that the assumption that large numbers of households can be saved with intensive services "just may not be the case."

Nevertheless, in the last decade, family-preservation programs have become so entrenched there's little chance they'll be junked. Health and Human Services Secretary Donna Shalala carefully sidesteps the question of whether it's possible to carry the reunification philosophy too far. Asked where she would draw the line in defining families beyond repair, she diplomatically suggests that the answers be left to child-welfare experts. "Nobody wants to leave children in dangerous situations," says Shalala. "The goal is to shrewdly pick cases in which the right efforts might help keep a

family together." So far, not even the experts have come up with a sure way to do that.

Where Do We Go From Here?

POLICYMAKERS BELIEVE THAT IF THEY could just remove the stresses from a family, they wouldn't have to remove the child. But critics argue that the entire child-welfare network must approach the idea of severing parents' rights as aggressively as it now approaches family reunification. That means moving kids through the system and into permanent homes quickly—before they're so damaged that they won't fit in anywhere. In theory, the Adoption Assistance Act already requires that, but no state enforces that part of the law. Illinois is typical: even in the most straightforward cases, a petition to terminate parental rights is usually the start of a two-year judicial process—*after* the 18-month clean-up-your-act phase.

Why does it take so long? Once a child is in foster care, the system breathes a sigh of relief and effectively forgets about him. If the child is removed from an abusive home, the assumption is that he's safe. "There's always another reason to give the parent the benefit of the doubt," says Daro. "They lose their job, the house burns down, the aunt is murdered. Then they get another six-month extension, and it happens all over again. Meanwhile, you can't put a child in a Deepfreeze and suspend his life until the parent gets her life together."

In the most blatant abuse and neglect cases, parents' rights should be terminated immediately, reformers say. In less-severe cases, parents should be given no more than six to 12 months to shape up. "You have social workers saying, 'She doesn't visit her child because she has no money for carfare'," says Murphy. "But what parent wouldn't walk over mountains of glass to see their kids? You know it's a crock. You have to tell people we *demand* responsibility."

And if parents can't take care of them, where are all these children supposed to go? With just 100,000 foster parents in the system, finding even temporary homes is difficult. For starters, reformers suggest professionalizing foster care, paying parents decent salaries to stay home and care for several children at a time. Long range, many believe that society will have to confront its ambivalence toward interracial adoptions. Perhaps the most controversial alternative is the move to revive orphan-

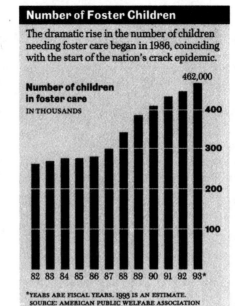

Number of Foster Children

The dramatic rise in the number of children needing foster care began in 1986, coinciding with the start of the nation's crack epidemic.

Number of children in foster care
IN THOUSANDS

462,000

400

300

200

100

82 83 84 85 86 87 88 89 90 91 92 93*

*YEARS ARE FISCAL YEARS. 1993 IS AN ESTIMATE.
SOURCE: AMERICAN PUBLIC WELFARE ASSOCIATION

ages, at least for teenagers, who are the least likely to be adopted. One of the fiercest supporters is Maddux, the new supervising judge of Cook County's abuse section. Maddux, 59, says that his own family was so desperately poor they once lived in a shanty with two rooms—one of which was an old car. When the family broke up, he and his younger brother went to live at Boys Town, Neb. He believes that many foster children today could benefit from the nurturing-yet-demanding atmosphere of group living. "I wasn't raised in a family after the age of 12," Maddux says. "I didn't miss it. Thousands of kids at Boys Town knew that being in a destitute, nonfunctioning family was a lot worse than not

being in a family." In Illinois, some are taking the idea seriously—among the proposals is turning closed military bases into campuses for kids.

Ironically, Illinois could wind up with one of the best child-welfare systems in the nation. Pressed by public outrage over Joseph Wallace's death, state legislators last year passed a law that puts the best interest of children ahead of their parents'. Foster parents will be given a voice in abuse and neglect cases. And the DCFS is beefing up caseworker training, so that those in the field will learn how to spot dangerous situations more quickly.

Some of the toughest changes are already underway in Cook County. The much-criticized Family First program has been replaced with a smaller, more intensely scrutinized family-preservation project known as Homebuilders. And the county's juvenile-court system has been expanded so that there are now 14 judges, not eight, hearing abuse and neglect cases; that cuts each judge's caseload from about 3,500 to about 2,000 children per year. But reform doesn't come cheap. The DCFS budget has tripled since 1988, to $900 million, and it could top $1 billion in the next fiscal year.

Whether any of this can save lives, it's too soon to tell. In its report on Joseph Wallace's death, the blue-ribbon committee was pessimistic. "It would be comforting to believe that the facts of this case are so exceptional that such cases are not likely to happen again," the panel wrote with a dose of bitterness. "That hope is unfounded." The temptation, of course, is to blame some faceless system. But the fate of children really lies with everyone—caseworkers, supervisors, prosecutors, judges—doing their jobs.

THE NEW OUTLAWS

Cities make homelessness a crime

Thomas O'Halloran played by the rules, and lost. The son of a San Francisco cop, he was born and raised in the Bay Area, attended parochial schools, and went to Stanford University. For nearly twenty-five years, he worked for Pacific Bell. In the latter part of his life, when his wife needed triple-bypass surgery, he spent their life savings—around $65,000—on her health care. After she died in 1991, O'Halloran became homeless.

GEORGE HOWLAND JR.

George Howland Jr. is the news editor of The Stranger, *a Seattle weekly newspaper.*

One day last August, he was sitting on a bench reading a book, with all of his worldly possessions beside him in a shopping cart, when several police officers rode up to him on their motorcycles. The police issued O'Halloran a $76 citation for camping in a public park. O'Halloran could not afford to use any of his $250-a-month phone-company pension to pay the fine. The penalty automatically increased to $180, and the police issued a warrant for his arrest.

Since August 1993, 4,300 citations like the one O'Halloran received have been issued under San Francisco's Matrix program. Mayor Frank Jordan has vowed that Matrix will clean up the streets through strict enforcement of laws against blocking the sidewalk, trespassing, and sleeping in public.

Around the country, similar harassment campaigns against the homeless are under way. The National Law Center on Homelessness and Poverty has documented crackdowns against the homeless in more than thirty cities since the late 1980s. In some cities, including Seattle, Atlanta, and Washington, D.C., new laws have been passed against begging, loitering, or sleeping in public. In other places, including Santa Monica, New York, and San Francisco, existing "public nuisance" laws, which have been ignored for decades, are suddenly being rigorously enforced.

Such efforts do nothing to address the complicated national crisis that homelessness has become. But politicians have found that cracking down on the destitute and "cleaning up" central shopping districts by moving the homeless to outlying neighborhoods wins votes.

Derrick Thomas learned the hard way

that cutting across parking lots is illegal in Atlanta. In May 1993, Thomas was staying in transitional housing near the Omni Stadium. In the evening he went out to make a call at a phone booth near a parking lot. While walking across the lot, Thomas was stopped by a man who was parking his car and wanted change. The parking-lot attendant witnessed the interaction and misinterpreted it. The attendant came "running and screaming, 'Don't pay him! Don't pay him!' " Thomas remembers. Thomas and the customer both attempted to explain but the attendant flagged down a motorcycle cop.

When the customer assured the police officer that Thomas had not been impersonating a parking lot attendant, Thomas was arrested under a different statute. "I was arrested for being an unauthorized person in a parking lot and taken to jail," he says. Thomas spent the weekend in jail because he had no money for bail. On Monday afternoon, the prosecutor informed Thomas that he could plead guilty and receive a five-day sentence which would include time served. If he pled not guilty, the prosecutor would ask the judge to delay the trial a week while the state prepared its case. Since Thomas can add, he chose the former. His story would have gone untold were it not for the efforts of the Atlanta Coalition for the Homeless, which has been documenting that city's "criminalization of poverty."

While the parking-lot section of Atlanta's 1991 antiloitering ordinance is bizarre, it is not unique; Jacksonville, Florida, has passed a similar statute. Not to be outdone, Seattle outlawed sitting on the sidewalk between the hours of 7 A.M. and 9 P.M. in certain designated commercial zones.

"This is not aimed at the homeless, it is aimed at the lawless," says Seattle City Attorney Mark Sidran. By "the lawless" Sidran and other city officials mean people

who, lacking anywhere else to go, sit down on the sidewalk or cross a parking lot or wander the city streets aimlessly. Jim Jackson, an Atlanta businessman, confidently declares that his city's new laws will "not punish anyone but the criminal." San Francisco's Mayor Frank Jordan assures us that "homelessness is not a crime. It is not a crime to be out there looking like an unmade bed. But if criminal behavior begins . . . then we will step in and enforce the law."

At least in Miami, this ever-expanding definition of criminal behavior ran into a wall. The city was arresting homeless people under a law which made it illegal to "stand, loiter, or walk upon any street or sidewalk in the city so as to obstruct free passage over." In 1992, U.S. District Judge C. Clyde Atkins ordered the city to create safe zones where homeless people could remain without fear of arrest for "innocent acts." In other cities, the homeless have not been so lucky.

In the fall of 1989, William Young, a homeless man, suddenly found himself evicted from New York City's subway stations and threatened with arrest. His crime? Asking people for money.

"I spend the money I receive soliciting on the basic necessities of life, that is, on food, shelter, clothing, transportation, and medicine," Young explains. Medicine is vitally important because Young is afflicted with a bleeding ulcer and high blood pressure. Young avoids public shelters because they are "dangerous places, where violence often occurs and the few belongings I have might be stolen." Instead, he chooses to try to earn enough money to rent a room for a night by begging subway fare and then riding to the loading docks in the Bronx: "If I am lucky I can make twenty dollars unloading trucks for the day."

Young ran afoul of Operation Enforcement in November 1989. In response to a drop in ridership, the New York City Metropolitan Transit Authority (MTA) targeted homeless people for eviction from subway and train stations. MTA's 3,800 transit cops began strictly enforcing rules that forbid littering, creating unsanitary conditions, blocking free movement, lying down on subway seats, and begging.

With the help of the Legal Action Center for the Homeless, Young took his fight for First Amendment protection of his right to ask people for money all the way to the U.S. Court of Appeals. The court ruled against him. "Begging in the subway often amounts to nothing less than assault, creating in the passengers the apprehension of imminent danger," Judge Frank X. Altimari wrote for the majority.

While beggars may seem annoying or even frightening to some people, how else are the homeless supposed to get money? Some do manage to hold steady jobs. Others, like Young, find casual work or day labor. The little extra money they can raise through alms may be what it takes to keep them alive. While no beggar should be permitted to threaten or physically harm people, New York has plenty of laws against extortion and assault on its books. Begging in and of itself should not be regarded as criminal behavior. Altimari's 1990 ruling, however, was among those that created the precedent for cities across the country to pass laws that restrict begging. Fortunately, another New York ruling (*Loper v. Brown*) overturned blanket prohibitions on begging on all streets and public ways in the entire state.

The lesson that city attorneys across the country have learned is that if begging is banned from a particular part of the city (i.e., the subway or near automatic teller machines) or defined somewhat narrowly (i.e., aggressive panhandling), the courts will generally uphold restrictions. Aggressive panhandling has been defined in Seattle as including the use of "profane or abusive language toward the person solicited," while in the District of Columbia it includes "continuously asking, begging, or soliciting alms after the person [being solicited] has made a negative response." Laws against begging have been passed in at least eleven other cities.

San Francisco's "Operation ASAP" (Aggressive Soliciting Abatement Program) illustrates the lengths to which police departments will go to protect monied citizens from beggars. Under Operation ASAP, the police department employed a host of expensive, state-of-the-art equipment, including bulletproof vests and video cameras, and spent 450 work-hours and $11,000 for an undercover sting operation aimed at netting aggressive beggars. The resulting fifteen arrests were seen as a disappointment by all involved. Sergeant William Henderson, ASAP's director, ex-plained the reasons for the meager results to his commander: "The overwhelming number of panhandlers . . . ask for money, then when refused say 'thank you, have a nice day!'or 'God bless you.' "

In 1992, Bobby Beamer, a fifty-nine-year-old man, was living under the Whitehurst Freeway in Washington, D.C. Beamer and about twenty-five other homeless people had constructed a shanty-town not far from the Kennedy Center and the Watergate Hotel.

On the morning of June 5, Washington police raided the shantytown. "The police who came down to the camp told me and the other homeless people who live in the camp to eat all of the food we had in five minutes," Beamer recalls. The police "took a mattress which we shared, and many of my clothes. They took the mattress, clothes, and food up the hill to the streets and put all of it in a truck." Beamer never saw his possessions again. Other homeless people from Beamer's shantytown and elsewhere in the city offer similar accounts of police seizing property, including flashlights, coats, blankets, "an interview suit," resumes, and umbrellas. One officer, Beamer says, "took my glasses and stomped on them. They were shattered and they are now useless. I paid a lot of money for those glasses. . . . I need a new pair very badly."

Attorney Michael Adlin wrote to Police Chief Addison Davis in behalf of the homeless. Adlin believes the police were not even acting "under the color of law" in these cases. Chief Davis replied, "It is our obligation to enforce the law and undertake actions which are necessary under appropriate circumstances. Understandably, then, what appears to be an unjustifiable seizure to some, is an appropriate disposal of property to others."

Such raids are not unique to Washington. In 1991, Atlanta police evicted sixty homeless people from one of the city's five "hutvilles," following a fire that damaged the viaduct which served as the hutville's roof. In Oakland, seven homeless people won a suit after the state police confiscated their property without warning during a raid in March 1992. Chicago's police spruce up Grant Park by clearing out homeless camps before city-sponsored concerts and events. In New York City, the Dinkins Administration bulldozed homeless shantytowns in Columbus Circle, Riverside Park, and vacant lots throughout the city. The best-known razing of a homeless encampment was Manhattan's 1991 action at Tompkins Square Park. Deputy Mayor Bill Lynch articulated the argument which is on the lips of city officials across the nation. "This [homeless camp] is not what the park is created for," he said. "It impedes the use of the park for all the community."

Lynch had no advice, however, on where homeless people should live. While estimates of homelessness in New York range from 70,000 to 90,000, the city says it has only 23,973 shelter beds. The shelter gap exists in all other cities that carry out destruction of homeless camps. Washington's 8,200 to 15,000 homeless people are provided only 6,700 shelter beds, Chicago's 12,000 homeless people have 4,590 shelter beds, and Atlanta's 15,000 homeless people have 3,500 shelter beds.

Nationwide, estimates of homelessness range from the Department of Housing and Urban Development's 600,000 to the National Coalition on Homelessness's two to three million. HUD's latest survey of shelter beds found 275,000 nationwide. If sleeping in public places—under freeways, in parks, or on heating grates—is illegal, that means at least 325,000 people are faced with the nightly choice of breaking the law or staying awake.

Since 1970, the United States has been faced with a simultaneous increase in the number of poor people and a decrease in places for them to live. The Federal Government has made it clear that it will not help cities solve the crisis. In the Reagan and Bush Administrations, cities faced deep cuts in Federal funding for low-income housing and services for the poor. The Clinton Administration shows little sign of improving things.

Meanwhile, mayors and city councils are under intense pressure from downtown business groups. Store owners, who are already losing customers to outlying malls, believe the presence of homeless people is hurting business. Business associations across the country have been flexing their political muscle and demanding that mayors do something to clean up the streets.

In the last few years, voters have also signaled their approval of crackdowns against the homeless, electing tough-talking mayors and supporting punitive campaigns. In 1990, Washington, D.C.'s voters turned down an ordinance that would have guaranteed shelter beds for every homeless resident. In 1992, San Franciscans approved Proposition J, an anti-begging ordinance which the Board of Supervisors had rejected as punitive.

In this political climate, it is easier for city officials to placate voters and businesses by locking up the homeless or moving them along, than it is to face the depth of the crisis.

Advocates for the homeless are responding to the crackdowns by organizing protests and filing lawsuits—with mixed success—while carrying on the day-to-day effort to feed, clothe, and shelter the poor.

One successful effort at fighting back was a recent grass-roots organizing campaign in Santa Monica, California. In the early 1980s, Santa Monica became known as one of the most compassionate cities for the homeless in Los Angeles County because of its generous social services, including a feeding program on the City Hall lawn. By the late 1980s the city's homeless population had grown to between 1,500 and 2,000 people. In response, a coalition of business owners, conservative citizens, the police chief, and members of the city council led a backlash against the homeless.

In June 1993, things came to a head when City Councilmember Kelly Olsen proposed enforcing an existing law which would close city parks from midnight to 5 A.M., denying homeless people a place to sleep. By the time of Olsen's proposal, homeless people and their allies had formed an organization, "We, the People," to fight back. Ron Taylor is one of the homeless people who led the fight. Taylor and others went to hear a speech by Olsen in which the councilman claimed there were plenty of other places to sleep besides the park. Taylor remembers. "Somebody called out, 'Well, can you name some?' Olsen said, 'Why not City Hall?' So that's where we all moved. . . . At one time there were about 100 people. . . . We just put our bedrolls everywhere and had the front steps of City Hall for our storage area. They didn't want to give us a bathroom, so City Hall began to smell pretty bad."

The City Hall sleep-in began to rally public opinion to the cause of the homeless. Among other things, the sleep-in showed the true face of homeless people. "We had a woman who was pregnant in her eighth month. We had a ninety-four-year-old woman who was out there and two other ladies in their late seventies. We had veterans of Desert Storm," Taylor says.

Two-and-a-half months after the sleep-in began, the city council agreed not to enforce the law closing the park between midnight and 5 A.M. In addition, Taylor says, "we managed to get two bathrooms opened twenty-four hours a day. I really and honestly think we gave them a wake-up call." Taylor encourages people to try similar tactics in other cities.

"Somebody has to take a stand," he says. "We should all be ashamed of ourselves for letting this [homelessness crisis] happen. If we don't stand up now, by the year 2000, it's just going to be mind-boggling how many people are going to be on the streets."

Crime, Delinquency, and Violence

The probability is becoming greater that every American will at some time in his or her life be subjected to a criminal act and that act will involve some degree of violence. With the ever-increasing crime rate, especially in major cities, confidence in law enforcement is declining, and citizens feel forced to arm themselves and turn their homes into minifortresses. What must be done to make our streets safe to walk, our highways safe to drive, and our homes safe from unwanted intrusions?

"Getting Serious about Crime" argues that it makes little sense to arrest offenders if the arrest is not associated with serious punishment. Attempts to rehabilitate these serious offenders do not work and, contrary to some reports, the cost society must bear to imprison these individuals is far less than the cost society must bear for their subsequent criminal activities.

"Ethics, Neurochemistry, and Violence Control" looks at the allure of a quick fix for violence. Medical scientists have been searching for a genetic link to violence that can be chemically controlled. The author questions the validity of such a notion because he believes that violence is a complex interaction of many social, psychological, and biological factors—therefore, any chemical attempt to control behaviors should be viewed with suspicion and caution.

"Crime Takes on a Feminine Face" examines the rapidly rising numbers of women engaging in violent criminal activities. The author reports that while much of women's criminal activities reflect the barriers faced by women in general in society, they are increasingly involved in malicious, vicious crimes.

"Danger in the Safety Zone" studies the impact that random violence is having on the sense of safety and security of individuals. Former havens of safety and security are no longer safe or secure. No one and no place are immune from violent acts. From the quiet solitude of a local library to a busy hospital emergency room, people are being beaten, shot, and killed. Amitai Etzioni, a major sociologist, observed, "There is a new level of fright, one that is overdone and realistic at the same time."

"Honey, I Warped the Kids" explores the interrelationship between violence on television and violence in society. The author argues that a massive amount of research data documents most clearly a direct cause-and-effect relationship between the two. While eliminating all violence on television will not eliminate all violence in society, it would make a significant impact. However, any attempt to limit violent television programing would run into issues of free speech, artistic expression, license, and censorship.

"The Economics of Crime" is costing American society more than $425 billion annually, which does not include the noneconomic costs of misery, fear, and insecurity that crime leaves in its wake. The author looks at various strategies that have been proposed to control crime, examines their effectiveness, and makes recommendations.

"The Global Crime Wave and What We Can Do about It" demonstrates that crime is a growing worldwide problem. The author discusses the roles that multiculturalism, the breakup of the traditional family, advances in technology, and growing alienation play in the growing wave of lawlessness and suggests steps to combat it.

Looking Ahead: Challenge Questions

Is there any relationship between the severity of punishment allotted a specific crime and subsequent deterrence?

What effect does being a victim of crime most likely have on the individual?

How can fear of becoming a victim actually make you a victim?

Is it possible to eliminate violence in a society? Explain.

In what major ways is delinquency the product of other social problems?

Do most delinquents grow up to become adult criminals? What evidence supports this?

Why do you believe violence is on the increase in the United States and around the world?

What social institutions seem to be the most effective in curbing violence?

Are there significant differences in the types of crimes committed by men and women? Explain.

How would a functionalist's approach to the problem of crime, delinquency, and violence differ from that of a conflict theorist?

Unit 2

Getting Serious About Crime

The system treats it like a game, and we're losing

George Lardner

George Lardner is a Washington Post reporter. This article is adapted from a speech delivered in October to the Kiplinger Midcareer Program in Public Affairs Reporting at Ohio State University.

"To wink at a fault causes trouble" is an old saying from the Book of Proverbs. It is also an apt description of what's gone wrong with our criminal justice system—especially when it comes to violent crime. Every day, in every courthouse across the country, we keep recycling the same criminals onto the streets to commit the same crimes again and again. The system keeps winking, as though the people who keep getting arrested, sentenced, convicted—and released—haven't learned how to play the game.

In fact, they know how to play it very well. They know they can count on being set free—on bond, on their own recognizance, for rehabilitation, for counseling, for supervision by probation and parole officers too busy to do any real supervising.

Consider, for example, a recent Washington Post report on the laxity accorded five of the seven men allegedly involved in a rash of fatal shootings and robberies in the Washington area. Two of them walked out of halfway houses, where one had been allowed to stay even after formal revocation of his parole. Another, who was the star of a jewelry store videotape that showed him pistol-whipping a woman and shooting a man, was free despite an outstanding charge of threatening to do bodily harm to two men, including a police officer. He had been released from custody on the strength of a promise to return for his trial in November. A fourth man was on parole from a Virginia prison—and also free on bond in a nearby county, on armed robbery charges. That robbery took place while he was still on parole for selling PCP and carrying a concealed weapon.

The fifth man was in a somewhat different category. He would have been better off if he had been required to serve more of his 1990 prison term for selling cocaine or if his parole had been revoked in light of a June 1993 arrest for trying to murder someone. Instead he was killed while watching a neighborhood football game. So was a 4-year-old girl standing nearby, leaving shock waves in the city that are still reverberating.

Something very much like this story could be written about the suspects in almost any rash of killings in any number of American cities. But it wasn't until my own daughter, Kristin, was murdered two years ago that I began paying closer attention to the supposedly routine violence that judges yawn at every day. It wasn't until then that I realized how hard it is to be put behind bars.

I've been covering courts and crimes for more than 30 years. But most of them were high-profile cases: Mafia figures in New York; contract killers in Cleveland; Teamsters in Chicago; Robert Kennedy's assassin in Los Angeles. These defendants were convicted and went to jail as they deserved. In the commonplace justice system, though, things work differently: Across the country, according to a recent Justice Department study, 62 percent of the 4.3 million people convicted of a crime and under active correctional supervision were on probation and another 12 percent were free on parole. Only 26 percent were in prisons or jails. In other words, three of every four people serving a criminal sentence on any given day in this country are rubbing shoulders with us.

This 75 percent is supposed to be under supervision of a probation or parole officer. But a 1990 study of three California programs found that the courts put many high-risk offenders on routine probation even though probation officers have caseloads of 150 or more. In Los Angeles County, the average caseload is reportedly as high as 600 per officer. Probationers in the three-county study saw their case officers an average of 15 minutes a month.

The results are about what you would expect. A Justice Department study of 79,000 felony probationers found that 43 percent of them were rearrested for another felony within their own state within three years of their sentencing, while still on probation. Half of the fresh arrests were for a violent crime or a drug offense.

Much is made of the costs of keeping a criminal behind bars. In fiscal 1990, the average annual cost was $15,603 per inmate—slightly less than that for federal prisoners and slightly more for state prisoners. But that's hardly bankrupting the system. As statistics compiled by the Justice Department show, state prisons cost only $41.91 per taxpayer, accounting for a measly 1 percent of all state and local spending. Federal prisons cost $3.46 for every U.S. resident, less than a tenth of 1 percent of federal spending. As a special committee of the American Bar Association found several years ago, "The entire criminal justice system is starved for resources."

Less than 4 percent of all U.S. government spending—that's federal, state and local—goes to support all justice activities, civil and criminal. That's less than 4 percent for everything—police, the courts, prosecutors, prisons, public defenders, the works. Barely more than 1 percent goes into the operation of our correctional system, including jails, prisons, probation and parole. In the year of the gulf war, U.S. taxpayers spent more on restoring Kuwait to its arguably corrupt rulers than they did on their federal justice system that year.

No doubt we'd much rather spend our money routing a villain like Saddam Hussein or building a new highway than we would on housing thugs. We need to overcome that reluctance.

◢

WE LIKE TO THINK THAT REHABILITATION WORKS, but there is no evidence, except in isolated instances, that it does. A landmark study in 1975 by the late Robert Martinson established that point. He reviewed the results of more than 200 separate efforts to measure the effects of programs designed to rehabilitate convicted offenders and concluded that rehabilitative efforts "have had no appreciable effect on recidivism." Harvard professor James Q. Wilson summed up the findings in his book "Thinking About Crime": "It did not seem to matter what form of treatment in the correctional system was attempted. Indeed, some forms of treatment (notably a few experiments with psychotherapy) actually produced an increase in the rate of recidivism."

By repeating these rather grim conclusions, I don't mean to suggest that I'm opposed to attacking the so-called "root causes" of crime. We need social programs to fight poverty and deprivation. Those conditions are unjust, whether they lead to crime or not. But social programs are not going to eradicate crime. As Wilson puts it, "If kindness, better housing, improved diets or lessened child abuse will reduce crime, I favor them. I only ask that the capacity of such measures to reduce crime be demonstrated and that their employment for crime-reduction purposes not be at the expense of society's desire to see justice done to those who have violated its moral imperatives."

And by that, Wilson means those who are guilty of predatory crime.

◢

VIOLENT CRIME MAY NOT BE AS FISCALLY COSTLY as, say, white-collar crime—and it may not produce such celebrity criminals as Michael Milken—but predatory crime is what worries most people and drives them apart from one another. It is—we have to face it—the biggest problem facing the country today.

The violence has not only grown in alarming quantity; it is also qualitatively more horrific. But what can we expect when movie and video heroes are glorified for electrocuting their foes, or tearing their hearts out? As President Clinton has said, "We have got to understand that we are raising a generation without the structure and order and predictability and support and reinforcement that most of us just took for granted."

Meanwhile, too many dangerous people are being set free. In Florida, a supposedly tough-on-crime state, the prisons have become so crowded that officials have been tossing more and more violent offenders into their "early release" program to meet federal court mandates.

In the District of Columbia, more than 1,500 individuals serving time for anything from murders to misdemeanors have strolled out of halfway houses since Jan. 1. About 500 of them are still at large. Weeks go by before the Corrections Department gets around to obtaining arrest warrants. The escapees often commit new crimes. An average of three to five defendants who are escapees appear in Superior Court each week, The Post disclosed in October.

Another important story certainly is the number of unserved warrants that pile up in every jurisdiction in the country. In Massachusetts, the commissioner of probation, Donald Cochran, told me that nobody knows how many outstanding warrants there are in his state. A probation officer who at one point supervised the man who stalked and killed my daughter told me of his frustrations in issuing warrants for probation violators. He said they just stack up at the police stations and are sometimes given lesser status because they didn't originate with the police.

Curiously, the press rarely seems to treat the failures of our justice system as real news. Rather, newspapers are too busy reporting what happened in Sarajevo or Mogadishu than domestic stories on violence, including family violence, battered women, spouse abuse, child abuse and assaults on the aged. The Washington Post, for example, printed 853 stories on Bosnia and Somalia from January through September, but only 38 stories in the categories of violence listed here. We've turned the news upside down. Events that we can do the least about command the biggest headlines. We forget that what our readers, or viewers, need is the news no one else can tell us about: the robbery at the grocery store, the mayhem on the playground, the shenanigans at City Hall.

◢

I AM NOT SUGGESTING THAT SERIOUS NEWSPAPERS put every grisly local crime on Page 1 as the tabloids do. I am suggesting that what we need on Page 1 are more stories that are as insightful about crime and the failures of our criminal justice system as the ones we run about foreign policy.

Those of us who cover the courts know that judges are a thin-skinned lot. When you scratch, they howl. But how many courthouse reporters, print or broadcast, tell their audience which judges are worth their salt, and which are not?

The same holds true for prosecutors and police. How many stories or newscasts challenge the plea-bargaining that goes on day after day? Is this justice? Or is it a cynical search for the least common denominator? The system is rarely questioned as U.S. involvement in Somalia may be questioned. But this is the system that released a Florida man who killed an 11-year-old boy after his early release for raping another. He should have gotten two life sentences, but they were plea-bargained down to an eight-year term, of which he served less than half.

Prosecutors argue that it already takes too long to bring cases to trial, that the system will collapse without pleas that won't be contested. That's an old lament, and I doubt the system would come anywhere near to collapse. But it certainly is a system that deserves to teeter a bit if that will expose its faults. Recent hearings in New York City have illustrated the corruption there. Police officers in some precincts take up to $8,000 a week for protecting drug dealers. They attack people with nightsticks, flashlights and lead-loaded gloves just "to show who's in charge." And they carry throwaway guns to explain away inconvenient homicides. Exceptions to the rule? Maybe. But how exceptional? And what have our news organizations done lately to find out?

"To wink at a fault causes trouble," the Proverbs say. The next line is, "A bold reproof makes peace."

ETHICS, NEUROCHEMISTRY, AND VIOLENCE CONTROL

Stephen G. Post

Stephen G. Post is assistant professor of medical humanities at the Center for Biomedical Ethics, Case Western Reserve University School of Medicine, Cleveland, Ohio.

The rapidly increasing human knowledge of neurochemistry is both medical miracle and moral muddle.

Today's so-called designer pharmacology involves the use of drugs to fine-tune mood, confidence, and anxiety levels even though no clinical condition exists. A useful analogy is to desired but unnecessary cosmetic surgery such as a slight modification of nose shape or perhaps yet another tummy tuck.

The question arises, then, will we gradually become a society of "happy" psychotropic hedonists? Or, on the other hand, should we be psychotropic Calvinists, striving hard to deal with the challenges of life by drawing on our inner resources and rejecting mind-and-mood-altering drugs? This is an old dilemma that can be raised at a new level, given the extent of recent scientific developments. How far shall we go in letting healthy people artificially fine-tune their sense of peacefulness and well-being?

Yet other questions surround new drugs that might eventually be proven useful in the control of socially undesirable and illicit behaviors. A debate, for example, has arisen over the possible use of serotonin to inhibit aggression.

Urgent questions mount over reliance on psychopharmacology to solve people's social and relational difficulties. They generally center around the concern that, although drugs are cheaper than psychotherapy, they absolve the individual of responsibility to sort out the underlying causes of his problem.

Anthony Burgess published his novella *A Clockwork Orange* in 1962, spawning the unforgettable Stanley Kubrick film in which Alex and his three "droogs" Pete, Georgie, and Dim engage in adolescent "ultraviolence" to strains of Beethoven's Ninth. Alex, prisoner 6655321, is eventually forced to undergo Dr. Brodsky's behavior-control process. Alex describes the doctor as "a malenky veck, very fat, with all curly hair curling all over his gulliver, and on his spuddy nose he had very thick otchkies" and as "all smiling as though to give me confidence."

For a fortnight, Alex is jabbed with syringes in his backside ("rooker") and made to view films of violence that, due to the injection, make him vomit repeatedly in anguished disgust. At the end of the process, Dr. Brodsky proclaims, Alex "will be your true Christian ready to turn the other cheek, ready to be crucified rather than crucify, sick to the very heart at the thought even of killing a fly."

Whatever one's interpretation of the novella's conclusions, it provides a fitting entry into the topic of this article, that is, the biologizing of human violence and the current debate over the possible role of psychiatry and neuroscience in eradicating the proclivity for wanton harm with new mind-altering drugs. I proceed by describing this acrimonious debate and providing some ethical analysis, although I am finally empirically skeptical of the genetic-biological interpretation of violence as well as suspicious of its political implications.

But before proceeding, clarity on the state of current biological science in relation to violence is essential. Thus far, *none* of the leads for a biological basis of violence have been scientifically verified.

One lead that has never panned out is the link between violence and low levels of serotonin, a brain chemical that affects behavior in some mental disorders. Based on some preliminary studies, biological psychiatrists loosely speculated that people in their early years might be treated with drugs to raise their serotonin levels. However, hundreds of recent studies indicate no consistent link between violence and serotonin levels. The leading researcher in this area, Dr. Klaus Miczek of Tufts University, has been widely quoted as denying that a serotonin-aggression link has yet been established.[1] Thus far, the attempt to biologize violence has failed. Even the studies carried out on criminals in the 1970s suggesting that high testosterone levels in males might be linked with violence and increased aggression proved inconclusive.

A phenomenon so multifactorial and complex as violence will probably never be reducible solely or even largely to genes and biochemistry. Yet there is a continuing tendency among some scientists and the media to overstate the biological hypothesis.[2]

This is probably because of the alluring simplicity of the notion of a possible link between genes and violence, such that violence-prone people would be found to have a distinctive neurochemistry that might be altered in the name of peace by physicians working for the state. Writing in the journal *Science*, Gary Taubes asks if scientists should be free to search for such a link and, if discovered, whether this knowledge would be misused: "Could it even lead to a sort of Holocaust—as nonviolent people who carry 'violence genes' were rounded up and dosed with drugs to ensure that they remain harmless to their law-abiding neighbors?"[3]

CURRENT DEBATE FOCUSES ON BLACK AMERICANS

The proposed "violence initiative" of the U.S. Department of Health and Human Services (HHS) was in large part the creation of then-HHS Secretary Dr. Louis Sullivan. In September 1992, the initiative was blasted by the Congressional Black Caucus, catching Sullivan, himself black, off guard. The Caucus feared that the research would focus on young inner-city blacks, who would be "discovered" to be biologically prone toward aggressive and violent acts, the solution for which could be the massive use of behavior-control drugs.

Sullivan accurately responded that in fact no race-specific studies of the genetic and biological basis of violence were contemplated, and that the HHS funds for such biological research were minuscule. Nevertheless, the initiative was halted for further review, which is still ongoing.

On January 15, 1993, HHS issued *The Report of the Secretary's Blue Ribbon Panel on Violence Prevention*, a project convened by Sullivan in December 1992. The panel was charged to advise him on the validity of allegations about inappropriate research, how to go about understanding violence, and how to assure that the HHS activities in violence research are open and supported by the wider community. Franklyn Jenifer, then-president of Howard University, served as chairman. The report found that HHS was neither attempting to establish any genetic correlation between race and violence nor

1. Richard Saltus, "Evidence That Genes Play a Role in Violence Is Weak," *Boston Globe*, 8 Feb. 1993.
2. Lisabeth DiLalla and Irving Gottesman, "Biological and Genetic Contributions to Violence—Wisdom's Untold Tale," *Psychological Bulletin* 109 (1991): 125–29.

3. Gary Taubes, "HHS 'Violence Initiative' Caught in a Crossfire," *Science* 258 (1992): 212–15.

Three neurosurgeons from Harvard, authors of a controversial letter
to the Journal of the American Medical Association *in 1967,*
associated the urban riots of that period with the brain
dysfunction of "slum dwellers."

targeting black American males, ages five to nine years, for purposes of medication. Moreover, the study recommended that blacks and other minorities be invited to join in ethical review of all research on violence and aggression.

Yet the black community, rightly suspicious of biomedical research in light of the decades-long Tuskegee studies in which black males were made to die of syphilis long after penicillin became available, is not easily calmed. Suspicions are exacerbated by recollection that three neurosurgeons from Harvard, authors of an extremely controversial letter to the *Journal of the American Medical Association* in 1967, associated the urban riots of that period with the brain dysfunction of "slum dwellers." These neurosurgeons, in 1970, with funding from the Department of Justice, performed experimental surgery on thirteen men and women in which they implanted electrodes to destroy tissue in the amygdala area of the temporal lobe, intending to quell violence.

Black civil rights leaders succeeded in having the funding halted. And the recent controversy over decades of radiation research by the Department of Energy has hardly mitigated minority suspicions of big science in collusion with government.

Clarification of the nonracist character of intended HHS studies might have been possible but for inflammatory remarks made in late 1992 by Dr. Frederick Goodwin, then director of the HHS Alcohol, Drug Abuse, and Mental Health Administration (ADAMH). A biologically oriented psychiatrist, Goodwin has long been a proponent of large-scale pharmacological interventions to control violence. In a speech that led to a national uproar, Goodwin stated that inner-city black youths are like jungle monkeys, capable

only of killing, sex, and reproduction. Sullivan removed Goodwin from his position.

The allegations that the "violence initiative" would try to link violence to race were firmly rooted in legitimate black suspicions of a history of government-sponsored racist research in the United States. Such allegations, although ultimately unfounded, were popularized by Dr. Peter Breggin, a well-known psychiatrist who categorically rejects the growing psychiatric emphasis on genetic-biological etiology of mental illness coupled with almost purely pharmacological treatment.

Breggin hit the talk-show circuit in 1992, charging that government-sponsored studies would lead to young black children being forced to take mind-numbing drugs to control their perceived proclivity for violence. He also brought this scenario to the attention of the Congressional Black Caucus, and, partly through his testimony to Congress, the "violence initiative" was shelved.

Recently, the influential *Journal of NIH Research* published a condemnation of HHS leadership for "caving in to political pressure," as no federal funds were ever approved for studies that link violence and race: "Over the course of a lifetime, one in 27 black males and one in 117 black females die from violent acts, compared with one in 205 white men and one in 496 white women. However, no studies supported by HHS even try to link violent or criminal behavior to race."[4]

4. Nancy Touchette, "Growing Inferno: Clearing the Smoke on Violence Research," *Journal of NIH Research* 4 (1994): 31–33.
5. Peter Breggin, *Psychiatric Drugs: Hazards to the Brain* (New York: Springer, 1983); *Toxic Psychiatry* (New York: St. Martin's Press, 1991).

"Increasingly, schools and parents accept the new approach that declares the youngster to be genetically defective and suitable for psychiatric treatment, including drugs and hospitalization."

CRITICISM OF BIOLOGICAL PSYCHIATRY

Biological psychiatrists are predictably critical of Breggin for what they consider to be his bias against the theory of brain-behavior interaction and for his allegedly antiscientific attacks on the use of pharmacologic medication. Breggin's two major books have the pointed titles *Psychiatric Drugs: Hazards to the Brain* and *Toxic Psychiatry*.[5] In these books, Breggin is critical of biological reductionism and treatment that impinges on individual rights.

Although Breggin has erroneously interpreted the HHS research initiative as racist and as gearing up for a totalitarian assault on antisocial behavior akin to that in George Orwell's *1984*, I nevertheless consider his critique of biological psychiatry as necessary, even if too one-sided. In a compelling article appearing in the *Wall Street Journal*, Breggin criticized the overuse of drugs and mental hospitalization to deal with emotional stress among the nation's children. This overuse is, he claims, financially driven. Hospitalization and pharmacological treatment based on diagnosis of mental illness are highly remunerative at a time when psychotherapy and family therapy are not well covered by health insurance. Breggin points to more than one million youngsters on Ritalin, a drug used to sedate unruly and rebellious schoolchildren, most of them boys.[6]

I hasten to add that there are some cases in which Ritalin is the only solution to hyperactivity and attention-deficit disorder, and it can work well. Yet it is overused, can have adverse side effects in some cases (although it is generally safe), and is a convenient technological substitute for the more time-consuming social, familial, and environmental interventions that often can mitigate such disorders.

Breggin argues that the etiology of such disorders lies principally in family trends: two working parents with a latchkey child, for whom drugs are more affordable than time. And Breggin points out that the single mother may find it impossible to handle the rambunctious boy, a task difficult for even the more sizable male mentor. A hasty diagnosis of hyperactivity and attention-deficit disorder comes in handy, as does Ritalin.

So Breggin concludes that by biologizing these so-called diagnoses we are

blaming the child for the problems of parents, families, schools, and society. Increasingly, schools and parents find it comforting to accept the new biological psychiatry approach that declares the youngster to be genetically and biologically defective, and suitable for psychiatric treatment, including drugs and hospitalization.

His remedy is for parents to "retake responsibility for our children." Although I would not take the case against biological psychiatry as far as Breggin does, I think that he is an important corrective voice.

There is absolutely no question that American psychiatry, once under the influence of Freud—and therefore psychoanalytic rather than biological-neurological in orientation—is now attempting

6. Peter Breggin, "The Scapegoating of American Children," *Wall Street Journal*, 7 Nov. 1989.

to regain scientific respectability and ensure research funding by focusing on the "hard" sciences of biochemistry, neuroanatomy, and pharmacology. Over the past decade, entire departments of psychiatry have been reshaped in accord with the hard-science model. Fortunately, the members of another school of psychiatry, the "ethnopsychiatrists," have been successful critics of the biological school, and we may see a partial swing back toward the psychosocial and analytic models.

LOCATING THE ROOTS OF VIOLENCE

It is not only legitimate but vitally important to question the psychiatric abuse of behavior-control drugs and the biological distraction from root social causes of violence. Biological psychiatry, in its attempt to gain scientific credibility in a time of tremendous growth in genetics, has looked to molecular biology to solve a problem that is located not so much within cells as within culture, injustice, and the history of human resentment. Any genetic predisposition toward violence, if discovered, would likely involve a number of genes in interaction with the environment and therefore would have little or no power to predict individual behavior.

Among the causes of violence are racism, poverty, poor schools, media inculcation, unemployment, cultural traditions that sanction forms of spouse and child abuse, religious fanaticism, and the brute "will to power" and domination characteristic of classes and nations. In addition, there are a host of other cofactors. The breakdown of the nuclear family, leaving young boys with no strong male role models, results in gang recruitment and immense wanton violence. The decline of the ethos of delayed gratification, coupled with greed, the striking visual contrast between the lives of the rich and the poor, the unfortunate sense among many adolescents that their value lies in the designer jackets and gold chains that some believe are worth killing for, the tremendous power of peer pressure, the sense of absolute power that comes with the taking of a life, the feeling that one's life is so hopeless that one may

as well kill with no concern for future punishment, and a general decline in the respect afforded human life explain why violence among adolescents is up. The images of *A Clockwork Orange* resonate with the fears that many experience in their neighborhoods.

There is no biomedical, technical fix for problems such as these. The only real solution is a familial, social, cultural, moral, religious, and economic transition that no syringe can supply. Despite technological progress, the close of the twentieth century leaves us with the antiprinciple "respect no life."

All criminal-justice professionals, like every first-year law student, know that violence cannot ultimately be controlled by law and the criminal-justice system. When the internal and characterological controls over violence are shattered, law is almost powerless. I say *almost* powerless because law in its most draconian form can succeed in controlling violence— though only by abrogating the human liberties of a free society. This is why freedom and virtue are inextricably linked, and why the annihilation of the latter inevitably entails the loss of the former.

ENVOI

Returning to *A Clockwork Orange*, just prior to Alex's undergoing of the Brodsky process, the prison warden states: "I shall have many sleepless nights about this. What does God want? Does God want goodness or the choice of goodness? Is a man who chooses the bad perhaps in some way better than the man who has the good imposed on him?" Would we want a state to achieve perfect peace, if it could, at the expense of human freedom?

The problem of violence should be solved in a manner that actively engages the entire person. To consider the widescale and routine use of mind-altering drugs makes a mockery of the human propensity for goodness and people's ability to recognize and condemn the evil in their own lives.

That our society has become so much more violent in recent decades has nothing to do with human biology but with the gradual inculcation of the spirit of violence, the rise of a "me-first" culture, growing economic pressures, and a crumbling of traditional family life. It would be a travesty to revictimize the young victims of all the social, economic, familial, and cultural factors that spawn violence by placing them on behavior-control drugs.

We all live in fear. A Hobbesian "war of all against all" prevails in our worst neighborhoods and floods into suburban enclaves. Some begin to speak of the cycle of civilizations and wonder if a nation with our degree of urban violence can long survive. As Lord Acton commented, social-political freedom is historically a thin veneer easily removed in times of social disintegration in favor of the absolute state. It is important that we preserve freedom and dignity in the struggle against violence, appealing to reason and shared values rather than to illusory biological solutions that intervene into the sacred neurological center of personal identity.

There is not one iota of evidence that race is relevant to the cause of violence. Nor is there any persuasive evidence of a consistent biochemical cause. But it is tempting to search for the "violence gene," although it will prove as nonexistent as the gene for schizophrenia that was announced with such media attention yet turned out to be utterly invalid. And if science ever discovers some genetic-biological link with violence, it will have varying expression and genetic penetrance, making it one vague cofactor among many others. Thus, it would be of little social value.

Yet the scientific desire to create the chemical imitation of human goodness through wide-scale medication is unlikely to diminish. As early as 1971, Kenneth Clark, in a presidential address to the American Psychological Association, proclaimed that society was on the verge of a new era in which biochemical intervention would stabilize human moral propensities. Dr. José Delgado had just dramatically tamed the aggression of bulls by implanting electrodes into the amygdala and caudate nucleus, the region of the brain presumed to be involved in their aggression. A wildly

charging bull came to a sudden stop with minor electronic stimulation. This, as previously stated, was for some neurosurgeons the fitting response to urban violence.

In Michael Crichton's *Terminal Man*, Harry Benson learns to love the electrical charge he gets from forty electrodes implanted in his brain. An article appeared in the *Yale Alumni Magazine* titled "Psycho-civilization or Electroliarchy: Dr. Delgado's Amazing World of ESB." All this suggested that mass behavior control was imminent and necessary and good. But as it turned out, electrostimulation of the brain was shown to produce completely different emotional responses in the brains of human subjects and to have no power to fine-control affect or function.

The issue of behavior control clearly informed the beginnings of bioethics in the early 1970s, faded from prominence, and may now be ready to reassert itself. Fundamental questions seem to be surfacing of whether chemical shortcuts should be used to control human behavioral problems that appear too expensive to solve at their root. As biological psychiatry continues to seek etiologies of violence and many mental disorders, violence may be subsumed under the medical model. Then, instead of teaching the perennial moral law of "do no harm" through religion and reason, we will have arrived at a technocratic society that to those lacking wisdom will appear utopian but will in fact be as dystopian as Orwell and Burgess suggested. In this society, the pills of technocrats will substitute for freedom, discipline, tradition, wisdom, and virtue. In a manner more total than Hannah Arendt predicted, *Homo faber* will have displaced and replaced *Homo sapiens*.

In his classic 1969 book, *Behavior Control*,[7] the late Perry London wrote that we were moving beyond the inculcation of values through "primitive" persuasion by education or inspiration to a world in which we "take over" people's lives by technological means. I confess a preference for the "primitive" way.

---

7. Perry London, *Behavior Control* (New York: Perennial Books, 1969).

Crime Takes On a Feminine Face

Chi Chi Sileo

Summary: Driven by economic need, self-defense or greed, more women are turning to crime, at a cost beyond the expense of incarceration. Often children are the losers. How should society handle female offenders? Some experts say the solution is in counseling and probation, not jail.

For more and more women, the legend "home sweet home" is being hung on the walls of a prison cell.

The increase in the rate at which women are going to prison has outpaced that of men. Since 1981, the number of men being put behind bars has gone up 112 percent; the number of women, 202 percent. This corresponds neatly with the upward trend in arrest rates; the rate of increase for women is now nearly double that for men.

What's behind these statistics? Are more women being drawn into a life of crime, or is the criminal justice system just getting more adept at catching and sentencing them?

"Both," says Rita Simon, a sociologist at American University in Washington and author of two books on women and crime. "Part of it is that just as women have more opportunities outside the home, they have more opportunities to fall into crime. And it's also true that in the past, judges tended to be more lenient with women, especially when they had children. But now justice is becoming more gender-blind."

The quasi-glamorous phrase "female criminal" conjures up the gun molls, femmes fatales and high-class madams beloved by tabloids and the movies. But the reality of women's criminality has far less to do with these captivating images and far more with the dreary exigencies of petty thievery, low-level drug dealing and small-time grifting. Women's growing presence in jails and prisons is being fueled by changing sentencing laws, a rise in white-collar crime and new legal tactics targeted at prosecuting women (in some cases, for nonexistent crimes).

In actual numbers, men still far outrank women in every type of crime, and even the wildest women don't indulge in the freewheeling activities that some male criminals do. FBI spokesman Kurt Crawford speculates that "there are maybe two" female serial killers at large (compared with estimates of as many as 500 males), and women are barely represented in crimes such as kidnapping, hostage-taking or terrorism. "These are just not female types of crimes," says Harvey Schlossberg, a former police officer and now the chief psychologist for the New York/New Jersey Port Authority. "Women tend to be motivated by economic concerns, while men are motivated by power and control."

Nancy Hollander, a past president of the National Association of Criminal Defense Lawyers, agrees that economics are at the root of women's fall from legal grace. "Women are going to jail for writing bad checks to get out of abusive homes," she asserts.

That's true of certain crimes, according to Simon, but not all: "Look at white-collar criminals; these are not poor women or abused women.

When I tell radical feminists this, they get furious. They believe that women are inherently more moral, that they only steal to feed their children. Well, the data just don't bear that out."

In fact, white-collar crime is where women seem to be flocking. The primary increase in arrests of women is for property offenses: larceny, fraud, embezzlement and forgery. And it isn't happening only in the United States: Reports are surfacing in Europe of female white-collar criminals, and a few years ago the Egyptian newsweekly *October* reported with alarm a rise in "the feminization of fraud."

When women take the money and run, they do so with much smaller amounts (an average of $50,000 compared with the $150,000 average that men take). Ironically, the barriers that hold women back here are the same ones that stall them in more legitimate professions. But as more women enter top executive circles, many experts predict, more of them will develop both the skills and the opportunity to play for larger criminal stakes. "Just give them time," says Simon.

Women who commit white-collar crime almost always act alone, and in this way such crimes stand out from other women's crimes. When a woman breaks the law it is usually through a personal connection — specifically, involvement with a man.

"Most women who are brought in for drug offenses have gotten there through their connection to a man," says Helen Butler, public affairs specialist at the Federal Bureau of Prisons. "Often their criminal involvement is very slight, so in the past judges would look more favorably on giving them things like probation." She adds that recent crime legislation which made drug dealing a federal offense and instituted mandatory minimum sentences has made sentencing stiffer all around, for both men and women. "Judges don't have any choice now. They have to hand down very tough sentences."

The war on drugs is packing prisons and jails with both male and female inmates. In Washington, D.C., for instance, 60 percent of the women held in jail are there for drug-related offenses; in the federal system the percentage is even higher. Most of these women are small-time, low-level accomplices who would have gotten probation or short sentences in the past.

According to Brenda Smith, director of the Women's Prison Project at the National Women's Law Center, women are highly vulnerable to involvement with drugs. "Women historically turn to crime to generate income. And drug dealing is a quick and easy way to do this. Also, because women are more low-level, they're more likely to get caught," says Smith, who has worked with imprisoned women for more than a decade.

In addition to accomplices in drug crimes and theft, there is also what Hollander calls "the most frightening group: women who are accomplices to men who abuse or kill other women or children." Stressing that these are a highly deviant minority of criminal women, Hollander differentiates them from women trapped in abusive relationships who end up abusing their children. In the latter situation, she says, "we have to be careful about assessing blame. . . . After all, these children had two parents. Where was the father? Also, it's possible that in these situations, the women are just so terrorized they can't think straight."

"I have a hard time accepting that," counters Schlossberg. He believes that women might abuse their children as a way of punishing their own abusers. "The child is his, too, and is an easier target. They may not be consciously aware that they're doing it, but at any rate, they still know right from wrong. They know they're harming that child."

Divorced or single mothers may become unwitting accomplices to abuse when they attempt to create a nuclear family. Studies have shown that stepfathers and boyfriends are more likely than natural fathers to abuse and neglect children living in their homes.

Family life in general doesn't seem to keep women out of the law's reach. Violent women rarely attack strangers, usually keeping their violent attacks close to home: Two-thirds of violent female offenders have attacked a family member, compared with 17 percent of violent male inmates. And while fewer than 6 percent of men serving time for homicide have killed a family member, more than 25 percent of women killers turned against what Justice Department statistics call "an intimate" — a lover, spouse, ex-spouse or pimp.

Those numbers have to be taken in context. According to even conservative estimates, about 40 percent of women who are charged with killing an intimate are women who found that deadly force was the only effective counteraction to long-term abuse. "Some of these women truly see no other option," says Smith of the Women's Law Center. "And in a purely technical sense, they are probably right. Think about it this way. A man can overpower a woman without killing her. He can beat her into submission and stop just short of killing her to make her stop doing something. A woman can't usually do that to a man. To stop him, she has to kill him."

Issues about spousal abuse and sticky legalistic questions of self-defense for battered wives are labyrinthine, but here certain facts bear consideration. The majority of women in prison report a history of physical or sexual abuse; almost all crime experts agree that learned violence begets later violence. And while it's true that battered women have more options now, and more awareness of those options, the fact remains that an abused woman's life is most in danger when she decides to leave the relationship.

According to Ann Jones, author of *Women Who Kill*, "There are cases on record of men still harassing and beating their wives twenty-five years after the wives left them and tried to go into hiding. If researchers were not quite so intent upon assigning the pathological behavior to the women, they might see that the more telling question is not 'Why do the women stay?' but 'Why don't the men let them go?'"

For women, if economic necessity, self-defense, punishing their abuser through their children or choosing to become an embezzler doesn't land them in jail, they might try this: getting pregnant.

A new trend in the war on drugs is accusing pregnant drug addicts of fetal abuse, a notion that is legally unclear. Pregnant women who are turned in by doctors when traces of drug use show up in tests are being hit with charges that range from illegal transport of narcotics (through the umbilical cord), child abuse and even assault with a deadly weapon.

"It's an abuse of prosecutorial power, plain and simple," says Lynn Paltrow, director of special litigation for the Center for Reproductive Law and Policy. "A complete misuse of criminal law. There is not one single state in which this law — fetal abuse — is even on the books." In fact, every challenge to these indictments in lower courts has been won, but the indictments keep coming anyway.

Minority women make up more than 70 percent of the 400 or more women charged with these offenses in cases currently before the courts. "These are the women most likely to use public health facilities instead of going to a private doctor who knows you personally," points out Smith. "If you're a middle-class white woman, your doctor would never even ask a question about drug abuse, certainly never administer a test for it."

Adds Paltrow, "These prosecutors claim that they just want the women to be forced into getting treatment. That's nonsense. There are no drug treatment programs for pregnant or parenting women with drug and alcohol problems."

The trend is particularly disturbing in light of new studies which indicate that while alcohol abuse during pregnancy is very dangerous, crack use actually inflicts limited damage on unborn children. And good prenatal care is universally acknowledged as the best way to ensure the birth of healthy children.

But, Paltrow says, "women are being scared away from both prenatal care and drug treatment because they don't want to be turned in. The fact is, if you care about the health of women or babies, you cannot adopt a punitive approach."

Poverty, drugs and physical abuse are the depressing trinity of women behind bars. The majority of them are mothers, and for many their real problems begin when they get out: finding a job and housing and reclaiming children in the care of relatives or foster parents.

Diana Hernandez, the director of counseling for the Fortune Society in

New York, an organization operated by former inmates that helps ex-offenders reintegrate into society, says these are the most difficult problems that many women face when they're released from prison: "Without a job, without a place to live, and a child or two depending on her, what is she supposed to do? Without help and support, chances are she's going to go back."

The impact on society goes beyond the costs of incarceration. The children, raised apart from their mothers and often in unstable conditions, are more likely to grow up with a host of problems—including a higher chance of becoming criminals themselves.

And, Hernandez says, some of the foster families who take care of these children get very attached to them; in some cases, women coming out of jail have lost their children as a result. "In either case, it's traumatic for mother, foster family and child," she says.

Women "getting out," like anyone with a criminal record, have an extremely difficult time finding employment and are more likely to return to crime or end up on welfare. Hernandez notes that just dealing with the bureaucratic red tape of life after imprisonment can be overwhelming.

"These are women whose behavior needs monitoring," Smith says. "But not to be locked up. I mean, they're not killers. What good does prison do them? If they weren't hardcore addicts or criminals when they went in, they sure will be when they get out." Smith, Hollander and other criminologists advocate probation and counseling in place of more-expensive jail terms. Because the majority of nonviolent female offenders (aside from white-collar crooks) do seem driven by economic need, such alternatives would probably be more sensible, they say.

Hollander, who has studied and worked with many child abuse cases, believes that imprisonment is a bad choice, particularly for family abusers — male or female. She cites one of her own cases, in which a year of intensive counseling was offered as an alternative for an abusive family. The family stayed together — without further violence.

"The more people we lock up," she says, "the fewer parents there are. Do we stop caring about 'the family' just because these people are poor and troubled? What's going to happen to those children without their parents? We're going to raise a generation of antisocial outcasts." Counseling does not work in every case, she concedes, but she believes it's worth a try.

"The real truth," Smith says, "is that you can't shut certain things out of your sight. You can't imprison away addiction or poverty or misery."

DANGER IN THE SAFETY ZONE

As violence spreads into small towns, many Americans barricade themselves

JILL SMOLOWE

"PAGING DR. STRONG. PAGing Dr. Strong." When that seemingly routine message squawked over the public address system last Monday evening at the Corona Regional Medical Center, nearly all employees froze. Just weeks earlier, the 148-bed hospital in Southern California had established new security precautions. Staff members now knew the potentially deadly meaning of those six words: someone with a gun was in the building.

The terrifying drama that unfolded over the next 10 minutes has become all too familiar not only in America's hospitals but in virtually all public places once regarded as safe havens. At 6:20 p.m., Sophia White, 31, entered the facility and calmly made her way to the third-floor nursery where six infants lay. Drawing a .38-cal. revolver, White wildly fired six shots at nurse Elizabeth Staten, striking her in the abdomen and hand. The wounded Staten fled down a stairwell to the first-floor emergency room, with White in pursuit. "She caught up with Liz at the chart desk and pistol-whipped her. Then she shot her," says veteran nurse Joan Black, 62, who was in the triage area at the time. "She said [to Liz], 'You've destroyed my life. You've taken my husband and my kids. Prepare to die. Open your mouth.'"

As White took aim yet again, Black crossed the room and wrapped her right arm around White. "I figured if she could feel my body, maybe she wouldn't kill me," Black recalls. Tightening the hug, Black placed her left hand over the gun and began a soothing patter. "You're in pain. I understand, and we can work it out." After five, maybe 10 minutes, White told Black she would give her the gun. Only after police handcuffed White did Black break down in sobs. "I don't know why the hell I did what I did," Black says. "It was just instinct." Instinct, that is, born of experience. "I've taken handguns out of the purses of little old ladies, and I've had people take a swing at me," she says. While this incident had no tragic ending—Staten survived the assault and is in stable condition—Black is wary of what may happen the next time. "You can't deny rapid access to an emergency room," she notes. "But nurses are terrified."

So, it appears, are most Americans. Bingeing on a diet of local news stories that graphically depict crime invading once safe ports—schools, restaurants, courtrooms, homes, libraries—Americans are rapidly coming to regard the summer of '93 as a season in hell. Indeed, a spate of events in the past two weeks seemed to argue that no one and no place was immune, not a respected schoolteacher living in a small town in Texas, not even the father of a megastar athlete driving a car down the highway.

The epidemic of shooting sprees in malls, McDonald's restaurants and movie theaters has fostered the perception that almost no place is safe anymore. Fear has led to a boom in the security industry and the transformation of homes and public places into fortresses. "People are worried more. They're worried sick," says Amitai Etzioni, a sociologist at George Washing-ton University. "There is a new level of fright, one that is both overdone and realistic at the same time."

Newly released FBI statistics show two different trends in crime rates: occurrences of violence in cities and towns with populations under 1 million are nudging upward, while such incidents are declining in the densest urban enclaves. In a TIME/CNN poll conducted last week, 30% of those surveyed think suburban crime is at least as serious as urban crime—double the number who said that was true five years ago.

The broadening of targets to include suburban and rural preserves—and the savageness of the crimes that fill the news—has left far more Americans feeling vulnerable. "The fear is getting worse because there is no pattern to the crime," says James Marquart, a criminal-justice professor at Sam Houston State University. "It is random, spontaneous and episodic." These days, everyone has a story to tell. Says Pam Lychner, 34, who six weeks ago founded a Houston-based citizens' action group called Justice for All: "People used to know one crime victim. Now they know five—or they are one themselves." According to the National Victim Center, victim-advocacy groups have multiplied nearly eightfold since 1985.

The past two weeks, in fact, provided a frightening new list of victims who found themselves suddenly vulnerable in places they thought they would be safe—a burger joint, a mall, the courtroom, a car. Here is a brief catalog of unexpected mortality: **A CAUSE CELEBRE** No one knew who "John Doe" was when they fished him from South Carolina's Gum Swamp Creek

A RHYTHM TO THE MADNESS

Is there a link between crime and population growth? And how does social change aggravate the current crime surge? James Q. Wilson, professor of management and public policy at UCLA and author of Thinking About Crime *and* The Moral Sense, *gave his views last week in an interview with* TIME *assistant editor Susanne Washburn. Excerpts:*

Any historian knows that crime waves, in fact, are cyclical. Earlier ones occurred in the 1830s, the late 1860s and the 1920s. The question is, What causes the cycles, and what affects their timing? Crime was abnormally low in the 1940s and 1950s and began to rise around 1963 and peaked in the late 1970s. The increase in crime from 1963 to 1980 was enormous—and it occurred in a period of general prosperity. Part of the explanation is that the population got younger, because of the baby boom—and younger men are more likely to commit crime than older ones.

Then in the early 1980s, almost all forms of crime began to decline for a while. The baby boom got old, so the baby boomers were no longer in the crime-prone years. We saw this in declining public-school enrollments. Now, however, if you look at what's happening in elementary schools, enrollments are going up because the children of baby boomers are starting to move through the cycle. My guess—and the guess of many other criminologists—is that by the end of this decade we will see an increase in the general crime rate regardless of what the government does.

Obviously, we want to do everything possible to moderate its severity. And public policy ought to be directed toward that end. The public expects it. I think politicians will face up to it. But we simply have to realize we are in an era when our ability to moderate the severity of crimes is substantially reduced from what it once was. We are much more reliant on public policy, which is a crude and not very effective

instrument. And we are much less dependent on informal social controls, which, when they work, are the most powerful controls.

The most significant thing in the last half-century has been the dramatic expansion in personal freedom and personal mobility, individual rights, the reorienting of culture around individuals. We obviously value that. But like all human gains, it has been purchased at a price. Most people faced with greater freedom from family, law, village, clan, have used it for good purposes—artistic expression, economic entrepreneurship, self-expression—but a small fraction of people have used it for bad purposes. So just as we have had an artistic and economic explosion, we have had a crime explosion. I think the two are indissolubly entwined. When that prosperity puts cars, drugs and guns into the hands of even relatively poor 18-year-olds, young people can do a great deal more damage today than they could in the 1940s or 1950s.

on Aug. 3. He had a bullet wound in his chest and no identification. Only two days later, after a car was found about 60 miles away, did clues and apprehensions start coming together. Last Friday, Chicago Bulls fans and friends went numb when they learned that John Doe was James Jordan, 57, the father of megastar Michael Jordan.

The senior Jordan disappeared after attending the North Carolina funeral of a friend on July 22. At the time, his family thought little of it: the elder Jordan often took off for days at a time without warning. Alarms began to sound on Aug. 5 when sheriffs in Cumberland County, North Carolina, found his car on a wooded back road. The red 1993 Lexus had been stripped of its tires, stereo system and vanity license plates. Though the windows were smashed, there was no evidence of foul play: no blood, no bullet holes, no ransom note. Then Cumberland County authorities learned of the John Doe corpse in a neighboring state.

Dental records confirmed the Jordan family's dread. Last week the FBI opened a kidnapping investigation, and a 16-year-old boy was arrested by sheriffs' deputies in connection with the stripped car. But as yet, the murder remains a mystery. What was the motive? Is there a link to the gambling allegations that have dogged the su-

perstar? James Jordan was an infectiously affectionate man, known as Pops not only to his famous son but to friends as well. The most chilling possibility is that his death was just the result of another carjacking—and that this could have been anyone's dad.

MC DONALD'S MASSACRE Kirk Hauptmann, 18, had just bitten into his cheeseburger last Tuesday in the no-smoking section of the McDonald's in Kenosha, Wisconsin, when he noticed Dion Terres, 25. "I looked up and said, 'Oh, he's got a gun,' but I thought it wasn't real," says Hauptmann. Moments later, Terres yelled, "Everybody out of here!" and began shooting a .44-cal. Magnum pistol. As 10 panicked patrons dove for the exit door, Terres unloaded four shots. Two middle-aged customers were killed, and Hauptmann was shot in the right forearm. Terres turned the fourth bullet on himself, splattering his brain on the walls and ceiling.

Later police found a 40-minute tape in Terres' apartment. The rambling message pointed to several possible motives. Terres spoke of being under psychiatric care a few years ago and admitted to fantasizing about killing people for more than a year. The tape made reference to several notorious mass murderers, including Jeffrey Dahmer and Ted Bundy. It also referred to a 1984 bloodbath at a McDonald's in San

Ysidro, California—and police speculated that Terres' rampage might have been a copycat massacre. On tape, Terres stated, "Society screwed me, and now it's payback time." He may have been referring to the company that he claimed fired him in March, or to the 16-year-old girlfriend who dumped him in July.

As police continue to gather details about the disturbed and reclusive young man, those who survived Terres' perverse revenge are trying to resume their lives. Hauptmann returned to the same McDonald's the next day. "I had to go back," says the college sophomore. "My stomach was in knots, but it's still a public place."

MURDER IN THE MALL Paula Clouse, 43, and her 15-year-old son were among the dozen patrons who turned up last Tuesday at the Metro North Mall in Kansas City, Missouri, for the 5:20 p.m. showing of *Robin Hood: Men in Tights*. About 25 minutes after the theater darkened, the teenager allegedly took out a handgun and pumped four bullets into his mother's head. The boy then left the theater and strolled into the mall, followed by stunned onlookers. An arrest swiftly followed, but police have yet to come up with a motive.

"Apparently the parents were going through a divorce, and it was a very bitter divorce," says Captain Vince McInerney. "There were arguments over custody. The

A CONVICT'S VIEW: "PEOPLE DON'T WANT SOLUTIONS"

Wilbert Rideau, 51, has been imprisoned since 1962 at the Louisiana State Penitentiary at Angola, serving a life sentence for murder. During that time, Rideau has gained renown as a journalist, author and advocate of prison reform. In a conversation with TIME *Houston bureau chief Richard Woodbury, Rideau gave a scathing critique of the prison system:*

Q. *What do you think of Clinton's crime package?*

A. Public fear is out of control, so he has to put more police on the streets. Boot camps can help, but often they're just another feel-good device for punishing criminals. I'd like to see more efforts aimed at really improving people. Crime is a social problem, and education is the only real deterrent. Look at all of us in prison: we were all truants and dropouts, a failure of the education system. Look at your truancy problem, and you're looking at your future prisoners. Put the money there.

Q. *How have the increases in violent crime over the years contributed to a tougher mood in the country?*

A. It's a self-fulfilling hypothesis. If you scare people enough and make them believe the world is crumbling around them, at some point they'll start reacting. The news media have helped set the tone of rabid crime, and the politicians just pick up the theme and go with the flow.

Q. *What has been the fallout on prisons of this get-tough mood? Is their basic role changing?*

A. Since the 1970s, they have increasingly become just giant warehouses where you pack convicts to suffer. Look around me in this place. It's a graveyard, a human wasteland of old men—most of them just sitting around waiting to die. Of the 5,200 inmates here, 3,800 are lifers or serving sentences so long they will never get out. America has embraced vengeance as its criminal-justice philosophy. People don't want solutions to crime, they only want to feel good. That is what politicians are doing, they're making people feel secure. They offer them a platter of vindictiveness.

Q. *You don't feel that the tougher sentences are in any way a restraining influence on the criminal mind?*

A. Not at all. The length of a prison sentence has nothing to do with deterring crime. That theory is a crock. I mean, I've lived with criminals for 31 years. I know these guys, and myself. That's not the way it works. When the average guy commits a crime, he's either at the point where he doesn't care what happens to him, or more likely he feels he is going to get away with it. Punishment never factors into the equation. He just goes ahead because he feels he won't get caught.

Q. *Then what will stop violent crime?*

A. Only one thing: the certainty of apprehension. If a criminal fears that he's going to get caught, he will think twice before he robs or steals. And it won't matter whether the sentence is one year or 100 years.

Q. *What would have deterred you?*

A. I've thought a lot about that. I know that if I hadn't been able to walk into a pawnshop and buy a handgun as easily as I did, I wouldn't have robbed that bank. That applies to just about everybody in this prison who ever held up anybody. Nobody robs a place with a knife or a can of Mace. I was 19, an eighth-grade dropout. If I'd known that things weren't as helpless as I thought they were, that would have stopped me. I wouldn't have felt so frustrated.

Q. *How would you go about paying for education programs you propose, given the cash-starved nature of most government budgets?*

A. By shortening sentences. Sure, that's a hot button, but the public must come to realize that it can't enjoy its full measure of vengeance and expect at the same time to reduce bulging inmate populations. The citizenry must determine the minimum amount of punishment that it is willing to settle for, and then channel the millions it has saved into schools and preventive programs.

Q. *Given the level of public outrage, how would you deal with those who do commit serious crimes?*

A. You don't go handing out 99-year, no-parole sentences all over the place. That's ridiculous. States can't afford to keep locking people away for eternity. It takes $1 million to house a lifer. Look at these convicts around me. They're old men at 50, like me, or even 40. The fire's been burned out of them years ago. Most of them you'll never have to worry about again.

Q. *Isn't the notion of shorter sentences an incendiary idea in today's political climate?*

A. Probably. But the public has been sold a bill of goods on prisons, just like it's been given a distorted, negative picture of recidivism and parole. Most of the guys in this prison will never return to Angola, I can tell you that from being here. And parole can and does work, and I would expand it. I'd much rather pay for parole officers to supervise nondangerous people than build $100,000 cells.

---

boy was living with his dad, and a younger sister lived with the mom and the mother's parents." The gun reportedly belonged to the boy's father; police have not determined whether the murder was premeditated or the father was involved. "Disputes used to be settled with a shouting match or a punch in the nose," sighs McInerney.

AN ASSAULT IN SMALL TOWN, U.S.A. Tomball, Texas (pop. 6,370), is the safe sort of town where many residents leave their front doors unlocked at night. The quiet middle-class community may rethink such nocturnal habits after the strangling death last Tuesday of 82-year-old Mildred Stallones, a retired schoolteacher. A respected member of the community who was known for her generosity to children, Stallones was found in her old frame house. Police are still trying to determine if rape was involved. Beyond a forced entry into the house, police have little to offer: no motive, no suspects, no signs of theft.

Until now Tomball has suffered only the occasional property crime. "This is a wake-up call for anyone in Tomball who may have got complacent about living here," says police chief Paul Michna. "Nowhere is safe." Since Stallones was found, some of the town's elderly citizens have asked to move in with their children. Stallones' former daughter-in-law, Kerri Harrington, has barely slept since learning of the murder. "Before, I felt safe," she says. "Now I know this horrible crime could happen anywhere to anyone."

COURTROOM CARNAGE Federal judges have been so jittery about courthouse crime that since the early '80s, most federal courts have been outfitted with airport-style X-ray machines, designed to detect concealed weapons. Even so, the bloodletting continues. On Aug. 6, a man scheduled to be sentenced for drug dealing stormed the federal courthouse in Topeka, Kansas, firing two guns and lobbing pipe bombs. Before Jack McKnight, 37, killed himself by detonating explosives strapped to his body, he killed a security guard and wounded five people. "There's now a tacit assumption that people can vent their frustrations almost anywhere," says Dr. Allwyn Levine, a New Jersey psychiatrist. "We've become a much more lawless society."

While experts agree that the summer's rash of too-close-to-home crimes has deepened Americans' anxiety, they disagree on the triggers that have touched off the violence. Some believe the crime waves are cyclical (*see box*). Many fault Hollywood, which rushes sordid re-creations to TV and cinema screens before the corpses are even cold. "We have created a culture that increasingly accepts and glamourizes violence," says Dewey Cornell, a clinical psychologist at the University of Virginia. "I don't care what the network executives say. It does desensitize you." Others point accusingly at the media. "Every crackpot out there knows that if he can take an automatic weapon into a fast-food restaurant, the more people he can shoot, the more attention he's going to get," says Houston homicide sergeant Billy Belk. "So it encourages these weirdos."

Many experts dig deeper—but the roots they pull up are a messy tangle of societal ills. "We have a whole generation of kids suffering from neglect," says sociologist Stephen Klineberg of Houston's Rice University. "There is no one at home when they return from school, and this neglect in socialization results in increased violence." Others cite neglect's twin evil, child abuse, or that distant relative, school truancy. Liberals decry poverty; conservatives fault the decline of family values.

As the experts argue, many Americans are taking safety matters into their own hands. "When people are besieged with new reports of crime every day, the perception grows that, by golly, maybe the cops are ineffective," says crime expert Marquart. "It reinforces the perception of the criminal-justice system not working,

and the next thing you know, people are mobilizing to protect themselves."

IN THE PAST FIVE YEARS SECURITY PRE-cautions have increased at hospitals, schools, shopping malls, offices, courthouses and even libraries. And for good reason. Within the past year, librarians have been attacked and killed behind their desk in Sacramento, California, and Buckeye, Arizona. Incidents of violence against health-care workers have increased 400% since 1982, says Ira A. Lipman, chairman of the National Council on Crime and Delinquency and head of Guardsmark, Inc., the nation's fifth largest security company. "Companies are very concerned because one incident in a shopping mall can destroy business."

Across the U.S., companies that offer security devices report booming sales in both low-tech paraphernalia (Mace, burglar bars, door alarms) and high-tech apparatus (video doorbells, motion-detection devices). Meanwhile, existing forms of high technology are being pressed into the services of security. Cellular phones are popular not only with businessmen but also with people who fear being stranded because of auto trouble or attacked while on the road. As their cost goes down, many are buying them for emergency use only.

Last year an estimated 16% of all U.S. homes installed electronic systems. Video surveillance is becoming more popular. Says Steve Gribbon of the Alert Centre Protective Services, a Colorado-based security company with 200,000 customers in 48 states: "Five or six years ago, only estates in the $700,000-to-$1 million range used them. We're now seeing them in $200,000 homes." Says Anthony Potter, a private security consultant in Atlanta: "In the past, people thought home-security systems were too expensive—that it was only for people with diamond collections." But, he adds, "they are seeing that it is not that expensive. It cuts their homeowner's insurance." Many are also thinking of gun ownership. Says Potter: "I know a lot of people who five years ago would not have thought about asking me about guns. Now they're asking me what kind they should buy."

"Many people who are most fearful of crime have the least reason to be fearful," says James Q. Wilson, a social scientist at

UCLA. "If you map the fear of crime and map the actual crime range, you note that they don't overlap." But, he says, "that doesn't mean people are irrational. It simply means that everyone is aware that we live in a far more dangerous society and, in fact, the self-protective measures they take do tend to protect them. They are acting correctly, rationally."

From coast to coast, people are sealing off their homes and neighborhoods with iron gates, razor-ribbon wire and iron spikes. The home of Billy Davis in Pico Rivera, southeast of Los Angeles, offers a glimpse of the paranoia that is fast turning homes into fortresses. His two-story frame house is outfitted with motion-sensitive floodlights, video monitors, infrared alarms and a spiked fence topped with razor wire. A metal cage surrounds the patio. Bars adorn every window. A Doberman pinscher guards the yard. And a security guard patrols the driveway. "The wrong people are behind bars," says Anne Seymour of the National Victim Center. "People are putting themselves behind bars because we as a nation have failed to put the right people behind bars."

While such precautions make some people feel safer, others worry about the "Balkanization" of America. "All of this leads to a breakdown of any sense of community," says Camilo José Vergara, who has been photographing the gradual fortressing of urban areas over the past 20 years. "Each family tries to make a living within its own fort and is unconcerned about what goes on outside." Moreover, homegrown solutions often breed new problems. When neighborhoods barricade themselves in, they often cut the access of police, ambulance drivers and fire fighters. When public institutions, like courts and libraries, erect barriers, the concept of access in a democratic society is threatened.

In the end, gates, gadgetry and gizmos may not be enough. "I don't think you can build gates high enough to eradicate the fear," says Los Angeles city councilwoman Rita Walters. "You've got to eliminate the source of the fear." Until then, the public arena can suddenly become a coliseum of blood sport. No place is sacred. All sanctuaries are suspect. —*Reported by Julie Johnson/ Washington, Elaine Lafferty/Los Angeles, Ken Myers/Cleveland, Lisa Towle/Raleigh and Richard Woodbury/Houston*

Honey, I warped the kids

Hollywood still doth protest too much, while the stats on video violence pile up.

Carl M. Cannon

Carl M. Cannon is the White House correspondent for the Baltimore Sun.

Tim Robbins and Susan Sarandon implore the nation to treat Haitians with AIDS more humanely. Robert Redford works for the environment. Harry Belafonte marches against the death penalty.

Actors and producers seem to be constantly speaking out for noble causes far removed from their lives. They seem even more vocal and visible now that there is a Democrat in the White House. But in the one area over which they have control—the excessive violence in the entertainment industry—Hollywood activists remain silent.

This summer, Washington was abuzz with talk about the movie *Dave,* in which Kevin Kline stars as the acting president. But every time I saw an ad featuring Kline, the movie I couldn't get out of my head was *Grand Canyon.* There are two scenes in it that explain much of what has gone wrong in America.

Kline's character has a friend, played by Steve Martin, who is a producer of the B-grade, violent movies that Hollywood euphemistically calls "action" films. But after an armed robber shoots Martin's character in the leg, he has an epiphany.

"I can't make those movies any more," he decides. "I can't make another piece of art that glorifies violence and bloodshed and brutality.... No more exploding bodies, exploding buildings, exploding anything. I'm going to make the world a better place."

A month or two later, Kline calls on Martin at his Hollywood studio to congratulate him on the "new direction" his career has taken.

"What? Oh that," Martin says dismissively. " . . . that. That's over I must have been delirious for a few weeks there."

He then gins up every hoary excuse for Hollywood-generated violence you've ever heard, ending with: "My movies reflect what's going on; they don't make what's going on."

This is Hollywood's last line of defense for why it shows murder and mayhem on the big screen and the little one, in prime time and early in the morning, to children, adolescents, and adults:

We don't cause violence, we just report it.

Four years ago, I joined the legion of writers, researchers, and parents

Passing the buck in Tinseltown

MICHAEL KRASNY

Michael Krasny is currently the host of San Francisco radio station KQED's "Forum," a weekday talk show. Priscilla Yamin of Mother Jones and Karen Daar contributed research to these interviews.

For seven years, Michael Krasny hosted a successful West Coast radio talk show widely recognized for discussing serious issues and showing respect for callers. Krasny left his commercial program to move to public radio in February 1993. Many saw Krasny's departure from commercial radio as symbolic of the industry trend toward sensationalism and controversy—and away from public trust and responsibility.

Mother Jones commissioned Krasny to explore the trend toward excess, particularly excess violence, in the entertainment industry. Film and TV producers, directors, and writers claim that they want to create works of artistic and social value, yet too often what we—and our children—see is only blood and gore. How can we reconcile the First Amendment with the cost to society of viewing such violence? And to what extent are these individuals responsible for the repercussions of their violent movies and television shows? Krasny asked a few players for their thoughts:

who have tried to force Hollywood to confront the more disturbing truth. I wrote a series of newspaper articles on the massive body of evidence that establishes a direct cause-and-effect relationship between violence on television and violence in society.

The orchestrated response from the industry—a series of letters seeking to discredit me—was something to behold.

Because the fact is, on the one issue over which they have power, the liberals in Hollywood don't act like progressive thinkers; they act like, say, the National Rifle Association:

Guns don't kill people, people kill people.

We don't cause violence in the world, we just reflect it.

THE FIRST CONGRESSIONAL HEARINGS INTO THE EFFECTS OF TELEVISION VIOLENCE took place in 1954. Although television was still relatively new, its extraordinary marketing power was already evident. The tube was teaching Americans what to buy and how to act, not only in advertisements, but in dramatic shows, too.

Everybody from Hollywood producers to Madison Avenue ad men would boast about this power—and seek to utilize it on dual tracks: to make money and to remake society along better lines.

Because it seemed ludicrous to assert that there was only one area—the depiction of violence—where television did not influence behavior, the television industry came up with this theory: Watching violence is cathartic. A violent person might be sated by watching a murder.

The notion intrigued social scientists, and by 1956 they were studying it in earnest. Unfortunately, watching violence turned out to be anything but cathartic.

In the 1956 study, one dozen four-year-olds watched a "Woody Woodpecker" cartoon that was full of violent images. Twelve other preschoolers watched "Little Red Hen," a peaceful cartoon. Then the children were observed. The children who watched "Woody Woodpecker" were more likely to hit other children, verbally accost their classmates, break toys, be disruptive, and engage in destructive behavior during free play.

For the next thirty years, researchers in all walks of the social sciences studied the question of whether television causes violence. The results have been stunningly conclusive.

"There is more published research on this topic than on almost any other social issue of our time," University of Kansas Professor Aletha C. Huston, chairwoman of the American Psychological Association's Task Force on Television and Society, told Congress in 1988. "Virtually all independent scholars agree that there is evidence that television can cause aggressive behavior."

There have been some three thousand studies of this issue—eighty-five of them major research efforts—and they all say the same thing. Of the eighty-five major studies, the only one that failed to find a causal relationship between television violence and actual violence was paid for by NBC. When the study was subsequently reviewed by three independent social scientists, all three concluded that it actually did demonstrate a causal relationship.

Some highlights from the history of TV violence research:

• In 1973, when a town in mountainous western Canada was wired for television signals, University of British Columbia researchers observed first- and second-graders. Within two years, the incidence of hitting, biting, and shoving increased 160 percent in those classes.

• Two Chicago doctors, Leonard Eron and Rowell Huesmann, followed the viewing habits of a group of children for twenty-two years. They found that watching violence on television is the single best predictor of violent or aggressive behavior later in life, ahead of such commonly accepted factors as parents' behavior, poverty, and race.

"Television violence effects youngsters of all ages, of both genders, at all socioeconomic levels and all levels of intelligence," they told Congress in 1992. "The effect is not limited to children who are already disposed to being aggressive and is not restricted to this country."

BRIAN GRAZER, Ron Howard's partner, has produced more than twenty movies. "Most of my films have been sweet-spirited: *Parenthood. Splash. My Girl.* I'm proud of them. Others I'm not so proud of. I learned a big lesson with *Kindergarten Cop.* No one objected to the violent confrontation scene, and there was no problem with it in our focus groups. Then I showed it to my five-year-old, and all of a sudden, reflexively, I put my hand over his eyes. I knew at that point that we'd made a mistake. It was too late to cut the scene, but I would cut it now.

"Usually bad movies aren't hits. I don't see Freddy Krueger [*Nightmare on Elm Street*] movies, and I wouldn't want my kids to see them. I don't know why people make such movies. They're sick."

BOB SHAYE, chief executive officer of New Line Cinema, is responsible for the *Nightmare on Elm Street* horror films. "There's an almost sardonic or dour humor to Freddy Krueger [the *Elm Street* killer], especially to fantasy horror buffs. The tales are useful and cautionary. They suggest that evil and harm are everywhere and that we need to be prepared. They're not intended for kids.

"We create a product. People buy it or they don't. It pains my aesthetic judgment, but I often feel a good movie is one that makes money. My interest is in entertaining people. *The Killers* and *Batman*? Too much for kids. I can draw my lines. Not everyone can."

SAM HAMM shares screenwriting credit for *Batman* and *Batman Returns.* "It was probably a bad idea to excite small children to see *Batman Returns.* The tie-in to McDonald's was the idea of marketing people.

"But I'm ambivalent about all of this. I can remember being scared as a kid at horror films and developing a craving for that sort of thing, but that's what may form imagination in a strong way and that's what creates narrative and inner life. It teaches you to look for stuff that's not safe in the art you enjoy later on.

"I'm not arguing to expose kids to *Friday the 13th* movies or porno, but I feel there's too much caution about what kids see. Gravitating toward the forbidden is a natural part of growing up.

"I'm dubious of stimulation and effect, wary of speaking of anyone's experience but my own. I knew as a kid very clearly the distinction between real violence and cartoon or film violence. I'm waiting for the legions of those affected by what they see to give testimony."

VIVIENNE VERDON-ROE directed the documentary film *Women For America, For The World.* "I can't go to most popular movies without checking them out with friends first, because I can't physically sit through [violent ones]. My body will not allow it. People really ought to think about the effects. They

• Fascinated by an explosion of murder rates in the United States and Canada that began in 1955, after a generation of North Americans had come of age on television violence, University of Washington Professor Brandon Centerwall decided to see if the same phenomenon could be observed in South Africa, where the Afrikaner-dominated regime had banned television until 1975.

He found that eight years after TV was introduced—showing mostly Hollywood-produced fare—South Africa's murder rate skyrocketed. His most telling finding was that the crime rate increased first in the white communities. This mirrors U.S. crime statistics in the 1950s and especially points the finger at television, because whites were the first to get it in both countries.

Bolder than most researchers, Centerwall argues flatly that without violent television programming, there might be as many as ten thousand fewer murders in the United States each year.

• In 1983, University of California, San Diego, researcher David P. Phillips wanted to see if there was a correlation between televised boxing matches and violence in the streets of America.

Looking at crime rates after every televised heavyweight championship fight from 1973 to 1978, Phillips found that the homicide rate in the United States rose by an average of 11 percent for approximately one week. Phillips also found that the killers were likely to focus their aggression on victims similar to the losing fighter: if he was white, the increased number of victims were mostly white. The converse was true if the losing fighter was black.

By the age of eighteen, the average child has witnessed eighteen thousand simulated murders on TV.

• In 1988, researchers Daniel G. Linz and Edward Donnerstein of the University of California, Santa Barbara, and Steven Penrod of the University of Wisconsin studied the effects on young men of horror movies and "slasher" films.

They found that depictions of violence, not sex, are what desensitizes people.

They divided male students into four groups. One group watched no movies, a second watched nonviolent, X-rated movies, a third watched teenage sexual-innuendo movies, and a fourth watched the slasher films *Texas Chainsaw Massacre, Friday the 13th Part 2, Maniac,* and *Toolbox Murders.*

All the young men were placed on a mock jury panel and asked a series of questions designed to measure their empathy for an alleged female rape victim. Those in the fourth group measured lowest in empathy for the specific victim in the experiment—and for rape victims in general.

THE ANECDOTAL EVIDENCE IS OFTEN MORE COMPELLING THAN THE SCIENTIFIC studies. Ask any homicide cop from London to Los Angeles to Bangkok if television violence induces real-life violence and listen carefully to the cynical, knowing laugh.

Ask David McCarthy, police chief in Greenfield, Massachusetts, why nineteen-year-old Mark Branch killed himself after stabbing an eighteen-year-old female college student to death. When cops searched his room they found ninety horror movies, as well as a machete and a goalie mask like those used by Jason, the grisly star of *Friday the 13th.*

Ask the families of thirty-five young men who committed suicide by playing Russian roulette after seeing the movie *The Deer Hunter.*

Ask George Gavito, a lieutenant in the Cameron County, Texas, sheriff's department, about a cult that sacrificed at least thirteen people on a ranch west of Matamoros, Mexico. The suspects kept mentioning a 1986 movie, *The Believers,* about rich families who engage in ritual sacrifice. "They talk about it like that had something to do with changing them," Gavito recalled later.

may not faint, like I do, but they're getting desensitized to violence, and it contributes to the social violence of gangs and the like.

"It's incredibly difficult when there are so few alternatives. Teens go to movies because there's often nothing else for them to do, and if they are gruesome or bad movies, no one in society seems to be saying so.

"I'm not an insider. I'm not living down there. But I know enough. It's all money. Everything's money. It's horrible."

RICHARD DONNER directed the *Lethal Weapon* movies, *Superman, The Omen,* and *The Goonies,* among others. "If people see gratuitous violence in any of the *Lethal Weapon* movies, I wonder if they've seen the same movie. It's entertainment. That's my obligation, I brought social issues into the *Lethal Weapon* movies, like when Danny Glover's family comes down on him for eating tuna, or the 'Stamp out the NRA' sign up in the LA police station. In the last one the daughter wears a pro-choice T-shirt.

"You've got to prove [a connection between film violence and real violence] to me. Movies do provoke. I won't do gratuitous or animal violence. We went a little too far in the first *Lethal Weapon,* but I wanted to move more after that toward a less real and more comic-book effect, despite the great reaction we had.

"Public trust comes into filmmaking. The filmmaker is ultimately accountable. I can defend my own work only on personal grounds. If I'm a provocateur of anything, I hope it's good emotion and humor. Censorship is in the ratings system. It works."

CALLIE KHOURI won an Academy Award for her screenplay of *Thelma and Louise.* "I have a hard time with violence just to entertain, but I believe it can be very effective in getting a point across. I resorted to it in my film, but there was a conscience to it. Thelma and Louise felt they had done something wrong, and there were big consequences—including psychic consequences.

"Outlaw movies have always been a catharsis for men, but denied to women. I was extremely frustrated with the literal interpretation of *Thelma and Louise.* Doesn't anyone read anymore or understand metaphor? The film was supposed to be complex, without easy answers, and with flawed characters. I thought when Louise shot that guy that there'd be dead silence in the theater. That scene was written carefully: it was an attempted rape, and I wanted to make what she did wrong. And yet people cheered. I was stunned."

LESLIE MOONVES is head of Lorimar Studios, often called the fifth network, which produced the TV movies "Jack the Ripper" and "Deliberate Strangers" (about serial killer Ted Bundy), as well as shows that Moonves has considerably more pride in, such as "I'll Fly Away" and "Home Front." "I'd love to do another 'I'll Fly Away,' but the corporate bosses won't let me.

2. CRIME, DELINQUENCY, AND VIOLENCE

Ask LAPD lieutenant Mike Melton about Angel Regino of Los Angeles, who was picked up after a series of robberies and a murder in which he wore a blue bandanna and fedora identical to those worn by Freddy, the sadistic anti-hero of *Nightmare on Elm Street*. In case anybody missed the significance of his disguise, Regino told his victims that they would never forget him, because he was another Freddy Krueger.

Ask Britain Home Secretary Douglas Hurd, who called for further restrictions on U.S.-produced films after Michael Ryan of Hungerford committed Britain's worst mass murder in imitation of *Rambo*, massacring sixteen people while wearing a U.S. combat jacket and a bandoleer of ammunition.

Ask Sergeant John O'Malley of the New York Police Department about a nine-year-old boy who sprayed a Bronx office building with gunfire. The boy explained to the astonished sergeant how he learned to load his Uzi-like firearm: "I watch a lot of TV."

Or ask Manteca, California, police detective Jeff Boyd about thirteen-year-old Juan Valdez, who, with another teenager, went to a man's home, kicked him, stabbed him, beat him with a fireplace poker, and then choked him to death with a dog chain.

Why, Boyd wanted to know, had the boys poured salt in the victim's wounds?

"Oh, I don't know," the youth replied with a shrug. "I just seen it on TV."

NUMEROUS GROUPS HAVE CALLED, OVER THE YEARS, FOR CURBING TELEVISION violence: the National Commission on the Causes and Prevention of Violence (1969), the U.S. Surgeon General (1972), the Canadian Royal Commission (1976), the National Institute of Mental Health (1982), the U.S. Attorney General's Task Force on Family Violence (1984), the National Parents Teachers Association (1987), and the American Psychological Association (1992).

During that time, cable television and movie rentals have made violence more readily available while at the same time pushing the envelope for network TV. But even leaving aside cable and movie rentals, a study of television programming from 1967 to 1989 showed only small ups and downs in violence, with the violent acts moving from one time slot to another but the overall violence rate remaining pretty steady—and pretty similar from network to network.

"The percent of prime-time programs using violence remains more than seven out of ten, as it has been for the entire twenty-two-year period," researchers George Gerbner of the University of Pennsylvania Annenberg School for Communication and Nancy Signorielli of the University of Delaware wrote in 1990. For the past twenty-two years, they found, adults and children have been entertained by about sixteen violent acts, including two murders, in each evening's prime-time programming.

They also discovered that the rate of violence in children's programs is three times the rate in prime-time shows. By the age of eighteen, the average American child has witnessed at least eighteen thousand simulated murders on television.

By 1989, network executives were arguing that their violence was part of a larger context in which bad guys get their just desserts.

"We have never put any faith in mechanical measurements, such as counting punches or gunshots," said NBC's Alan Gerson. "Action and conflict must be evaluated within each specific dramatic context."

"Our policy," added Alfred R. Schneider of ABC, "... makes clear that when violence is portrayed [on TV], it must be reasonably related to plot development and character delineation."

Of course, what early-childhood experts could tell these executives is that children between the ages of four and seven simply make no connection between the murder at the beginning of a half-hour show and the man led away in handcuffs at the end. In fact, psychologists know that very young children do not even understand death to be a permanent condition.

But all of the scientific studies and reports, all of the wisdom of cops and grief of parents have run up against Congress's quite proper fear of censorship. For years, Democratic Congressman Peter Rodino of New Jersey chaired the House Judiciary Committee and looked at calls for some form

When you get burned with quality programming you get gun-shy—you feel you need to stick to the shows that make money. You know what the problem is? Network change. Somebody like Bill Paley [former chairman of CBS] used to say that he didn't care if he got a twelve share, because there was a public trust and social responsibility to put on an 'I'll Fly Away.' GE buys a network, and you've got a different agenda.

"Network presidents don't keep their jobs based on the number of Emmy awards. Let's face it: there is more sensation and violence because it works. The movie of the week has become the killer of the week story.

"Do we have a responsibility to our public? Of course. I honestly don't know what to do about it. How's that for an answer?"

JOE ESZTERHAS has written the scripts for such major Hollywood films as *Betrayal, Jagged Edge, Basic Instinct*, and *Sliver*. His work has been criticized as sexist and homophobic. "I don't like to be a Monday morning quarterback on my own work."

DAWN STEEL became the first woman to head a major studio when she was made president of Columbia Pictures in 1987. During her career, she has worked on such films as *Top Gun, Beverly Hills Cop II, Casualties of War, When Harry Met Sally*, and *Look Who's Talking*. She now runs her own production company. "I believe I've never made a movie in bad taste or with excessive violence. But for profit, I've had to make movies not from my soul. If I want to make a film for passion, I have to make it for less money.

"I'm more cynical about the violence in LA than about violence in our business. It's unanswerable whether movies reflect the culture or vice versa. I monitor my kid's movies and won't let her see what's not appropriate for her. There's no way you can censor any movie in this country that's being made. That's our First Amendment."

MATT GROENING is creator and executive producer of the TV hit "The Simpsons." "Anytime you visualize something, it's difficult not to glorify it. Every antiwar film is prowar, because its violence is stylized and an audience can be removed from it and enjoy it. Stylistically, violence is almost invariably glorified, even when you have an antiviolent point of view. Look at *Platoon*. Violence is invariably used in movies and TV as punctuation, and it does have a numbing effect on people after a time.

"Most TV, most movies, really, are less pernicious than tedious and boring. What's bad for kids is bad storytelling. Tell better stories."

BARRY DILLER, ex–chief executive officer and chairman of Fox and Matt Groening's former boss, now heads QVC Network. He couldn't disagree more with Groening about television's being mostly bad. "I can't imagine why he would say that. Pound for of censorship with a jaundiced eye. At a hearing five years ago, Rodino told witnesses that Congress must be a "protector of commerce."

"Well, we have children that we need to protect," replied Frank M. Palumbo, a pediatrician at Georgetown University Hospital and a consultant to the American Academy of Pediatrics. "What we have here is a toxic substance in the environment that is harmful to children."

Arnold Fege of the national PTA added, "Clearly, this committee would not protect teachers who taught violence to children. Yet why would we condone children being exposed to a steady diet of TV violence year after year?"

Finally there is a reason to hope for progress.

Early this summer, Massachusetts Democrat Edward Markey, chair of the House Energy and Commerce subcommittee on telecommunications, said that Congress may require manufacturers to build TV sets with a computer chip so that parents could block violent programs from those their children could select.

He joins the fight waged by Senator Paul Simon, a liberal Democrat from Illinois. Nine years ago, Simon flipped on a hotel television set hoping to catch the late news. "Instead," he has recalled many times, "I saw a man being sawed in half with a chainsaw, in living color."

Simon was unsettled by the image and even more unsettled when he wondered what repeatedly looking at such images would do to the mind of a fourteen-year-old.

When he found out, he called television executives, who told him that violence sells and that they would be at a competitive disadvantage if they acted responsibly.

Why not get together and adopt voluntary guidelines? Simon asked.

Oh, that would be a violation of antitrust law, they assured him.

Simon called their bluff in 1990 by pushing through Congress a law that allowed a three-year moratorium on antitrust considerations so that the industry could discuss ways to jointly reduce violence.

Halfway through that time, however, they had done nothing, and an angry Simon denounced the industry on the Senate floor. With a push from some prominent industry figures, a conference was set for this August 2 in Los Angeles.

This spring, CBS broadcast group president Howard Stringer said his network was looking for ways to cut back on violence in its entertainment, because he was troubled by the cost to society of continuing business-as-usual.

"We must admit we have a responsibility," he said.

Jack Valenti, the powerful head of the Motion Picture Association of America, wrote to producers urging them to participate in the August 2 conference. "I think it's more than a bunch of talk," Simon said. "I think this conference will produce some results. I think the industry will adopt some standards."

The federal government, of course, possesses the power to regulate the airwaves through the FCC, and Simon and others believe that this latent power to control violence—never used—has put the fear of God in the producers. He also thinks some of them are starting to feel guilty.

"We now have more people in jail and prison per capita than any country that keeps records, including South Africa," Simon says. "We've spent billions putting people behind bars, and it's had no effect on the crime rate. None. People realize there have to be other answers, and as they've looked around, they have settled on television as one of them."

Maybe Simon is right. Maybe Hollywood executives will get together and make a difference.

Or maybe, like Steve Martin's character in *Grand Canyon*, producers and directors from New York to Beverly Hills will wake up after Simon's antitrust exemption expires December 1, shake off the effects of their holiday hangovers, and when asked about their new commitment to responsible filmmaking, answer:

"What? Oh that. . . . that. That's over. We must have been delirious for a few weeks there."

pound, the hour and half-hour television series are very good. There's a lot of junk, but much more in the movie business, the record business, even legitimate theater. It's snobbery to call a show like 'Roseanne' lowbrow or vulgar. It's funny and interesting and has a good moral value and tone.

"TV movies are crummy. 'Hard Copy' is a lying, thieving, lowlife program of hideous, cynical purpose. It's not serious television. There are only a few tabloid shows, but they speak loudly.

"I think you look at society, and you see what is reflected on television in terms of violent action. Absolutely, [there is too much violence]. But we can be thoughtful and reasonable and change that, reduce it. I think plans over the last few years will help. Senator Simon's work with the networks will help."

PHILIP KAUFMAN co-wrote and directed *The Wanderers*, *The Unbearable Lightness of Being*, and *Henry and June*, and wrote and directed *The Right Stuff*. "There is a fascist edge to a lot of the violence we see. I'm in favor of pushing the envelope, but when you push it in romance or eroticism you get an NC-17 rating. It's easier to get an R rating if you use senseless violence, because the ratings board is largely conservative and embraces violence before sex."

JOSH BRAND, along with his partner, has produced the TV hits "St. Elsewhere" and "Northern Exposure." "If something gets a high rating, say, 'The Amy Fisher Story,' then advertisers pay more money. Now, did the networks create the audience for it, or do they pander to what the audience wanted? Is it okay to pollute the emotional and spiritual environment?

"Now there are studies [that show] that violent images don't affect people, just as the tobacco industry has studies showing that cigarette smoking doesn't cause cancer. And they use the First Amendment to evoke their rights and get into this study versus that study, and the whole thing becomes a wash, a miasma of moral mud. But I think that there is absolutely no question that the profusion of these kinds of images has a negative effect, not only on children but on human beings in general.

"But regulations are dangerous, particularly when dealing with the free expression of ideas. I do believe that some of those ideas are like pollutants, but there isn't one thing you can do. A panacea doesn't exist."

Although there may be no panacea, we must still look for solutions. How would you resolve the conflict between excessive violence in entertainment and the protections guaranteed under the First Amendment?

Write to *Mother Jones*, 1663 Mission St., 2nd Floor, San Francisco, CA 94103. Or fax us at (415) 863-5136.

THE ECONOMICS OF CRIME

The toll is frightening. Can anything be done?

Americans are scared. The fear of crime permeates their lives. They worry about being mugged or raped in a parking lot or while walking home from work. They're afraid of being robbed at a highway rest stop or having their children kidnapped at a suburban mall. They put bars on their windows, alarms in their cars, and cans of tear gas in their pockets. And they should be frightened. All told, some 14 million serious crimes were reported to the police last year, a number that surely understates the actual magnitude of America's No. 1 problem.

But the daily reality of muggings and murders that make the headlines and TV news shows is hurting the public in a far different, yet no less destructive, way. Crime in America is exacting an enormous economic toll on the nation—far bigger than anyone realizes.

New estimates by BUSINESS WEEK show that crime costs Americans a stunning $425 billion each year. That figure comes from a detailed analysis of all of the direct and indirect costs of both property and violent crimes, from emergency-room care for a mugging victim to the price of a new alarm system for a home to the income lost to the family of a murdered cab driver.

Human misery aside, from a purely dollars-and-sense perspective, the U.S. isn't devoting enough resources to the fight against crime—and is frittering away many of the resources it is using.

The U.S. spends some $90 billion a year on the entire criminal-justice system. That includes $35 billion for police protection, less than the country is spending on toiletries each year. Indeed, anticrime policy over the years has been a series of quick, cheap fixes: New prisons are being built, but the number of police has barely kept pace with the growing population. Meanwhile, economic and social programs that could quickly bring down crime have been largely ignored.

Even the spate of crime-fighting legislation going through Congress falls far short of what is needed. The Brady Bill, just signed into law, simply requires a five-day waiting period for the purchase of handguns. And the highly acclaimed anticrime bill recently passed by the Senate would add a meager $4.5 billion a year to total criminal-justice spending.

TV VIOLENCE. Why is the nation underspending on crime-fighting? The public may well believe that there's little more money can do short of putting the Army on every street corner. Some have blamed crime and violence on the decline of "family values" or the loss of inner-city manufacturing jobs, neither of which can be solved by government action. Most recently, excessive violence on TV has been fingered as a key culprit by Attorney General Janet Reno and Surgeon-General M. Joycelyn Elders.

Economists, on the other hand, view crime as a choice that can be affected by changes in punishments and rewards. Recent research by economists shows that higher levels of anticrime spending, if well-directed, can make a big dent in crime. Crime can be reduced by increasing what economists call the "expected punishment"—the

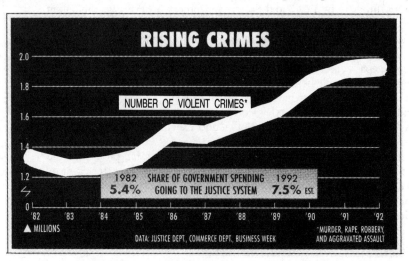

RISING CRIMES

NUMBER OF VIOLENT CRIMES*

| 1982 | SHARE OF GOVERNMENT SPENDING | 1992 |
| 5.4% | GOING TO THE JUSTICE SYSTEM | 7.5% EST. |

'82 '83 '84 '85 '86 '87 '88 '89 '90 '91 '92

▲ MILLIONS

*MURDER, RAPE, ROBBERY, AND AGGRAVATED ASSAULT

DATA: JUSTICE DEPT., COMMERCE DEPT., BUSINESS WEEK

average prison time served for a crime, adjusted for the chances of being caught and convicted. Today, the expected punishment for committing a serious crime is only about 11 days—half what it was in the 1950s. At the same time, job prospects for young adults and teenagers have soured, lowering the economic rewards for staying straight. "Criminals are sensitive to incentives," says Morgan O. Reynolds, a Texas A&M University economist who studies the economics of crime. Adds Ann Witte, a Wellesley economist: "The carrot can work, and the stick can work."

What's needed is a cost-effective way of raising the punishment that potential criminals can expect, argue these economists. That means the U. S. needs to devote many more resources to every aspect of law enforcement, not just prisons. That means more police on the streets, tougher sentences for young criminals, and closer monitoring of criminals on probation.

At the same time, it's crucial that the U. S. boost spending for job training and other programs in order to give teenagers and young adults better alternatives to crime. Typically, these programs are cheaper than the $20,000-to-$30,000-a-year cost of imprisonment. "We will never be able to afford enough prisons if that's our only approach to the criminal-justice problem," says Stephen Goldsmith, the Republican mayor of Indianapolis and a district attorney for 12 years. "You have to give people some hope for jobs and housing."

Such sentiments are far more common today than they were just a few years ago. In the 1980s, politicians were quick to call for longer, harsher sentences for all types of crimes. And one of the most damaging labels for a local politician in those years was "soft on crime." Yet for all the harsh rhetoric, few additional resources were devoted to fighting crime on the streets. Spending on prisons and the judicial system soared in the 1980s, but the number of police per 10,000 people barely rose. Indeed, in the second half of the decade, the total number of state and local police increased by only

16%, while the number of violent crimes jumped by 37%.

Now, fiscally strapped local officials find themselves begging for federal help and admitting defeat. District of Columbia Mayor Sharon Pratt Kelly unsuccessfully sought to deploy National Guard troops on the capital's streets, saying: "We're dealing with a war, yet people don't seem to want to win this war." After 300 stores were robbed and 52 people killed during holdups this year, Kelly's police chief recently suggested that a good way to cut crime was to close stores earlier.

The best deterrent is the simple presence of police

The analogy to war is a good one. By BUSINESS WEEK's calculation, the real cost of violent and property crime—when properly toted up—far exceeds the $300 billion defense budget. Spending by businesses and consumers on private security alone—including alarms, guards, and locks—comes to some $65 billion, according to William Cunningham, president of Hallcrest Systems Inc., a McLean (Va.) security-industry consulting firm. "People are more fearful, and they're taking a greater stake in their own protection." This has turned into a bonanza for companies such as Winner International Corp. in Sharon, Pa., which engineers and markets The Club, a steering-wheel lock to discourage auto theft. From 1990 to 1992, Club sales grew from $22 million to $107.3 million.

But Winner's bonanza is just another burden for business and consumers. "I call this the 'security tax' that business now has to pay because government hasn't been able to make us feel safe at home, work, or play," says Frank J. Portillo Jr., chief executive of Brown's Chicken & Pasta Inc., a 100-store fast-food chain based in Oak Brook, Ill. He had to install security cameras and hire guards for some of his stores in rougher neighborhoods after seven employees were massacred on Jan. 8 at a

Brown's Chicken outlet in Palatine, Ill.

The security tax hits urban areas particularly hard. According to BUSINESS WEEK's analysis of FBI crime statistics, most large cities have violent crime rates from two to seven times higher than their suburbs. As a result, many businesses and residents of crime-prone areas move to safer surroundings. That can quickly become a self-perpetuating cycle, since as jobs move out, the area becomes even more hopeless for the people who remain. BUSINESS WEEK estimates that annual damage to large urban economies from high crime rates is about $50 billion.

MIAMI VISE. Because of Miami's dependence on tourism, it is probably the urban area facing the clearest threat from crime. The city "has two problems," says Joseph P. Lacher, president of Miami-based Southern Bell-Florida and chairman of the Greater Miami Chamber of Commerce. "We have a serious crime problem to deal with and an even worse perception of crime." Dade County, where Miami is located, has one of the highest crime rates in the country. "People are scared to come to Florida," says Roberto Willimann, owner of Specialized Travel Systems, a Miami travel agency that caters to Germans. His business fell to about half of last year's after the Sept. 8 murder of a German tourist.

But crime's most devastating impact is measured in more than lost jobs and added security costs. The victim of a mugging or a rape carries the physical and emotional scars for years. Moreover, the damage to friends, family, and society from every murder is enormous.

Economists are able to measure the economic value of such intangible damages of violent crime using techniques originally developed for the cost-benefit analysis of safety regulations. According to newly published estimates by Ted R. Miller, a health-and-safety economist at National Public Services Research Institute in Landover, Md., and two colleagues, the value of a human life cut short by murder is about $2.4 million. They estimate the economic damage of a rape

ARREST AND PRISON: WHAT COPING WITH CRIMINALS COSTS

NUMBER OF VIOLENT CRIMES
1,932,000

1992 DATA

PRISONERS HELD FOR VIOLENT CRIMES
410,000

ARRESTS FOR VIOLENT CRIMES
742,000

DATA: JUSTICE DEPARTMENT, BUSINESS WEEK

ALL ARRESTS
14,075,000

AVERAGE COST PER ARREST*
$4,000

*POLICE AND COURT SYSTEM

ALL PRISONERS
900,000

AVERAGE ANNUAL COST PER PRISONER
$27,000

to average about $60,000, while the typical robbery or assault costs more than $20,000. With more than 20,000 murders committed each year plus 2 million other crimes of violence, the so-called intangible damages come to a mind-numbing $170 billion, says Miller and his co-authors.

If America really wants to bring down violent crime, there's simply no way of dealing cheaply with a problem of this magnitude. "If you are going to have an effect, you have to spend a lot of money," says Wellesley economist Witte. But in a time of belt-tightening, it's essential to make every dollar as effective as possible. The ultimate goal is to reduce the incentives for criminal behavior. "We need the positives from participating in the legitimate economy to go up and the negatives from participating in the criminal economy to go up," says Goldsmith. "We've got the mix exactly backward."

DIMINISHING RETURNS. Spending on corrections has quadrupled over the past decade, rising far faster than spending on police or the courts. In part, that has been because of court-ordered up-grades of existing prisons, but actual incarcerations in state and federal prisons have tripled since 1980. And some economists, like Texas A&M'S Reynolds, believe that this prison boom has helped boost expected punishment a bit, keeping the crime problem from getting even worse than it already is.

But now the law of diminishing returns is setting in. Building and staffing prisons is extremely expensive, especially as sentences get longer and older inmates require increased medical care. Imprisoning a 25-year-old for life costs a total of $600,000 to $1,000,000. So putting someone in prison for life puts a huge financial

burden on the next generation—just as a big budget deficit does.

For that reason, much of the additional spending on law enforcement should go toward beefing up police forces rather than building new prisons. Indeed, evidence from economic studies shows that putting more police on the front lines has more of a deterrent effect than longer prison sentences. Explains Judge Richard Fitzgerald of Jefferson District Family Court in Louisville: "Most cops I know think that what really deters is the certainty of apprehension, not the sanction that would be imposed."

Even so, any concerted attempt to raise expected punishment will necessarily mean spending more on prisons. Every year, more than 60,000 violent criminals receive probation, largely because of overcrowding, according to Michael Block, a University of Arizona economist who was a member of

---

A COST-EFFECTIVE PLAN FOR REDUCING CRIME

Removing the incentives for criminal behavior can make Americans safer. Here's how:

1 IMPROVE ENFORCEMENT
Boost spending on police and courts by one-third, or $15 billion, to make apprehension and conviction much more certain. Increase spending on prisons and jails by 20%, or $5 billion

2 FOCUS PUNISHMENT
Release juvenile records at the first adult felony conviction so that longtime offenders can be quickly identified. In-

crease use of boot camps for youthful offenders.

3 CONTROL DRUG-RELATED CRIME
Test convicted criminals on probation for drug use on a regular basis, which could cut down on repeat offenders. Boost spending on drug rehabilitation.

4 EXPAND JOB TRAINING
Give teenagers an alternative to crime by doubling the size of the Job Corps, which has a proven crime-reducing record. Expand funding for privately run remedial

education and socialization programs.

5 SUPPORT NEIGHBORHOOD SAFETY
Encourage a shift to community policing, which puts more cops on the street instead of behind desks. Use police to prevent problems, not just respond to emergencies.

6 LESSEN LEVELS OF VIOLENCE
Expand violence-prevention and conflict-reduction programs in the schools. Toughen federal gun control, and buy back illegally owned handguns in cities.

the U. S. Sentencing Commission. That means one of the cheapest solutions to the crime problem, he says, is to "punish those people who are already captured."

FEW WORRIES. But the largest holes are in the juvenile-justice system. Violent-crime rates among young people have been rising far faster the among adults. "We are seeing juveniles committing more of the violent crimes at a younger age and with more destructive force and impact," says Judge Fitzgerald.

Part of the problem is that expected punishment for juveniles is very low. Young people often get little punishment for the first three or four felonies. "Juveniles have been getting the message that they can get away with anything," says Marvin Wolfgang, a criminologist at the University of Pennsylvania. Adds Mark A. Kleiman, an expert in the economics of crime at Harvard University:"It trains people to be criminals."

In addition, teenagers have little worry that crimes committed as juveniles will hurt them as adults. In most states, juvenile criminal records are permanently sealed. So a cost-effective way of identifying multiple offenders would be to unseal juvenile criminal records at the first adult felony conviction.

America's solution for dealing with illegal drug use has cost it dearly, too. In the 1980s, draconian sentencing laws were used to combat the drug problem, putting tens of thousands of people—and not necessarily the most violent ones—in prison. Currently, 60% of inmates in federal prisons and 20% of inmates in state prisons are there on drug charges. That helped drive up spending on prisons without doing much to deter violent crime.

One alternative strategy to keep down drug use and related crime without filling up scarce prison cells is to monitor more closely the nearly 3 million convicts on probation. Kleiman argues that regular drug-testing of criminals on probation could dramatically reduce drug use, at a cost of perhaps $5 billion annually. That can be combined with increased funding

for drug-rehab programs like the one at DC General Hospital in Washington, which treats 900 people each year at a cost of about $1,800 per person. "Most people who are heavy users can and will quit if they are under heavy pressure," says Kleiman, "and you'll reduce the criminal activities of the people you're testing."

But by itself, increased enforcement will not be enough to stem the tide of violence. "Short term, we need more cops and more aggressiveness in enforcement and prosecution," says Louisville Mayor Jerry Abramson, chairman of the U. S. Conference of Mayors. "But when a police officer gets involved that's too late. The focus has to be not just on catching criminals but on preventing criminals."

Moreover, giving young people alternatives to crime can multiply the effectiveness of the existing criminal-justice system. For every person not committing crimes, police can concentrate more resources on hard-core criminals. For example, if job training and education programs lowered the crime rate by 25%, that could mean an increase of as much as one-third in the expected punishment for lawbreakers.

Unlike many social programs, intensive training and education have already provided good evidence that they can reduce the crime rate. "Crime is a young man's game," says Witte. "Keep them busy and doing things that are not illegal, and they don't get in trouble."

For example, studies of the federal Job Corps, which is a residential program for basic education and hands-on vocational training, show a big drop in arrests for program participants. "There are few programs for young men that we can document as working well," says David Long, a senior research associate at Manpower Demonstration Research Corp., a nonprofit research organization in New York. "The Job Corps stands out as strikingly effective."

A NEW WORLD. The key to the success of the Job Corps and similar private programs is providing kids with a whole new environment. That

makes such programs expensive to run: A year in the Job Corps costs about $22,000. Adding enough slots in these programs to make a difference could cost billions. About 650,000 juveniles were arrested in 1992 for violent and property crimes. To provide programs for half of them would cost about $7 billion annually.

These programs are cheaper than the prisons they could replace, though. Average per-inmate cost for all juvenile facilities nationwide runs at about $30,000 annually. That's far more than the yearly cost of a slot in the Job Corps. In some cases, the difference can be even bigger. Take City Lights School in Washington, with 100 inner-city adolescents, many of them violent juvenile offenders. According to Stephen E. Klingelhofer, development director at City Lights, the $53-a-day cost is a bargain compared with the $147 daily tab at Lorton Reformatory Youth Center in Lorton, Va. Treatment at City Lights can be as simple as setting a good example. "A lot of these kids have never seen anyone getting up in the morning and going to a job," says Klingelhofer. "A lot of them come here not knowing any other way to settle disputes than by violence."

More and more police departments are focusing on prevention as well. This new philosophy goes under the name of "community policing," which means reorganizing police departments to put more officers in the field and focusing on helping neighborhoods prevent crime rather than just reacting to emergencies. That approach may include having more police out walking beats, working with social service and community agencies, and generally getting to know the residents. "We want to improve the quality of life in the neighborhoods," says Jerry Galvin, police chief of Vallejo, Calif., which has used community policing for six years and seen violent crime drop by 33%.

If combined with organizational reforms, a shift to community policing need not mean a huge expenditure of new resources, advocates say. "Community policing has nothing to do with new officers or more money," says Galvin. "But you have to remake the

AN ANGUISHED CRY OF 'ENOUGH' IN AMERICA'S KILLING FIELDS

Crime is an American tragedy, especially for blacks. African Americans are disproportionately both perpetrators and victims of criminal violence. Blacks make up almost half the country's prison admissions, and nearly one in four black men between the ages of 20 and 29 is in prison, on parole, or on probation. And homicide is the leading cause of death among black youths. Says Marian Wright Edelman, president of the Children's Defense Fund: "We lose more black men to guns in our cities in one year than we lost to all the lynchings after the Civil War."

Fear stalks inner-city streets. And in recent months, political leaders, ministers, and academics have all begun a crusade against crime, crying out to young black men to stop the violence. The Reverend Jesse Jackson rails against the lethal combination of guns and drugs in inner-city high schools. President Bill Clinton invokes the legacy of Dr. Martin Luther King Jr. in a plea to stop killing "each other with reckless abandonment." Increasingly, both liberals and conservatives are crossing racial and ideological divides to find common ground on policies that nurture families, support communities, create jobs, and provide more police protection in America's ghettos.

What's so discouraging is that black crime has become pervasive in many cities even as black politicians have gained power throughout the land, as the ranks of the black middle class have expanded, and as black high school graduation rates have risen.

CRIME PAYS. The reasons for the increase in violent crime are multifaceted, but the starting point is economic: The rewards for honest work for the less-educated have fallen, while the payoff for crime has risen. Urban jobs declined sharply beginning in the early 1970s, as foreign competition heated up. Inner cities began a downward spiral as work disappeared.

At the same time, explosive growth in the drug trade and other illegal pursuits

offered jobs and good money. A 1989 survey of youth crime in Boston shows that average hourly pay from crime ranged from $9.75 to $19 an hour (and no taxes), vs. the $5.60 an hour that youths earned after taxes from legitimate work, according to Richard B. Freeman, an economist at Harvard University. "Essentially, what is happening is that wage and employment opportunities have declined dramatically, and opportunities in the criminal sector have grown," says Harry J. Holzer, an economist at Michigan State University.

The sharp decline of the two-parent family is also part of the crime problem.

BLACKS AND CRIME

Blacks make up 12% of the nation's population but have high arrest rates...

SHARE OF ALL ARRESTS, 1992

MURDER AND NONNEGLIGENT MANSLAUGHTER	55.1%
ROBBERY	60.9%
AGGRAVATED ASSAULT	38.8%
BURGLARY	30.4%

...make up an increasing share of prison admissions...

WHITE		BLACK	
'86	'91	'86	'91
40%	35%	45%	49%

...with nearly one in four under correctional supervision...

MEN, AGES 20 TO 29, IN JAIL, OR ON PAROLE OR PROBATION

WHITE	HISPANIC	BLACK
6.2%	10.4%	23.0%

VICTIMS (1991)

...and are more likely to be crime victims

	WHITE	BLACK	WHITE	BLACK
HOMICIDE PER 100,000	4.9	34.0		
VIOLENT CRIME PER 1,000			29.6	44.4

DATA: FEDERAL BUREAU OF INVESTIGATION, THE SENTENCING PROJECT, JUSTICE DEPT., NATIONAL CENTER ON INSTITUTIONS AND ALTERNATIVES

These days, 56% of black families are headed by women, and the figure increases significantly in inner-city neighborhoods. A large part of the decline in marriage rates is traceable to male joblessness and extraordinary poverty levels. The welfare system encourages female-headed households by providing financial support to unmarried mothers. The upshot: Juveniles from single-parent families have a greater chance of being involved in crime—especially murder and robbery.

Young criminals are devastating many inner-city communities, and throwing them into jail for short periods only seems to make things worse in the long run. When they return to their communities, they bring back the violent ethics of the cell block. Drugs, violent crime, and prisons are a part of everyday life. "If you haven't been arrested, you haven't gone through a rite of passage," says Marvin Dunn, a psychology professor at Florida International University.

FEW ROLE MODELS. The ecology of crime isolates inner-city communities in other ways. Few entrepreneurs open businesses in high-crime districts, where they can easily become murder or robbery victims. Middle-class blacks have fled for safer streets, too. In racially segregated, poverty-stricken neighborhoods, young people are less exposed to the work ethic, and informal networks of church and community groups are being drained of their most prominent middle-class members.

To make even a dent in the violence will require policies ranging from family support networks to more police. Most important, there must be jobs to compete with the lure of crime. Without jobs, high levels of violence in America's cities will continue, along with disproportionate black incarceration—and unimaginable suffering.

By Christopher Farrell in New York, with bureau reports

department to make community policing work." In Vallejo, 80% of police officers are in the field vs. the national average of about 60%.

New Haven, Conn., has had the same experience. In early 1993, New Haven shifted to community policing rather than just having officers answer 911 calls. That required more police on the street. The solution: substitute civilian staff for cops who used to pump gas into police cruisers and hand out billy clubs and clip boards. It's cost-effective as well. An officer costs about twice as much as a clerical worker and is much more expensive to train.

VICIOUS CYCLE. Part of what's scary about the latest wave of crime is not just the numbers but the brutality involved, especially the rampant use of firearms. From 1986 to 1991, robberies increased by 27%, but the use of a fire arm during a robbery increased by 49%. And in a vicious cycle, crime is escalating the number of guns in private hands, as frightened Americans search for protection. At Colt Manufacturing Co. in Hartford, Conn., commercial handgun sales are running about 25% higher in 1993 than they were in 1992. "A whole gamut of industries are supplying the services that are being created by the crime statistics," says Colt Chairman R. C. Whitaker.

The job corps works—and it costs a lot less than prison

Can this spiral of violence be broken? Certainly a federal law making handguns illegal would sharply decrease the number of guns being sold and make their street price much higher, though, like Prohibition in the 1920s or the war against drugs in the 1980s, it might be very expensive to enforce. But with 60 million handguns already in private hands, even an effective ban on guns might not be enough. One intriguing possibility is to return to an approach that has been tried successfully in the past—buying back handguns. In 1974, the City of Baltimore decided to offer $50 per gun. In three months, 13,792 guns were turned in. A similar program today could help get illegally owned guns off the street, especially if combined with national gun control.

Some groups are trying to stamp out juvenile crime before it starts by teaching kids that violence simply is not the only way to settle disputes. That approach can be cost-effective, experts say, if it is started early. For example, Howard University's Violence Prevention Project is trying to teach 40 troubled 4th, 5th, and 6th graders to cope with boredom, frustration, and anger without reaching for a weapon. "Is it working? It's too early to tell," admits Hope Hill, director of the program. "It appears to be, but it will take several years to know."

In the end, no one solution will work, and no cheap and easy cure is possible. But the tremendous cost of crime to Americans demands that we not give up. The country's great wealth can surely be harnessed in an effective way to provide the remedies that will allow people to walk the streets without fear again.

By Michael J. Mandel in New York and Paul Magnussan in Washington, with James E. Ellis in Chicago, Gail DeGeorge in Miami, Keith L. Alexander in Pittsburgh, and bureau reports

THE GLOBAL

CRIME WAVE

And What We Can Do about It

Around the world, nations are reporting more murders, rapes, and robberies. A criminologist explains the underlying causes of this wave of lawlessness and suggests steps to combat it.

Gene Stephens

Gene Stephens is a professor in the College of Criminal Justice, University of South Carolina, Columbia, South Carolina 29208. Telephone 803/777-7315; fax 803/777-9600. He is also criminal-justice editor of The Futurist *and a frequent contributor. His last article, "Crime and the Biotech Revolution," appeared in the November-December 1992 issue.*

Crime is increasing worldwide, and there is every reason to believe the trend will continue through the 1990s and into the early years of the twenty-first century.

Crime rates have always been high in multicultural, industrialized, democratic societies such as the United States, but a new phenomenon has appeared on the world scene—rapidly escalating crime rates in nations that previously reported few offenses. Street crimes such as murder, assaults, rape, robbery, and auto theft are clearly escalating, particularly in some formerly communist countries such as Hungary and in western European nations such as Scandinavia and the United Kingdom.

U.S. crime rates remain the highest in the world overall, but some offenses, such as breaking and entering, have actually decreased over the past decade. Other offenses, such as

murder, rape, and robbery, have stabilized. In adjacent Canada, property crime rates decreased significantly in all categories in the 1980s.

Statistics on white-collar crime are harder to find, but every indication is that this, too, is rapidly increasing worldwide and can be expected to spiral upward well into the twenty-first century.

What is driving this crime explosion? And what steps can be taken to curb it?

There are no simple answers. Crime is a lot like cancer: It is serious, potentially deadly, comes in many varieties, is difficult to diagnose, hard to treat, and almost impossible to eradicate.

Still, there are certain conditions associated with rising crime: increasing heterogeneity of populations, greater cultural pluralism, higher immigration, realignment of national

borders, democratization of governments, greater economic growth, improving communications and computerization, and the rise of anomie—the lack of accepted social norms.

These conditions are increasingly observable around the world. For instance, cultures that were previously isolated and homogeneous, such as Japan, Denmark, China, and Greece, are now facing the sort of cultural diversity that has been the norm in the United States for most of its history.

Meanwhile, the breakup of the Eastern Bloc has led to attempts to democratize formerly communist countries and has also put many citizens on the move, in a search for a better life.

International migration has hit an all-time high and will not peak for several more years.

From *The Futurist*, July/August 1994, pp. 22-28. © 1994 by the World Future Society. Reprinted by permission of *The Futurist*, 7910 Woodmont Avenue, Suite 450, Bethesda, MD 20814.

The Challenge of Multiculturalism

Multiculturalism can be a rewarding, enriching experience, but it can also lead to a clash of values and frequent warfare if peaceful systems of conflict resolution are not established and accepted. Heterogeneity in societies will be the rule in the twenty-first century, and failure to recognize and plan for such diversity can lead to serious crime problems, especially in emerging multicultural societies.

The connection between crime and culture cannot be overemphasized: There are high-crime and low-crime cultures around the world. In the years ahead, many low-crime cultures may become high-crime cultures because of changing world demographics and politicoeconomic systems. In general, heterogeneous populations in which people have lots of political freedom (democracy) and lots of economic choice (capitalism) are prime candidates for crime unless a good socialization system is created and maintained.

To understand why this is so, we can begin by recognizing that the very nature of crime is culturally defined. What is legal and desirable in one culture may be viewed as a serious crime in another; for instance, making a large profit on a business transaction is highly acceptable in the United States but, until recently, considered "profiteering" in China, where the government executed those found guilty of it. Even within a single culture, the definition of a crime may change through space and time. Gambling is legal in a number of U.S. states but illegal and imprisonable in others. Over the past two centuries, the use of alcohol, marijuana, opium, and other drugs has been legal and illegal at various times in all U.S. states.

A culture in which the citizens are very similar—sharing similar ethnicity, religious beliefs, income levels and values, such as Denmark—is more likely to have laws that represent the wishes and desires of a large majority of its people than is a culture where citizens come from diverse backgrounds and have widely disparate income levels and lifestyles, as in the United States. For this reason, homogeneous cultures normally have a lower level of law violation than heterogeneous cultures.

In addition, some cultures have a tradition of discipline—a belief that laws ought to be obeyed and that offenders (including you personally) should own up to violations and pay the penalty. Usually these are homogeneous cultures in which the citizens are well socialized and believe the laws represent their best interests. In some island cultures, violators of laws and customs actually penalize themselves, even in instances where their offenses would never have been discovered. By contrast, in cultures where individualism is strong, and belief and respect for law is low, laws are often broken and violators go to great lengths to avoid capture and conviction. If caught, they often deny responsibility and continue to combat charges even after conviction (through repeated appeals). Usually these are heterogeneous cultures, where the citizens disagree about the laws and are poorly socialized to obey them.

The Importance of Parenting

Critical to crime rates in any culture are the parenting and child-care philosophies and methods. Most street crimes such as larcenies, burglaries, robberies, and assaults in all societies occur among adolescents and young adults. Thus, the socialization process used to rear children becomes directly related to the types and amount of crime that can be expected.

In some societies, parents are seen as primarily responsible for their children, but all citizens share in that responsibility, since everyone's welfare is affected by the proper socialization of each child. In other societies the child is treated as chattel—the property of the parents—and only gross negligence or abuse brings societal pressure on the parents. The first type of society assures that parents receive preparation for infant care and provides support for parents in caring for their children. In the second type, no such support system exists and helter-skelter, catch-as-catch-can child care is the rule. In these societies, nothing is required to be a parent—no knowledge, no skills, no income—and regardless of economic circumstances, the parent is on his or her own to care for the child. The law only steps in to punish the parent who cannot

cope or protect the child in extreme circumstances. It is not difficult to determine which system is more likely to produce a law-abiding young adult.

The disparity between the wealthiest and poorest citizens is narrow in some cultures. People may be poor by world standards, but the little available wealth is shared fairly evenly. In other societies, the differences between the wealthy and the poor are enormous: The people at the top may have hundreds, even thousands, of times more wealth than those at the bottom. This disparity may lead to a high crime rate except when stern methods of re-

"In [some] societies, nothing is required to be a parent—no knowledge, no skills, no income."

pression are used, as under totalitarian regimes.

In some cultures, law breaking is seen as due to improper socialization and the remedy is viewed more as resocializing the offender into the society (either while in custody or in the community). In other cultures, retribution is sought against the offender, who is held individually responsible for his actions. The remedy applied is usually imprisonment and/or community control and surveillance for revenge and deterrence. Socialization may or may not be attempted but, if it is, the justification is to protect society, which accepts no blame for the individual's "failings."

China and Japan have far less reported crime than other nations. China's low rate may be attributed in part to its long tradition of respecting elders and paying attention to family and community. The communist regime built on this tradition, adding neighborhood councils, which clearly establish the standards for behavior and meet often with citizens to reinforce those expectations. There is little chance for anomie or doubt about community standards. Unlike China, Japan is a democratic, highly industrialized state, but its long cultural heritage encourages citizens to succeed through team work and accommodation; open hostility and confrontation are unacceptable.

The Information Society

Besides increasing heterogeneity, the world is changing in other fundamental ways that affect crime rates. One major shift is the rise of high-tech societies whose economies are interdependent and based on creation, collection, analysis, synthesis, dissemination, and utilization of information. Already, two-thirds of U.S. jobs are dependent in some way on information technology and the total is expected to rise to 80% by the turn of the century.

The emerging information society is bringing with it new crimes such as computer-assisted theft, but its more significant influence on crime is indirect: More people are turning to street crime and violence because they find themselves unprepared, educationally or emotionally, to cope with the requirements for success in the new era.

Looking ahead, we can anticipate that improved computer network systems will lead to a proliferation of organized crime syndicates. Unlike ethnic-based criminal groups like the Mafia, the emerging international "mobs" of the twenty-first century will be united by their interests and skills as they provide new black-market services such as replacement body parts for wealthy clients.

The Problem of Anomie

Currently, much of the world is in a state of what French sociologist Émile Durkheim called *anomie*, or normlessness. In most societies, the traditional social order has broken down, and there is a lack of clear-cut, well-established laws and limitations on behavior. As sociologist Robert K. Merton emphasized, society must institutionalize the means (such as work, investment, or inheritance) for achieving material well-being or other goals if that society is to avoid the state of anomie and resultant crime and disorder.

Some nations, such as the United States, face pervasive anomie due to their lack of restraints on human desires. In the United States, people feel that anyone can become a millionaire or President. With the demise of communism, dictatorships, and colonialism and the emergence of democracy in different forms around the world, many peoples are now experiencing boundless expectations amid increasingly fluid societal standards and regulations. Cultural diversity and the absence of effective guidelines on how to succeed in the emerging information era intensify this anomie. Moving from an authoritative society to a democracy also creates anomie, because the old rules and norms are abandoned before new laws and norms have evolved and become accepted. Democracy itself offers the citizens a cornucopia of expectations: Anything is possible, and the methods for achieving one's goals are vague, allowing individuals to "innovate." Their innovations, unfortunately, often constitute crimes.

Increasing criminal activity is not only appearing in many countries but crossing international borders.

CRIME AND THE ELDERLY

Handling crimes against the growing numbers of elderly will require new approaches and training of police. Older people are especially vulnerable to crimes such as con games, frauds, and assaults. Their fear of crime often makes them prisoners in their own homes. Now, police are responding with a new field of specialization—law-enforcement gerontology.

Gerontologists still give little attention to the crime problems of the elderly, says Wilbur L. Rykert, director of the National Crime Prevention Institute at the University of Louisville. But now, many U.S. states, including Illinois, Rhode Island, Florida, and Delaware, are developing programs that will familiarize police with the specific issues related to crimes against the elderly, such as assault and abuse by family, health-care providers, and others and the elderly's vulnerability to fraud. Law-enforcement gerontologists are also making efforts toward closer cooperation with the elderly community.

"By developing a rapport with the elderly, officers . . . can pinpoint specific problems that impact that segment of the population and then recommend ways to minimize the risk of victimization," says Rykert. Communities can also be advised to watch out for known fraud-related operations that specifically target the elderly. Another strategy is to enlist volunteers from the elderly community to advise police departments on their specific needs, according to FBI special agent Joseph A. Harpold.

"As the number of senior citizens in the United States increases, the need for law-enforcement gerontology becomes more apparent," says Rykert. The key, he says, is to properly combine existing gerontological research with crime-fighting techniques. By familiarizing themselves with the issues faced by the elderly community, "law-enforcement gerontologists can improve the quality of life for senior citizens across the country."

Source: "Law Enforcement Gerontology" by Wilbur L. Rykert and "Focus on Cooperation: The FBI and the Elderly" by Joseph A. Harpold, *FBI Law Enforcement Bulletin* (February 1994), United States Department of Justice, Federal Bureau of Investigation, 10th Street and Pennsylvania Avenue, N.W., Washington, D.C. 20535.

An international car-theft ring operates from Poland; child pornography via computer operates globally from Europe; violent organized-crime groups are arriving in the United States from formerly communist countries in Europe and Asia.

To a large extent, anomie results from a breakdown in the "bonding" process, long recognized by criminologists as important to the health and safety of society. The individual who is closely in congruence with social expectations over a long period of time is unlikely to commit a serious crime, because he or she has developed a "bond" or stake in society. Believing that society offers the good life and that it can be obtained by reasonable actions, the individual is unlikely to stray far from established rules of conduct. Some cultures socialize citizens to its expectations and rewards through family, religion, school, and community. Other societies have unclear or competing goals and lifestyles, and each citizen comes into contact with contradictory rewards and expectations. Laws may differ from one area to another, and law enforcement may be strict in one neighborhood, lax in another. In these societies, lawbreaking is likely to be frequent.

Wide freedom of choice combined with little or no direction as to how to make one's choices responsibly is also a formula for high crime rates. Socializing citizens to adopt and obey a common set of laws is quite different from allowing citizens wide freedom of choice with no socialization other than penalties for violating laws against the choices many individuals wish to make (fornica-

CRIME RATES AROUND THE WORLD (PER 100,000 POPULATION)

	Murder 1980	Murder 1990	Rape 1980	Rape 1990	Breaking & Entering 1980	Breaking & Entering 1990	Robbery 1980	Robbery 1990	Motor Vehicle Theft 1980	Motor Vehicle Theft 1990
Austria	1.0	2.3	0.2	7.0	748.0	1,152.0	31.0	52.0	18.0	27.0
Canada	2.6	5.7	14.1	—	1,497.0	1,343.0	103.0	98.0	437.0	383.0
Chile	5.7	5.8	12.1	9.6	1,894.0	—	24.0	34.0	8.0	11.0
China	—	1.9	—	3.2	—	17.0	—	8.0	—	—
Costa Rica	4.5	5.3	9.9	7.8	—	232.0	22.0	47.0	—	23.0
Czechoslovakia	1.1	2.0	2.9	8.0	—	621.0	5.0	2.0	—	96.0
Denmark	1.4	4.6	7.0	9.4	1,893.0	2,383.0	29.0	41.0	411.0	576.0
Egypt	2.1	1.6	—	0.006	9.0	—	—	0.03	2.0	3.0
England & Wales	2.3	2.7	2.5	6.7	1,264.0	1,991.0	31.0	72.0	659.0	977.0
Finland	2.4	0.6	7.7	7.6	762.0	1,432.0	41.0	56.0	163.0	364.0
France	1.0	4.5	3.5	8.1	512.0	712.0	66.0	106.0	399.0	520.0
Germany	1.4	3.9	11.2	8.2	1,188.0	1,749.0	39.0	56.0	104.0	115.0
Greece	0.7	2.0	1.0	1.9	67.0	265.0	1.0	11.0	0.3	68.0
Hungary	2.6	3.1	4.4	4.5	148.0	743.0	10.0	28.0	35.0	78.0
Ireland	0.7	0.8	1.4	2.5	647.0	822.0	33.0	46.0	15.0	32.0
Israel	—	2.2	—	5.4	—	912.0	—	15.0	—	316.0
Italy	1.4	6.4	1.1	—	43.0	—	19.0	64.0	230.0	546.0
Japan	0.8	1.0	0.2	1.3	248.0	184.0	2.0	1.0	28.0	28.0
Norway	1.1	2.6	3.2	9.0	—	116.0	8.0	24.0	178.0	608.0
Peru	—	12.0	2.3	8.9	8.0	24.0	19.0	24.0	12.0	—
Portugal	1.6	2.8	1.5	1.1	86.0	72.0	1.0	36.0	49.0	48.0
Scotland	1.6	9.2	3.2	9.7	1,522.0	3,804.0	72.0	91.0	626.0	708.0
Spain	1.0	2.4	2.3	4.5	357.0	1,212.0	64.0	271.0	215.0	343.0
Sweden	1.6	7.0	10.6	16.4	1,682.0	1,801.0	41.0	69.0	412.0	879.0
U.S.	10.0	9.4	36.0	41.2	1,669.0	1,235.0	244.0	257.0	495.0	658.0
U.S.S.R.	—	8.7	—	7.8	—	—	—	44.0	—	47.0

Crime Rates in Selected Countries. Crime statistics are notoriously unreliable, says author Gene Stephens, who prepared this chart. Even when gathered and presented "in good faith"—with no political agenda—crime rates are difficult to compare because of different definitions of and emphasis on crime and different methods of collecting data.

Two major methods of gathering data exist: Collecting crime reports from police and polling people on whether they have been victimized. Overall, only about one in three crimes in the United States is reported to police, according to surveys of the population.

The data in the chart are primarily from the International Police Organization (INTERPOL). Some figures come from the World Health Organization or the United Nations. In some instances, figures for 1981 or 1989 were used rather than 1980 or 1990.

tion, gambling, alcohol or drug use, abortion, loitering, sodomy, tax evasion, etc.).

Some cultures choose proactive ways to control crime while others adopt reactive approaches. In proactive cultures, care is taken to see that all citizens take part or are well represented in building a consensus of support for laws, and all citizens are taught and socialized and resocialized from birth to obey these laws. In reactive societies, laws are often the product of group conflict, and since there is often disagreement about the law, little socialization—or contradictory socialization—takes place. Thus, the individual is left confused about what is expected or is even socialized to disobey. Society's only contribution is to punish the violator if captured and convicted, and even this is generally done ineffectively.

Worldwide Crime Wave

Reported crime rates around the world (see chart) are rising in most countries for which we have data. Though the statistics must be interpreted with extreme caution, certain observations may be offered. Overall, the United States is the crime capital of the world, and other western nations, such as Scotland and Canada, are not far behind. These high rates may be due to high levels of heterogeneity and industrialization in North America and Scotland's long history of "individualism"—self-reliance and an expectation of confrontation.

While violent crime rates show no clear trends, property crime rates were stable (though high) in the United States and even decreased in Canada between 1980 and 1990 while escalating rapidly in the European countries. What explains this discrepancy? One possible interpretation is that conditions in the European nations are moving closer to those long associated with the United States.

The United States was the first industrialized, democratic, heterogeneous nation and thus the first to face the crime problems associated with anomie. At the same time, the other nations are following the United States into the Information Age. So we can theorize that crime

will be a growth industry in many countries as they find themselves gripped by the same social forces that have long affected the United States. The decline of crime rates in North America during the early 1990s is encouraging, but we should postpone cheering until it becomes clearer what is really happening. Since crime rates are associated with youth, specifically the ages 15 to 25, the rising age of the North American population may adequately explain stabilizing or declining crime rates. The percentage of adolescents is expected to increase by the end of the twentieth century, however.

Creating a Safe, Sane World

The outlook for global crime is disturbing, if not alarming. However, much can be done to improve the prospects for eventually reducing crime rates. Let's begin by asking, What is the formula for changing a high-crime culture—heterogeneous, poorly disciplined, and culturally pluralistic with helter-skelter parenting and child care, large disparities in wealth, choice without direction, punishment without socialization—into a low-crime culture?

First, we need to move from a "war" model to a "peace" model in

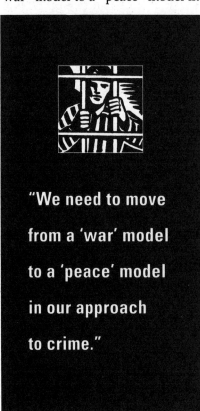

"We need to move from a 'war' model to a 'peace' model in our approach to crime."

our approach to crime. Already some scholars are suggesting such a change, as shown by a recent book entitled *Criminology as Peacemaking*, edited by criminologists Harold E. Pepionsky and Richard Quinney (Indiana University Press, 1991). At present, police treat a community as if it were enemy territory: They drive around it in patrol cars looking for troublemakers to arrest; friendly contact with the inhabitants is often negligible, and citizens respond by regarding the police as an occupying army.

The peace model, exemplified by community policing, fits well with the emerging information era, where success will depend more on cooperation than competition, reconciliation more than retribution. Under the peace model, we will search in this shrinking, multicultural world for a consensus of values on certain big issues, such as murder and theft, and on fair and effective ways of resolving the inevitable conflicts of values in less critical areas (noise levels, sexual preferences, gambling, drug use, religious rituals) without imposing one group's preferences on another group. Legal sanctions need to be reserved for acts that truly endanger the citizenry rather than simply fit one group's lifestyle preferences.

Second, the world's most valuable resource—its children—need to be treated with the respect they deserve. Children need and deserve tender loving care and attention. When they feel wanted and gain attention and approval for socially desirable activities, they are unlikely to become serious lawbreakers as adolescents or adults. The research is clear on that point, but many societies are failing to make sure children get what they need. A useful first step is universal training for parents. A number of low-crime cultures have already taken this step, and the beginning may be seen in some high-crime cultures such as the United States, where many school districts are offering Parent Effectiveness Training (PET) at the puberty-level grades as well as nonviolent conflict-resolution techniques at all grade levels, beginning in preschool.

Third, proactive rather than reactive methods must be used in reducing crime. If a crime is prevented, there are no victims and no costly repercussions such as trials and incarceration. However, a preventive approach would require a change in the traditional structure, role, and methods of criminal-justice systems. In the traditional system, violators are apprehended, taken before a court, and, if convicted, sent to institutions or placed under supervision. Such a system does relatively little to prevent crime since most convicted criminals are eventually turned loose without having been cured of their criminal tendencies.

Under a reformed criminal-justice system, the traditional law-enforcement agencies would expand their scope to create partnerships with other social-service units and expand the role of the police to include crime prevention. Police officers often can anticipate when someone is likely to commit a crime, but they feel now largely powerless to do much about it. An officer on patrol may, for instance, spot an unemployed, homeless teenager on the street; from experience, the officer knows the youth will probably run out of money and then shoplift at a nearby supermarket, or worse, snatch a woman's purse, break into a home, or mug a pedestrian, but the officer traditionally has done nothing until a crime takes place. Under a reformed criminal-justice system, the officer would be able to contact social-service-agency workers to see that the youth was settled for the night (at a home or in a shelter) before he turned to crime to survive. Furthermore, the officer could help the social-service people follow up to make sure the teen got continuing shelter and educational/vocational assistance.

The community-policing approach involves a return to the nineteenth-century role of the police—protecting and serving the community by being constantly aware of neighborhood problems and ever ready to help solve them in cooperation with their employers—the citizenry. Police would get back to their roots in the community by communicating with citizens through neighborhood councils and meetings, foot patrols, crime-watch organizations, etc. In addition, security agencies hired by business and private organizations would cooperate with public police to jointly establish and preserve the peace.

Fourth, when disputes arise—and many can be expected in a multicultural society—the forum for address-

> "Police officers often can anticipate when someone is likely to commit a crime, but they feel now largely powerless to do much about it."

ing them must change from adversarial to nonadversarial. In the emerging Information Age society, power is becoming diffused horizontally. The new communications can create potent new political blocs almost instantaneously as geographically and culturally separated individuals are galvanized to act. When conflict occurs, disputes need to be settled by mediation or arbitration in a nonadversarial environment rather than by a courtroom combat that pits the defendant against the hierarchical power structure. Further, most disputes are among people who know each other and/or interact frequently. To create adversarial relationships among such persons can have negative consequences.

Emerging in the United States today is a wide network of approaches toward mediation and solution through mutual agreement. These approaches include the Multidoor Courthouse, where disputes are evaluated and referred to the most appropriate forum, and Neighborhood Justice Centers, to which courts, social-service agencies, and even neighbors can refer disputes (including assaults, theft, and other criminal incidents). Evaluations of mediation programs find client satisfaction to be far higher than in the adversarial proceedings. Even law schools now are taking heed and teaching mediation/arbitration skills. One excellent program now emerging provides conflict-resolution training in U.S. school districts so children can learn how to handle disputes without violence.

The remedy sought for crime must turn from punishment aimed at retribution (revenge) and deterrence to socialization based on restitution and reconciliation. Restitution following mediation means the victim's losses are paid for by the offender (if possible) or compensation is provided through personal service, job training followed by repayment, etc. Reconciliation means the parties involved in a dispute meet, vent their anger, determine an equitable solution, carry out the agreement, and then accept each other with a better understanding of ways to prevent future conflict.

In summary, the 1990s and beyond will likely be a time of escalating crime rates in much of the rapidly changing world. But high-crime cultures can be changed into safe, sane, desirable twenty-first-century societies. The key techniques include an emphasis on proactive rather than reactive approaches, tolerance of cultural differences, mediation followed by reconciliation when disputes occur, and special attention to the need of children to be reared with tender loving care by all and bonded to society through effective socialization. In such a society, government agencies are clearly controlled by the citizens and responsive to their needs. Partnerships of individuals and institutions are essential, and creating symbiosis ("You scratch my back and I'll scratch yours" or "We're all in this together") is the main goal. Only then will wars on crime be replaced by peace in the 'hood.

Aging, Health, and Health Care Issues

- **Aging (Articles 15 and 16)**
- **Health and Health Care (Articles 17–21)**

The prospect of one's later years of life becoming the traditionally anticipated "golden years" is becoming increasingly doubtful for many Americans. Health, the economy, and other factors may make retirement and the daily lives of older Americans far from what they had expected. Even organizations that were created to help the elderly may not have the best interests of the elderly at heart.

"Old Money" illustrates the fact that the largest nonprofit organization in the United States, and perhaps the world, is one ostensibly committed to the needs of retired persons, yet apparently is more interested in its corporate holdings and image than in providing quality services for the elderly.

"The New Face of Aging" attempts to break through the stereotypes surrounding aging and to show that "conscious aging" can make the latter years productive and that the experience and wisdom of the older generation can help solve many societal ills.

Individuals must be healthy in order to be happy, productive, and active. But at some point nearly everyone has problems with his or her health and requires help. For some this help is readily available, affordable, and effective. But to a growing number of Americans, becoming sick is frightening and devastating because these individuals cannot afford or are not eligible for health insurance. Any illness requiring hospitalization will destroy them financially. For a society that boasts one of the highest standards of living in the world, it is paradoxical that America cannot provide adequate health care for all of its citizens regardless of ability to pay. In the United States, health care is not a right but a privilege, and the numbers of privileged individuals is rapidly shrinking.

"Risky Business" has moved into the health insurance industry. To maximize earnings for its investors, managers of health insurance companies have engaged in questionable business ventures that are placing their companies in financial jeopardy. Thus thousands of individuals could find themselves facing significant increases in their health insurance premiums or even without any health coverage at all.

"Deadly Migration" discusses the impact of extensive health and environmental regulations on many industries in industrialized nations. To escape these regulations and their associated high costs, major industries are relocating to less-developed countries. This unregulated migration is spewing massive amounts of sewage and pollutants into the air and the groundwater, which can only cause long-term ill effects for the residents of these countries.

"Confronting the AIDS Pandemic" looks at the toll in lives, resources, and economic costs that AIDS will take by the year 2000. Entire societies will be decimated, causing significant repercussions around the world. The problem of AIDS necessitates a coordinated worldwide effort, which is not occurring because many industrialized nations are electing to tackle "their" problem independently.

The author of "Mental Illness Is Still a Myth" is a most vocal critic of psychiatry and its treatment of those displaying unusual and dysfunctional behaviors. Thomas Szasz cogently argues that psychiatry, and the activities of most psychiatrists, could be best understood if viewed as a branch of law or as a type of secular religion rather than as "science."

"Who's Protecting Bad Doctors?" examines the degree to which professional organizations, such as the American Medical Association, systematically weed out incompetent and unscrupulous doctors. The problem as the author sees it is that they do not eliminate bad doctors. The reasons she has uncovered should concern every person in the United States who wants to be assured that he or she will receive quality and up-to-date medical care.

Looking Ahead: Challenge Questions

Why is it important that today's young people focus on the problems of the elderly?

What would you say are the most significant problems and issues facing those over the age of 65?

What should be done to ensure that organizations created to represent the needs and interests of the elderly really do so?

What steps must those approaching retirement take if they want to be sure that their later years will be the golden years of life? What steps must our society take to help them?

In what ways would the symbolic interactionists', functionalists', and conflict theorists' approaches to the study of the problems of aging differ?

Is adequate health care in the United States a right or a privilege? In your estimation, which should it be?

What activities of the health insurance industry might be threatening your health?

What reforms, if any, should the government of the United States be making in health care?

Is it the responsibility of the American Medical Association (AMA) to weed out bad doctors? Why is this an issue the AMA has always tried to steer clear of, and are its members justified in doing so?

How might AIDS impact on the world's economy? What threat does the AIDS pandemic pose for the rights and freedoms of those with AIDS or the HIV virus? What can each individual do to contribute to the solution or control of AIDS?

What are the implications of thinking of psychiatry as a branch of law or as a type of secular religion rather than as a branch of scientific medicine?

In what significant ways would the approaches of the three major types of sociological theorists differ in relation to the study of health issues?

What conflicts in values, rights, obligations, and harms seem to underlie the issues and problems covered in both parts of this unit?

Old Money

Why the mighty AARP spends as much furnishing its offices as it does on programs to help the elderly

Christopher Georges

Christopher Georges is an editor of The Washington Monthly. *Research assistance was provided by Greg Bologna.*

The American Association of Retired Persons (AARP) receives approximately $75 million annually from the federal government to run a pair of job training and placement programs for older Americans—two of the largest of their kind. A recent phone call to AARP's Washington, D.C., headquarters to inquire about enrollment in the programs led to the following:

The caller, after unsuccessfully attempting to explain the programs to two befuddled receptionists, was bounced to Jack Everett, an official in the organization's Senior Employment Office, who cheerfully explained that AARP offers no federally funded job placement or training programs. Everett suggested calling the Department of Labor (the agency that pays AARP $52 million to run one of the programs) for help. He also offered other ideas, like, "Try the phone book under the senior citizens section," and suggested contacting the National Council on Senior Citizens, another, smaller advocacy group for older Americans. He even threw in some job-training advice: "You'll need a resumé. That's always a good first step. . . ."

Everett's not alone. Similar inquiries at AARP offices in major cities in 16 states turned up like responses: Only six of the offices were aware that these programs even exist, although AARP literature boasts that they're offered at 108 sites across the nation. One office suggested calling Elder Temps, a privately run job-placement firm. Another advised calling the Jewish Council for the Aging. Several others suggested enrolling in an AARP job search workshop and seminar—for a fee of $35.

In a way, those phone calls distill what's wrong with AARP, one of America's largest and most influential nonprofit organizations: In its brochures, it's dedicated to helping seniors work, play, and wield power. In real life, however, helping itself seems to be Job One. "It's no more than a big business," grumbles Virginia Fine, who until last year was an officer of a California AARP chapter. "The whole Washington operation is simply geared toward making money." A close look at the mammoth nonprofit's Washington command central offers a fair amount of evidence to back Fine's charge. In 1990, for example, AARP spent about as much on office furniture and equipment as it did on programs to help its 33 million elderly members.

The world according to AARP

Why should you care? If you're over 50, odds are you're a member: More than half the over-50 population has paid the $5 dues to belong. Next to the Catholic Church, it's the largest membership organization in America. But even if you're not an AARP card-carrier, you're paying for the organization's extravagance anyway, because AARP receives, in addition to its federal grants, a federal subsidy equivalent to nearly $20 million a year.

Of course, AARP's nonprofit status also grants it something money can't buy—the trust of millions of older Americans: trust to represent their interests in Washington, to sell them worthy products, and to use their dues and fees in their best interest. For most of the organization's 34 years, the media and AARP members have accepted that trust at face value. But a peek at AARP's finances and lobbying efforts suggests that this trust may not always be well-earned.

AARP describes its mission as threefold: to lobby on behalf of seniors; sell them products and offer them discounts on other goods and services; and provide them with the chance to both volunteer their services and benefit from the volunteer work of others. For their $5 investment, members get an assortment of goodies: a subscription to *Modern Maturity,* AARP's bimonthly magazine (far and away America's largest, with a circulation five times that of *Time*); discounts from car rental companies, major hotel chains, airlines, and on American Express travel packages; and, of course, the opportunity to save money on health insurance, prescription drugs, and other products sold by AARP.

And sell it does. AARP's nine business enterprises sustain a cash flow of about $10 billion annually and revenues of nearly $300 million, with the greatest portion coming from AARP's centerpiece enterprise: group health insurance. With more than 5 million policy holders, it's the largest of its type. Last year, AARP profited nearly $100 million from this business alone. AARP's only role in selling the policies is as a middleman: AARP's partner, Prudential Insurance, offers the policies, which are promoted through AARP publications and direct mail solicitations. For every policy sold, AARP receives a 4 percent administrative allowance simply for collecting the premium and passing it on to Prudential.

AARP'S mail-order pharmacy, one of the nation's largest, brings the organization about $3 million per year. Its direct mail operation is so massive that AARP sends more than 1 percent of the entire nation's nonprofit third-class mail. Add to this the $100 million it collects each year in membership dues and the interest on about $50 million from Treasury bills, and total annual revenues add up to about 10 times the take of the United Way.

The United Way: Come to think of it, the comparison doesn't end there. AARP devoted about $30 million last year, and just $14 million in 1990, to programs aimed at directly assisting the elderly—a pittance compared to the funds it lavished on itself. Perhaps the most conspicuous symbol of AARP's use of resources is its new 10-story Washington headquarters. Leased for about $16 million a year, the 500,000-square-foot building is one of Washington's most alluring. Fellow lobbyists refer to the structure as the "Taj Mahal"; *The Washington Post*'s architecture critic described it last year as "a knockdown surprise, a classical package whose odd vigor is at once apparitional and relentless."

It's little wonder he was impressed: The structure, crowned with a medieval-style turret, boasts a state-of-the-art radio and TV broadcast studio, a fitness center, and a beautifully appointed marble lobby. Office lights are guided by motion sensors; even the stairwells are wallpapered and carpeted.

Nor was expense spared in furnishing the thing. Dozens of mahogany bookcases costing $1,800 each, for example, are built in throughout, and stained-glass windows adorn every floor. Total costs for furnishings and equipment came to $29 million in 1990.

"Even people here wonder if it's proper for a nonprofit for the elderly to be housed this way," says one

---

The AARP pays out nearly $2 million annually in lawyers' fees, which is more than it devotes to all but four of its more than a dozen elderly assistance programs.

AARP insider. As for the old furniture, it now sits idle in a Virginia warehouse rented at AARP expense. AARP officials defend the costs, saying that they sought to construct a building that would last for years to come. Also, they say, internal calculations showed that moving the old furniture to the new building would have cost just as much as the new decor.

Still, the decor is chump change compared to the $43 million spent on salaries for the 1,100 headquarters employees. "There are layers of people here, many of whom have little or nothing to do," says one D.C. insider. Busier, apparently, are the organization's lawyers. AARP pays out nearly $2 million annually in lawyers' fees, which is more than it devotes to all but four of its more than a dozen elderly assistance programs. AARP, in fact, retains two sets of lawyers: an in-house counsel and a team of lawyers from the New York firm of Miller, Singer, Raives, and Branden. The two lead attorneys, Alfred Miller and Lloyd Singer, have been closely associated with AARP since 1971, when the firm was formed specifically to provide legal counsel to the organization. Former AARP executive director Jack Carlson, who was fired after a 15-week tenure in 1987 following a dispute with the board of directors, explains that the lawyers' roles range from overseeing the business enterprises to monitoring committee meetings. "They permeate the whole organization," Carlson says. "There's a heavy-duty orientation to the commercial side and they didn't want anyone to come in and sabotage it."

Overseeing the empire today is executive director Horace Deets, a former Jesuit priest who joined

AARP in 1975. He is described as a low-key leader who travels frequently and who views his mission as decentralization of AARP and "intergenerational expansion" (that is, recruiting younger members). His salary is $200,000—not in the Aramony stratosphere, but at the high end of the spectrum of nonprofit executives' salaries. Deets reports to a 15-member board of directors and six national officers—all of whom are unpaid volunteers with roles limited mostly to making ceremonial appearances at functions representing AARP, attending conventions, and sitting on various committees that oversee AARP's commercial enterprises. Board members and about 250 other top-level volunteers scattered throughout the country enjoy expense accounts, free travel, and other perks that were worth about $11 million in 1990 alone.

Back in Washington, the 1,100 paid staffers are apparently not enough to get the job done at AARP-central. Every year, nearly $10 million is doled out to an army of consultants brought in to write public opinion polls, newsletter copy, and radio scripts and to perform other odd jobs, like providing "media training" to top-level volunteers preparing for radio and television appearances. AARP officials say they are unsure how many consultants are hired each year, but insiders place the number in the hundreds. Last spring, AARP paid nearly *2 million* to a consulting firm to run an in-house workshop called "communicating with co-workers." Another consulting firm, Synectics of Cambridge, Massachusetts, was called in to instruct AARP employees on how to better provide input on projects and set priorities in the office. The amount Synectics received is unknown, but it was enough to prompt the firm to set up a satellite office in Alexandria to serve AARP. And last July, as staffers prepared to move from the old AARP building to the new headquarters, more hired guns were ushered in—in this case to help train employees in how to pack their belongings into boxes for moving.

Hot for profit

While the Washington crowd enjoys the riches of the organization, the level of support that flows back to members is rather paltry. Of the approximately $30 million spent assisting the elderly in 1991, $4 million went to coordinate programs such as educational forums and diet and exercise activities, $4 million was spent on the biennial convention, and $3.7 million was devoted to "education of older workers **and employers in matters of obtaining employment . . . keeping employment and retirement planning.**" With respect to the last program, what AARP neglects to mention in its public financial records is that it also *charges* members $35 to enroll in such courses.

AARP has a penchant for charging members for services. One of the organization's most popular assistance programs is its 55/Alive driving education course for seniors. It is, of course, an important and useful service, but while AARP spends about $2.8

million to run it, it also *collects* an $8 fee from most of the 450,000 enrollees.

Leaders of local AARP chapters across the country also charge that the national office, despite its bulging bankrolls, does little to support them beyond printing pamphlets and offering moral encouragement. Many chapters hold bake sales or fundraisers to scrape up money for meetings or events. The scant support shows. So disorganized were local chapters that when phone inquiries were made regarding three of AARP's most vaunted volunteer programs (legal aid, services, Medicare/Medicaid advice, and a widow support ser-

> *Its 33-million-name list is the heart of AARP's financial empire; alone it's worth millions of dollars, since direct mail solicitations are the corner stone of its fortunes.*

vice), only about a third of the offices contacted had any idea that the programs exist.

The response wasn't much better when similar inquiries were made to the Washington headquarters about its Medicaid/Medicare assistance program and the Financial Information Program (offering advice on money-related topics). In each case, callers were told that no such programs exist. But inquiries about purchasing health insurance and prescription drugs were handled promptly.

Another example of AARP's emphasis on profits over service occurred last year when chapter officer Virginia Fine of the Sacramento, California, AARP asked AARP's national office for a list of all AARP members in her region in an attempt to encourage members to become more active in the local chapter. AARP refused to release the list, saying it was confidential. Eventually she and other local leaders petitioned the state attorney general to force AARP to release the names. Why the hesitancy from Washington? Its 33-million-name list is the heart of AARP's financial empire; alone it's worth millions of dollars, since direct mail solicitations are the cornerstone of its fortunes. So protective of this list is AARP that its bylaws call for expulsion or suspension of any member who releases "a complete or partial list of members" without written permission from AARP's president.

Capitol crimes

Of course, direct services to the elderly aren't

AARP's only game, as officials there are quick to tell you. AARP's real forte is helping its members on Capitol Hill. AARP's legendary lobbying arm, which absorbs about $18 million of its budget, includes a team of 18 lobbyists and researchers in its policy shop, the Public Policy Institute. As expected, chief among AARP's causes are averting cuts in benefits for the elderly, protection of pensions, and various health care initiatives. AARP's lead lobbyist, John Rother, describes his team's lobbying style as "low key," presenting carefully researched data rather than holding press conferences or issuing "damning reports."

AARP has in past years been charged with neglecting the elderly poor in favor of the well-to-do, who are more likely to buy its services. More and more congressional aides and lobbyists, however, now credit AARP with placing greater emphasis on issues like low-income housing, as well as reemphasizing long-time causes like age discrimination, Social Security, and consumer-related issues. Yet some congressional AARP watchers still argue that the lobby has been conspicuously silent in several recent battles over bills designed to assist the elderly that could, coincidentally, also threaten AARP's financial empire.

►*Medigap insurance reform:* In 1990, after investigations into Medigap insurance (policies designed to offer seniors coverage in areas not covered by Medicare), Congress, convinced that insurance sellers were swindling many seniors into buying protection they didn't need or already had, moved to clean up the mess. The reform legislation, which called for a fairer system for seniors but a less profitable one for insurance providers, won the hearty support of all seniors groups—except, according to congressional aides involved in enacting the legislation, AARP. AARP officials today insist that they fully backed the legislation. But one senior-level aide to a congressman who sponsored the measure disagrees. "They met with us and gave some suggestions, but most of these were on how to *soften* the bill."

►*Prescription drug prices:* After congressional hearings in 1990 found that drug companies were overcharging Medicare for pharmaceuticals, legislation was introduced to force lower fees. The bill aimed not only to save the government billions of dollars, but also to help people insured through Medicare, who often faced out-of-pocket costs of 50 cents to a dollar per prescription, limits on the types of medications covered, and in some cases restrictions on the number of times they could refill those prescriptions. The losers were, of course, the drug sellers, who'd see their profit-margins diminish. Again, full support came from almost every seniors group except—you guessed it. While Rother insists that AARP worked hard to enact the bill, Hill staffers close to the legislation again disagree. "Sure, we wished AARP would have supported it, but they weren't involved," says a senior Senate staff aide instrumental in the bill's enactment.

►*National health insurance:* Instead of endorsing any of the nearly one dozen plans introduced in Congress, AARP recently released a preliminary draft of its own health insurance plan, one it claims is best for all Americans, not just the elderly. While it includes a few "Canadian-style" features like universal long-term care coverage, the plan is, first and foremost, a "play-or-pay" model that calls for employers to provide insurance to employees or pay into a public fund. Employer-based programs have received criticism from other elderly groups because they do less for seniors than Canadian-style systems. As a result, elderly advocates question AARP's motives in eschewing any of the proposed Canadian-style plans, noting that an employer-based model, unlike nationalized health care, would allow AARP's $100 million insurance-selling enterprise to survive.

If the profitmaking impulse occasionally affects AARP's lobbying efforts, it also sustains the group's flagship publication, *Modern Maturity*, which the organization considers a crucial tool in its mission to educate seniors. While the magazine is filled with innocuous service pieces, there is a seamier side to the publication: its thinly masked mission to promote AARP's business enterprises. A survey of recent issues showed that on average more than a third of the advertising inches promoted AARP-sponsored products or services offered by its discount partners. In fact, about one in every 10 pages featured an ad pushing an AARP product. (Competing products and services almost never appear in the magazine.)

Of course, *Modern Maturity* doesn't run articles that outright endorse any of AARP's products or services. Instead, what you'll find on, say, the page opposite the health column is a full-page ad for the organization's insurance plan. And while articles offering advice on how to wisely invest money don't make specific mention of AARP's investment service (and of course omit mention of other plans, no matter how highly rated), they do appear close to ads for AARP's Scudder investment plan. "They wouldn't write a piece on a trip to the Second Coming unless it was operated by American Express tours," says Leonard Hansen, a New Orleans-based syndicated columnist on elderly affairs.

You might think some of AARP's members would get wise to self-promotion like this and do something about it. But while there are nearly 4,000 local AARP chapters across the nation, each with its own elected leadership, members have little voice in setting AARP policy. Washington keeps a tight grip on the selection of both regional and state leaders. State directors, area vice presidents, and state coordinators are all appointed by AARP's Washington-based executive committee. In the past, members attempting to assert their own opinions on political issues have faced the wrath of the Washington office. Ted Ruhig, who served several terms as an officer of AARP's Carmichael, California, chapter, was a regional director of AARP's voter education drive in 1989. Unhappy with AARP's position on catastrophic care legislation, Ruhig spoke out publicly against the lobby. A few weeks later, he received a letter from the Washington headquarters thanking him for his years of service to AARP and dismissing him from his leadership post.

"Occasionally we have to terminate people," Rother explains, "although it's not a pleasant thing to do."

Elder hostile

From the headquarters to the magazine, AARP seems a lot more of a business than a charity or grassroots lobby. In fact, the organization has in many respects evolved into a giant merchandising company that taxpayers subsidize to the tune of millions of dollars. "If I could, I'd walk into AARP and immediately shift the money around," Kurt Vondran, a lobbyist with the National Council on Senior Citizens, says enviously, thinking of the services and programs that could be created with that glorious $300 million budget.

Of course, Vondran's wishes aside, AARP doesn't *have* to chuck the mahogany bookcases, the box-packing consultants, the $11 million executive perks, or the selling obsession. It doesn't *have* to start functioning as a nonprofit, running programs on behalf of the seniors it's chartered to serve. There's another reasonable option. AARP can keep on peddling those products and living as baroquely as it likes —just as long as it drops the charitable cover and pays its taxes like other American businesses. That'd mean, hmmm, millions of dollars saved every year by the federal government—probably a bigger help to America's older people than the AARP will ever be.

The New Face of Aging

From intergenerational friendships to elder activism, the "conscious aging" movement offers a new concept of what's possible in the second half of life.

Jonathan Adolph

Jonathan Adolph is New Age Journal's *senior editor.*

Even after all these years, the memory still haunts Barry Barkan. It was his first visit to the nursing home where his grandmother had recently been placed, one of several such institutions that lined the beach front in Long Beach, New York. The place was "smelly, dark, dirty, and unfriendly," Barkan recalls. As for his grandmother, "nobody knew her for who she used to be, as a parent, as a mother, as a wife, as a person with a life and a vision, with a spiritual life. She had no identity." It was two in the afternoon and his grandmother lay on a hospital bed wearing a nightgown. Her teeth were not in her mouth.

"As a boy, I used to spend hours on end sitting in Grandma's rocker, talking with her about family and world affairs, especially as they related to the Jews, and about the old days—just chatting," he would later write. "Now there wasn't much to say. I couldn't find a way to transcend the sorrow that now became a barrier between my grandmother and the rest of us. She didn't want to live anymore. She said it again and again. Not as a person letting go of the sweet gift of life and preparing for a mysterious connection to the God to whom I remember her frequently praying, but as a person betrayed."

As the years passed, Barkan would recall that image of his grandmother—and see himself. And he realized that if he was going to age in a more humane world, change had to begin now. Drawing upon the empowerment and consciousness-raising techniques he had learned as a civil-rights and anti-war activist in the '60s, Barkan took his work right into the belly of the beast—the nursing homes themselves. Through what he came to call the Live Oak Project, he and his partners began establishing "regenerative communities" among residents and staff. "What we did, essentially, is we went in and organized a culture, a life, among the people in the home, by bringing them together at the same time every day and talking about what was going on in the home, in their lives; what was meaningful." In March 1986, the group took the work a step further and became owners of a nursing home of their own: the Live Oak Living Center at Greenridge Heights in El Sobrante, California. Today, the center's eighty-five residents use the regenerative-community model to take an active role in their own affairs, gathering regularly to plan meals, help produce books of poetry, or memorialize members who have died.

Old age. No issue touches more people and stirs less public debate. In a culture so enamored of outward appearance, aging is a reality many of us would simply rather not face. But, say Barkan and others working to redefine what is possible in our later years, by closing ourselves off from this integral stage of life we also deny ourselves a crucial opportunity for self-understanding. For along with wrinkled skin, gray hair, and sagging flesh, they argue, old age can also bring the wisdom, insights, and inner peace that often prove elusive in younger years. "All the emphasis on aging tends to be negative, because we tend to look at people from an external, material point of view," notes Rick Moody, deputy director of Hunter College's Brookdale Center on Aging and a leading thinker in the field. "If you just define people that way, you're never going to look at what the strengths of aging are, because the strengths really are inner."

From *New Age Journal*, March/April 1992, pp. 62-66. © 1992 by New Age Publishing, Inc. Reprinted by permission of *New Age Journal*, Watertown, MA.

Breaking Stereotypes
EXTRAORDINARY, ORDINARY OLDER AMERICANS

Twelve years ago, public radio reporter Connie Goldman posed a question to a group of kindergartners for a supposedly light feature for Mothers' Day: What is old? The young students' answers—innocent reflections of cultural stereotypes—would set Goldman on a professional quest that continues to this day: to explode the myths and misconceptions about aging.

"There were an overwhelming number of negative responses," recalls Goldman, whose subsequent interviews with "extraordinary, ordinary older Americans" became the series "Late Bloomer" heard on National Public Radio and whose most recent work, a book of interviews with forty prominent older Americans titled *The Ageless Spirit*, will be published by Ballantine this May. "The children said, 'Old people, they fall asleep a lot,' or 'They keep saying the same thing over and over,' or 'They sit around, they don't do nothing.' "

In her interviews for NPR and elsewhere over the years, Goldman has been presented with quite another picture of aging: people who were using their old age—and the greater self-knowledge that comes with it—to explore new pursuits, learn new skills, give back some-thing to their communities. The stories Goldman's work has brought to light can be powerful inspiration: The recent retiree, say, who at his wife's suggestion dug out the accordion he hadn't played since their courting days and eventually found himself with a new volunteer career—playing for gleeful kids at nursery schools. Or the man who tutored kids in reading (even though he was legally blind) and was welcomed into a whole community of teachers and students in the process. "I sat in while he was tutoring these two little boys, and I said, 'How can you do that when you can't even see what they're reading?' And he laughed and said, 'Listen, I read for plenty of years before I lost my sight. I can tell if a sentence is being read right.'

"It's a matter of attitude," Goldman concludes. "It's how you deal with what life gives you. It's how you integrate it into your life. It's how you keep it from taking charge of your life. I mean, there *is* sadness. There is loss that comes with age—loss of mates and friends and family and often loss of mobility and loss of health. It isn't all freedom and it isn't all fun. But it also isn't all sadness and loss and grief and wrinkles."

Activism
GATEKEEPERS TO THE FUTURE

They meet in living rooms or gather around kitchen tables operating under the provocative nom de guerre Gatekeepers to the Future. Most often, they come together to simply discuss a topic of local significance—water issues, say, or the fate of the rainforests—but almost inevitably the talk leads to action. Soon, they're supporting a referendum or organizing a letter-writing campaign. As they become more and more informed about the problem," explains group founder Martin Knowlton, "they tend to become activists."

Wide-eyed teen-agers out to change the world? Not quite. Knowlton's Gatekeepers are almost exclusively of retirement age, people who are using their spare time and life experience to, in his words, "become active representatives of the people of the future." So far, the five-year-old group has some 450 members, roughly 150 of whom take part in the informal discussion/activism groups that the organization helps form and supports with background papers, a quarterly newsletter, and other resources.

Knowlton—a teacher, research engineer, world traveler, and social activist—is no stranger to the concept of organizing elders. In the mid-'70s, together with his colleague David Bianco, he founded Elderhostel, the hugely popular international travel and study program that now serves more than 200,000 over-fifty-five student-adventurers. If Elderhostel was Knowlton's "think globally," Gatekeepers to the Future is his "act locally." He is quick to note, however, that the organization does not have any political agenda other than encouraging elders to represent the interests of the generations to come. The individual discussion groups choose what they want to study and how they want to follow up on what they've learned.

The power of Gatekeepers, Knowlton explains, lies in "having an informed body of people who are influential dealing with these things." Under the group's watchful eye, the slow process of social change is given new importance. "We're doing things as a society today that we're probably not going to see the results of in our lifetime," Knowlton notes. "But they are going to have a possibly profound effect on the lifetime of our grandchildren's generation."

Intergenerational Relationships
THE MEETING OF PAST AND FUTURE

Nothing breaks down fears and misconceptions about aging, Nancy Henkin believes, quite like face-to-wrinkled-face contact. As head of Temple University's Center for Intergenerational Learning, Henkin has seen firsthand how our society's segregation of the ages strips both young and old of vital roles, and how restoring those roles—through intergenerational programs such as the ones she offers—can bring remarkable results. "There's nothing as special as going into a nursing home and seeing a kid who may be pretty wild at school wheeling a frail old woman around or feeding her lunch," she says. The old woman gains a companion, but just as important, "this kid feels terrific, because he's really helping someone who's worse off than he is."

But the Center's programs (there are now eleven) are not just about the young helping the infirm. One of Henkin's most successful—Linking Lifetimes—is a mentoring program, now in place in nine cities around the country, that matches adults aged fifty-five and older with kids beginning to slip through the social service cracks. The program specifically looks for mentors who can share a common bond of experience—men who faced the same pressures growing up on the same neighborhood streets, say, or women who themselves were teen-aged mothers. "They can connect with the kids," notes Henkin, "in a way other people can't."

Uniting all the Center's programs—from Homefriends (in which high school students help house-bound elders) to Project WRITE (in which college students teach reading and writing to elders) to ECHO (a training program for elders interested in child care)—is the idea that both the young and the old are often untapped resources whose various skills and knowledge can be mobilized to meet community needs. At the same time, the meeting of past and future can have consequences that are even more far-reaching.

"If we start at a young age realizing that we're all connected," Henkin says, "and that someday I'm going to be like Grandma and that years ago Grandma was like me, then maybe we won't fear the aging process so much and maybe we'll be able to reach out to each other in more meaningful ways."

Housing
FINDING COMMUNITY

In her frequent talks around the country, gerontologist and housing expert Jane Porcino has been hearing an increasingly common complaint: People tell her they don't feel connected to other people. They feel alone. They miss a sense of community. And they worry about becoming even more isolated in their old age.

Fortunately, Porcino has some solutions. In *Living Longer, Living Better: Adventures in Community Housing for Those in the Second Half of Life,* she outlines dozens of innovative housing options now available that blend the privacy of home ownership with the companionship of group living. Ultimately, she says, housing is not simply a matter of shelter. "What we're doing here in a sense is developing a new form of family."

The options for older people vary widely, from informal collaborative arrangements (where one person may have a large house and another needs a place to stay) to intergenerational small-group living (where as many as a dozen unrelated people share a large house or apartment building) to larger intentional communities (which attract people who share a common interest, often a spiritual perspective). Still, Porcino says, when it comes to elder housing, "people think its only a nursing home, retirement community, or living alone."

One of the most promising new ideas to Porcino is cohousing, an arrangement imported from Denmark in which members buy their own units within a larger housing or condominium complex but share meals, activities, and space in a common building. These intergenerational settings would seem to offer an ideal environment for an older person—with friends, entertainment, meals, and people of all ages nearby. As many as one hundred cohousing groups (including one started by Porcino's son) are now in various stages of formation in the United States, and Porcino predicts that many more will be created as people see the satisfaction that community living can bring. "It's healthier to live with others," she says. "Not only will we live longer, but we'll live better.

Spiritual Eldering
SAVING YOUR LIFE

For Rabbi Zalman Schachter-Shalomi, founder of the Spiritual Eldering Project at Philadelphia's P'nai Or Religious Fellowship, the key to gaining the wisdom and self-understanding that make one a true elder lies in the willingness to face death head-on.

"People who don't want to look ahead as they grow older *back* into the future rather than walk into the future," explains Schachter-Shalomi, who in his "From Aging to Sage-ing" seminars uses a range of self-exploration, imaginal, and group-discussion exercises to help older people confront their fears of aging. "When they back into the future, they look at the past. And when they look at the past, they see their failures."

Only by making peace with mortality, he says, can we keep open a path to the future. And with the future before us, we can then review our past in a more healthy light. "One sees that the painful memories aren't necessarily failures," he says, "but that the memory is like the grain of sand in the oyster that grows the pearl."

This process of life review—of exploring, in Schachter-Shalomi's words, "the obstacles, the emotional hot spots, the freak-outs and anxieties that shut down consciousness"—can be difficult for many people. But it can be made easier, he says, by viewing our lives as having a greater purpose than our Earthly existence may suggest. "When a person finds out, I have been a cell in the global brain, I have made Earth become conscious of herself, this was my privilege—to be conscious and to be alive and to have loved and shared—that gives a different ambience to the person. It shows that the later years can be delightful rather than sad."

Maintaining a forward-looking attitude becomes all the more important as we head into the "October, November, and December" of the lifetime—the crucial period in our social and spiritual development when we can assess what our lives have taught us. "When you are working on a computer, sometimes you type a whole page and then the power goes out," Schachter-Shalomi observes. "If you have not saved your work to disk it is all lost. A lifetime asks the same question, 'Are you saved?' You must write into the global awareness what it is that you have accumulated in your lifetime and who you have become."

In Schachter's cosmology—a rich blend of Eastern spiritual ideas and Western transpersonal psychology as well as Jewish mysticism—the "saving" of each life has tremendous significance. "I believe there is more good in the world than evil—but not by much," he says. "The task of each of us is to help tip the scale. Every life matters immensely and every well-lived and completed life helps in *tikkun olam* (healing the world)."

That limited view of old age may be ready to give way, however, say Barkan, Moody, and other advocates of what is being called "conscious aging." Perhaps the greatest force behind this shift is demographic: The baby boom, that generational bulge that has shaped so much of cultural life in the late twentieth century, is now inching toward fiftysomething—and finding itself face-to-face with aging parents, failing health, and other hard-to-rebut evidence of human mortality. At the same time, this "age wave" of older Americans threatens to put new pressure on already overburdened health care systems and social services. In short, we have seen the elderly, and they are us—and our uncertain future is giving us pause. Notes Mark Gerzon, author of the forthcoming *Coming Into Our Own: Understanding the Adult Metamorphosis:* "There is this age group that is trying to say, 'Wait a minute. We lived our youth differently than our parents did. How do we live the second half of our life differently than our parents did?'"

That such concerns are on the rise is further evidenced by the creation of a three-day conference dedicated entirely to the alternative aging movement. Titled "Conscious Aging: A Creative and Spiritual Journey," the first-of-its-kind gathering, to be held in New York City May 1 through 3, will bring together more than two dozen prominent teachers, researchers, doctors, and spiritual leaders—from Yale surgeon Bernie Siegel to Rabbi Zalman Schachter-Shalomi to Gray Panthers founder Maggie Kuhn—all of whom are working to give old age new meaning. Hosted by the Omega Institute, a holistic education center in Rhinebeck, New York, the conference is being seen as something of a watershed event, a signal that the generation that once hoped to die before it got old may be ready to change its tune. "As it is now, we look on the elder years as worthless and even contemptible," notes Omega cofounder Elizabeth Lesser. "That kind of thinking robs so much from so many of us, no matter how old we are. We need a new way of looking at and experiencing aging."

For many people, however, thinking about growing old is still about as pleasant as contemplating extensive dental work. The reasons for this, notes University of Texas scholar Thomas R. Cole, author of *The Journey of Life: A Cultural History of Aging in America*, are often as much cultural as personal.

RESOURCES

Live Oak Living Center at Greenridge Heights
2150 Pyramid Dr.
El Sobrante CA 94803
(415) 222-1242

Spiritual Eldering Project
P'nai Or Religious Fellowship
7318 Germantown Ave.
Philadelphia PA 19119
(215) 242-4074

Center for Intergenerational Learning
Temple University
1601 N. Broad St.
Philadelphia PA 19122
(215) 787-6836

Gray Panthers
6342 Greene St.
Philadelphia PA 19144
(215) 438-0276

Gatekeepers to the Future
Fort Cronkhite, Building 1055
Sausalito CA 94965
(415) 331-5513

Omega Institute
RD 2, Box 377, Lake Dr.
Rhinebeck NY 12572
(914) 338-6030

Living Longer, Living Better: Adventures in Community Housing For Those in the Second Half of Life by Jane Porcino (Continuum, 1991); $15.95.

Coming Into Our Own: Understanding the Adult Metamorphosis by Mark Gerzon (Delacorte Press, 1992); $19.

The Journey of Life: A Cultural History of Aging in America by Thomas R. Cole (Cambridge University Press, 1992); $27.95.

"Aging and the Human Spirit Newsletter"
The University of Texas Medical Branch, M-11, Institute for the Medical Humanities
Galveston TX 77550-2764

"It never has been fun to grow old and frail and sick," Cole notes. "But before the middle of the nineteenth century, people had a sense, rooted in their religious traditions, that aging was part of a natural process that one could not change. One *could*, however, transform its meaning—depending on one's religious convictions—and live it as a journey to salvation."

That existentially comforting philosophy, however, was soon replaced by the scientific and medical views of growing older—ideas that are still with us today. "People consider aging as a problem that can be solved just as any other disease can be solved," says Cole. "You have an endless number of tummy tucks, eat the right foods, or run enough, and you'll be able to avoid the debilitating aspects." That idea, however, is only half true. What's more, Cole notes, by believing we can "solve" aging, instead of coming to terms with it, we lose a powerful opportunity for gaining self-knowledge. Our mortality, once accepted, he says, "can become the existential ground for compassion, solidarity, and spiritual growth." And it's not just the StairMaster set that may have trouble accepting aging. Explorers of self-development may get hung up as well, says Rick Moody. "In many ways the whole new age sensibility has often been centered around issues of personal control—being in charge of your life, mastering your destiny, acquiring higher states of consciousness, that sort of thing," he says. "And in many ways aging represents the antithesis of that. It represents coping with finitude, loss of control, coming to terms with limits, but not necessarily in a negative way."

Moody, in fact, sees a close parallel between the difficulty we as individuals have in coming to terms with the limits of aging and the difficulty our society now has in coming to terms with the ecological limits of the planet. "In both cases," he says, "we're witnessing the collapse of the idea of unlimited growth."

For Barry Barkan, the task of breaking through denial and honestly facing issues of aging represents nothing less than the central social challenge of our time. In his latest project, Barkan intends to show his peers exactly why this is so. The book he is writing—"a wake-up call to the '60s generation" entitled *Live Oak Reveille*—will lay out the future as it might occur if action isn't taken: a future in which the baby boomers find themselves aging amid dwindling government resources; substandard health care, housing, and transportation; and unprecedented intergenerational strife. "For the first time in history we have the potential to turn over a world that's less good than the one we got from our parents," he cautions. "There's going to be a lot of anger about this."

That's the bad news. The good news is that we may have time to change things—to reprioritize the way our government spends its money, to resolve long-denied social problems, to create a society that respects its elders as we would like to be respected when we reach that age.

"We've got a very small window of opportunity," Barkan says. "And we have to work on a number of levels. We have to become conscious about the way we're relating to this generation of elders. We need to develop a vision of our own sense of elderhood, about what it means to be an elder, so we can age toward that vision. And we need to promote and develop a pro-elder public policy agenda."

"On a macro level," he continues, "we need to pacify the world. Because if we don't do it now, if we don't move from a militaristic world to a world that uses its resources for peace, then we're not going to have the kind of world that we can age into."

Barkan believes that the same demographic forces that are helping to create the approaching aging crisis can help head it off, if the baby boomers recognize what they stand to gain—and lose. "Many of my peers think back to the '60s and '70s as having been the heyday of our generation," he says. "But that's not the best day of our generation. The best day of our generation has got to be ahead of us.

"What we need to do now is gather our energies and our attention, thinking about ourselves, our lives, our future, and the lives of future generations," he continues. "We have to reorganize ourselves as a generation so that we can take power. Those of us who are now in our forties and fifties—this is the period in life when people ordinarily have become the movers and shakers of society and taken over the institutions of society. This is our power period."

Still, the task seems daunting: How can we break through our denial and confront aging in a more healthy way? More specifically, how can we learn to become not simply old people, but societal elders—people whose years on the planet are seen not as a burden to be borne but as a source of wisdom? And how can we create a society that will respect and honor that wisdom? The programs profiled on these pages—developed by advocates of "conscious aging"—suggest some first steps we can take toward that goal.

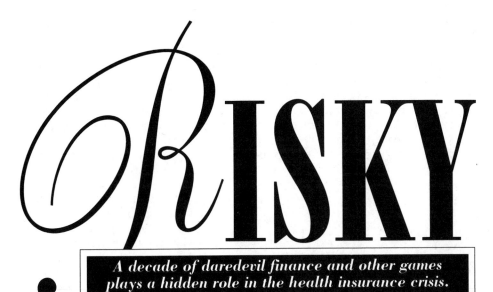

RISKY BUSINESS

A decade of daredevil finance and other games plays a hidden role in the health insurance crisis.

Jeffrey Denny

Jeffrey Denny is executive editor.

Like many small-business proprietors, Jan and Phil Fenty of Washington, D.C., fret constantly about the cost of health insurance. Owners of Fleet Feet, a running shoe and clothing franchise, the Fentys pay dearly to cover themselves and their two full-time employees under the Washington-area Blue Cross/Blue Shield Health Plan. Just recently Blue Cross gave notice that Fleet Feet's premium would be increased 28 percent, bringing their monthly payment to $1,800.

So the Fentys were outraged to read in the *Washington Post* that Blue Cross had raised rates partly because of some $100 million in losses from various for-profit business ventures, many unconnected to medical coverage. For example, one of its subsidiaries reportedly now owns Cape Cod beachfront property and a

rock-and-roll recording studio on a 145-acre New England farm—the unintended result of having loaned $11.1 million to a student travel agency that defaulted.

"It made me angry to see those big shots wasting our money and our rates going up and up and up," says Jan Fenty.

The Fentys are among the untold number of health insurance policyholders nationwide who may have suffered higher rates, reduced coverage, unpaid bills or cancellation because of a little explored factor in the nation's health insurance crisis: The same kind of 1980s-style go-go investment practices, questionable business dealings, lavish spending and help-yourself ethics that brought down the savings and loan industry also have undermined the insurance industry.

Under a tattered patchwork of state laws and virtually no federal oversight, health insurance underwriters have lost billions of dollars investing in high-yield, low-grade "junk" bonds, real estate and other dubious ventures. Sporadic cases of fraud have compounded the losses.

"It's been a well-told tale here," says Lester Dunlap, a consumer advocate for the Louisiana Department of Insurance. "You find this in almost every state."

Until recently, there was little concern about how health insurers invested their assets as long as they provided an efficient system for spreading out the cost of medical care. But increasingly their financial management is a matter of public policy.

"I don't think the public is aware of what could happen to their health insurance because of some of these problems," says a congressional aide who investigated life/health insurance company failures.

A review of insurance industry reports, ongoing congressional investigations, newspaper articles and pending lawsuits, as well as interviews with insurance regulators, financial analysts and other industry observers reveals a disturbing picture:

GAMBLERS' MENTALITY. A 1990 paper by Investors Diversified Services (IDS) named "imprudent investment management" among the "major factors" in the failure of the 48 largely health and accident insurers it studied. "Over half...had an investment portfolio significantly different from the industry norm," the report noted.

AILING INSURERS. The number of life/health insurer insolvencies tripled during the 1980s "and this trend appears to be continuing," the U.S. General Accounting Office (GAO) concluded in a recent report. And 14 of the 72 Blue Cross health plans nationwide, the country's largest health insurer with 94 mil-

other than...the explosion in health care costs," says John Maginn, chief investment officer at Mutual of Omaha, the nation's premier underwriter of individual health plans.

But logic dictates that when an insurance company's overall financial picture is weakened by investment losses, it leaves less room to hold back rate hikes or keep risky policyholders. "Everything that affects the bottom line" affects health policies, says a National Association of Insurance Commissioners (NAIC) official.

panies started selling financial services, competing with S&Ls, banks and brokerages to give customers top returns. This encouraged insurers to sink their assets into high-yield ventures. By the end of 1990, the average life/health insurance company had a quarter of its assets in junk bonds, real estate and mortgage loans, according to A.M. Best. Life insurance companies in fact held about 30 percent of the outstanding junk bonds, a separate 1990 analysis estimated.

By then the roof was falling in. Between 1988 and 1990 the junk bond default rate (the portion rendered worthless) tripled from 3 percent to 10 percent. The real estate market also collapsed, littering the landscape with vacant office buildings, unfinished subdivisions and unmet mortgage payments.

COST TO ADMINISTER MEDICARE, PER BENEFITS PAID: 1.4%...

...TO ADMINISTER PRIVATE HEALTH INSURANCE: 17%

Source: Congressional Budget Office

lion policyholders, are in "weak" or "very weak" financial condition, according to an independent analysis.

POLICYHOLDERS STUCK. In addition to facing higher rates or cancelation, policyholders also may be saddled with unpaid medical claims because the system of state "guaranty funds" designed to clean up after insurance company failures is full of holes, according to the GAO. And with rare exception, the guaranty funds do not cover Blue Cross policyholders, members of health maintenance organizations (HMOs) or employees of self-insured businesses — more than 120 million policyholders.

On top of that, the rash of failures has contributed to the increase in health insurance premiums because the guaranty fund system is financed by insurance rate increases, as well as tax revenues. The cost of covering unpaid life/health insurance claims from insurers that failed between 1976 and 1991 is expected to reach $4.2 billion, according to A.M. Best, an insurance rating agency.

The health insurance industry insists that it's financially stable on the whole, arguing that most of the 1,500 medical underwriters in business today are healthy and that fraudulent operators are rare. And executives with the nation's largest health insurers reject the notion that investment losses have harmed policyholders. "Absolutely nothing else contributes to [the health insurance crisis]

This is particularly true for Blue Cross plans and small health insurers operating near the margin, according to Robert Hunter, president of the National Insurance Consumers Organization (NICO), a leading industry watchdog. "If you're already having trouble, and then your investments start to go bad, then it puts critical pressure on you to get rid of people [and] raise rates," Hunter says.

THE PARTY'S OVER

The health insurance business is fairly straightforward. Companies take in premiums based on policyholders' medical histories, set aside reserves to cover expected claims and "surplus" for unexpected claims, and keep a share for overhead and profit.

Surplus and reserve accounts are invested. Companies that sell several lines of insurance — most health policies are sold by life insurance companies, for example — typically sink their money into a mixture of investments of various risk, maturity and payoff.

Life/health insurance companies try to carry some low-risk, liquid investments, such as money market securities, that can be converted quickly into cash to reimburse the continuous stream of medical claims. These tend to offer low returns. They also try to carry as many high-return investments as possible, which tend to be riskier. That's where the trouble began.

During the 1980s many insurance com-

The collapse in 1991 of two major life insurance companies—Executive Life of California and New York (because of junk bond losses) and New Jersey's Mutual Benefit Life (real estate losses)—focused national attention on the insurance industry's investment woes. But little attention was paid to the impact on health insurance, even though life insurers are the largest underwriters of health policies.

For example, Travelers and CIGNA each reported reductions in health division net income because of sharply devalued real estate investments. A third of Travelers' mortgage and real estate holdings—$5.2 billion worth—were "underperforming" as of last fall while 6.3 percent of its investment portfolio was in junk bonds. Aetna Life & Casualty posted an 18 percent decline in net income overall for 1991 largely due to commercial mortgage losses. Aetna had $1.5 billion in junk bonds and $1.6 billion in problem mortgages last fall.

Company officials deny that their health policyholders have been hurt as a result. But critics say the same investment strategies that helped to sink the S&L industry are playing an indirect role in the health insurance crisis. "First they take our money with a false promise of safety," Martin Weiss, a Palm Beach, Fla., financial adviser who analyzes the health insurance industry, maintains. "Then they invest it in junk bonds and speculative real estate, and now they're trying to make us, the consumers, pay for their blunders."

E.F. HUTTON SPOKE

While Blue Cross health plans are nonprofits, many still couldn't resist the go-go investment game.

One eager participant was Blue Cross of West Virginia. In early 1987, Shearson Lehman Brothers, the big Manhattan brokerage house, and E.F. Hutton, the financial adviser, offered to loan the Blue Cross plan $25 million to buy 30-year U.S. Treasury bonds on credit and make futures and options trades at the Chicago commodities exchanges, according to a pending lawsuit filed in state court by the West Virginia insurance commission.

Convinced, the Blue Cross plan bought the Treasury bonds and over the next 10 months undertook a frenzy of high-risk commodities trades, at times making a dozen or more transactions a day. It stopped only after it had lost $2.3 million — plus $150,000 it had paid Shearson and Hutton for their financial services. Shearson Lehman (which later acquired Hutton) refused to comment for this article.

Partly because of its losing investments, West Virginia Blue Cross became the first in the Blues network to collapse, stranding 51,000 policyholders with unpaid medical claims and others with reduced or canceled coverage. Local doctors have defied court orders and ignored pleas from state officials not to dun patients. Some policyholders' credit ratings have been ruined. One medical group with $114,000 in unpaid claims reportedly insists that patients needing non-emergency surgery pay half their bill in advance. "I lost a total of over $23,000 myself," one policyholder told Congress. "How could a health insurance company simply go bankrupt and leave over $41 million worth of claims unpaid?"

West Virginia Blue Cross also hemorrhaged an undetermined sum of money through a number of for-profit subsidiaries and affiliates, some of which were set up for the personal gain of the health plan's executives, a Senate investigations subcommittee chaired by Sen. Sam Nunn (D-Ga.) found in a 1992 probe. An offshoot of one subsidiary set up to invest in real estate and travel agencies sold computer equipment back to the health plan at mark-ups of 80 to 130 percent, the state insurance commissioner found later.

Nationwide many Blue Cross plans have financed the creation of for-profit ventures, some health-related and some not, in an effort to earn extra money to hold down premiums. The Blue Cross

national association in Chicago defends this practice and argues that subsidiaries altogether cleared some $195 million in profits in 1991 (although a Blue Cross spokesperson could not say how it affected premiums).

But the Nunn subcommittee's ongoing probe of the Blues has revealed a "tendency...to devote inordinate amounts of time, monies and resources on subsidiaries not directly related to their primary task of providing low cost, quality health care coverage," a staff report notes. For example:

INSURANCE FAILURES DUE TO UNDERPRICED PREMIUMS: 23%...

...DUE TO INVESTMENT LOSSES AND ALLEGED FRAUD: 45%

Source: A. M. Best Company

■ Washington, D.C.'s Blue Cross plan operated 45 subsidiaries, including a group of far-flung companies that provided travel services such as evacuating ill travellers, finding lost luggage and selling trip-interruption insurance. It lost $32 million; the health plan was close to failing when a neighboring Virginia plan agreed to take it over.

■ The Maryland plan is in trouble partly because of $120 million in subsidiary losses. One subsidiary did make money: In 1989 (the same year health premiums rose more than 25 percent), the health plan invested $14.7 million to set up BCBSM Finance, which bought and sold stock. Before shutting down in December, BCBSM Finance cleared $500,000 in profits — but that was far less than the $2.4 million it could have cleared had the $14.7 million been sunk into a passbook savings account paying 4 percent interest.

BRANDO'S LIFE MASK

It's not always risky ventures that hurt health policyholders. According to industry studies, alleged internal fraud has played a noticeable role in the rash of insurance company insolvencies.

Consider allegations involving George Washington Life of West Virginia, a $40 million commercial life/health insurer that state regulators seized more than two years ago. Regulators charge that John Wilbur of Jacksonville, Fla., and other

executives of the insurer and its parent company skimmed $14 million in premiums from George Washington for their private enrichment and conspired to mislead examiners about their activities.

"GW Life's money and assets were systematically looted...from 1981 through at least 1991," West Virginia's insurance commissioner charged in a $45 million fraud and civil racketeering lawsuit filed in September. That, as well as "systematic fraud and breaches of fiduciary duty" by company officers, directors and lawyers, caused the company to fail, the suit charges. Wilbur did not respond to requests for comment.

That's nothing compared to what emerged from the rubble left by the collapse of World Life and Health of Pennsylvania in 1991. It was licensed to sell health, life and accident insurance in 18 states, had 64,000 policyholders — and will cost $28 million to clean up. Here's what Senate staff investigators and state regulators found:

Some of World Life's policyholders actually were covered by two reinsurance companies whose principal assets were laughably bogus. Among them were so-called "treasury bills" issued by something called "Sovereign Cherokee Nation Tejas." State regulators contacted the purported Indian tribe's office in Atlanta, Ga., to check out the treasury bills. They wound up speaking with the treasurer, who called himself "Wise Otter" and spoke with a pronounced British accent.

Wise Otter turned out to be Dallas Bessant, a British citizen and owner of the two companies. "Cherokee Nation Tejas is neither sovereign, Cherokee nor a nation," Nunn subcommittee investigators later reported. "It is a sham, run by a group of 'white' or 'Anglo' Americans for the sole purpose of financial self-enrichment."

And what backed the Cherokee Nation Tejas treasury bills? Items included a "life mask" of Marlon Brando the company claimed was worth $1.5 million; titles to movies such as *Computer Beach Party*, *Distant Drums* and *My Girl Tisa*; gold mineral leases, valued at nearly $100 million, for a site under a municipal parking lot in Central City, Colo.; and certificates of deposit from nonexistent financial institutions. The "tribe" was in such sorry financial shape that at one point its officers were denied credit to rent rooms at the Motel 6 in Dallas.

Small-business owners Jan and Phil Fenty were outraged that their Blue Cross plan spent $44,000 on golf outings.

WASTING AWAY

The years of financial mistakes and misdeeds are playing out with a vengeance.

According to Blue Cross national association spokesperson Julie Boyle, an internal "watch list" of endangered plans includes six: Maryland, New Hampshire, New Jersey, Empire of New York, Vermont and Washington, D.C., which together cover some 15 million people. (Only the Washington, Maryland and New Jersey plans are reported to have suffered large subsidiary losses.)

But health insurance analyst Martin Weiss says that number may be too low. According to his financial rating system, which was submitted in testimony to the Nunn subcommittee, 14 Blue Cross plans were still "weak" or "very weak" as of early December. "Weak" means that policyholders could be at risk, Weiss says; "very weak" means they already are. Another 14 received only "fair" ratings.

Because the Blues are nonprofit and often required to insure people whom commercial insurers refuse as too risky, they tend to be hit harder by rising medical costs and operate close to the edge.

But many commercial, for-profit health

insurance companies haven't fared much better. The incidence of life/health insurer failures has increased sharply since the mid 1970s; more than 140 failed between 1989 and 1991. On top of the failed firms, "a significantly greater number of insurers had affiliate or overstated asset problems resulting from overexposure in low-quality assets, typically, [junk] bonds, commercial mortgages or commercial real estate projects," A.M. Best notes.

The health segment has been hit hardest. The cost of covering unpaid medical claims left by failed insurers far exceeds that of other insurance claims — $190 million in 1989 and 1990 alone, according to the GAO.

OUT IN THE COLD

Often health insurers that suffer investment losses play games with policyholders, challenging claims, delaying payments and refusing to cover portions of medical bills deemed beyond "usual or customary" costs, which become increasingly arbitrary, state regulators say. "The net effect on the consumer is he doesn't get the response he expects," says Lester Dunlap of the Louisiana state insurance department.

And while health insurers downplay any connection, investment losses have been linked to rate increases when company books are laid bare. Examining the Washington and Maryland Blue Cross plans in the wake of their financial woes, insurance regulators found that both increased their premiums to help cover subsidiary losses. "The only way you can get [the money] back is through rates…," John Picciotto, the Maryland plan's chief legal officer, told the *Washington Post*.

When banks fail, the federal government covers depositors' money. When health insurers fail, the only place policyholders can take their medical bills is to the system of state-administered guaranty funds, which are designed to pay bills the failed insurance company had promised to cover. Unfortunately, the system is full of holes (see box, next page).

And for some policyholders, there's the ultimate nightmare if their insurance company fails: cancelation. When World Life and Health was seized by Pennsylvania insurance regulators in 1991, the firm had already spun off its 30,000 individual health and accident policies to another Pennsylvania insurer. But most group health plans were terminated. "[Policyholders] had to go find another

health insurer," says a Pennsylvania insurance commission spokesperson.

State insurance liquidators often try to find another insurer to take over policyholders of failed companies. "We've been pretty successful at selling off these blocks," Oklahoma Insurance Commissioner Cathy Weatherford says. Indeed, it can be relatively easy to find new carriers for healthy policyholders, especially large employee groups.

But many insurers will not assume those with poor medical histories, preexisting health conditions or contracts that limit rate hikes. And "nobody wants the little groups," says a Pennsylvania insurance department spokesperson. When Michigan's HMO West failed in 1988 the state liquidator had to twist arms to get other health plans to accept two women left stranded days before they expected to give birth. "Under these conditions, a significant number of individuals…may be unable to obtain new health insurance," the GAO noted.

There is practically no protection when an insurance company decides to cancel or sell off health policies before it goes under. As California's Great Republic Life Insurance Co. suffered financial problems that led to its liquidation in 1991, it canceled a health plan with 14,000 policyholders, including Stan Long, 38, of Los Angeles, who had been diagnosed with HIV, the AIDS virus.

Long went more than a year without coverage, but "lucked out" because his condition was stable, his doctor was a close friend and his pharmacist refused to charge him. Now Long is covered under California's health insurance risk pool, which is financed by cigarette taxes. But he's still angry.

"My business has more regulations than health insurance does," says Long, a partner in an interior design firm.

ASLEEP AT THE SWITCH

Who let the insurance industry gamble with people's medical security? Perhaps it's not surprising to find many of the same players from the S&L debacle:

THE ACCOUNTANTS. Recently, the Big Eight accounting firm Ernst & Young agreed to pay $400 million to settle federal lawsuits charging the firm with failing to adequately audit four large thrifts that subsequently failed (costing taxpayers $6.6 billion) and to call off any more federal suits.

Ernst & Young currently is being sued for $55 million in damages by the West

Virginia Blue Cross liquidator in connection with its auditing of the local Blue Cross plan. "Ernst & Young repeatedly told the department that the plan would not fail, but that its problems were only cyclical," West Virginia Insurance Commissioner Hanley Clark testified in July. Ernst & Young says the suit is "totally unfounded and will be dismissed."

On the whole, the Nunn subcommittee investigation found, accountants "played a significant role for [the] sham deals" that resulted in insurer failures.

FLAWED OVERSIGHT. The insurance industry has fought any reform of the 1945 McCarran-Ferguson Act, which flatly outlaws federal regulation, leaving an uneven state-by-state system.

An insurance company licensed in a dozen states may be subject to a dozen different state laws and regulatory approaches. NAIC, the state regulators' association, attempts to set nationwide standards and in the last two years has recommended tougher laws and regula-

tions to head off insurance failures — and federal regulation. But until recently the association did little about the problem because it was primarily concerned with keeping ailing insurers afloat, critics say.

"Monday morning quarterbacking in the regulation of financial interests is really quite easy," a NAIC official responds. "Look at federal regulation of banks and thrifts. We think our regulation stacks up quite well against these."

Many state insurance regulators continue to lack the legal power, political backing or resources to oversee the industry, however. "Current U.S. insurance regulations are replete with a number of significant loopholes," the Nunn subcommittee noted. Most states' investment regulations have been passive, allowing insurers "to invest in virtually any type, quality or concentration of asset without limitation," Minnesota insurance regulator Thomas Borman testified in 1990. And regulators had an average of only $250 to investigate each complaint they receive and $4,000 to ex-

amine each company they regulate, according to a 1990 study by an insurance agents' association. Until last September, the federal charter of Washington, D.C.'s Blue Cross plan actually limited the local insurance commissioner's authority to regulate the health plan; the District government has never audited its books.

The Blue Cross system has been accused of stonewalling and thwarting regulators "by either putting politically powerful individuals on their boards or by making contributions to certain campaigns," according to a Nunn subcommittee staff report. West Virginia's Blue Cross spent $102,000 between 1987 and 1990 "in lobbying and attorneys' fees …primarily to fight the department's attempt to strengthen the state's laws and jurisdiction over" the health plan, according to state Insurance Commissioner Clark. "Not included in this figure," he added, "is the salary for current and former state legislators who were also on the plan's payroll."

CO-OPTED REGULATORS. Some regula-

No Guarantee

ABOUT A YEAR AGO, the American Council of Life Insurance placed a large advertisement in the *Wall Street Journal* proudly announcing that all 50 states had established life and health insurance guaranty funds, which are designed to protect policyholders from getting stuck with unpaid medical bills or death claims should their insurer fail.

Noting that the funds are financed by assessing insurers a percentage of their income from life and health insurance premiums, the council proclaimed, "The fact that life insurers have to help pay for the mistakes of other companies gives them a powerful incentive to maintain the financial strength of the industry."

Nice try. Insurers actually contribute little to the funds. Who really pays? We do. In all but a handful of states, insurers are permitted to recover their guaranty fund payments by raising premiums or filing for tax breaks. Eighty-six percent of the guaranty fund assessments in 1990 will be reimbursed by the public.

"The guaranty funds are used as a massive tax benefit for the companies," a Missouri state senator told the *St. Louis Post-Dispatch*. "People should know that they are the ones paying...for the insolvent insurance companies."

Another problem: The guaranty system isn't as airtight as the ad implied. "The term 'state guaranty fund' is a misnomer masking the system's faults," Mary Lynn Sergeant, a General Accounting Office (GAO) researcher, testified last spring.

As the GAO noted in a 1992 report, "Some policyhold-

ers of multi-state insurers may have no protection at all should their insurer fail," particularly if a policyholder moves to a state where his or her insurer is not licensed to operate. And 28 states place some limit on medical claims left by defunct health insurers; in 22 states, the cap is $100,000. In Utah, policyholders have to absorb the first $500. Guaranty funds have failed — or refused — to cover unpaid medical claims right away.

The insurance council's ad also didn't note that millions of health insurance policyholders aren't covered at all by the guaranty fund system. These include people covered by unlicensed, fly-by-night operators. Or employees of companies that insure themselves through third-party administrators, a growing but barely regulated trend in medical coverage. Most of the 94 million Blue Cross policyholders aren't covered either. And only four guaranty funds cover health maintenance organizations (HMOs), which represent some 38 million people and which the insurance industry sees as the future of health coverage in America. HMO coverage "is something the states ought to be considering," says Michael Surguine, a legal specialist with the National Association of Insurance Commissioners.

"With the rising number of failures of small insurers and the recent regulatory takeover of large life/health insurers, there is a growing likelihood that even more policyholders...will face the prospect of falling through the safety net and landing without the benefits promised by their insurers," the GAO reported. —*J.D.*

CRISIS? WHAT CRISIS?

JOHN WILBUR OF JACKSONVILLE, FLA., sure knew how to live. For years Wilbur charged his firm for several annual trips to Europe, dropping some $100,000 on travel and entertainment in one year alone, a state official who reviewed company documents confirms. At one point Wilbur spent 12 weeks at the Marriott Marquis hotel in Manhattan, which wasn't itemized but would cost about $12,000 today. Wilbur also charged virtually all his personal expenses to his firm — including laundry bills. All that on top of a $350,000 annual salary.

Generous perks aren't unusual in many blue-chip corporate suites. But Wilbur was chair of George Washington Life Insurance Co., a relatively small life and health underwriter chartered in West Virginia and headquartered in Florida. Until September 1990, that is, when George Washington folded — in part, state insurance examiners say, because of Wilbur's lavish spending habits.

The crisis in affordable medical coverage makes it hard to stomach the way some insurers spend money.

Take salaries, for instance. In 1991, CIGNA chair and CEO Wilson Taylor received $1.3 million in compensation, then-Aetna board chair James Lynn received $1 million and Travelers CEO Edward Budd got $923,000. Or political contributions: In 1991-92, Aetna made $46,000 in corporate contributions to various Republican committees.

And for a nonprofit entity, the Blue Cross network seems to have a lot of money to throw around, according to an ongoing probe by the Senate investigations subcommittee.

To begin with, Bernard Tresnowski, president of the Blue Cross and Blue Shield Association, which represents the nation's locally based Blue Cross health plans, drew $622,000 in salary, benefits and allowances in 1991. Tresnowski in fact was the second-highest paid executive of all 37 medical trade groups tallied by *National Journal*, besting even the affluent American Medical Association.

At policyholder expense, executives of the Washington, D.C.-area Blue Cross plan, which is in deep financial trouble, flew to exclusive international resorts to investigate restaurants, beaches and accommodations for future business meetings. Top executive Joseph Gamble spent $447,000 on travel from 1987 through 1992, including 22 trips to Europe aboard the Concorde. During a 1989 jaunt to London, Paris and Zimbabwe, which cost $7,900, Gamble attended a conference to give a speech on fraud in the insurance industry. When he retired last fall, Gamble was presented with a three-dimensional collage commissioned from a local artist. Cost: $29,000.

Salary and compensation for former Maryland Blue Cross president Carl Sardegna increased 284 percent between 1986 and 1991. And while the Maryland plan was seeking rate hikes and its "financial picture was dark," state insurance commissioner John Donaho testified, the health plan annually pitched hospitality tents at the Preakness horse race — at a cost of more than $65,000 in 1992 alone — "under the guise of being a good corporate citizen," Donaho said. To entertain guests, the Maryland Blue signed a $300,000, four-year lease for a 14-seat exclusive luxury sky-box suite at the Baltimore Orioles baseball stadium, complete with private elevator and bathrooms, wet bar, two color TVs and an internal telephone to order refreshments. Food and drink wasn't included — that came to an extra $588 per game, on average.

Before it collapsed in 1990, stranding 51,000 policyholders, the West Virginia Blue spent at least $102,000 in lobbying and attorneys' fees, mostly to fight regulators' attempts to strengthen state laws and oversight of Blue Cross. Policyholders paid $340,000 in settlement costs and attorneys' fees in connection with two cases of sexual harassment filed against two officers. They kept their jobs.

West Virginia policyholders also unknowingly bought the health plan's president a new Lincoln Continental. But when other executives decided it would look bad — after all, the health plan was in the middle of a financial crisis — the car was traded for a cheaper Pontiac. The president ended up "not really liking the Pontiac," however, so the plan re-purchased the Lincoln. *—J.D.*

tors are too close to the industry. Many are former industry employees and vice versa. According to another study by the insurance agents' group in 1990, 49 percent of the insurance commissioners who left office between 1984 and 1989 went on — some immediately — to positions in insurance companies or provided legal, accounting or consulting services to the industry. In 1976, for example, West Virginia insurance department examiner Michael Davoli was assigned to audit George Washington Life. Three years later Davoli was hired by the insurer's **parent company as assistant to the chairman of the board, according to the West Virginia insurance commission suit.**

Insurance companies often pick up the tab for food, drinks and entertainment at regulators' quarterly meetings, sometimes because regulators ask them to, according to published reports.

A QUESTION OF TRUST

Sensing that change is inevitable, the insurance industry recently softened its opposition to any major reform of the health care system. The Health Insurance Association of America has endorsed a plan in which the government would require employers to buy a standard employee health insurance package and tax more generous health benefits.

"[F]orcing some employers to buy your product seems a helluva lot better than having your industry shut down by the government," a *National Journal* columnist noted.

But given the industry's stewardship of scarce medical resources, many people have a gut-level distrust of any health care reform plan that leaves insurance companies in control.

"If they decide to change and not concentrate on profits but on people's health, then it's possible I could trust them," says small-business owner Jan Fenty of Washington, D.C. "But for the past 12 years everybody had license to go crazy and forget the average person."

Deadly Migration

HAZARDOUS INDUSTRIES' FLIGHT TO THE THIRD WORLD

JOSEPH LaDOU

JOSEPH LaDOU, M.D., is chief of the Division of Occupational and Environmental Medicine at the University of California, San Francisco. As a director of the International Commission on Occupational Health, he has traveled extensively to investigate working conditions and to establish training programs in occupational and environmental medicine in newly industrialized countries.

In 1988, a California manufacturer of epoxy coating materials decided that it could no longer afford to make its products in the United States. The cost of complying with new emission standards for the solvents the products contained would simply have been too high. Yet the company learned that if it set up shop in Mexico, it not only could use the same solvents but could dump wasted solvents at no cost into the arroyo behind the plant.

It's no secret that the low cost of manufacturing in Third World and newly industrialized countries has prompted thousands of First World corporations and investment groups to set up manufacturing operations there. The biggest lure, of course, is cheap labor—factory wages in countries such as Thailand, Bangladesh, Ghana, Guatemala, and Bolivia are often as low as 5 percent of those in industrialized countries. Companies also manufacture abroad to be closer to foreign markets and to overcome trade barriers. In return, the host countries reap significant benefits. According to the U.N. Environment Programme, foreign companies and investors have provided 60 percent of all industrial investment in developing countries over the past decade. For many nations, such investment is the primary source of new jobs.

But the industrial migration has a perverse side, the extent of which the California epoxy case can barely hint at. As developed nations enact laws promoting environmental and occupational safety, more and more manufacturers are moving their hazardous and polluting operations to less developed countries, most of which have either no environmental and worker-safety regulations or little power to enforce those that are on the books. Hazardous industries have migrated to many parts of Africa, Asia, and Eastern Europe. Japan, for example, with its limited land and dense population, has a pressing need to export manufacturing industries such as electronics, chemical production, and metal refining. And many European nations have exported hazardous industries such as textiles, petrochemicals, mining, and smelting.

There is an ironic twist to the problem. Countries that spend little on things like sewage systems, water treatment plants, and enforcement of environmental and occupational safety can offer tax rates dramatically lower than those in the industrialized world. Foreign-based manufacturers take the bait and move in, polluting waterways and endangering workers. Yet the host government can't afford remedies because of the low tax rate.

Pollution and working conditions are so bad that, in effect, the Industrial Revolution is taking place all over again, but with much larger populations of workers and in many more countries. And many of the resulting deaths and injuries are taking place with the complicity of First World companies.

The Faces of Exploitation

The practice of using less developed nations as a dumping ground for untreated factory waste is but one of many forms the export of industrial hazards can take. Industries whose markets in developed countries are shrinking because of environmental concerns are vigorously promoting their products in the less health-conscious Third World. DDT is a compelling example. Its worldwide production, led by U.S. and European companies, is at record levels, even though it has been illegal to produce or use the pesticide in the United States and Europe since the 1970s.

Asbestos is another distressing example. To stimulate the development of companies that will produce asbestos products, Canada's government sends free samples of the material to a number of poorer countries, where many workers and communities are still unaware of the mineral's dangers. (Bangladesh received 790 tons, worth $600,000, in 1984.) Partly as a result of such promotion, Canadian asbestos exports to South Korea increased from 5,000 tons in 1980 to 44,000 tons in 1989. Exports to Pakistan climbed from 300 tons to 6,000 tons in the same period. Canada now exports close to half its asbestos to the Third World.

The First World also exports entire industries—including most lead smelting, refining, and product manufacture—that present occupational hazards. In developed nations, companies using processes that involve lead are required to take costly precautions to protect workers. U.S. lead workers must receive special training, have proper work clothes and changing facilities, and go on paid leave if tests reveal high lead levels in the blood. But in the lax regulatory climate of Malaysia, most lead-acid battery workers—at both foreign- and locally owned plants—have lead levels three times as high as allowed in U.S. workers. And lead plants exported to India continue operating even though 10 percent of the workers have lead poisoning.

Even a migrating industry that doesn't involve toxic materials can be hazardous, because First World corporations often apply a double standard to worker safety. At home, they might comply rigorously with health and safety regulations. Abroad, the same companies let safety standards plummet to the levels prevailing in the less developed host country.

Those levels are miserably low. Worker fatality rates are at least twice as high in industrializing countries, and workplace injuries occur with a frequency not seen in the developed nations since the early years of the Industrial Revolution. Workers in poor countries—usually with limited education, skill, and training—tend to labor in small, crowded factories with old, unsafe machinery, dangerous noise levels, and unsound buildings. Protective gear is seldom available. The companies also tend to be geographically scattered and inaccessible to health and safety inspectors.

On learning of such conditions in India or Malaysia, we in the First World may wince but may also be tempted to put them out of mind—to regard them as a Third World problem from which we are comfortably remote. Yet Americans need look no farther than their own southern border to find some of the worst instances of migrating industries' disregard for human health and environmental safety. Many of the factories that U.S. and other foreign interests operate in northern Mexico freely pollute the water, the air, and the ground and subject workers to conditions nothing short of Dickensian.

The Siesta of Reason

In 1965, Mexico sought to overcome chronic unemployment through the Border Industrialization Program, designed to lure foreign manufacturing business—mainly from the United States—into Mexican border states. The country's government hoped that foreign capital would flow into the economy along with modern production methods that would help create a skilled workforce.

Under the program, manufacturers send raw materials and equipment to Mexico. If they agree to take back the finished products, they need pay taxes only on the value added in Mexico instead of on the value of the entire product. Another big draw is that factory wages average about $5.40 per nine-hour day, less than in Korea, Taiwan, Hong Kong, and other countries long favored for off-shore manufacturing. For U.S. investors, the cost of transporting goods and materials to and from northern Mexico is lower as well.

Today, nearly 1,800 factories operate under this program in northern Mexico, employing about half a million workers. The plants, known as "maquiladoras," extend from Tijuana in the west to Matamoros on the Gulf of Mexico. Their owners include some of the largest U.S. corporations: IBM, General Electric, Motorola, Ford, Chrysler, General Motors, RCA, United Technologies, ITT, Eastman Kodak, and Zenith. Japan's Sony, Matsushita, Hitachi, Yazaki, and TDK also run maquiladoras, as do numerous European companies.

Most maquiladoras are small plants with fewer than 100 workers. In the program's early years, they were largely clothing manufacturers and hand assembly operations, employing mostly women. Today maquiladoras manufacture or assemble a wide range of products, from automobile parts to high-technology electronic components. Men now account for close to 40 percent of the workforce.

No one disputes that the main goal of the Border Industrialization Program has been met. The estimated $3 billion in foreign exchange earnings that maquiladoras pump into the Mexican economy each year now exceeds revenues from tourism and is second only to Mexico's oil and gas exports. Virtually all the new manufacturing jobs created in Mexico in the past decade—and a fifth of the country's manufacturing jobs overall—resulted from the rapid growth of the maquiladoras.

Yet these benefits have come at a high cost. The Border Industrialization Program has created serious social and environmental problems in both countries, but especially in Mexico. The prospect of employment in maquiladoras has caused the populations of border towns and cities to swell. Since 1970, for example, Nogales (south of Tucson) has grown fourfold to 250,000, and Juarez (across the Rio Grande from El Paso) has grown from 250,000 to 1.5 million.

Overcrowding strains these municipalities beyond their limits. Tens of thousands of workers subsist in cardboard huts in squatters' camps without heat or electricity, and sewage is dumped into the arroyos, through which it flows to the nearest river or estuary. At least 10 million gallons of raw sewage from Mexico flows into the Tijuana River every day, polluting San Diego's beaches. The Mexican government is so hard pressed to deal with the problem that the U.S. government, the state of California, and the city of San Diego have agreed to pay most of the $192 million cost of a treatment plant on the border.

But maquiladoras do more than just overburden sewers. Many owners and managers—especially of small maquiladoras engaged in metal working, plating, printing, tanning, and dyeing—readily admit that they moved their operations to Mexico partly because hazardous processes are unwelcome in the United States and other developed countries, and that Mexico is not creating any serious obstacle to their activities. As one owner of a furniture factory explained to me, "I can find lots of Mexican workers in the United States. What I can't find here in Tijuana is the government looking over my shoulder."

Indeed, the very terms of the Border Industrialization Program seem to encourage recklessness. Many foreign companies or investment groups set up maquiladoras through the Mexican government's "shelter program," whereby the parent company—typically known only to the government—maintains control of production and a Mexican company forms to act as co-manager. This shelter firm recruits, trains, and pays all the Mexicans in the workforce. It also manages relationships with the local community and with the Mexican government. In short, foreigners run the business while their Mexican partners see to the social tasks. Because it is a Mexican corporation, the shelter operator shields the foreign company from liability in case Mexico ever cracks down on violators.

Consequently, the foreign operators have little incentive to make sure the 20 million tons of hazardous waste that maquiladoras generate each year is properly disposed of. No data are available on how much of this waste is deposited in rivers and streams, the air, or the ground, but the volumes are enormous. For example, the New River flows northward from Baja California into California contaminated by industrial wastes such as chloroform, benzene, toluene, xylene, and PCBs, and by agricultural runoff that contains various pesticides,

including DDT. The river also carries more than 20 million gallons of raw sewage each day.

California has evaluated numerous alternatives to protect community health and Imperial Valley agriculture. The cheapest solution is to provide the Mexican city of Mexicali with a wastewater collection and treatment system, following the approach proposed for Tijuana sewage. The U.S. Environmental Protection Agency may eventually have to take similar action for all the major cities and towns along the U.S.-Mexico border. In that event, the U.S. taxpayer would ultimately pay for the reduced cost to industry of manufacturing in Mexico.

Mexico's lax monitoring of industrial practices encourages dumping of hazardous waste. Under Mexican law, toxic materials brought in by plants for use in manufacturing—such as paints, cleaning solvents, oils, and acids—must be returned to the country of origin or recycled in Mexico. But according to the Texas Water Commission, only about 60 percent of these waste materials leave Mexico. The other 40 percent—much of it toxic, the commission reports—is disposed of illegally in Mexico's sewers, drainage systems, and landfills. When waste is returned to the United States, it is often transported in improperly packaged and labeled containers.

Dirty Work

Just as the amount of illegally dumped waste is difficult to pin down, so too is hard information on working conditions in maquiladoras. Not only do U.S. and Mexican maquiladora managers deny investigators access to their plants and their workers, but the Mexican government discourages inquiries and health studies. What's more, the U.S. Department of Commerce refuses to share its list of companies participating in the maquiladora program so as not to discourage them from complying with reporting procedures.

High worker turnover rates—6 to 15 percent per month in the states of Chihuahua, Sonora, and Baja California—also make it difficult to survey health effects in maquiladoras. Controlled studies are almost impossible with such an unstable employee population.

What investigators have been able to piece together is that while working conditions in the maquiladoras vary greatly, they are in most cases far inferior to those required in developed countries. Many plants are inadequately ventilated and lighted. Accidents resulting from inattention to safety procedures and the absence of safety equipment are frequent. Nogales maquiladoras reported more than 2,000 accidents in 1989—three times the accident rate of comparable factories on the U.S. side of the border. Sanitation is poor, production quotas are high, noise is often excessive, and machinery is often unsafe.

Workers also receive few rest periods and must perform long hours of microscopic assembly work. And even though many workers regularly handle hazardous materials—especially organic solvents—protective clothing, gloves, and other safeguards routinely required of U.S. industry are rare. To make matters worse, the workers lack safety instruction on the hazardous materials they are using—again a U.S. requirement.

Some plants even allow workers to take home empty contaminated steel drums that once contained hazardous chemicals such as pesticides, solvents, acids, and alkalies. Thousands of these containers are used to store water for domestic purposes throughout the industrial regions of Mexico.

Because of a dearth of studies, the amount of harm caused by such exposure is essentially unknown. But the case of Matamoros, the town where the former U.S. company Mallory Capacitors operated a maquiladora for many years, raises alarming possibilities. The Matamoros School of Special Education has identified 20 retarded children whose mothers were pregnant while employed by Mallory and required to work with PCBs, highly toxic chemicals used in the company's products. PCBs were banned in the United States in 1977 because of their toxicity.

The Matamoros exposures occurred for full workdays over many months. The women often had to reach into deep vats of PCBs with no protection other than rubber gloves. Many of the workers developed the chloracne rash these chemicals typically cause. Recent medical studies in Taiwan and Japan of pregnant women exposed to PCBs reveal the same sort of retardation as in the children of Matamoros. It is very likely that many more children damaged by their mothers' work at Mallory live in other Mexican towns that health researchers have not yet studied. And Matamoros may not be the only town in Mexico where PCBs have caused retardation.

Why does Mexico allow these environmental and occupational abuses to continue? One reason is a lack of resources to combat the problem. SEDUE (Secretariat of Urban Development and Ecology), Mexico's environmental oversight agency, faces financial constraints that limit its ability to regulate the maquiladora industry.

But political constraints play a role as well. The Mexican government enthusiastically supports the maquiladora program. Should SEDUE become too agressive in its efforts, the government might withdraw the meager environmental funds the agency does receive. Municipal governments also operate from a precarious position. If they complain about hazardous waste dumping or unsafe working conditions—or if they press for taxes to support better sewage treatment facilities, schools, and medical care—the owners might move the plants to other cities or even other countries.

Despite these problems, Mexico has made some progress in environmental regulation. In May 1989,

SEDUE required all plants to obtain water discharge permits indicating their compliance with Mexico's rather liberal laws on toxic waste treatment. They may then dump the treated water into the sewer system. Any plant violating this requirement can be fined up to $70,000, and those responsible face a prison sentence of six years. But like most environmental laws in developing countries, this threat is made by an agency that lacks the full backing of its government and the resouces to carry out its mission. So far, this effort has produced few results, although a number of companies are now consulting with industrial hygienists and safety engineers to ensure that they will not be fined.

The U.S. government, too, is inching toward cleaning up the border—likewise with few concrete signs of progress. The federal Rio Grande Pollution Correction Act of 1988 aimed at dealing with that river's problems. But its limited scope and lack of financial support led to widespread disappointment and an array of further legislative attempts. Congress is now considering legislation to set up a permanent U.S.-Mexican environmental health commission, in which the EPA and SEDUE would work jointly to evaluate the maquiladoras and explore ways of preventing or punishing environmental abuse along the border.

Unfortunately, none of these proposals addresses the fundamental flaws of the maquiladora program, such as its failure to raise enough taxes to improve infrastructure. Given both governments' acceptance of the present system, no law that would attack the problems at their roots has any serious likelihood of enactment in the near future.

An International Approach

The slowness of the United States in dealing with abuses by the maquiladoras is typical of the way First World nations have responded to the problems caused by the export of hazardous industries. Like the EPA, which devotes only about a tenth of a percent of its budget to its Office of International Affairs, the environmental agencies of other wealthy countries are just beginning to develop concern for the consequences of industry's actions abroad. Nevertheless, it is the exporting nations that need to take the initiative.

The host countries, hungry for jobs and foreign capital, cannot be expected to make the first moves to end unsafe and polluting practices—and they often resent outside pressure to do so. Poorer nations take the position that only after they have attained the standard of living that rich countries enjoy will they adopt the restrictive environmental policies of the First World. What's more, these countries generally lack large, well-funded environmental groups like those in Europe and the United States. Popular support for actions that may impede the growth of the job market and a rise in living standards is virtually nonexistent.

Thus the world's industrialized nations will have to work together to end the shameful practice of exporting obsolete and hazardous technologies and industries. International agreements must replace the perverse incentives that threaten the world's environment.

International environmental organizations could help stem many of these problems. The U.N. Environment Programme, for example, has been working with a number of Third World countries to introduce siting requirements for hazardous industries. UNEP is also developing information centers on hazardous materials. The U.N. World Health Organization (WHO) and International Labour Office (ILO) provide some guidance to developing countries on occupational health and safety. But the combined annual budgets of these agencies is only about $3 million, severely hampering their ability to fund environmental research and provide worker education and health inspections. And WHO and ILO have confined their activities mainly to larger employers, while the vast majority of worksites in developing countries are small.

Other global bodies have made laudable attempts to control industry's behavior. The OECD Guidelines for Multinational Enterprises, the U.N. Code of Conduct on Transnational Corporations, and the ILO Tripartite Declaration of Principles Concerning Multinational Enterprises and Social Policy attempt to provide a framework of ethical behavior. The ILO declaration of principles, for example, recommends that multinationals inform worker representatives about hazards and protective measures. But stronger medicine is needed.

When industry migrates to developing countries, governments and international lending institutions could require environmental impact assessments. The World Bank, along with other international lenders, now offers to produce such assessments when the host country can't. The bank has also taken steps toward requiring poor countries to put occupational and environmental protections in place as a condition for receiving development capital. Similarly, industrialized countries must insist that companies apply the same safety and environmental regulations to their manufacturing operations abroad as they do at home.

As part of this effort, countries need to cooperate to set global standards for occupational and environmental exposures to dangerous substances. Some newly industrialized countries have formulated lists of chemicals and metals that should receive priority regulation and enforcement. Yet these lists often contain laboratory reagents, rarely used chemicals, and other materials not likely to pose occupational and environmental problems, while omitting many highly toxic substances that see broad use. Industrialized countries therefore need to adopt one set of standards with which all companies manufacturing in poorer countries must comply.

So far, both rich and poor nations see the short-term advantages in the export of hazardous industries but turn a blind eye to long-term harm. In the Third World and the First World alike, the risk of future accidents like Bhopal, the cost of environmental cleanup, and pollution's toll on public health are seldom discussed with candor. But as the developed countries have found, the longer environmental damage and hazardous working conditions continue, the greater the cost of remedying these problems once regulations and enforcement are in place. By disregarding such concerns, First World industries are shifting substantial burdens to those least able to bear them.

ANALYSIS

Confronting the AIDS Pandemic

**Daniel J. M. Tarantola
and Jonathan M. Mann**

*Daniel J. M. Tarantola, M.D., is a
lecturer in international health at
the Harvard School of Public
Health. Jonathan M. Mann, M.D.,
is director of the International
AIDS Center of the Harvard AIDS
Institute.*

In 1986, the world undertook to mobilize against the AIDS pandemic in an effort that continued to grow until the beginning of this decade, when it began to stall. Today, the global HIV/AIDS pandemic is spinning out of control—its broad course has yet to be influenced in any substantial way by policies and programs mounted against it.

In 1991–1992, the Harvard-based Global AIDS Policy Coalition undertook a review of the state of the AIDS pandemic. The findings of this review, which appear in our new book *AIDS in the World* (Harvard University Press, December 1992), raise the alarm and call for an urgent revival of the response to AIDS.

The magnitude of the pandemic has increased over 100-fold since AIDS was discovered in 1981. From an estimated 100,000 people infected with HIV worldwide in 1981, it is estimated that by early 1992, at least 12.9 million people around the world (7.1 million men, 4.7 million women, and 1.1 million children) had been infected with HIV. Of these, about one in five (2.6 million) have thus far developed AIDS, and nearly 2.5 million have died.

The spread of HIV has not been stopped in any community or country. In the United States, at least 40,000 to 80,000 new HIV infections were anticipated during 1992; in 1991, more than 75,000 new HIV infections occurred in Europe. In just five years, the cumulative number of HIV-infected Africans has tripled, from 2.5 million to over 7.5 million today. HIV is spreading to new communities and countries around the world—in some areas with great rapidity. An explosion of HIV has recently occurred in Southeast Asia, particularly in Thailand, Burma, and India, where, within only a few years, over one million people may have already been infected with HIV. HIV/AIDS is now reported from areas that, so far, had been left relatively untouched, such as Paraguay, Greenland, and the Pacific island nations of Fiji, Papua New Guinea, and Samoa. The global implications are clear: During the next decade, HIV will likely reach most communities around the world; geographic boundaries cannot protect against HIV. The question today is not *if* HIV will come, but only *when*.

INCREASED COMPLEXITY

The pandemic becomes more complex as it matures. Globally it is composed of thousands of separate and linked community epidemics. Every large metropolitan area affected—Miami, New York, Bangkok, London, Amsterdam, Sydney, Rio de Janeiro—contains several subepidemics of HIV going on at the same time. The impact on women is increasing dramatically, as heterosexual transmission accounts for almost 71 percent of HIV infections. Worldwide, the proportion of HIV infected who are women is rising rapidly, from 25 percent in 1990 to 40 percent by early 1992. The epidemic also evolves over time: In Brazil, the proportion of HIV infections linked with injection

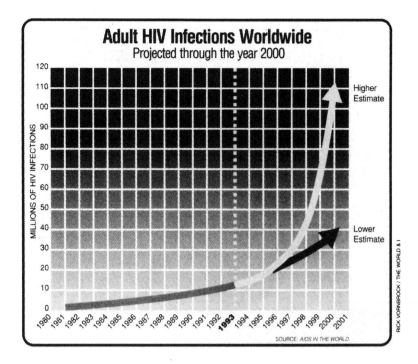

Adult HIV Infections Worldwide
Projected through the year 2000

drug use has increased over ten-fold since the early 1980s; in the Caribbean, heterosexual transmission has now replaced homosexual transmission as the major mode of HIV spread.

The pandemic's major impacts are yet to come. During the period 1992–95 alone, the number of people developing AIDS—3.8 million—will exceed the total number who developed the disease during the pandemic's history prior to 1992. The number of children orphaned by AIDS will more than double in the next three years: from approximately 1.8 million today to 3.7 million by 1995. The pandemic has not peaked in any country—no community or country can claim "victory" against HIV/AIDS. By 1995, an *additional* 5.7 million adults will become infected with HIV. Thus, from 1992 to 1995, the total number of HIV-infected adults will increase by 50 percent. During the same period, the number of children infected with HIV will more than double, from 1.1 million to an estimated 2.3 million.

By the year 2000, the Global AIDS Policy Coalition has projected that between 38 million and 110 million adults—and over 10 million children—will become HIV infected. The largest proportion of HIV infections will be in Asia (42 percent), surpassing sub-Saharan Africa (31 percent), Latin America (8 percent), and the Caribbean (6 percent). By the end of this decade, 24 million adults and several million children may have developed AIDS—or up to 10 times as many as today.

Only a few years ago, tuberculosis was considered a stable problem that was endemic mostly in the developing world. If it was also prevalent in certain socioeconomic groups in industrialized countries, there was a common belief that the situation was largely under control. This general sense of complacency, denounced by many who had been fighting the disease, led to a decline in resources allocated to surveillance, prevention, and treatment services. When HIV came on the scene, it found a vulnerable population.

There is a dangerous synergy between HIV and tuberculosis that makes the combined effects of both worse than their separate effects added together. HIV makes individuals and communities more vulnerable to tuberculosis; it increases the rate of reactivation of tuberculosis infection, shortens the delay between TB infection and disease, and reduces the accuracy of diagnostic methods. Recent outbreaks of multiple-drug resistant tuberculosis have occurred in New York City and in Miami, especially in hospitals and prisons. Combining its projections with estimates made by the World Health Organization, *AIDS in the World* estimates that, by early 1992, there were more than 4.6 million people with both TB and HIV infection worldwide, 81 percent of them in Africa.

Geographic boundaries cannot protect against HIV. The question today is not *if* HIV will come, but only *when*.

TAKING STOCK

Confronting the growing pandemic are national AIDS programs. These actions may involve governmental institutions and agencies, nongovernmental organizations, and the private sector.

Almost invariably overseen by ministries of health, they are generally implemented through government agencies and health services.

The success of a national AIDS program involves the extent to which it helps curb the course of the HIV epidemic and provides quality care to those already affected. On this basis, no program in the world can yet claim success.

Of the 38 countries surveyed by the Global AIDS Policy Coalition, 24 reported having conducted an evaluation since the inception of their national program. In general, the evaluation findings can be summarized as follows:

• Once created, programs become operational rapidly.

• They were successful in raising public awareness on AIDS issues although they did not always prevent (and at times they even generated) misperceptions among certain communities.

• They raised appropriate human rights issues and in some instances managed to prevent violations of these rights.

• They exchanged information—and in some cases made funds and skills available—at the international level.

Industrialized countries were generally able to secure the financial, human, and technological resources required to increase drastically the safety of blood and blood products, and establish diagnostic and treatment schemes reaching most (but not all) people in need. The same could not be said, however, about developing countries, which are constrained by lack of resources, weak infrastructures, and multiple developmental or even survival issues.

Common criticisms of these programs are their lack of focus and priority setting, their weak management, their lack of inte-

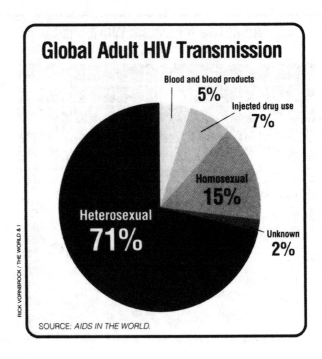

Global Adult HIV Transmission

Blood and blood products **5%**

Injected drug use **7%**

Homosexual **15%**

Heterosexual **71%**

Unknown **2%**

RICK VORNBROCK / THE WORLD & I

SOURCE: *AIDS IN THE WORLD.*

gration with existing disease prevention and control services, and their inability to actively involve other health programs, sectors, and nongovernmental organizations. Denial persists about the pandemic's impact upon women; prevention and research efforts worldwide still inadequately involve them.

In its report, the Global AIDS Policy Coalition suggests indexes that can be applied at the national or regional levels. Similar indexes are being developed for the assessment of community vulnerability.

THE COST OF AIDS

AIDS policies and programs used to be guided by two motives misperceived by many as antagonistic: a human rights/humanitarian approach and a public health perspective. The economic argument was seldom raised because it was not politically advantageous to make the cost of AIDS a major public issue. It did not conform to the humanitarian agenda (cost is secondary to human rights) nor to the public health perspective (the population must be protected). But with

the rising number of people and communities affected by the pandemic, the cost of prevention and care and the general economic impact of AIDS have become critical issues.

The economic perspective considers the impact of AIDS in a decade that began in a worldwide recession. It can be argued that the impact of HIV/AIDS on young, productive adults and their children will jeopardize the national development of many countries. In July 1992, a study conducted by an American team estimated the economic impact of the pandemic by feeding epidemiological projection data into a computer model of the global marketplace. It concluded that by the year 2000, the pandemic could drain between $356 billion and $514 billion from the world's economy, and developing countries are expected to be the hardest hit.

The Global AIDS Policy Coalition estimated that money spent on AIDS in a one-year period during 1990–91 was in the range of $1.4–$1.5 billion for prevention, approximately $3.5 billion for adult AIDS care alone, and $1.6 billion for research, for an adjusted total of $7.1 to $7.6 billion (including costs for treating those persons with HIV before AIDS occurs). Interestingly, about 95 percent was spent in industrialized countries that have less than 25 percent of the world's population, 18 percent of the people with AIDS, and 15 percent of HIV infections worldwide.

For HIV prevention activities in 1991, about $2.70 was spent *per person* in North America and $1.18 in Europe. In the developing world, spending on prevention amounted to only $0.07 per person in sub-Saharan Africa and $0.03 per person in Latin America. Of the $5.6 billion spent on AIDS research since the discovery of AIDS in 1981, $5.45 billion, or 97 percent, has been spent in industrialized countries. The United States is the biggest contributor to global AIDS research spending, with $4.8 billion, or 86 percent of the world total. Domestic and international research have led to a considerable advancement of knowledge. Research funds benefited from annual increases in the late 1980s, but resources support-

---

**The United States
is the biggest contributor to
global AIDS research spending,
with 86 percent
of the world total.**

---

ing this research are reaching a plateau.

For AIDS care, 89 percent of world spending in 1990 was used to help less than 30 percent of the world's people with AIDS—those living in North America and Europe. And yet, the cost of medical care for each person with AIDS—roughly equivalent to annual per capita income in developing countries—is overwhelming individuals and households everywhere. Inequities in treatment and prevention are growing. The cost of one year's treatment with AZT is about $2,500, while per capita income in all developing countries averages $700—in sub-Saharan Africa the

figure is $470—or less than one-fifth the cost of AZT for one year. Individual studies have indicated that the annual cost of care for an adult with AIDS varied in 1990–91 from $32,000 in the United States to $22,000 in western Europe, $2,000 in Latin America, and a mere $393 in sub-Saharan Africa.

These figures translate into the harsh reality of length of survival and quality of life of people with AIDS. The need for AIDS care and the inequity in access to quality services will continue to grow: The number of AIDS treatment years for adults alone will increase from an estimated 433,000 in 1992 to 619,000 in

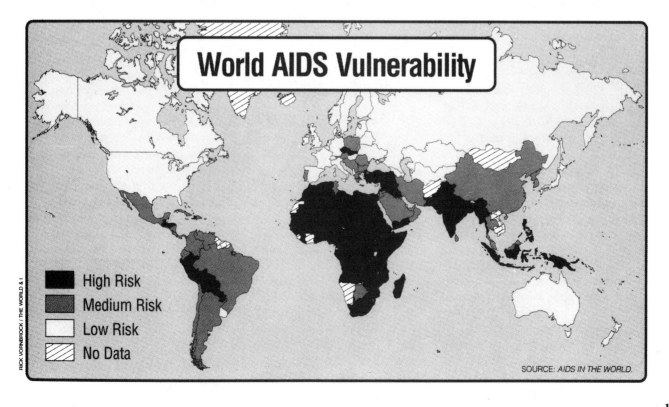

World AIDS Vulnerability

High Risk
Medium Risk
Low Risk
No Data

SOURCE: *AIDS IN THE WORLD.*

RICK VORNBROCK / THE WORLD 8.1

1995; almost 60 percent of these will be in Africa and 26 percent in the industrialized world. Built into these estimates, however, is the average duration of survival of an adult with AIDS, which in Africa is estimated at about one year after diagnosis, less than half of the survival duration of an adult with AIDS in the industrialized world.

Despite the introduction of HIV diagnostic tests over seven years ago, unscreened blood is currently responsible for at least 5 percent of global HIV infections. Most sub-Saharan African countries still cannot afford a safe blood supply. And even if an AIDS vaccine became available today, its impact on the world would be limited by inequities in access to it.

NEED FOR A GLOBAL VISION

Where efforts have been made to provide a coordinated response to the growing crisis, there are clear signs of positive individual responses. But where programs are confronted with weak national commitment, declining resources, and a growing sense of complacency, national AIDS programs are in jeopardy and, together with them, the people they are intended to serve. Many governments, constrained by their lack of resources, continue to avoid the reality of the pandemic: More people become infected because they do not have sufficient access to information and services; more individuals require care that they cannot afford; more families and communities are affected by the impact of a pandemic that has only begun.

Industrialized nations are turning away from coordinated efforts, showing a growing preference to work independently, on a bilateral basis, with chosen developing countries. Fragmentation of efforts by industrialized countries has led to competition among donors in some countries. It is clear that as the pandemic continues to worsen, AIDS programs will be forced to struggle with insufficient funds.

Global efforts have failed to motivate low-prevalence countries to act before the epidemic reaches them in force. India, Burma, and the Sudan are examples of a delayed response and a failure to learn from the experience of heavily affected countries.

Overall, the world has become more vulnerable to HIV and AIDS. On the basis of the societal factors that create vulnerability to spread of HIV, *AIDS in the World* has identified 57 countries as *high risk* for HIV spread—including countries that have thus far escaped the brunt of the pandemic, such as Indonesia, Egypt, Bangladesh, and Nigeria. An additional 39 countries are considered to be at *substantial* risk of a major HIV epidemic, including 11 Latin American countries, 8 in the southeast Mediterranean, 7 in Asia (including China), 4 in the Caribbean, and 9 in other regions.

We *are* at a critical juncture in the confrontation with AIDS, but we are not helpless. By revitalizing leadership, by addressing prevention and the needs of the affected, by formulating clear, international strategies, by accelerating effective, safe, and affordable treatments and vaccines, it *is* possible to stall the future spread of the pandemic.

At a time when many countries are undergoing major geopolitical transitions and are facing severe economic recessions, HIV/AIDS is not simply fading away. The world will continue to experience a rapid increase in the number of people developing AIDS until there is a cure. In the meantime, a troubled world population can unite together to fairly and equitably make available prevention and treatment programs until that day comes.

Mental Illness Is Still a Myth

Thomas Szasz

Thomas Szasz is professor emeritus of psychiatry at the State University of New York in Syracuse, New York. He is author of The Myth of Mental Illness; Our Right to Drugs: The Case for a Free Market; *and* A Lexicon of Lunacy: Metaphoric Malady, Moral Responsibility, and Psychiatry (*the latter published by Transaction Publishers*). *His most recent book is* Cruel Compassion: Psychiatric Control of Society's Unwanted.

In a memorable statement C. S. Lewis once remarked, "Of all the tyrannies a tyranny sincerely exercised for the good of its victims may be the most oppressive. . . . To be 'cured' against one's will and cured of states which we may not regard as disease is to be put on a level with those who have not yet reached the age of reason or those who never will; to be classed with infants, imbeciles, and domestic animals." These words still apply to psychiatry today.

Anyone with an ear for language will recognize that the boundary that separates the serious vocabulary of psychiatry from the ludicrous lexicon of psychobabble, and both from playful slang, is thin and permeable to fashion. This is precisely wherein lies the richness and power of language that is inexorably metaphoric. Should a person want to say something sensitive tactfully, he can, as the adage suggests, say it in jest, but mean it in earnest. Bureaucrats, lawyers, politicians, quacks, and the assorted mountebanks of the "hindering professions" are in the habit of saying everything in earnest. If we want to protect ourselves from them, we had better hear what they tell us in jest, lest the joke be on us.

As far back as I can remember thinking about such things, I have been struck by the analogic-metaphoric character of the vocabulary of psychiatry, which is nevertheless accepted as a legitimate medical idiom. When I decided to discontinue my residency training in internal medicine and switch to psychiatry, I did so with the aim of exploring the nature and function of psychiatry's metaphors and to expose them to public scrutiny as figures of speech.

During the 1950s, I published a score of articles in professional journals, challenging the epistemological foundations of the concept of the mental illness and the moral basis of involuntary mental hospitalization. In 1958, as my book *The Myth of Mental Illness* was nearing completion, I wrote a short paper of the same title and submitted it to every major American psychiatric journal. Not one of them would accept it for publication. As fate would have it—and because the competition between psychologists and psychiatrists for a slice of the mental health pie was then even more intense than now—*The American Psychologist* published the essay in 1960. The following year, the book appeared. I think it is fair to say that psychiatry has not been the same since.

Responses to my work have varied from lavish praise to bitter denunciation. American psychiatrists quickly closed ranks against me. Official psychiatry simply dismissed my contention that (mis)behaviors are not diseases and asserted that I "deny the reality that mental diseases are like other diseases," and distorted my critique of psychiatric slavery as my "denying life-saving treatment to mental patients." Actually, I have sought to deprive psychiatrists of their power to involuntarily hospitalize or treat competent adults called "mental patients." My critics have chosen to interpret this proposal as my trying to deprive competent adults of their right or opportunity to seek or receive psychiatric help. By 1970, I had become a non-person in American psychiatry. The pages of American psychiatric journals were shut to my work. Soon, the very mention of my name became taboo and was omitted from new editions of texts that had previously featured my views. In short, I became the object of that most effective of all criticisms, the silent treatment—or, as the Germans so aptly call it, *Totschweigetaktik*.

In Great Britain, my views elicited a more favorable reception. Some English psychiatrists conceded that not all psychiatric diagnoses designate *bona fide* diseases. Others were sympathetic to the plight of persons in psychiatric custody. Regrettably, that posture rested heavily on the misguided patriotic belief that the practice of psychiatric slavery was less common in England than in the United States.

Not surprisingly, my work was received more favorably by philosophers, psychologists, sociologists, and civil libertarians, who recognized the merit of my cognitive challenge to the concept of mental illness, and the legitimacy of my questioning the morality of involuntary psychiatric interventions. I thus managed to set in motion a controversy about mental illness that is still raging.

When people now hear the term "mental illness," virtually everyone acts as if he were unaware of the distinction between literal and metaphoric uses of the word "illness." That is why people believe that finding brain lesions in some mental patients (for example, schizophrenics) would prove, or has already proven, that mental illnesses exist and are "like other illnesses." This is an error. If mental illnesses are diseases of the central nervous system (for example, paresis), then they are diseases of the brain, not the mind; and if they are the names of (mis)behaviors (for example, using illegal drugs), then they are not diseases. A screwdriver may be a drink or an implement. No amount of research on orange juice and vodka can establish that it is a hitherto unrecognized form of a carpenter's tool.

Such linguistic clarification is useful for persons who want to think clearly, regardless of consequences. However, it is not useful for persons who want to respect social institutions that rest on the literal uses of a master metaphor. In short, psychiatric metaphors play the same role in therapeutic societies as religious metaphors play in theological societies. Consider the similarities. Mohammedans believe that God wants them to worship on Friday, Jews that He wants them to worship on Saturday, and Christians that He wants them to worship on Sunday. The various versions of the American Psychiatric Association's (APA) *Diagnostic and Statistical Manual* rest on the same sort of consensus. How does behavior become illness? By the membership of the American Psychiatric Association reaching a consensus that, say, gambling is an illness and then issuing a declaration to that effect. Thereafter "pathological gambling" is a disease.

Obviously, belief in the reality of a psychiatric fiction, such as mental illness, cannot be dispelled by logical argument any more than belief in the reality of a religious fiction, such as life after death, can be. That is because, *inter alia*, religion is the denial of the human foundations of meaning and of the finitude of life; this authenticated denial lets those who yearn for a theo-mythological foundation of meaning and who reject the reality of death to theologize life and entrust its management to clerical professionals. Similarly, psychiatry is the denial of the reality of free will and of the tragic nature of life; this authenticated denial lets those who seek a neuro-mythological explanation of human wickedness and who reject the inevitability of personal responsibility to medicalize life and entrust its management to health professionals. Marx was close to the mark when he asserted that religion was "the opiate of the people." But religion is not the opiate of the people. The human mind is. For both religion and psychiatry are the products of our own minds. Hence, the mind is its own opiate; and its ultimate drug is the word.

Freud himself flirted with such a formulation. But he shied away from its implications, choosing instead to believe that "neuroses" are literal diseases, and that "psychoanalysis" is a literal treatment. As he wrote in his essay "Psychical (or Mental) Treatment":

> Foremost among such measures [which operate upon the human mind] is the use of words; and words are the essential tool of mental treatment. A layman will no doubt find it hard to understand how pathological disorders of the body and mind can be eliminated by 'mere' words. He will feel that he is being asked to believe in magic. And he will not be so very wrong. . . . But we shall have to follow a roundabout path in order to explain how science sets about restoring to words a part at least of their former magical power.

I took up the profession of psychiatry in part to combat the contention that abnormal behaviors are the products of abnormal brains. Ironically, it was easier to do this fifty years ago than today. In the 1940s, the idea that every phenomenon named a "mental illness" will prove to be a bona fide brain disease was considered to be only a hypothesis, the validity of which one could doubt and still be regarded as reasonable. Since the 1960s, however, the view that mental diseases are diseases of the brain has become scientific fact. This contention is the bedrock claim of the National Alliance for the Mentally Ill (NAMI), an organization of and for the relatives of mental patients, with a membership in excess of one hundred thousand. Its "public service" slogan, intoned like a mantra, is: "Learn to recognize the symptoms of Mental Illness. Schizophrenia, Manic Depression, and Severe Depression are Brain Diseases.

Diagnoses are social constructs which vary from time to time and from culture to culture.

Psychiatrists and their powerful allies have thus succeeded in persuading the scientific community, the courts, the media, and the general public that the conditions they call "mental disorders" are diseases—that is, phenomena independent of human motivation or will. This development is at once curious and sinister. Until recently, only psychiatrists—who know little about medicine and less about science—embraced such blind physical reductionism.

Most scientists knew better. For example, Michael Polanyi, who made important contributions to both physical chemistry and social philosophy, observed: "The recognition of certain basic impossibilities has laid the foundations of some major principles of physics and chemistry; similarly, recognition of the impossibility of understanding living things in terms of physics and chemistry, far from setting limits to our understanding of life, will guide it in the right direction." It is no accident that the more firmly psychiatrically inspired ideas take hold of the collective American mind, the more foolishness and injustice they generate. The specifications of the Americans With Disabilities Act (AWDA), a federal law enacted in 1990, is a case in point.

Long ago, American lawmakers allowed psychiatrists to literalize the metaphor of mental illness. Having accepted fictitious mental diseases as facts, politicians could not avoid specifying which of these manufactured maladies were covered, and which

were not covered, under the AWDA. They had no trouble doing so, creating a veritable "DSM-Congress," that is, a list of mental diseases accredited by a congressional, rather than a psychiatric, consensus group. Thus, the AWDA covers "claustrophobia, personality problems, and mental retardation, [but does not cover] kleptomania, pyromania, compulsive gambling, and. . .transvestism." It is reassuring to know that the Congress of the United States agrees with me that stealing, setting fires, gambling, and cross-dressing are not diseases.

Thus, the various versions of the APA's *Diagnostic and Statistical Manual of Mental Disorders* are not classifications of mental disorders that "patients have," but are rosters of officially accredited psychiatric diagnoses. This is why in psychiatry, unlike in the rest of medicine, members of "consensus groups" and "task forces," appointed by officers of the APA, make and unmake diagnoses, the membership sometimes voting on whether a controversial diagnosis is or is not a disease. For more than a century, psychiatrists constructed diagnoses, pretended that they are diseases, and no one in authority challenged their deceptions. The result is that few people now realize that diagnoses are not diseases.

Diseases are demonstrable anatomical or physiological lesions, that may occur naturally or be caused by human agents. Although diseases may not be recognized or understood, they "exist." People have hypertension and malaria, regardless of whether or not they know it or physicians diagnose it.

Diagnoses are disease names. Because diagnoses are social constructs, they vary from time to time, and from culture to culture. Focal infections, masturbatory insanity, and homosexuality were diagnoses in the past; now they are considered to be diagnostic errors or normal behaviors. In France, physicians diagnose "liver crises"; in Germany, "low blood pressure"; in the United States, "nicotine dependence."

These considerations raise the question: Why do we make diagnoses? There are several reasons: 1) Scientific—to identify the organs or tissues affected and perhaps the cause of the illness; 2) Professional—to enlarge the scope, and thus the power and prestige, of a state-protected medical monopoly and the income of its practitioners; 3) Legal—to justify state-sanctioned coercive interventions outside of the criminal justice system; 4) Political-economic—to justify enacting and enforcing measures aimed at promoting public health and providing funds for research and treatment on projects classified as medical; 5) Personal—to enlist the support of public opinion, the media, and the legal system for bestowing special privileges (and impose special hardships) on persons diagnosed as (mentally) ill.

It is no coincidence that most psychiatric diagnoses are twentieth-century inventions. The aim of the classic, nineteenth-century model of diagnosis was to identify bodily lesions (diseases) and their material causes (etiology). The term "pneumococcal pneumonia," for example, identifies the organ affected, the lungs, and the cause of the illness, infection with the pneumococcus. Pneumococcal pneumonia is an example of a pathology-driven diagnosis.

Diagnoses driven by other motives—such as the desire to coerce the patient or to secure government funding for the treatment of the illness—generate different diagnostic constructions and lead to different conceptions of disease. Today, even diagnoses of (what used to be) strictly medical diseases are no longer principally pathology-driven. Because of third-party funding of hospital costs and physicians' fees, even the diagnoses of persons suffering from *bona fide* illnesses—for example, asthma or arthritis—are distorted by economic considerations. Final diagnoses on the discharge summaries of hospitalized patients are often no longer made by physicians, but by bureaucrats skilled in the ways of Medicare, Medicaid, and private health insurance reimbursement—based partly on what ails the patient, and partly on which medical terms for his ailment and treatment ensure the most generous reimbursement for the services rendered.

As for psychiatry, it ought to be clear that, except for the diagnoses of neurological diseases (treated by neurologists), no psychiatric diagnosis is, or can be, pathology-driven. Instead, all such diagnoses are driven by non-medical, that is, economic, personal, legal, political, or social considerations and incentives. Hence, psychiatric diagnoses point neither to anatomical or physiological lesions, nor to disease-causative agents, but allude to human behaviors and human problems. These problems include not only the plight of the denominated patient, but also the dilemmas with which the patient, relatives, and the psychiatrist must cope and which each tries to exploit.

My critique of psychiatry is two-pronged, partly conceptual, partly moral and political. At the core of my conceptual critique lies the distinction between the literal and metaphorical use of language—with mental illness as a metaphor. At the core of my moral-political critique lies the distinction between relating to grown persons as responsible adults and as irresponsible insane persons (quasi-infants or idiots)—

the former possessing free will, the latter lacking this moral attribute because of being "possessed" by mental illness. Instead of addressing these issues, my critics have concentrated on analyzing my motives and defending psychiatric slavery as benefiting the "slaves" and society alike. The reason for this impasse is that psychiatrists regard their own claims as the truths of medical science, and the claims of mental patients as the manifestations of mental diseases; whereas I regard both sets of claims as unwarranted justifications for imposing the claimants' beliefs and behavior on others. Because the secret to unraveling many of the mysteries of psychiatry lies in distinguishing claims from assertions, descriptions, suggestions, or hypotheses, let us briefly examine this concept.

Psychiatrists have the power to accredit their claims as scientific facts and rational treatments.

Advancing a claim means seeking, by virtue of authority or right, the recognition of a demand—say, the validity of an assertion (in religion), or entitlement to money damages (in tort litigation). To use my previous example, Muslims, Jews, and Christians all claim that God created the world in six days and on the seventh He rested. However, each faith names a different day of the week as the day of rest. Similarly, (some so-called) psychotics assert that they hear voices that command them to kill their wives or children; psychiatrists assert that such persons suffer from a brain disease called "schizophrenia," which can be effectively treated with certain chemicals; and I claim that the assertions of psychotics and psychiatrists alike are claims unsubstantiated by evidence. The point, however, is that psychiatrists have the power to accredit their own claims as scientific facts and rational treatments, discredit the claims of mental patients and psychiatric critics as delusions and denials, and enlist the coercive power of the state to impose their views on involuntary "patients."

The difference between a description and a claim is sometimes a matter of context rather than vocabulary. For example, the adjective "schizophrenic" may describe a man who asserts that his wife is trying to poison him (assuming that she is not); but it functions as a claim when, after shooting his wife, the killer's court-appointed lawyer, desperate to "defend" him (perhaps against his nominal client's wishes), claims that the illegal act was caused by schizophrenia and that the killer should therefore be "acquitted" and treated in a mental hospital, rather than punished by imprisonment. Because psychiatrists view mental diseases and their treatments as facts rather than as claims, they reject the possibility that the words "illness" and "treatment" may, as all words, have a literal or metaphorical usage. Although some psychiatrists now concede that hysteria is not a genuine disease, they are loath to acknowledge that it is a metaphorical disease, that is, not a disease at all. Similarly, many psychiatrists acknowledge that psychotherapy—that is, two or more persons listening and talking to one another—is radically unlike surgical and medical treatment. But, again, they do not acknowledge that it is a metaphorical treatment—that is, not a treatment at all.

Psychiatry is a branch of the law and a secular religion rather than a science or a therapy.

Finally, psychiatrists, who potentially always deal with involuntary patients, delight in the doubly self-serving claim that their patients suffer from brain diseases and that these (psychiatric) brain diseases (unlike others, such as Parkinsonism) render their sufferers incompetent. This claim lets psychiatrists pretend that coercion is a necessary, yet insignificant, element in contemporary psychiatric practice, a claim daily contradicted by reports in the newspapers. Understandably, psychiatrists prefer to occupy themselves with the putative brain diseases of persons called "mental patients" than with the proven social functions of psychiatric diagnoses, hospitals, and treatments.

Lawmakers do not discover prohibited rules of conduct, called crimes, they create them. Killing is not a crime; only unlawful killing is—for example, murder. Similarly, psychiatrists do not discover (mis)behaviors, called mental diseases, they create them. Killing is not a mental disease; only killing defined as due to mental illness is; schizophrenia thus "causes" hetero-homicide (not called "murder") and bipolar illness "causes" auto-homicide (called "suicide").

My point is that psychiatrists, who create diagnoses of mental diseases by giving disease names to personal (mis)conduct, function as legislators, not as scientists. It was this sort of diagnosis making alienists engaged in when they created masturbatory insanity; that Paul Eugen Bleuler engaged in when he

created schizophrenia; and that the task force committees of the American Psychiatric Association engage in when they construct new psychiatric diagnoses, such as body dysmorphic disorder, and deconstruct old ones, such as homosexuality.

I am not arguing that rule making, such as politicians engage in, is not important. I am merely insisting on the differences between phenomena and rules, science and law, cure and control. Treating the sick and punishing criminals are both necessary for maintaining the social order. Indeed, breakdown in the just enforcement of just laws is far more destructive to the social order than the absence of equitable access to effective medical treatment. The medical profession's traditional social mandate is healing the sick; the criminal justice system's, punishing the lawbreaker; and the psychiatric profession's, confining and controlling the "deviant" (ostensibly as diseased, supposedly for the purpose of treatment). This is why I regard psychiatry as a branch of the law and a secular religion, rather than a science or therapy.

I want to add a brief remark here on the so-called anti-psychiatry movement with which my name is often associated. As detailed elsewhere, I consider the term anti-psychiatry imprudent and the movement it names irresponsible. As a classical liberal, I support the rights of physicians to engage in mutually consenting psychiatric acts with other adults. By the same token, I object to involuntary psychiatric interventions, regardless of how they are justified. Psychiatrists *qua* physicians should never deprive individuals of their lives, liberties, and properties, even if the security of society requires that they engage in such acts. In adopting this view, I follow the example of the great Hungarian physician Ignaz Semmelweis who believed that obstetricians, *qua* physicians, should never infect their patients, even if the advancement of medical education requires that they do so.

I do not deny that involuntary psychiatric interventions might be justified vis-à-vis individuals declared to be legally incompetent, just as involuntary financial or medical interventions are justified under such circumstances. Individuals who are disabled by a stroke or are in a coma cannot discharge their duties or represent their desires. Accordingly, there are procedures for relieving them—with due process of law—of their rights and responsibilities as full-fledged adults. Although the persons entrusted with the task of reclassifying citizens from moral agents to wards of the state might make use of medical information, they should be lay persons (jurors) and judges, not physicians or mental health specialists. Their determination should be viewed as a legal and political procedure, not as a medical or therapeutic intervention.

I have sought to alert the professions as well as the public to the tendency in modern societies—whether capitalist or communist, democratic, or totalitarian—to reclassify deviant conduct as (mental) disease, deviant actor as (psychiatric) patient, and activities aimed at controlling deviants as therapeutic interventions. And I have warned against the dangers of the destruction of self-discipline and criminal sanctions which these practices create—specifically the replacing of penal sanctions with psychiatric coercions rationalized as "hospitalization" and "treatment." To describe the confusion arising from the use of the metaphorical term "mental disease," I have suggested the phrase "the myth of mental illness." For a political order that uses physicians and hospitals in place of policemen and prisons to coerce and confine miscreants and which justifies constraint and compulsion as therapy rather than punishment, I have proposed the name "therapeutic state."

The personal freedom of which the English and American people are justly proud rests on the assumption of a fundamental right to life, liberty, and property. This is why deprivations of life, liberty, and property have traditionally been regarded as punishments (execution, imprisonment, and the imposition of a fine), that is, legal and political acts whose lawful performance is delegated to specific agents of the state and is regulated by due process of law. No physician *qua* medical healer has the right to deprive another of life, liberty, or property. Formerly, when the clergy was allied with the state, a priest had the right to deprive a person of life and liberty. In the seventeenth century, the state began to transfer this role to psychiatrists (alienists or mad-doctors), who eagerly accepted the assignment and have served as state agents authorized to deprive persons of liberty under medical auspices. Now, we are witnessing a clamor for granting physicians the right to kill persons—an ostensibly medical intervention euphemized as "physician-assisted suicide."

It is a truism that the interests of the individual, the family, and the state often conflict. Medicalizing interpersonal conflicts, that is, disagreements among family members, the members of society, and between citizens and the state, threatens to destroy not only respect for persons as responsible moral agents, but also for the state as an arbiter and dispenser of justice. Let us never forget that the state is an organ of coercion with a monopoly on force—for good or ill. The more the state empowers doctors, the more physicians will strengthen the state (by authenticating political preferences as health values), and the more the resulting union of medicine and the state will enfeeble the individual (by depriving him of the right to reject interventions classified as therapeutic). If that is the kind of society we want, that is the kind we shall get—and deserve.

Who's Protecting Bad Doctors?

Judith Warner

Judith Warner, author of "Hillary Clinton: The Inside Story" (Signet Books), is a freelance writer based in New York City.

The fact that the United States is in dire need of a national health care plan is beyond dispute. That approximately 37 million people, the majority of them women and children, are without any form of health coverage is a national disgrace, as is the fact that health costs continue to skyrocket. Equally outrageous—despite all the ballyhoo about the superiority of U.S. health care providers—the present system makes it all too easy for unqualified and potentially dangerous doctors to practice medicine on unsuspecting patients.

At any moment, on any given day, countless doctors with long paper trails of serious malpractice charges are practicing with impunity, often protected by law from public scrutiny while a state medical board makes up its mind about what to do with them. All too often, the state does nothing or ends up doing too little too late. For medical consumers, who are systematically kept in the dark about doctors' malpractice and disciplinary records, too little too late can mean death.

"Malpractice is not an aberration. It's one of the leading health epidemics in this country," says Laura Wittkin, executive director of the National Center for Patients' Rights. "But unless there's a couple of hundred dead bodies around, the state does nothing." Wittkin's criticism is well grounded in fact. There are nearly 400,000 serious incidents of medical malpractice committed in U.S. hospitals annually—100,000 of which result in death. Yet in 1992 only 200 doctors out of the approximately 585,000 licensed physicians in the U.S. were disciplined on malpractice-related charges by state medical boards. It's obvious that the present system is not working. And as a result of this "health epidemic," unsuspecting patients are left vulnerable.

In July 1993 Guadalupe Negron, a 33-year-old Honduran immigrant, bled to death after a routine second-trimester abortion at the Metro Women's Center in Queens, New York. Her death appeared suspicious, but when investigators discovered that her attending physician had been Dr. David Benjamin, it became a scandal. Benjamin had a 12-year history of medical malfeasance. In 1985 New York State's medical board had found him guilty of mutilating and maiming 12 women during non-abortion-related gynecological surgery. He'd begun operations he didn't know how to finish, had sutured together unrelated parts of the body, and had performed unnecessary hysterectomies. In 1986 the state suspended his license for three months and put him on proba-

Countless doctors with long paper trails of serious malpractice charges are practicing with impunity.

tion. Benjamin then changed cities, changed his name, lied on an application for new hospital privileges (which was never checked), and went on to harm at least five more women during surgery. In June 1993 the board finally voted to revoke his medical license, but still allowed him to practice medicine while he prepared his appeal. One month later, Guadalupe Negron was dead.

Until recently, consumers in New York City could have been warned about Benjamin. But in June 1993 an appellate court ruled to prohibit the release of information about doctors charged with malfeasance until final disciplinary action is taken and the doctor has a chance to appeal. The result is that the kind of information that could have saved Negron's life is now inaccessible.

"Any doctor you go to today could be in a situation like Benjamin's, and you wouldn't ever know it," says Ilene Merdinger, a spokeswoman for the law firm representing Negron's family, which is currently mounting the first-ever negligence suit against the State of New York. "How many more doctors like Benjamin are there out there, freely victimizing patients because we're not privy to information about them?"

The problem is endemic to every state in the nation. State systems for regulating and disciplining doctors—usually run through one or more agencies linked to a state department of health—are disorganized, underfunded, understaffed, backlogged, and controlled largely by a powerful and hostile medical community.

"The system is not working well anywhere," says Arthur Levin, director of the Center for Medical Consumers. "The disciplinary process affords doctors every opportunity to come out O.K., and it's not in the public interest. That has a lot to do with the political influence of organized medicine and also reflects a more general psychological mind-set that bends over backward to be good to the physician. People tend to think of doctors as a valuable resource to the community and believe that every effort should be made to keep them in practice."

Even when the system works, it can still take up to two years or more to investigate complaints and bring charges, ranging from murder to Medicaid fraud. Lack of funding, repeated appeals, and endless logistical hurdles designed to protect doctors from the smear of false charges make the process even longer. And when the system doesn't work, there are cases like Benjamin's, or like that of Dr. Ivan C. Namihas, a Tustin, California, gynecologist. It took 22 years of complaints against Namihas, who is known to have mistreated or sexually abused patients in at least 140 cases, before the state revoked his license in 1992. In Oklahoma, Dr. Joe Bills Reynolds, an obstetrician and gynecologist, lost his license in the spring of 1990. That was two years after his hospital privileges had been suspended and his malpractice insurance canceled, and more than six months after his wife died on his in-office operating table from massive blood loss during liposuction.

Women are often most at risk, because so many of these bad doctors tend to cluster in women's specialties like gynecology or plastic surgery, in which procedures are routinely performed in unregulated outpatient settings. Women fall prey to botched surgical procedures, sexual abuse, unnecessary operations, and the overprescribing of drugs. And all too frequently, doctors ascribe psychological causes to women's physical complaints and treat them with Valium instead of running more medical tests. Says Merdinger, "We've seen cases of women with stomachaches going to the emergency room, where they're given Maalox and sent home, and the next morning they're dead."

Poor women are the most frequent users of hospital emergency rooms for family medical care, and as a result they suffer disproportionately from the frequent misdiagnoses committed there. Undocumented immigrants, fearful that hospitals will report them to the government, are the easy prey of inept, unscrupulous doctors, who set up shop in their neighborhoods and advertise in their native language newspapers. Native Americans living on reservations are at risk of being treated by doctors who, according to Charon Asetoyer, executive director of the Native American Women's Health Education Resource Center, would not otherwise be able to practice medicine in the U. S. at all. Asetoyer says the Indian Health Service (a federal agency) is notorious for hiring physicians who have so many malpractice suits and disciplinary actions against them that they can't practice in any state, so instead serve on Indian reservations that, as federal lands, are not subject to state regulations.

Although women have, in the past ten years, begun to take a much more active role in questioning their doctors and making choices about their medical care, their ability to protect themselves against shady practitioners has remained sorely limited. Despite years of lobbying at the state and federal levels by patients' rights groups, the most important information about who doctors are and what they've done wrong in the past is still off-limits to the public.

It isn't that hard to find out where a doctor went to medical school, was licensed, or is accredited. In all medical libraries and many large public libraries consumers can find this information in the *American Medical Directory* (which lists only members of the American Medical As-

The lack of public disclosure of information about dangerous doctors stems from a single source.

sociation) and the *Directory of Medical Specialists*. They can also call the American Board of Medical Specialties at (800) 776-CERT. State medical boards, the agencies responsible for licensing and disciplining doctors, can disclose if an action has been taken. But often finding out *what* disciplinary actions and malpractice suits have been filed is another story.

To investigate her doctor, a patient must find out which state agency is responsible for licensure and discipline. That isn't easy. In Florida, for example, licensing is the province of the state department of business and professional regulation, and disciplining is done by the board of medicine; in Michigan, requests go through the bureau of occupational and professional regulations. After finding the proper agency, she must know the right questions to ask. As a rule, if she doesn't specifically ask whether any disciplinary action has been taken, the agency won't tell. And it will only disclose *current* actions—no prior actions will be disclosed unless a complete history is requested. And she won't be told about action taken by another state unless her state is taking disciplinary action based upon it. "Consumers must be taught how to ask the questions," says patients' rights advocate Laura Wittkin. "The board may have an enormous amount of information, but if you don't ask, they'll never tell. They are far more an instrument of the medical community than advocates for consumers, and they have been very successful at keeping consumers from getting any information until the bitter end."

It shouldn't be this difficult: since September 1990, state medical boards have been required to report all their disciplinary actions against physicians, doctors' malpractice payments to patients, and disciplinary actions taken by hospitals to a single information clearinghouse—the National Practitioner Data Bank. The data bank was created by Congress in 1986 as a way to aid state medical boards in tracking and flagging repeat-offender doctors who jump from state to state, reestablishing themselves with new licenses each time they are barred from practicing. Founded over the vociferous opposition of the medical community, it was hailed as a way to protect consumers from the likes of such practitioners as the infamous Dr. Nabil Ghali, a gynecologist who was convicted in Kentucky in 1983 for having sex with a 14-year-old girl and who went on to practice and lose medical licenses in New York, Florida, Utah, California, and Ohio.

But consumers *don't* benefit from the data bank because the medical lobby made the law's passage contingent upon the stipulation that the information it contains *not* be available to the public. And too little is actually reported. Hospitals are required to report disciplinary actions taken against doctors when privileges are suspended for 30 days or more, so they frequently skirt the law by imposing 29-day suspensions. Doctors settle malpractice claims out of court and make their payments in the names of their insurance companies or group practices as a way to exempt themselves from being reported to the data bank. State boards are required to check an out-of-state doctor's record before granting licensing privileges, but they're not required to act upon what they find. And though boards are mandated to collect malpractice information on doctors, few will release it to consumers.

The lack of public disclosure of information about dangerous doctors stems from a single source: powerful political pressure upon state and federal agencies by physicians and their trade groups, like the AMA and state medical societies. At its national meeting in 1993, the AMA voted to recommend that the National Practitioner Data Bank be disbanded. The AMA's stance is not surprising given that the organization has long argued against public disclosure of doctors' records on the grounds that consumers do not understand them and that it unfairly damages physicians' reputations.

"What they're saying is that the reputation and positions of physicians are more important than the public interest," says consumer advocate Levin. "And that's the underlying political and philosophical difference here: Whose well-being comes first, physicians' or patients'?"

The biggest losers in this tug-of-war—now weighted strongly in favor of physicians—are women. And under President Clinton's proposed managed health care plan, things may get worse. The plan will most likely bind everyone seeking affordable health care into HMO-type systems that will severely limit choice of doctors. Although no formal statistics are available yet, patients' rights advocates say that there is strong anecdotal evidence to indicate a high incidence of misdiagnoses and inadequate care in HMOs, where the bottom line is, ever and always, profit-making.

Like hospitals, HMOs are supposed to do periodic background checks on their doctors, but there's no standard government regulation stipulating how frequently or how well they must do them. Two years ago Aetna Health Plans of New York, one of the state's largest HMOs, got a slap on the wrist for failing to adequately check and recredentialize its doctors. This came as a result of a complaint filed by a patient who discovered that her obstetrician, Dr. John Poglinco, was neither a member (as he claimed) of the American College of Obstetrics and Gynecology, nor registered to practice in the state, and had lost all hospital privileges for delivering babies. Aetna had not checked his credentials since 1986.

Although President Clinton had talked about requiring regional health plans to issue "report cards" on their doctors and hinted he might try to open up the National Practitioners Data Bank to the public, there was no mention of this in the current health plan at press time. And consumer advocates are skeptical about it being put forward in the future. Says Levin, "It's hard to believe the administration would go to battle on the National Practitioner Data Bank when any such provision would be so violently opposed by organized medicine, and when they've been trying so hard to play up to organized medicine."

In fact, the AMA, which vociferously opposes the release of malpractice information, has presented its own compromise plan. The organization proposes creating an information system within the data bank, which would provide consumers with information only on a doctor's licensure, education, and certification status—information, in other words, that any patient could get from reading the plaques in a physician's office. And there has been no further discussion of report cards. All of which leaves consumers no better off when it comes to ensuring that we not fall prey to dangerous doctors. If we are to avoid little more than a Band-Aid approach to the problem, now is the time to press for making the data bank live up to our needs.

Poverty and Inequality

It is not clear whether poverty is the result or cause of inequality but where one is found, so is the other. Most individuals, regardless of how little or how much they have, would agree that poverty is bad, but they do not necessarily agree that inequality is bad. To those raised in capitalistic societies, inequality is seen as the driving force behind the American success story. The ability to improve one's economic position, the chance to move up through corporate hierarchies, and the opportunity to have access to the best that life offers has made America great. Conversely, the lack of any real upward mobility is the direct cause of the fall of Communism. It is not inequality that is bad, but the degree of inequality. It is when the gap between the top and bottom becomes extreme, when the number of individuals at the bottom greatly exceeds that of those at the top, and when the opportunity for improving one's self is removed, that questions of inequality as a social problem emerge.

President Clinton has vowed to end welfare as we know it, a declaration that appeals to many Americans. But his ability to achieve his vow is highly problematic. "Old Traps, New Twists" identifies six traps that have frustrated all prior attempts at welfare reform and assesses the probability that President Clinton, or anyone, will ever be able to accomplish meaningful reform.

"Does Welfare Bring More Babies?" Many critics of the existing welfare system argue that it does. But empirical evidence does not indicate this. The author discovered, after conducting detailed statistical analysis of data collected on African Americans, that moderate differences in welfare benefits produce only small differences in childbearing behaviors.

"Going Private" has been proposed as one way of reducing the cost of doing much of the business currently conducted by state and federal governments. Businessman and presidential candidate Ross Perot and others argue that private industry can do almost anything better and cheaper than most government bureaucracies. This may be true in some cases, but the author argues that cheaper is not always the best when the lives of poor, sick, aged, and extremely vulnerable people are involved.

"No Exit" is what many individuals trapped in isolated urban ghettos discover. No matter what they desire, no matter how hard they work, they cannot escape the inner city environment of unemployment, crime, violence, drugs, and inadequate services. This article examines the social conditions that have turned their American dream into a nightmare.

"When Problems Outrun Policy" examines the effect of economic growth and inflation on American lifestyles. Many Americans find their lifestyles essentially unaffected, but growing numbers are finding it difficult to stay above the poverty line. The author discusses why this trend is occurring and what difficult choices and changes must be made to reverse it.

Looking Ahead: Challenge Questions

How is the distribution of poverty changing?

What are the major problems facing a president who wants to eliminate or reduce poverty significantly?

What societal-level problems are ensuring that the poor stay poor?

What problems must President Clinton resolve if he is serious about "reinventing" government and winning the war on poverty?

How might programs designed to eliminate or alleviate problems associated with poverty actually perpetuate them?

How might privatization hurt those it is designed to help?

Are private organizations always better than public ones?

Why will many students find it difficult to rise above their parents in wealth, status, and influence/power?

How would sociologists differ in the ways they go about studying problems of inequality and poverty?

What are the conflicts in rights, values, obligations, and harms that seem to be underlying each of the issues covered in this section?

OLD TRAPS NEW TWISTS

Kent Weaver

Kent Weaver, a senior fellow in the Brookings Governmental Studies program, is the author of Automatic Government: The Politics of Indexation. *This article is adapted from his Brookings book,* Welfare Reform.

One of President Clinton's boldest and most popular electoral pledges was to "end welfare as we know it." He promised to place time limits on receipt of benefits in the Aid to Families with Dependent Children program and to require recipients to undergo training and move into public- and private-sector jobs within two years. His objectives are clear: to give a new set of incentives to welfare recipients, lessen long-term dependence on welfare, move poor families into America's economic mainstream, and reduce poverty among American children.

The president's call for welfare reform should not come as a surprise. Rising AFDC costs and caseloads and increasing percentages of out-of-wedlock births have widened the perception that current policies have failed and have increased public and policymaker interest in reform.

Welfare reform is an unusually knotty policymaking task, however. Critics of AFDC have long lamented the "welfare traps" that bedevil efforts to help poor families. David Ellwood, co-chair of the administration's task force on welfare reform, has pointed out three "helping conundrums"—problems with no satisfactory solutions. First, providing support to poor families is likely to reduce the rewards to work, as well as work effort—in some cases, increased work actually makes them worse off. Second, focusing support on families most likely to need help, single-parent families, can encourage out-of-wedlock births and divorce or separation. Finally, targeting aid to those who need it most tends to isolate recipients politically, while diminishing the relative status of those who are doing a bit better—notably working, two-parent families.

That these traps in policy design are a serious obstacle to welfare reform is widely acknowledged. Less often recognized is that reform poses a set of *political* traps, outlined below, that are equally serious and hard to avoid. All these traps have contributed mightily to the repeated failure or watering down of past efforts to reform AFDC. And all loom large in the current round of reform, often with new and more perilous twists. Thus while the public may be ready for a big change, it is far from certain that policymakers will be able to deliver it. And if welfare reform does get through Congress, it is far from clear that it will take a form that will aid poor children.

The Clinton Proposal and Its Rivals

Although details of the administration's plan remain to be worked out, its outlines are clear. Efforts to establish paternity and enforce child support payments will be stepped up. Teenage mothers will be required, in most circumstances, to live with their parents rather than set up new households. AFDC recipients will sign contracts that specify reciprocal obligations: the state will provide education and job training; the recipient will participate in these programs and take a job when it becomes available. After two years, recipients who have not found private-sector jobs will take community service jobs. These new obligations will be phased in gradually, beginning with younger AFDC mothers, in a bow to the budgetary reality that it is cheaper to pay benefits than provide jobs and support services, notably child care and transportation. Finally, state welfare offices will be reoriented—away from checking on eligibility and toward helping recipients gain job skills and find work.

The administration does not have the field to itself. The House Republican Welfare Reform Task Force has proposed a more expensive package with a greater emphasis on work requirements. They would pay for it primarily by cutting off most means-tested benefits to legal residents of the United States who are not citizens. Another Republican proposal, backed by the conservative group Empower America, would cut off all AFDC, food stamp, and housing benefits to unmarried mothers under age 21 and encourage states to establish "orphanages" for children and group homes for unwed mothers. Both Republican plans would cap most spending programs for low-income Americans.

The shape—indeed the existence—of any final legislation depends on how these proposals thread their way through the political traps in store for welfare reformers.

The Dual-Clientele Trap

Perhaps the central political problem for American family support policy is the dual-clientele trap: policymakers can't help poor children (which is popular) without also aiding their parents (which is unpopular); they can't dramatically increase disincentives for out-of-wedlock childbearing without also risking making poor children worse off. Recent welfare reform debates have featured a continuing clash between concerns about ensuring the welfare of children and concerns about the behavior (and how to alter it) of parents and prospective parents. That the AFDC caseload, like the poverty population generally, is made up heavily of racial and ethnic minorities has made the debate even more contentious and inflammatory.

Many of those focusing on parental behavior are convinced that stiff punitive reforms in AFDC's incentives structure are necessary to force recipients to change their behavior. Punitive incentives, however, would seriously harm those unable or unwilling to make the necessary changes. More important, they would hurt their children. This prospect has, until recently, kept discussions of the most draconian welfare reforms—for example, Charles Murray's proposal to end AFDC—on the fringes of the welfare debate. But as illegitimacy rates continue to rise and other solutions elude reformers, proponents of punitive policies have begun to dominate the public debate and to deride those who voice concern for children as "paleo-liberals." The administration has not bought into this rhetoric, but its talk of "ending welfare as we know it" has allowed concern over children to be nearly forgotten in the focus on parents' behavior. By soft-pedaling children's welfare, it has facilitated the weakening of the political dual-clientele trap without changing the social reality that precipitous, poorly thought out welfare reforms could lead to a social disaster for many poor children.

The Perverse Incentives Trap

The perverse incentives trap flows from the helping conundrums noted earlier. Giving cash to unmarried mothers lowers their incentives to marry or forgo childbearing. Providing them with Medicaid health insurance or child care makes it harder for them to leave AFDC and accept low-paying private-sector jobs that offer no such benefits: if they do, they may suffer real income declines.

Perverse incentives also feed on themselves: efforts to eliminate or reduce one set can lead to a new set. For example, providing temporary access to Medicaid or child care benefits to families who leave welfare helps them make the transition—but it also encourages people who lose their jobs to go on welfare to take advantage of these benefits before returning to work. The fact is that no plausible reform of the existing system can avoid creating some new perverse incentives or worsening some existing ones.

The political trap posed by perverse incentives is this: if policymakers ignore those incentives in their reform proposals, public confidence is likely to falter when critics of reform point them out—as they surely will. But actually coming to grips with perverse incentives may be very expensive and may make reform harder to pass, as scarce resources are diverted from core reform initiatives.

The Clinton plan encounters the perverse incentives trap in several ways. First, it relies on health care reform to extend health insurance to the working poor,

WHY WELFARE IS SO HARD TO REFORM IN 1994

thus easing the way for AFDC recipients to leave welfare for low-paying jobs. But this seems to argue for delaying action on AFDC, because the projected costs and caseload estimates for welfare reform are likely to be higher (and thus harder to sell politically and harder to get through the budget scorekeeping process) now than they would be after a comprehensive health care reform package is in place—if that ever happens. Second, recent drafts of the Clinton plan propose substantial spending on child care for the working poor to lessen AFDC's attractions for this group. But spending more on the working poor will not please lawmakers who want to concentrate resources on current recipients. Nor will it suit those fearful of making more people dependent on government aid or those who simply don't want to spend more money.

The Money Trap

The AFDC money trap is simple: any reform likely to improve the prospects for poor children means spending more money than the public thinks is necessary or Congress wants to spend. Most people already think that too many people receive AFDC and that it is too costly. They think welfare reform should save money immediately. But few reform proposals would do that. Almost inevitably, they require at least short-term spending increases for education, job training, or other services. But to increase spending, government must increase taxes, increase the deficit, or cut other programs—all anathema to legislators. So even when Congress adopts welfare reform initiatives, they are underfunded—and therefore hobbled from the start in achieving their goals. The JOBS program of the Family Support Act of 1988, for example, was supposed to have a dramatic impact on the AFDC clientele while increasing spending only $3 billion over five years for education, training, and employment.

The money trap is made even worse this year by the financing proposals already on the table. The proposal by the Republican Welfare Reform Task Force would pay for its work program by stopping almost all means-tested transfers and social services to noncitizens, both legal and illegal. The Clinton plan is likely to call for a more targeted restriction on Supplemental Security Income benefits for "sponsored aliens"—family members who join earlier immigrants and are eligible, after five years, to apply for the SSI program. But both proposals raise serious political problems. States fear that they will inherit the job of caring for the immigrants. And the Hispanic Caucus in the House opposes the proposals because many affected immigrants are from Latin America.

The Overselling Trap

With AFDC so unpopular, its clientele so politically weak, and the record of derailed reform so long, legislators are reluctant to undertake reform for only modest policy gains. Thus to get welfare reform on the agenda, much less pass it, advocates must promise far more than they can deliver.

But overselling has serious costs. Not only does it threaten the credibility of specific reform proposals, it also increases public cynicism about *any* reform. If reform didn't live up to expectations last time, why will it do so this time? Thus politicians grow even more reluctant to wade into the welfare reform swamp, necessitating yet more overpromising—and so the cycle goes.

The overselling trap this time began with the president's promise to end welfare as we know it and to limit recipients to two years of benefits before being expected to work. The image conveyed to the public was that of an income transfer program being transformed into a work program. But the reality is different. Many welfare mothers will not be expected to work, either because they are caring for infants or because they are seriously disabled or care for children who are. But the biggest hurdle is money. Providing jobs, even low-skilled jobs, takes lots of it—upwards of $20 billion a year for administration, transportation, and child care for all AFDC families. Thus recent drafts of the Clinton plan call for a slow phase-in and many exemptions. By 1999 fewer than 170,000 parents—out of almost 5 million AFDC families— are expected to be at work in government-provided or -subsidized jobs. Such phase-ins may be fiscally and administratively prudent, but they will not end welfare as we know it. Pressure will no doubt be felt in Congress to increase work requirements while simultaneously lowering funding levels.

The Fragile-Coalitions Trap

Too weak to make its own way, AFDC is also too unpopular to be quietly tucked into a legislative package featuring more popular programs. Its precarious political situation, together with the money trap and the perverse incentives trap, dooms reformers to face the fragile-coalitions trap: no legislative majority can be built for reform without including lawmakers who disagree with some part of the package and who would probably defect if a separate vote were held on that part. The risk of a collapsing coalition can be minimized if reform sponsors can limit amendments, but they usually cannot, especially in the Senate.

Clinton's coalition is particularly prone to collapse. Child advocacy groups may oppose the plan if they think it will deprive many families of cash benefits without guaranteeing a job or if it fails to provide adequate child care. Conservative Democrats may not approve its slow phase-in of work requirements. The Hispanic Caucus may oppose its financing provisions. Public-sector unions worry that a large public jobs program would displace their workers. Others fear that it could turn into another CETA public service employment program, which was so unpopular that it, almost alone among social programs, was killed outright by the Reagan administration in 1981. Limiting payments to women who have children while on AFDC is likely to be opposed by right-to-life groups, who fear it would encourage abortions, *and* by pro-choice groups in states that do not allow Medicaid funding of abortions.

How these conflicting pressures would affect lawmakers' votes is hard to predict, but they could certainly provide ample reason for wavering legislators to oppose welfare reform. Neither a generous nor a highly punitive version of reform is likely to command a congressional majority, and it is far from clear that there is adequate middle ground for significant reform. Pressure for more punitive, less expensive reform is likely to grow if Congress waits until after the fall congressional elections, when Republicans are likely to gain seats, at least in the House.

The Federalism Trap

States have great leeway both in the AFDC benefits they pay and in the obligations they impose. They can also apply for waivers to deviate from existing national standards. That freedom allows states to be responsive to local conditions, such as differences in the cost of living, and to experiment to find out how changes in incentives affect recipients' behavior. Wisconsin, for example, is testing two-year limits on benefits. New Jersey denies AFDC mothers additional payments for children conceived while the mothers are on the program.

But allowing state flexibility also poses a trap: it can subject individuals to extremely unequal treatment based on where they live, and it can start a "race to the bottom," as states scale back benefits and impose ever more onerous obligations to avoid becoming welfare magnets.

THE KEY TO MAKING PROGRESS IS SUSTAINED WORK—AND NOT JUST BY WELFARE RECIPIENTS, BUT BY THOSE WHO DESIGN AND IMPLEMENT POLICY.

The extent to which this federalism trap leads to reforms that hurt the poor depends in part on the other traps. If state budgets are tight—as many are because of exploding Medicaid spending—state innovations are more likely to emphasize punitive measures. And Washington's leeway in rejecting punitive state reforms will be affected by commitments it has made. Having promised to "end welfare as we know it," will the administration be able to reject state efforts to impose time limits without providing jobs to those that hit the limits?

Prognosis and Recommendations

What then is the prognosis for this round of welfare reform? And what *should* welfare reform include and exclude? By their very nature, the political traps in welfare policymaking cannot be avoided. Choices must be made. And there is no such thing as welfare reform that does not pose risks for the welfare of children. But by choosing carefully, the administration and Congress can both improve the prospects for maneuvering through the traps to secure significant reform legislation *and* improve the prospect that reform will genuinely improve the life chances for poor children.

While Congress must make choices on hundreds of specific issues, four broad possibilities seem most plausible as outcomes in this round of reform. The first, and most likely, is stalemate. Second is a phased work and time limits plan, similar to the Clinton plan and perhaps allowing more flexibility to the states. Third is a stronger set of work requirements and time limits, along the lines of the House Republican task force plan. Fourth is legislation heavy on sanctions and time limits and light on funding to finance work.

Among these options the last comes closest to ending welfare as we know it, but it poses the greatest risk of leaving many poor children destitute and homeless. Nor do conservative prescriptions to rely on residential facilities (orphanages for non-orphans) for children taken away from indigent mothers make this option more palatable, even if the process of becoming homeless were an efficient way to sort unfit mothers from fit ones. Running group facilities on a large scale is difficult, and financially strapped states lack the resources to make them work well. The American experience in running programs ranging from mental hospitals to reform schools to foster care suggests that such "orphanages" would more closely resemble Bleak House than Boys Town.

The first option, stalemate, is little better than the last, if for no other reason than that it is likely to end up in the same place. By reinforcing the perception that nothing is being done about welfare, stalemate may eventually lead to radical, heavily punitive reform.

That leaves options two and three. Option three has much to recommend it—but also a powerful argument against it. We don't know much about how time limits are likely to work. Imposing them on a nationwide scale is "Thelma and Louise" policymaking: shoot without considering the consequences, then drive off a cliff. Experiments on time limits are under way, but the results are not yet in. What combinations of time limits and sanctions for noncompliance work best, for example? Which segments of the welfare population should be targeted first? How much is homelessness likely to increase? At present, decisions about these issues are likely to be the product of guesswork informed by varying combinations of theory and prejudice, rather than by solid data. To minimize the risk that this giant policy leap into the unknown will result in social disaster, we should be cautious in both policy design and implementation.

The second possibility, cautious and phased reform, is thus the best option—but not necessarily the most likely one. What can the administration do to improve the prospects for its plan?

First, it can change its rhetoric. With its promise to end welfare as we know it, the administration has fallen into the overselling trap in a big way. At this point, the best thing it can do is emphasize the need to make solid progress on a problem that cannot be ended overnight. It can also reemphasize the importance of children's welfare.

The administration can do much to avoid the fragile-coalitions trap. It can state, as it did with health care, a set of bottom-line conditions—in particular, adequate funding for child care and training to accompany any broad-scale time limits—that, if not met, will provoke a veto. The risk is that the minimum will become the maximum that Congress will pass. But at least such a move would ensure that welfare reform does not become a political cover for abandoning poor children.

The administration should also recognize that the lack of money to undertake a nationwide time-limits-plus-jobs program presents an opportunity as well as a problem. In the absence of good data on time limits, the administration should continue to encourage experimentation by states. It should make sure the results are carefully evaluated so that the lessons learned can be applied more broadly. But it should also clearly signal the sorts of state plans that it cannot accept—in particular, statewide time limits on benefits without an adequate jobs program at the end.

The problem of welfare dependency has, in short, no magic solutions. The key to making progress, as conservatives are fond of saying, is sustained work—and not just by welfare recipients, but by those who design and implement policy.

DOES WELFARE BRING MORE BABIES?

CHARLES MURRAY

Charles Murray is Bradley fellow at the American Enterprise Institute.

ast October, I published a long piece on the op-ed page of the *Wall Street Journal* entitled "The Coming White Underclass." Its thesis was that white illegitimacy—22 percent of all live births as of the latest (1991) figures—is now moving into the same dangerous range that prompted the young Daniel Patrick Moynihan to write about the breakdown of the black family in 1964, and that the ensuing social deterioration in lower-class communities may be as devastating for whites in the 1990s as it was for blacks in the 1960s. The centerpiece of my solution was to abolish all federal support for single women with children.

The response was, for me, unique. It is not just that the piece aroused more intense reaction than anything I have written since *Losing Ground*, but that so many people agreed with me. This is not normal. After I publish something, my mail and phone calls are usually split about 50/50 pro and con. This time, almost everyone agreed that the problem of illegitimacy was just as bad as I described, and a surprising number of people, including some ordinarily prudent people in the public eye, endorsed my radical notion of ending welfare altogether.

All this leads me to believe that illegitimacy is about to replace abortion as the next great national social debate. It should; not because the nation spends too much on welfare but because, as Moynihan said first and best, a community that allows a large number of young men to grow up without fathers "asks for and gets chaos." I believe it is not hyperbole but sober fact that the current levels of illegitimacy already threaten the institutions necessary to sustain a free society.

And so I want to end welfare. But this raises an obvious question: do we have any reason to believe that ending welfare will in fact cause a large-scale reduction in illegitimacy? Does welfare cause illegitimacy?

The answer has seemed self-evident to people ranging from the man in the street to Nobel laureate economists. The answer has not been nearly so clear, however, to social scientists who have studied the problem, nor has the search for an answer been conducted with stately scholarly detachment. It has instead been a hard-fought battle stretching back many years. Almost everyone has brought convictions about what the answer ought to be, for few issues have been so politically charged. But with a few lapses, the combatants have played by the technical rules in making their points, and, after all this time, we have learned at least a few things on which we can agree.

Two detailed reviews summarize the academic evidence. One, by Brown University economist Robert Moffitt, is called "Incentive Effects of the U.S. Welfare System: A Review," and it appeared in the *Journal of Economic Literature* in March 1992. I wrote the other one, called "Welfare and the Family: The U.S. Experience," as part of a special issue of the *Journal of Labor Economics* in January 1993, devoted to a set of articles comparing the American and Canadian social policy sponsored by the William H. Donner Foundation.

What follows summarizes the major area of agreement that has developed over the last 10 years—necessarily simplifying many findings and ignoring nuances. Then I turn to the major remaining area of disagreement. It brings to the attention of a general audience—for the first time, to my knowledge—a major technical error in the understanding of black illegitimacy that has large consequences for the subsequent debate. Bluntly: an important and commonly used argument of those who say that welfare does not cause illegitimacy is 180 degrees wrong.

Where Analysts Agree: Studies of Differences Among States

If the agreement could be summed up in a single sentence, it is that moderate differences in welfare benefits produce some differences in childbearing behavior, but only small ones. The main research strategy for reaching this conclusion has been to explore the effects of variations in AFDC (Aid to Families with Dependent Children) benefits across states. The hypothesis has been that since benefits vary widely, there should be differences in childbearing behavior as well, if indeed welfare is a culprit in producing illegitimacy.

Back in 1983, David Ellwood and Mary Jo Bane—both now senior officials in Clinton's Department of Health and Human Services—wrote the early version of a paper (still being circulated in typescript) during the debate over *Losing Ground* that everyone interpreted as proving that welfare doesn't cause increases in illegitimacy. That's not exactly what the analysis found—their approach to the issue was indirect and used a methodology so complex that evaluating the results is difficult even for specialists—but "Ellwood and Bane" is nevertheless still cited in the media as the definitive study that welfare does not affect illegitimacy.

Since then, several studies have explored the issue more directly, and the consensus has shifted to a tentative conclusion that welfare is implicated, but not dramatically. The results from the recent studies have many differences, and it would be unrealistic to try to draw a consensus from them about the magnitude of the effect of welfare. One study found a fairly large effect on childbearing behavior (for example, a predicted increase of 16 percent in the probability of teen births if welfare benefits rose 20 percent), but the effect was statistically insignificant. (This can happen when samples are small or the variation in results is very large.) Another found an effect that was in the same ballpark (a 6 percent increase in childbearing by unmarried women in response to a 10 percent increase in welfare benefits) and was also statistically significant. Other studies have found statistically significant effects without reporting the magnitude.

Until recently, studies of this issue have concluded that the effects of welfare are much easier to find among whites than among blacks. In two of the studies mentioned above, all of the apparent effect of differing welfare benefits on childbearing behavior was accounted for by the behavior of whites. An additional study that was limited to black teenagers found only a small, statistically insignificant effect.

But the situation is changing. A recent detailed study by Mark Fossett and Jill Kiecolt in *Journal of Marriage and the Family* using 1980 census data found a substantial and consistent relationship between the size of public assistance payments and illegitimacy among black women ages 20–24, even after controlling for a wide variety of economic, social, and demographic factors. Why did this study find a relationship where others had not? Partly because the analysis was more tightly focused than the others, using metropolitan areas rather than states; partly because the study focused on a particular

IF THE AREA OF AGREEMENT [IN THE WELFARE/ ILLEGITIMACY DEBATE] COULD BE SUMMED UP IN A SINGLE SENTENCE, IT IS THAT MODERATE DIFFERENCES IN WELFARE BENEFITS PRODUCE SOME DIFFERENCES IN CHILDBEARING BEHAVIOR, BUT ONLY SMALL ONES.

age group (women ages 20–24) instead of lumping all women together. Much more work remains to be done regarding black illegitimacy and welfare, but the best bet at this time is that the results for blacks and whites will converge. Using what the social scientists call "cross-sectional data"—comparing different places at the same historical moment—it seems likely that welfare will be found to cause some portion of illegitimacy, but not a lot.

The area of agreement, limited though it may sound, has important policy implications. Even taking the studies showing the largest statistically significant effect of welfare on childbearing, there is no reason to suppose that reducing welfare benefits by 10 percent will produce more than about a 6 percent drop in

childbearing among single women. This is not enough to make much difference in anything. More generally, if you were to ask scholars of various political viewpoints in the welfare/illegitimacy debate about the prospective effects of other welfare proposals that have been in the news recently—stopping the increase in benefits that kicks in when a second child is born, toughening workfare requirements, linking welfare to school attendance, and so forth—almost all of us would be pessimistic. We have different reasons for thinking that such changes would be good or bad, but the available data do not give much cause to think that such small changes will produce more than small effects.

Where Analysts Disagree: Variation Across Time

The favored way of examining the effects of welfare, taking advantage of the natural variation in AFDC payments across states, has a number of defects.

One problem with drawing comparisons across states is that state-by-state differences in welfare benefits are not so great as they seem. When you are first told that Louisiana has an average monthly AFDC payment of $169 and California has a monthly payment of $640 (the 1990 figures), the difference looks huge. But some federal benefits (such as food stamps) are more generous in low AFDC states, and Medicaid is available everywhere. Adding in everything, the proportional differences in the welfare packages available in different states shrink. And when you then put those differences in terms of the local economy, the difference nearly disappears. When the General Accounting Office compared the value of welfare packages in 13 locations across the country in the late 1970s, when state-by-state AFDC differences were near their peak, the agency found that the San Francisco package turned out to provide an income equivalent to 66 percent of the median household income in San Francisco, while the New Orleans package provided an income equivalent to 65 percent of the median household income in New Orleans. Should we be surprised to find that welfare differences between Louisiana and San Francisco do not produce much difference in out-of-wedlock childbearing?

Another problem is that a powerful factor masks the effects of welfare on blacks when scholars base the analysis on states. The black-white difference in illegitimacy goes back to the earliest post-Civil War data. No scholar has ever succeeded in explaining away this racial difference with any combination of economic, social, or educational control variables. The residual difference is astonishingly large. In a large national database (the National Longitudinal Study of Youth), the probability that a baby will be born to a single woman is more than twice as high for blacks as whites *after* controlling for age, education, socioeconomic background, and poverty. For reasons that are still not understood, something in black culture tolerates or encourages birth out of wedlock at higher rates than apply to white culture in any given year, and this has been true before and after welfare was introduced. The problem is that "black culture" (a term I am using because no one knows how to describe it more specifically) is not spread evenly across the United States. The states in which blacks have the very lowest illegitimacy ratios are places like Idaho, Montana, North and South Dakota, Alaska, Hawaii, New Hampshire, and Maine, where AFDC payments are often well

above the national average, but a very small black population lives in the midst of a dominating white culture (with its much lower illegitimacy ratios). Most of the states with the very lowest AFDC payments are in the Deep South, where blacks not only constitute a major portion of the population, but are densely concentrated in given areas—also, in other words, where whatever-it-is about black culture that produces high illegitimacy is likely to permeate the world in which black youngsters grow up. In statistical terms, this means that a great deal of noise is introduced when one analyzes the effect of varying AFDC payments. The same data that show no relationship between welfare and illegitimacy among blacks across states suddenly show such a relationship when one controls for the size and density of the black population.

The main problem with comparisons across states is that they ignore the overriding historical reality that welfare went up everywhere in the United States in a concentrated period of time, producing an overall national change that dwarfs the importance of between-state differences. Focusing on differences between states ignores the main effect.

Even when one takes a historical perspective, the story is a complex one. Here,

pictorially, is the main battleground in the debate over whether welfare causes illegitimacy (see Figure 1).

There are many things to argue about in this figure. Probably the one you have heard most often involves the size of the welfare package. I have shown it as a combination of AFDC, food stamps, Medicaid, and public housing subsidies, using conservative methods for valuing these components. Those who argue for an expansion of welfare benefits would have shown a much different figure, showing just the AFDC benefit, which in real terms has retreated to 1950s levels.

But to focus on just the AFDC cash payment is an example of the bogus part of the welfare/illegitimacy debate that most parties to the debate are now beyond, at least when they talk among themselves. Statements such as "welfare benefits are now back to 1950s levels" often show up in congressional testimony and the network news shows, but no serious student will deny that food stamps, Medicaid, and housing benefits are part of the relevant package available to a young woman with a baby and that those have expanded dramatically, along with a hodge podge of other benefits both federal (the Women, Infants, and Children's Supplemental Feeding Program, for example) and state or municipal (heating fuel subsidies, eviction protection, for example). Arguments about the specific value of Medicaid and public housing subsidies could result in minor shifts in the trend line shown in the figure, but the overall shape must remain the same by any method of computation: a very large increase in the last half of the 1960s, a smaller drop in real value in the last half of the 1970s (because of inflation—the nominal value of benefits continued to rise), and only small changes since the early 1980s, when inflation subsided. This basic shape of the trend in welfare benefits sparks the authentic part of the debate, which may be summarized as follows.

Looking at the figure, we see that the real value of the AFDC benefit first available in 1936 begins to rise in the mid-1940s. By the end of the 1940s, the illegitimacy ratio begins a modest rise too. The increase in AFDC steepens somewhat in the mid-1950s, and within a few years the slope of the illegitimacy ratio steepens as well. Then in the mid-

FIGURE 1
WELFARE BENEFITS AND ILLEGITIMACY
A SIMPLE COMPARISON

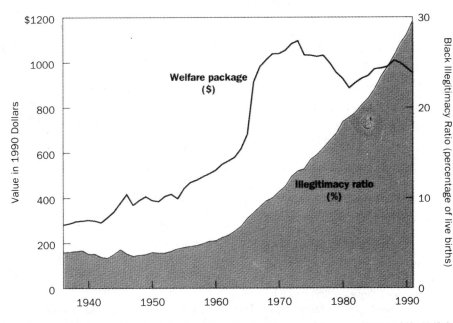

Source: Illegitimacy data since 1960: National Center for Health Statistics, "Advance Report of Final Natality Statistics," *Monthly Vital Statistics Report*, vol. 42, no. 3(S) (Sept. 9, 1993), table 16, and comparable tables in earlier volumes. Data prior to 1960: National Center for Health Statistics. *Vital Statistics*. Computation of the welfare package uses budget data from U.S. Bureau of the Census on AFDC, food stamps, public housing, and Medicaid, *Statistical Abstract of the United States*. The method of computation is described in Charles Murray, "Welfare and the Family: The American Experience," *Journal of Labor Economics*, vol. 11, no. 1, part 2, (Jan. 1993).

1960s the trend lines for both the value of the welfare package and illegitimacy shoot sharply upward. All of this is consistent with an argument that welfare is an important cause of illegitimacy.

But there is another side to this story, as shown in the graph after the early 1970s. After 1973, the value of the welfare package begins to drop, while illegitimacy continues to increase. This is inconsistent with a simple relationship of welfare to illegitimacy. Why didn't illegitimacy decrease a few years after the value of welfare began to decline?

At this point, the published research literature is little help. The "research," if it may be called that, has consisted mostly of pointing to the part of the graph that is consistent with one's position. But the contending parties in the debate must hold certain underlying assumptions about how causation is going to work in such a situation. Let's suppose you want to argue that the trend in illegitimacy should have flattened and reversed when the real value of welfare benefits stopped climbing. It seems to me that this implies two assumptions: (1) fertility behavior is highly sensitive to incremental changes in welfare benefits, independent of existing fertility trends among single women, and (2) young women accurately and quickly discount nominal increases in welfare according to changes in the Consumer Price Index.

I do not find either of those assumptions plausible. In the late 1970s, social

I WAS PERSUADED BY THE EVIDENCE THAT A CASE COULD NOT BE MADE THAT WELFARE CAUSED MORE ILLEGITIMATE BIRTHS, ONLY THAT WELFARE RAISED THE PROBABILITY THAT A GIVEN BIRTH WOULD BE ILLEGITIMATE. I WAS WRONG.

scientists knew that the real value of the welfare benefit was declining, but the young woman in the street probably did not. She was, after all, seeing her friends on welfare get checks that were larger every year, and health care and housing benefits that were more important every year as prices went up.

People like me also have to meet a burden, however. The main one, as I see it, is to spell out how a complex causal sequence is working, for, clearly, a simple causal link (fertility behavior among single women goes up and down with the value of the welfare check) doesn't work. One of the key features of my explanation is the assumption that many of the social restraints on illegitimacy erode as out-of-wedlock births become more common. Thus we may argue that the very large increase in benefits in the 1960s was indeed a major culprit in jacking up the illegitimacy ratio, but that the increased prevalence took on a life of its own in the 1970s. I find this plausible but, obviously, many who use the 1970s as evidence that welfare does not cause illegitimacy must not find it plausible. Here, the prescription to improve the quality of the debate is for both sides to spell out the assumptions that go into their causal arguments and test them against the data.

The Great Black Fertility Illusion

This brings us to the issue I mentioned earlier, that on one argument crucial to the debate, the accepted wisdom is 180 degrees wrong. It involves black illegitimacy, which has always been at the center of public concern about illegitimacy, and at the center of debate about causes. Many of you who have followed the welfare debate will recognize it, for the argument is made frequently and volubly. It goes like this:

Yes, the *proportion* of black children born to single women started to shoot up rapidly during the 1960s. But during that same period, the *incidence* of births among single black women was actually going down. If the increases in welfare during the 1960s had such terrible effects, why were fewer single black women having babies? Here are the trend lines for the proportion (represented by the line labeled *proportion*) and incidence (represented by the line labeled *incidence*) (see Figure 2).

As one writer put it: "Unmarried black women were having babies at a considerably lower rate in 1980 than they were in 1960. Further, the birth rate among black single women had fallen almost without a break since its high in 1961." The author? Me, writing in *Losing Ground.* At that time, like everyone else involved in the welfare/illegitimacy debate, I took for granted that the production of black illegitimate babies was falling, even though the proportion of black children born to single women was rising, and that this was something that those who would blame welfare for illegitimacy would have to explain away.

Such explanations are available because fertility rates were falling for married women as well. One may acknowledge that broad social forces can have an overriding influence on the propensity of women to have children and still argue that welfare has an independent role in shaping the marital circumstances surrounding the children who are born. But, given the figure shown here, it becomes implausible to make the more ambitious argument that welfare bribes women to have children, no matter how often social workers tell you that they know of many such cases. That is why, in the example of Harold and Phyllis, which became one of the best-known sections of *Losing Ground,* I was careful to begin the scenario with Phyllis already pregnant. I was persuaded by the evidence summarized in the paragraph above that a case could not be made that welfare caused more illegitimate births, only that welfare raised the probability that a given birth would be illegitimate.

I was wrong. Figure 2 reflects a statistical illusion. Here is the appropriate way to view the production of black babies out of wedlock from 1960 to 1990 (see Figure 3).

The line for the proportion remains unchanged, but what a dramatic difference in the measure of incidence. The incidence of black illegitimacy did not peak in 1960; on the contrary, it remained roughly steady until 1967, when suddenly it shot up and continued increasing with only short breaks through the end of the 1980s.

What statistical game has been played? If you take a careful look at the labels in the figures, you may be able to figure it out for yourself—notice the slight

FIGURES 2 & 3
TWO WAYS OF LOOKING AT BLACK ILLEGITIMACY

Illegitimacy can be represented by two measures: the *proportion* and the *incidence* of babies born out of wedlock. Figures 2 and 3 show identical upward lines for the *proportion* (the illegitimacy ratio). Figure 2, however, shows that the *incidence* of out-of-wedlock births has trended downward unevenly until the mid-1980s, while Figure 3 shows an upward trajectory. Both figures measure the *incidence* of births to single black women, but they do so in different ways. Which is the more useful measure to understand the rate at which illegitimate babies are being born?

In Figure 2, the number of illegitimate births to black women is expressed in terms of the population of single black women. That measure would be appropriate if the proportion of single women in the black population held constant. But it didn't; it soared over the period shown here. To get an accurate measure of the changing "production of illegitimate babies," we need to compare illegitimate births to the black female population. The slope of the line in Figure 2 reverses.

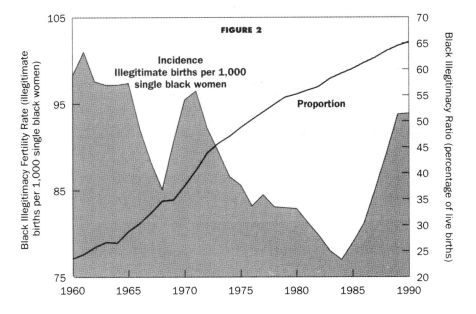

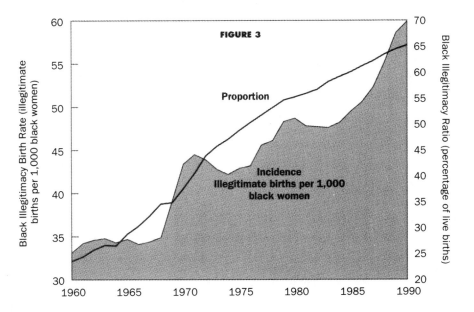

Source: Computed from National Center for Health Statistics, "Advance Report of Final Natality Statistics," *Monthly Vital Statistics Report,* vol. 42, no. 3(S) (Sept. 9, 1993), Figure 2: tables 1 and 17, and comparable tables in earlier volumes. Figure 3: tables 1 and 16, comparable tables in earlier volumes.

difference in wording between "illegitimate births per 1,000 single black women" in the first graph and "illegitimate births per 1,000 black women."

Statistics don't lie, as long as everyone is clear on precisely what question is being asked and precisely what the statistic measures. Here, we are interested in two separate phenomena: proportion and incidence. Proportion can be measured only one way (divide the number of illegitimate babies by the total number of live births). But in Figures 2 and 3, we used two different ways of measuring incidence, and they showed utterly different results. They cannot both be right. Which one is?

The underlying sense of "incidence" is "frequency relative to a consistent base." If the size of a population were constant, then we could simply use the raw number of illegitimate births as our measure of incidence. But populations do not remain constant. Therefore we need to divide the number of births by some denominator that will hold the population factor constant. The usual way to do this is by using the number of single women as the denominator. This makes intuitive sense, since we are talking about illegitimate births. But it is an inferior measure of incidence because the real issue we are interested in is the production of illegitimate babies per unit of population. What few people, including me, thought about for many years is that it is possible for the production of illegitimate babies per unit of population to go up even while the probability that single women have babies goes down.

This seeming paradox can occur if the number of single women suddenly changes far out of proportion to the increase in the overall population, and that's what happened to blacks during the 1960s. In a mere five-year period from 1965 to 1970, the proportion of black women ages 15–44 who were married plummeted by 10 percentage points, from 64.4 to 54.6 percent—an incredible change in such a basic social behavior during such a short period of time. (During the same period, the comparable figure for whites fell from 69 to 66 percent.) Black marriage continued to fall throughout the 1970s and 1980s, hitting a low of 34 percent in 1989—barely more than half the proportion that prevailed in 1960.

FIGURE 4
BLACK BIRTHS INSIDE AND OUTSIDE OF MARRIAGE AND WELFARE

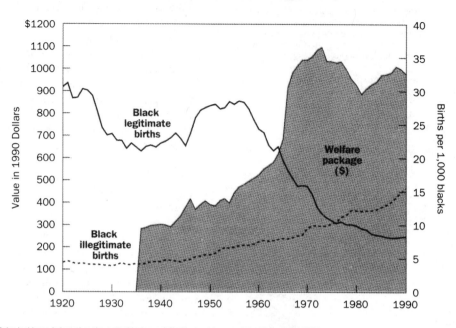

Note: Incidence is based on the entire black population to provide a consistent base since 1920.
Source: Same sources used in Figure 1, plus population data from *Historical Statistics of the United States, Colonial Times to 1970*, vol. 1 (Washington, DC: U.S. Bureau of the Census, 1975), Table A23–28, and U.S. Bureau of the Census, *Statistical Abstract of the United States.*

To see what this does to the interpretation of fertility rates, think of the familiar problem of interpreting Scholastic Aptitude Test (SAT) scores. Whenever the scores go down, you read news stories pointing out that maybe education isn't getting worse but that more disadvantaged students (who always would have scored low, but had not been taking the SAT) have entered the SAT pool, therefore causing the scores to fall. It is a similar scenario with the pool of black single women: By 1970, a large number of black women who would have been married in the world of 1960 were not married. The pool was being flooded. Did these new additions to the pool of single women have the same propensity to have babies out of wedlock as the old pool of single women? The contrast between the two figures suggests that the plausible answer, no, is correct.

The crucial point is that the number of illegitimate babies in the black population—not just the proportion, but the number—produced in any given year among a given number of blacks nearly doubled between 1967 and 1990, even though the fertility rate among single black women fell. It increased most radically from 1967 to 1971, tracking (with a two-year time lag) the most rapid rise in welfare benefits. Or in other words, black

behavior toward both marriage and out-of-wedlock childbearing during the period in which welfare benefits rose so swiftly behaved exactly as one would predict if one expected welfare to discourage women from getting married and induce single women to have babies.

When we then take the same measure and look at it over the 70-year sweep from 1920 to 1990, comparing black incidence of birth within marriage and outside marriage, all against the backdrop of the value of the welfare package, this is how the picture looks (see Figure 4).

The figure is not in any way "proof" of a causal relationship. But it is equally important to confront the plain message of these data. At the same time that powerful social and economic forces were pushing down the incidence of black children born to married couples, the incidence of black children born to unmarried women increased, eventually surpassing the rate for married couples. Something was making that particular behavior swim against a very strong tide, and, to say the least, the growth of welfare is a suspect with the means and opportunity.

This new look at black illegitimacy, then, knocks the legs out from under one of the main arguments that has been used to exculpate welfare's role in promoting illegitimacy 20 years from now. This will not stop the debate. The map linking welfare and illegitimacy still has big gaps. Optimistically, the progress we have been making in the last decade will continue. Pessimistically, it had better. For if illegitimacy is as serious a problem as I think, we cannot afford to waste much more time in deciding what needs to be done.

Going Private

States pawn off public services

CAMILLE COLATOSTI

As clinic workers protested, armed security guards forcibly evicted emotionally and mentally impaired patients from Detroit's Lafayette Clinic last October. Closed since then, the clinic was the only public psychiatric research hospital in Michigan.

"Patients were treated like cattle," according to the United Auto Workers' magazine *Solidarity*. "Ordered to pack their bags, they were herded into buses as friends and relatives called tearfully from behind fences."

"I'll never get over what I saw," says Deborah Dell'Orco, spokeswoman for UAW Local 6000, which represents 22,000 state employees. "It was a holocaust for the mentally ill."

The patients and workers at Lafayette Clinic were the latest casualties of privatization—the process of selling public services to private firms. Naming privatization as one of his guiding principles of government, Michigan Governor John Engler promised to "return to the private sector those state operations that can be more effectively and efficiently performed by the private sector."

Patient dumping, transferring state clients to corporate providers, saves the state the cost of running its own institutions. It also benefits the private facility, which accepts the patient's Medicaid and Supplemental Security Income. But it can prove dangerous for patients.

Stories abound of substandard care received at private institutions. Patients are neglected; they live in dangerous conditions and suffer physical abuse. Beverly Enterprises, for example, the nation's largest for-profit nursing-home chain, has been cited for 173 major patient-care violations and class-action suits alleging wrongful death are pending in Michigan, Georgia, and Florida.

But Governor Engler claims that Michigan, facing a budget deficit for the third year in a row, has no choice but to pare down. And Michigan is not alone in its decision to reduce state services and rely on the private sector instead. Trying to trim the size of state and local government is a national trend.

In part, this trend results from a severe economic crisis. In 1991, forty-seven states spent more than they took in. And 1992 wasn't much better: thirty-five states that had adopted balanced budgets again confronted deficits.

The reasons for the deficits include:

¶ The recession. "During tough economic times," says Mike Ettlinger of the Washington, D.C.-based Citizens for Tax Justice, "high unemployment means declines in personal income tax and increases in welfare and social-service costs."

¶ The decline in Federal aid to states and cities. Between 1980 and 1989, the real value of grants to state and local governments dropped by 38 per cent. In 1979, Federal aid accounted for 22 per cent of state and local budgets; in 1989, it made up only 16 per cent.

¶ Regressive tax systems. States raise revenue primarily from low- and middle-income people, not the wealthy and corporations. According to *A Far Cry from Fair*, a report by Citizens for Tax Justice, "Forty-four states and the District of Columbia tax the very rich at lower rates than they tax the poor. In five states—Nevada, Texas, Florida, Washington, and South Dakota—the poor pay five times as great a share of their incomes in state and local taxes as do the rich."

As Ettlinger explains, "Soaking the poor just doesn't raise enough money to support a modern economy, especially when you consider the current distribution of wealth in the United States. The richest 1 per cent of all families make more than the bottom 40 per cent. The top fifth make more than everyone else put together."

Still, budget crises alone don't explain the privatization trend. An ideology gaining popularity among policymakers—and articulated in *Reinventing Government*, by David Osborne and Ted Gaebler—holds that local governments need to be remade.

The authors cite conservative economist Peter Drucker, who wrote that "the purpose of government is to make fundamental decisions and to make them effectively. . . . Any attempt to combine governing with 'doing' on a large scale paralyzes government's decision-making capacity." In other words, governments should not provide services but instead oversee them.

Government works best, claim economists Michael Mills, Charles Van Eaton, and Robert Daddow of the Heartland Institute, a conservative research group in Detroit, "when it employs, under its oversight, someone else to do the doing."

So, beginning from the assumption that government is bureaucratic and ineffective, proponents of "reinventing government" focus not on increasing revenues but on two other areas.

Sometimes they eliminate services completely. *The States and the Poor*, by the Center on Budget and Policy Priorities, reports that the last two years have seen forty-four states cut or freeze benefits in the Aid to Families with Dependent Children program; twenty-two states eliminate or severely reduce general assistance ben-

---

Camille Colatosti, the author of "Stopping Sexual Harassment: A Handbook for Union and Workplace Activists," is a free-lance writer and a member of UAW Local 1981. She lives in Detroit.

From *The Progressive*, June 1993, pp. 29-31. © 1993 by Camille Colatosti, director of the Working Women's Project in Detroit. Reprinted by permission of the author.

efits; twenty-six states freeze or cut supplemental benefits to poor, elderly, and disabled recipients of Supplemental Security Income.

At other times, they propose transferring public services to private contractors and promoting competition. While this does not exactly mean running government like a business, it does involve introducing corporate concepts to public service.

"Government and business are fundamentally different institutions," explain Osborne and Gaebler. "Government is democratic and open. Hence it moves more slowly than business, whose managers can make quick decisions behind closed doors. Government's fundamental mission is to 'do good,' not to make money. . . . Government must often serve everyone equally, regardless of their ability to pay or their demand for a service; hence it cannot achieve the same efficiencies as business."

Yet, they conclude, "The fact that government cannot be run just like a business does not mean it cannot become more entrepreneurial."

While Osborne and Gaebler claim that "entrepreneurial" means "creative and flexible," the positive examples they ask politicians to emulate emphasize lean production techniques. The key to success involves finding ways to provide services at little cost. Usually, this requires paying workers low wages with no benefits.

Reinventing Government points to Frank Keefe, former secretary of administration and finance in Massachusetts, who argues: "Contracting with private vendors is cheaper, more efficient, more authentic, more flexible, more adaptive. . . . Contracts are rewritten every year. You can change. You cannot change with state employees who have all sorts of vested rights and privileges."

"The state can't fire anybody," is the way Alan Flory puts it. Executive director of the Community Organization for Drug Abuse, Mental Health, and Alcoholism Services, a private corporation managing $17 million in state contracts in Arizona, Flory continues, "My people—I can push 'em; I can make 'em work hard."

Employed on a year-to-year basis, contract workers are too vulnerable to expect "rights and privileges." Over 35 per cent of public-sector workers, on the other hand, belong to unions and demand certain compensation standards.

Detroit Mayor Coleman Young has put Flory's philosophy into practice. Blaming most of the city's fiscal crisis on overpaid public employees, he laid off more than a thousand clerks and typists and contracted their work to private firms.

But the laid-off workers, most of whom are African-American women, are among the lowest-paid employees in the city. They average only $22,000 a year—hardly an outrageous salary. Giving these jobs to private contractors meant forcing many workers onto the unemployment rolls, while compelling others to accept significantly lower wages.

Even with such wage and benefit cuts, it remains unclear that privatization really saves money. The costs of converting to the private sector and administering the contract can run high. For example, eleven out of twelve contracted services were more expensive than in-house costs, according to a 1992 study by the General Accounting Office.

"The actual savings gained in public contracting out are razor thin," says Elliot Sclar, a professor at Columbia University. "Studies suggest that when everything goes well, real cash savings are less than 10 per cent. However, things frequently do not go well."

> **Often, contractors will 'low-ball' bids for the first year or two—until the government loses its ability to provide people with the service.**

Often, too, contractors will "low-ball" their bids for the first year or two—until the government loses its ability to provide the service. Once the government has become dependent on the private sector, the contractor will raise its price.

Privatization also results in increased opportunities for corruption. "There's bribery, kickbacks, conflicts of interest, and charges for work never performed," says Bobbi Rabinowitz, vice president for publicity at AFSCME Local 371 in New York City. Local 371 recently won a victory against privatization. City administrators wanted to contract out an important health-care service: evaluating hospital patients as they are released to determine the need for home care.

"Our members were doing a fine job," says Rabinowitz. "There was nothing wrong whatsoever. Contracting wouldn't save money, stop waste, or improve efficiency. The service is already efficient."

So why switch? Workers believe that administrators wanted to return favors to individuals who stood to gain from the contracts.

Newsweek magazine reported similar cronyism in Massachusetts. One-fourth of the 1,300 firms the state contracts with each year turn out to be technically insolvent. "Some agencies do a fine job," concluded *Newsweek.* "Some—including a medical-services firm whose owner billed the state for his Lincoln Continental and his chauffeur—slip past official scrutiny."

On top of such abuses, services often suffer. Take the example of public hospitals. Today, the private management of public health facilities is a booming business. Contractors show profits of 15 to 30 per cent. But public accountability disappears, and the quality of patient care deteriorates.

Typically, public hospitals feel a budget crunch not because they are mismanaged but because patients lack insurance and funds to pay. Management can eliminate fiscal problems only by scrimping on service and limiting public access. Private management firms have been known to screen uninsured patients before admitting them, turning away those who cannot pay. Some require deposits before providing care. Others eliminate or reduce unprofitable services. All told, these tactics call into question the mission of public hospitals: to provide health care for the indigent.

When, ten years ago, Chicago's Cook County General Hospital hired Hyatt Medical Management Services, Inc., to consult on its budget and administration, public service began to suffer. Unconcerned about the hospital's mission, Hyatt began to charge the poor for inpatient and outpatient services. It increased room rates and intensive-care rates to obtain higher insurance reimbursements and turned away people who were ineligible for Medicaid.

"Within eight months after Hyatt came to Cook County Hospital to improve efficiency," says Geraldine Dallek of the National Health Law Program, "the situation had deteriorated. Under Hyatt's direction, the hospital regularly lacked such basic supplies as aspirins, paper towels, urine-specimen cups, syringes, blood culture bottles, and similar items. Then the entire computer recording system for hospital supplies broke down—supplies like insulin were rationed and wards began hoarding whatever they had, in fear of running out."

While services to the poor suffered, Hyatt profited and the hospital's deficit increased. A 1990 complaint that former Massachusetts finance director Peter Nessen made to then-Governor Michael Dukakis seems relevant: Of contracting out, he said, "We often made decisions when we knew nothing at all about the product, the outcome, and most important the effect of the program for the client."

"Privatization certainly isn't the wrong choice in every case," concedes Kathleen Gmeiner of the Michigan Fair Budget Action Coalition, a group of labor, community, and religious activists fighting to restore state services. "Doctors at public hospitals receive a fee for service, for example. And this works relatively well. But if public-health services themselves, or even the Medicaid system, were privatized, the government would lose its capacity to contain competition and to contain costs. The state would lose its capacity to provide Medicaid and would be at the mercy of the private sector."

For Gmeiner, the test of good government is how it treats its most vulnerable citizens. "Government must provide each citizen opportunities for self-sufficiency," she argues. "And for those citizens who are incapable of self-sufficiency, government must assume the role of permanent provider of economic support, social support, and protection to enable them to live with dignity."

Such a statement reveals, perhaps more than any other, the difference between those who favor effective and responsive public service and those who advocate privatization. To proponents of "reinventing government"—politicians like Governor Engler of Michigan, Governor William Weld of Massachusetts, former President Ronald Reagan, and, to some extent, President Bill Clinton—the number of people "incapable of self-sufficiency" appears extremely low. To some degree, all discuss the need to pare down government, to make it smaller.

"Politicians are selling off government services—and eliminating government it-self," says Bob Lathrop, Michigan political director of the Service Employees International Union. "Engler, for example, is shirking his responsibility to govern at the same time that he's trying to make government as small as possible."

Gmeiner agrees. "Proponents of privatization, politicians like Engler, aren't reforming government," she says. "They're not making it more efficient or more responsive to human need. They are simply slashing benefits without compunction. Engler, for example, has shown no creativity in making system changes. He's created no new jobs and no new job-training programs. He's simply denied people access to services they need."

Along with activists across the country, the Michigan Fair Budget Action Coalition is trying to move the debate from sheer economics to a people perspective. "We want people to decide what services they need," says Gmeiner. "Then we'll discuss funding."

Citing a 1992 Milbank Memorial Fund Report called *Hard Choices in Hard Times*, Gmeiner proposes that "the principles of fairness and liberty guide the choices that state and local officials make."

"Fairness and liberty have several meanings," the Fund reports. "Fairness includes taking care of the least advantaged, removing impediments to opportunity, and accommodating competing interests. Liberty connotes decisions about social needs that will have priority over individual decisions to dispose of income. Both fairness and liberty require that government be involved in assuring well-being. At times, government is the agent of first resort; sometimes, it is the guarantor of health and safety."

To fund the services that people need, the Michigan Coalition proposes cutting corporate tax breaks by 10 per cent to increase revenue for human services.

This would generate $700 million to $1 billion, which does not seem unreasonable to Gmeiner, who says Michigan has cut 20 per cent of its social-services budget since 1990. But businesses oppose it. In particular, General Motors, Ford, and Chrysler have implied they'll take their business elsewhere if their tax breaks are slashed.

Some states are taking other measures to balance their budgets, including increasing taxes on the wealthy. In 1992, for example, Ohio, a state whose cuts in general-assistance benefits were second only to Michigan's in 1991, actually raised income taxes for families earning over $200,000 a year. This helped fund small increases in Aid to Families with Dependent Children and in Medicaid.

Kansas made a similar income-tax change and, at the same time, reduced taxes for poor families. Unfortunately, these tiny increases in tax revenue are nowhere near enough. And says Marian Kramer, leader of Up and Out of Poverty, the national advocacy group for the homeless, people shouldn't settle for them.

"The people are losing," she says, "losing in the courts and in the legislature. When the government ceases to take care of its people, then the people have to do something to set things straight. We have to take matters into our own hands. It's time for us to fight back—and to fight now, as hard as we can for as long as it takes."

No Exit

In isolated urban ghettos, a better life seems a world away

Barbara Vobejda

Washington Post Staff Writer

CLEVELAND

Five years ago, Adrienne Walker set out to work at the Stop N Shop. It was a shining moment for her. She was a single, inner-city mother living on welfare who had applied for a job in the suburbs, interviewed and been hired, easy as that. All she had to do was get there.

That wasn't so easy. She convinced a friend to drive her, but it took 45 minutes, and after a few days her friend "got lazy," she says. She took the bus, but to make the right connections she had to leave home 3½ hours before her shift began.

In the meantime, her grandmother was struggling to take care of Walker's 1-year-old son. And then the final straw: she found out she was pregnant with a second child.

It all just seemed too much, and after 10 days on the job, she quit.

Now that suburb, that job and the fleeting promise of deliverance seem a world away from Walker's neighborhood, a battered landscape of public housing projects and boarded-up factories.

For Walker and those who live around her, escape seems impossible. They are isolated from jobs and services, surrounded by poverty and threatened by crime. They pray that a troubled, overburdened school system can lift their children out.

"I would like to move," says Walker, now married and the mother of three. But even with that $5-an-hour job in the suburbs, she says, "it would not be easy."

Neighborhoods like Walker's reflect a new dimension to urban life in America: Never before have inner-city residents been so isolated from mainstream society.

Scholars argue that this isolation is at the heart of the worst ills of the inner city, a tangle of crime, unemployment and stubborn poverty, all of which President Clinton has pledged to attack.

But repairing the cities, which have come to embody the nation's most intractable problems, could prove to be more complex and difficult for Clinton than fulfilling any other campaign promise. It entails overhauling health care and welfare, improving schools, curbing the drug trade and revitalizing the economy.

And in big cities, those daunting tasks are made even more complicated by the chasm—psychological, physical, economic and social—that separates the urban ghetto from virtually all other facets of American life.

"Getting in there with programs is more difficult" because of this chasm, says Health and Human Services Secretary Donna E. Shalala, who will oversee many of the Clinton programs aimed at urban problems.

"The issue is not just that people have moved, but the jobs have moved," she says. And for this and other reasons, inner-city residents "don't have the resources to deal with these issues."

In neighborhoods from Cleveland and Detroit to Chicago, New York, Washington and Los Angeles, inner-city isolation takes many forms.

It is economic. Cities have lost millions of manufacturing jobs, leaving urban residents like Walker with few work opportunities. They are unprepared for the white-collar jobs downtown, and service jobs outside the city are far away and pay too little to allow a move to the suburbs.

It is physical. Urban sprawl has moved more of the population, employment, shopping and services farther from the urban center. Middle-class suburbanites have less reason to drive into the central city, leaving neighborhoods distinctly separated by class, with little interaction or empathy among their residents.

For residents of the inner city, the new glass towers downtown and the suburban brick houses sit beyond reach, like elusive visions of prosperity.

It is racial and social. The flight of the middle class—black and white—from the inner city has left a population that is overwhelmingly black and poor, devoid of healthy businesses, strong schools or other institutions that contributed to stability in the past. This concentration of poverty means that children grow up with little exposure to steadily employed adults, making it easy for them to see unemployment as a way of life.

From the *Washington Post National Weekly Edition*, March 15-21, 1993, pp. 6-7. © 1993 by the Washington Post. Reprinted by permission.

"In short, the communities of the underclass are plagued by massive joblessness, flagrant and open lawlessness and low-achieving schools, and therefore tend to be avoided by outsiders," wrote University of Chicago sociologist William Julius Wilson in his 1987 book, "The Truly Disadvantaged," which first laid out in detail the increasing concentration of poverty in the inner cities.

The result, he argued, is that those who live in these neighborhoods, "whether women and children of welfare families or aggressive street criminals, have become increasingly socially isolated from mainstream patterns of behavior."

Walker is not personally isolated; she has a supportive, extended family. Many of those around her have strong ties to their churches. But they have virtually no social interaction with suburbanites or middle-class society. And as a group, they exist in a stunningly hopeless and solitary milieu.

"I knew about this neighborhood, but I never thought I'd be living here," says Francie Tate, who lives a few doors from Walker in the same public housing complex. "When I told everybody I was moving to 79th [Street], everybody said that's really bad."

Tate, the single mother of two sons, Martel, 1, and Robert, 6, was frightened at first. Television violence, she says, pales in comparison to what children here see in the parking lot. Walker tells of her husband discovering a woman's strangled and beaten body in a car just outside their front door.

Another time, she woke to the sound of a burglar smashing her picture window. She still is not sure whether he made it into the apartment or was frightened off by her screams.

As she tells the tales of daily life in the ghetto, one of her sons listens impassively, the TV flashing in the background.

The isolation of the community makes even the most prosaic chores more difficult. There are no supermarkets nearby, only expensive corner stores, so shopping requires a long bus ride.

Tate waits for a "jitney," an unofficial taxi service, to bring her home with her groceries. She shops once a month when she gets food stamps, hauling home six gallons of milk, four of which she freezes.

She now feels comfortable in the neighborhood, she says, "but I don't want my kids to grow up here." Tate dreams of moving to North Carolina, living in a "gorgeous" house, with a country kitchen and a big back yard where her sons can run.

In her neighborhood, she says, "it's going to get worse before it gets better. There are people on the street. More jobs are closing now. And there's going to be more people on the streets."

The daily trials of inner-city residents like Tate and Walker are well known to Housing and Urban Development Secretary Henry Cisneros, who as former mayor of San Antonio was forced to grapple with urban ghettos. "People have nothing—nowhere to go for food or services," he says.

The new administration may explore some policy proposals, he says, including conversion of the first floors of high-rise buildings into supermarket and shopping complexes to create a place "of common activity and contact." In the meantime, he says, "isolation is a very serious problem."

Cleveland's inner city has spiraled down quickly and dramatically over the past decade, largely the result of the collapse of the area's manufacturing base.

Since 1979, metropolitan Cleveland lost 88,000 manufacturing jobs, a phenomenon that has left long stretches of city geography dotted with abandoned factories, crumbling shells that were once the economic heart of the community.

Even in metropolitan areas where the number of jobs has increased, virtually all of the employment growth has been not in the city but in the suburbs, says Mark Alan Hughes, an urban geographer and coauthor of a recent Urban Institute study on the subject. This is true in Washington, D.C., Chicago, Los Angeles, Philadelphia and Detroit, among others.

At the same time, population moved out of many cities and inner-city poverty rates grew. In Walker and Tate's neighborhood, known as "Central," the poverty rate is 63 percent.

Cleveland's neighborhoods are among the most segregated in the nation, according to University of Michigan demographer William Frey. And the city is much worse off than its surrounding suburbs. When "dissimilarity" between suburbs and city is measured in terms of unemployment, income, poverty and other statistics, the contrast is greater here than in most of the nation's other major metropolitan areas. The division between city and suburbs is true across America, accompanied by a sharp alienation between suburbanites and the inner-city poor.

Lewis West, who runs a social service agency near King-Kennedy Estates, a notorious public housing project, says the Cleveland suburbs are full of people who are "scared to death" of Central. "The public perception is that it's a bad place to be. The local paper described it as 'Dodge City,' " he says.

But many of those who live in Central say it is not the high crime rates, but the lack of jobs that has inspired the deepest desperation.

"There were times when I just lost hope. I got a trade as a machinist but I can't get a job," says Robert Bey, who was laid off from his factory job in 1982. "Big industry doesn't care about the people they leave in the inner city."

Robert Agnew, a recovering addict who has been unable to find work, remembers when auto and machine factories were vital here, along with huge bakeries and a General Electric plant. "The steel mills was happening," he says. Today, "we live in a jungle. This is a war."

At Vocational Guidance Services, a job training facility in Central, a project is underway to encourage employers in the neighborhood, among them a metal stamping factory, storage business and print shop, to hire local residents. But officials at the training center warn that they face an enormously difficult task.

The loss of jobs and the soaring rates of unemployment are most to blame for the isolation of the inner city, says Claudia Coulton, director of the Center for Urban Poverty and Social Change at Case Western Reserve University here.

Neighborhoods elsewhere in the city that were stable only a short time ago, she says, are facing the same prospect: As factory workers have lost their jobs and have less money to spend, property values have declined, housing stock has deteriorated and drug trafficking, especially in crack cocaine, has moved in.

"That's when you began to see areas losing their more middle-class population and a rise in other problems, delinquency, crime, infant mortality," she says.

In Central, a black neighborhood that has been impoverished for a generation, economic segregation worsened considerably over the 1980s, she says. While just a quarter of poor people in Cleveland were living in impoverished areas—neighborhoods in which there are virtually no middle-class people—in 1980, that figure doubled to half by 1990.

Poverty rates increased in many big cities over the 1980s: in Detroit, from 22 percent to 32 percent; in Los Angeles, from 16 percent to 19 percent; in Milwaukee, from 14 percent to 22 percent.

And even in cities where the poverty rate fell—including Washington, D.C., where it slipped from 19 percent to 17 percent—the rates declined more in the suburbs, meaning that poverty became more concentrated in the central cities, according to urban geographer Hughes.

The concentration of poor people makes it even harder to find jobs, sociologists argue. In nonpoor neighborhoods, people often find work through neighbors, friends and relatives. But when an entire community is impoverished, those who are looking for work have no connections to help get jobs.

Coulton contends that children suffer too when they are outside the mainstream. Unlike their peers in middle-class neighborhoods, they are exposed to behavior, from dress and attitudes to delinquency and teenage childbearing, that keeps young people from getting ahead.

Tracie Glenn, a single mother who has been struggling to find steady work, says she was struck by a sad contrast recently when she was cleaning the suburban house of a professional couple.

The house, says Glenn wistfully, "was beautiful. All these awards and certificates were hanging there. . . . I heard the daughter talking to her mother, and I knew she was going someplace."

WATCHING THE MAINSTREAM MOVE

Over the past decade, the inner cities have become increasingly isolated as population and jobs have moved out.

In some places, the number of jobs inside the city declined, to the benefit of the suburbs:

The result has been a significant increase in inner-city poverty, especially in:

METRO AREA	SUBURBAN JOB GROWTH 1980-86	CITY	POVERTY RATE 1980	POVERTY RATE 1990
Chicago	100%	Detroit	22%	32%
Cleveland	100	New Orleans	26	32
Dayton	100	Cleveland	22	29
Detroit	100	El Paso	21	25
Greensboro	100	Milwaukee	14	22
Louisville	100	Houston	13	21
Seattle	99	Los Angeles	16	19
Newark	97	Dallas	14	18
Los Angeles	95	Fort Worth	14	17
Providence	95	Denver	14	17
Youngstown	93	Oklahoma City	12	16
Washington, D.C.	91	Phoenix	11	14

SOURCE: U.S. Census Bureau and Urban Institute

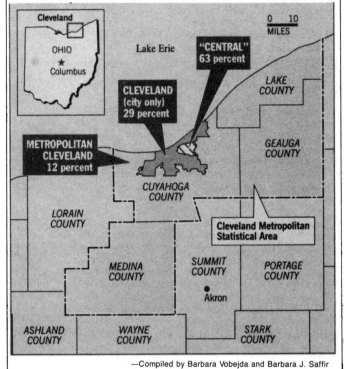

POVERTY CONCENTRATION IN CLEVELAND, 1990

—Compiled by Barbara Vobejda and Barbara J. Saffir

BY JAY LIEBENOW FOR THE WASHINGTON POST

But then she thought of her own neighborhood. "Kids 12 and 13 are selling drugs. And a lot of [the parents] have their kids doing it."

Of her own 11-year-old son, she says, "I don't know what he'll grow up to be. . . . I'm in a lot of fear."

For children, says Harvard University sociologist Gary Orfield, the effects of being sequestered in a ghetto are worse than for adults.

Those children "most dependent on education are concentrated in places with the most rotten education," he says. "When you concentrate poverty, you concentrate health problems, family problems, school populations are very unstable, kids are exposed to criminal problems."

At George Washington Carver Elementary School in Cleveland's inner city, the children need only look out the classroom window to see gang fighting, prostitution and drug dealing, principal Theodore Carter says.

He says he has watched as the community around the school crumbles, literally and figuratively. Across the street, for example, just one structure stands on a block that once had 10 houses.

Carter tries to get the parents involved, but at his monthly parent-teacher meetings, he is lucky to get a dozen parents in a school that enrolls 460 students.

He has come to a bleak conclusion about his students, 80 percent of whom live in poverty. "If they can't get out of the projects, I don't think there's much hope. Some will be productive, but when it's generation after generation in the projects. . . ."

Their parents may know they should move, but they are stuck, he says. "They don't have the resources."

The hope of leaving the ghetto dances constantly before Adrienne Walker.

Her mother, a clerk with the federal government, fled to the Cleveland suburbs 13 years ago after Walker fell into a troubled high school crowd and began skipping classes. Walker says she excelled in her new suburban school, earning a high school diploma with A's and B's.

But Walker did not stay in the suburbs. When she was forced to find her own place six years ago, the easiest option seemed to be a public housing unit in the same complex with her grandmother, back in the inner city.

The road into the ghetto was easy. Leaving, she knows, will not be. It will require a much higher income, enough to cover rent on an unsubsidized apartment. And it will take savings, for security deposits and other moving expenses.

And then there are the well-known bureaucratic traps: If she or her husband, Dwayne Jennings, finds work, she loses Medicaid coverage and welfare benefits. If they amass savings, her assistance is jeopardized.

When Walker and Jennings were married last year, he was getting $6 an hour as a cook at a downtown restaurant. Her resident manager learned of the marriage, and the monthly rent on the apartment rose from $55 to $300. Walker's welfare check fell from $359 to $296.

Jennings was laid off and has been out of work since July. He heard of a good job at a factory in Twinsburg, a suburb to the south, but there was the same hitch.

"How was I going to get there? How was I going to get back?" he says.

Like most residents here, Walker and Jennings have an escape plan, however abstract and tenuous. They say they will buy a small apartment building when Jennings receives an $8,000 settlement for a work injury. Walker plans to sign up for courses at the local community college.

In the meantime, they live in a world circumscribed by boundaries middle-class Americans never face: avoiding corner markets where residents say prices shoot up the day food stamps are issued; waiting until relatives can drive them Christmas shopping, so their packages don't get stolen on the bus ride home; letting their children play in parking lots because the playground next door has been overrun by drinking, gambling teenagers; facing a $5 fine if their children play on the housing project grass.

Walker thinks she knows what it feels like to be freed from the trap. For a short time this year, when her husband was working and she was receiving benefits, they caught up with the bills. For the first time, they went to the grocery store once a week.

"People would say, 'Dang, didn't you just go to the grocery store?' " she says. "I could take the kids downtown, buy them blue jeans, buy them a meal at McDonald's."

For some reason, the liberty of buying that Happy Meal seems to haunt her. She says now when she takes her children shopping, her oldest son, Greggory, inevitably pleads with her: "Mommy, can we get this? Can we go to McDonald's?'

"I'll say, 'No! Don't ask me that. . . .' He'll look at me like, 'I just asked you for McDonald's.' "

It is that exchange, more than anything else, that she dreads. It is then, she says, that she feels stuck.

Washington Post staff writer Guy Gugliotta contributed to this report.

When Problems Outrun Policy

Returning to rapid economic growth and taming the market's tendency to create both wealth and poverty requires a new vision of domestic policy.

Robert Haveman

Robert Haveman is John Bascom Professor of Economics and Public Affairs at the University of Wisconsin-Madison and the Robert M. La Follette Institute of Public Affairs.

Recent events have brought many Americans face to face with a series of harsh realities. While economic life for many of us remains prosperous, a growing number—and an increasing proportion—of adult Americans are living below the poverty line.

For this group, especially for those on the bottom rungs of the nation's income ladder, conditions are especially severe. Their incomes have, in unprecedented fashion, failed to rise with economic growth. Their neighborhoods have become crime-infested and drug-dominated. The schools which their children attend are able neither to sustain order nor maintain educational standards. The social institutions that were vital to them in their youth—their churches, clubs, neighborhoods—seem irrelevant today. Their families have been broken up (or never put together) and the values with which they navigate life have little resemblance to those dominant in earlier times.

Unresponsive government

In addition to these economic, social, and value changes, poor people and minorities have experienced others as well. Many now perceive one of the fundamental institutions in their lives—the government—to be inimical to their interests. In the past, they viewed the government as being protective. They depended on it to maintain minimal standards of physical and social order. They felt assured it would be responsive in time of crisis.

Welfare was considered a "safety net" by poor people and minorities. They had faith that the police would sustain order, the parks department would maintain parks, the roads department would fix roads, the sanitation department would clean the streets, and that public employment would offer job opportunities. This view by poor people—that government was an ally in improving their lot and making their neighborhoods habitable—may often have been more an apparition than a reality, but it was their belief.

One reason for poor people's past affirmation of government was that public officials then seemed clearer in their statements about the responsibilities of the public sector. What government was all about, according to the words of the political leaders, was the setting and enforcement of acceptable standards of income, education, sanitation, safety, and access to services.

Moreover, government people backed up their words with actions and money. Programs designed to meet people's needs—for development of skills, legal counsel, safety, mental and physical health services, and access to shelter—were visible. And the civil servants within these public programs either cared or pretended to care, and, more often than not, believed that they and their programs mattered.

From *Challenge*, May/June 1993, pp. 28-35. Reprinted with permission of the publisher, M. E. Sharpe, Inc., 80 Business Park Drive, Armonk, NY 10504, USA.

Even if there was often little real evidence that economic security was increasing, or that neighborhoods were safer and schools better, or that there were more job opportunities, or that housing conditions were improving, the press and community leaders regularly cited efforts by government to make things better. The services provided may not always have been cost-effective, but they were palpable, and announced that government was trying.

Many of today's poor no longer perceive government in this way. Few political leaders offer clear statements about government's responsibility and its role. Indeed, the main theme of many government leaders is that government has little, if any, responsibility for personal and community well-being. Few budgets providing services to the poor have increased, and rarely do news stories report government's attempts to improve the lot of the poor. Increasingly, public institutions once viewed as protective appear punitive and threatening.

Perhaps equally important, private standards have also changed for the worse. Family values, judgments about individual responsibility, perceptions of appropriate personal behavior and appearance, and expectations of the good will of neighbors have all eroded. The roots of these changes are not clear. Has it been a more permissive environment led by public acceptance of changed personal standards? Can it be the availability of cheap drugs and weapons, and the opening of "markets" in drugs and other illicit goods, generating substantial returns to criminal activity? We can only guess. We cannot really know.

The role of the economy

My thesis here is that the performance of the U.S. economy should not be omitted from any list of the causes of our problems. A further thesis is that this poor economic performance did not occur in a vacuum; more precisely, that governmental policy contributed significantly to its failure. If these two theses contain truth, then it follows that government has a responsibility to change its course, and I offer some suggestions for such a redirection.

The future of the American economy is high on everyone's list of concerns. While there are some encouraging signs regarding macroeconomic performance—a dwindling trade deficit, low inflation, a "solved" savings and loan crisis—other signs are less favorable. Unemployment remains stubbornly high. Saving, investment, and economic growth remain at historically low levels. The public deficit rises. The health of the banking and insurance sectors seems increasingly fragile. The macroeconomic future is surely not rosy.

This macroeconomic scenario is relatively well known, but another set of facts regarding the American economy is less clearly perceived. They involve the performance of the "micro" parts of the economy—the labor market, income flows and their distribution, the changing composition of jobs, and the changing character of the requirements and delivery of education.

I offer a few microeconomic perspectives about the American economy in order that we may understand more clearly whence we have come and where we should be going. They suggest that social problems have indeed overwhelmed policy. Moreover, I contend, much of federal government social policy—welfare, Social Security, health policy, and tax policy—has contributed to these developments. And I shall take the opportunity to indicate several fundamental policy changes that might contribute to narrowing the gap between problems and policy.

Decline in productivity growth

The median worker in the U.S. economy has experienced no increase in his or her real wage and salary earnings since the mid-1970s—a period of almost twenty years. Only when fringe benefit increases are included does real median worker compensation appear to have held approximately even. Moreover, capital per worker—plant, machinery, and equipment—has also sagged.

Why this dismal performance? While we cannot identify the causes with certainty, many have been suggested, often bearing supporting evidence. At its crux, this dismal earnings and investment performance is linked to the changes that have occurred in the rate of productivity growth—the rate of increase in the ratio of output to labor inputs—in the American economy.

In the 1950s, productivity grew annually by 2.64 percent. It remained at a high 2.5 percent in the 1960s. In the 1970s, however, the bottom dropped out, and the productivity growth rate fell to 1.24 percent. The 1980s were even worse, recording a dismal 1.09 percent annual growth.

But identifying the slowdown in productivity growth as the culprit only masks the root cause. What has caused the decline in productivity growth, a decline that most analysts mark as having begun about 1973? Again, several factors seem to be at work, arguably the most important being the oil price shocks that occurred in 1973 and again in 1976. Among other things, the radical change in the price of this input rendered obsolete a significant share of the U.S. capital stock designed, as it was, for an energy-intensive production process.

But, other factors contributed as well. Among them were the tilt in the composition of U.S. workers toward the less experienced (women, youth, and immigrants); the impact of environmental and other regulations diverting some capital investment funds from normal plant and equipment toward emissions reduction; and the declining quality of the education of an ever younger work force relative to the needs of industry. While one can compile a catalogue of potential factors with ease, assigning a specific share of the blame to any one is more difficult.

Owing to the stagnation of productivity and wages, American families have secured rising incomes almost exclusively by working more. Women's labor-force participation has increased, resulting in some growth in total family income. But even this income growth has not been significant, and what expansion we have experienced should properly be attributed to increased work effort and increased work time. There is clearly an upper limit to this source of family income growth.

One fact stands out ominously: American families no longer look forward to increasing standards of living, or to a world in which sons and daughters live better than their parents.

Growing gap between rich and poor

The gap between rich and poor has greatly increased over the past twenty years. The wages of a high school graduate, relative to those of a college graduate, have fallen by 15 percent since 1980. Since 1975, the income of the top 20 percent of the nation's households has risen from 41 percent to 44 percent of the total income pie—an historic increase. What lies behind this unsettling trend? As before, there is no sure explanation, but a few of the most important factors seem clear.

New jobs in the American economy have appeared with technical requirements beyond the abilities of an increasing share of the nation's job entrants to meet them. Those with little or inadequate education have done very poorly, both relative to their earlier experience and relative to others with more education and skills. These workers—some

new entrants to the job market and others being recycled from other jobs—have been forced into low- or minimum-wage slots requiring little skill. The wages of many of these jobs are insufficient to lift a family of four out of poverty. By any standard, the living standard of the families of these workers has shrunk.

On the other hand, those with substantial education or skills have experienced relatively high demand for their services, and their wages have been bid up, their family income following close behind. The result has been a growing gap between the economic status of families headed by high school graduates and those headed by college graduates.

A second factor is related to changes in the structure of American industry. The manufacturing sector has long been in decline, and the distribution of jobs has become tilted toward that part of the labor force where wages are typically lower—the service and trade sectors. The decline of manufacturing is also associated with the fading numerical strength and negotiating power of American trade unions. As a result, a pool of physically difficult (but high-paying) jobs has disappeared and has been replaced by part-time, seasonal, and low-paying jobs.

A third factor lies in important changes in U.S. tax laws that have made financial transactions extremely lucrative, with or without any clear view that they represent real efficiency gains. These tax law provisions have encouraged leveraged and hostile takeovers capable of generating huge returns to those who have engineered them. They have reduced the effective tax rate on high-income people while allowing it to creep upward for middle- and low-income people. Not only did this process generate huge incomes for those involved in arranging these corporate reorganizations, they often resulted in business failures, plant closings, and the shift of production capacity to other countries with lower labor costs. It is this shift that lies behind the stories of workers who, despite long experience in and dedication to firms and plants, have lost their jobs, exhausted their unemployment benefits, and been forced into either early retirement or low-paying, unskilled work.

Because of this widening of the nation's income distribution, we have seen a decline in social cohesion among America's diverse groups. More people with sagging living standards and little hope for future prosperity have come to see the enormous accumulation of income and wealth by others as having occurred at the expense of their own lagging prospects.

One manifestation of diminished social cohesion

is the increase in officially defined poverty, rising from about 12 percent in the 1970s to 14 percent in the 1980s. Another example is the growth in minority youth unemployment rates to the 40 percent range, resulting in alienation, frustration, hopelessness, and anger. Yet another manifestation, though far more difficult to document, is the apparent ability of the rich to convert their income and wealth into economic power and political influence.

As a result, the nation is showing signs of polarization stemming from this growing inequality. We see dissolution and frustration among the losers, and position and power among the winners. The analogy between the structure of some our large cities, encumbered with abject poverty enclaves isolated in and surrounded by palatial wealth, to those of some third world countries has been suggested with increasing frequency.

The "New Poor"

Those who have filtered to the bottom of the income distribution include some of the nation's most economically vulnerable citizens. These households contain a disproportionate share of the nation's children, on whose shoulders the nation's economic future depends. The groups of "new poor" that now populate the bottom of the income distribution include families headed by unwed mothers, children, minority youth, and families headed by young workers with little education. While other groups, notably the elderly and older workers, have bubbled up from the bottom of the distribution over time, the new groups have sunk down into it.

What factors account for this pattern of gainers and losers over the past several decades? Again, several factors are at work, and again, the precise role played by any of them remains in doubt. One indisputable factor is the growth in single-parent families, due in large part to the explosion in divorce rates and the increased number of women choosing to give birth although unmarried. Today, over 350,000 children are born each year to teen unmarried mothers, up from less than 200,000 per year in 1970. A typical pattern for the majority of these mothers is to join the welfare rolls within a few years of giving birth. Indeed, from 1970 to 1989, mother-only families grew from about 10 percent of all families to about 21 percent.

A second factor is the declining relative economic status of single-parent families during the past 20 years. While intact families registered income gains due to the advantage of having two working mem-

bers, the primary sources of income support for single parents—government assistance programs and the low-skill labor market—eroded significantly. The per capita income of single-parent families fell from 67 percent of that of intact families to 55 percent.

A third factor can be found in the elevated rate of childbearing among younger people, especially those with low education, low skills, and low earnings. Not surprisingly, the nation's population of children has become concentrated in young families, often economically disadvantaged. The children's poverty rate has increased from a par with other age groups in the nation in 1965 to about 150 percent of that level today. The children's poverty rate today stands at over 20 percent.

Finally, due to the rapid rise during past decades in the real level of Social Security benefits, government entitlement resources have become increasingly skewed toward the older population and away from children. By most estimates, the level of public support to children has fallen in real terms. As a result of this shift, the poverty rate of the elderly, which was much higher than the general poverty rate in the 1960s, now stands below that of the rest of the nation's citizens.

Because of this widening gap between children of younger families and members of the older population, the level of intergenerational animosity has increased. The elderly fight tenaciously for the maintenance of governmental Social Security and medical-care benefits. Younger families observe the publicly supported prosperity of older people and they resent it. Citizens, more generally, have come to recognize the declining level of investment in America's children, and have begun to face up to the serious implications of this trend for the future economic performance of the nation.

Can anyone doubt the increasing evidence that the nation is seriously misallocating resources among generations, being provident to older citizens whose working days are largely done, while skimping on young people whose later productivity will determine the nation's economic future? The implications of this for the nation's continued prosperity and for continued harmony among its different generations are serious.

The present versus the future

Consistent with the elderly having done well relative to youth and children, the nation has become more consumption-oriented and less investment-oriented, more concerned with the present than with the future, and increasingly ready to pass along the costs of our current living standards to future generations.

Manifestations of the nation's present-mindedness are ubiquitous. Nearly all the most prominent issues currently on the nation's agenda reflect a concern with neglected investments in our future. The enormous and persistent deficits and the growing debt imply a public sector willingness to borrow from the future in order to support consumption today. The concern with the quality of education at all levels suggests a perception that we have not been paying enough attention to the preparation of our children and youth for participation in a technologically advanced economy. Our savings and investment rates have, in recent years, fallen substantially relative to earlier levels.

From 1950 to 1979 the nation's saving rate averaged between 8 percent and 9 percent of GNP. Since 1980, it has averaged 4.2 percent. We clearly have been unwilling to forgo consumption in order to save and invest in future productivity and output gains. We decry the reduction in the quality of our roads, bridges, and parks. And we marvel at the ability of other nations to construct rapid rail systems and advanced technology communications networks, while we apparently cannot. We collectively judge that environmental degradation has gone too far, a numbing realization that here too we have used our legacy to support current living standards, apparently discounting the implications for our future.

Perceiving the problem, however, is easier than identifying its causes. Tastes—indeed, changing tastes—no doubt play an important role in this overconsumption and misuse of our inheritance. Perhaps we are passing through an era in which self-gratification dominates concern for our children and the world in which they shall live. Patterns of delayed marriage and low birth rates are consistent with this. The desire of women for an established career prior to childbearing, high divorce rates (often carrying painful lessons on the risks of early marriage), and a bleak horizon for income gains in middle age have made early childbearing and family-forming less attractive than it once was. For a variety of reasons, young people have reserved time to fulfill their own desires before entering into more enduring work and personal relationships.

Affluence, too, has played a role. Those at the top of the nation's income ladder, who have done well despite a slow-growing economy, have tended to engage in more leisure activities than when their incomes were lower. A choice of this nature, almost by definition, involves satisfying immediate desires at the expense of work, diligence, and productivity.

Observers of recent developments in Japan report the dissatisfaction of young people there with a life of long work hours and self-sacrifice in the interests of production. The call for more leisure and consumption grows louder there too. And perhaps perversely, a predictable concomitant of increased leisure is that it is consumed jointly with a variety of goods and services ranging from cars to campers to cruises to cottages. The likelihood that the increased demand for them has squeezed out both saving and investment is strong.

Moreover, the present-oriented nature of our private choices has probably influenced choices made in the public sector. One can see the increasing generosity of Social Security benefits over the past decades as being driven by just such a desire for more consumption in old age.

The implications of this drift toward "present orientation" are not difficult to see. Because investment is the "engine" propelling economic growth, the prospects for rapid future growth are not good. Few analysts forecast a return to growth rates of the sort we experienced in the two decades after World War II. With slow economic growth comes a lower rate of technological change and continued sluggish patterns of productivity improvement. If our performance on these fronts is inferior to that of our competitors, we will continue to prejudice our competitive economic position and our ability to participate in the production of those goods and services that lie on the cutting edge of technological change. Perhaps most discouraging is the fact that our profligacy will tend to saddle our children today, and those yet to be born, with the costs of our consumption.

A recent study estimates that the continuation of our current public-sector policies will require the typical child born next year to sacrifice at least $50,000 of his or her future earnings (in present-value terms) to pay for the present- and consumption-orientation of existing policy.

There can be no doubt that the consumption binge in which we participate will inhibit our future growth and prosperity, erode our international competitive position, and leave a legacy to our children which includes poor prospects for increases in economic well-being. It will leave responsibility for the support of a large and growing pool of nonworking dependents to our children as well as a large bill for the unpaid-for consumption which we have enjoyed.

What role has the federal government played?

In part, the direction taken by the American economy reflects the impact of demographic changes in our own society and international developments beyond our control. However, some of these disturbing trends are our own fault. A significant portion of the responsibility for them must be allocated to decisions made by U.S. citizens, either personally or collectively through the public policies they have implicitly supported. There is little doubt that the federal government by its policies, and the U.S. citizenry by its support of those policies, have been major contributors to the economic malaise we are now experiencing.

In essence, government policy has served as an engine of consumption—not of investment, nor work, nor productivity. It has been a primary source of the intergenerational conflicts in which we now find ourselves embroiled. And it has contributed to the growing inequality in income and wealth.

These are strong assertions, and have to be buttressed with some facts. To support these propositions, I offer a number of examples of policies that, in my judgment, have played an important role.

• The increasing generosity of Social Security benefits and medical-care coverage through Medicare has improved the standard of living of older citizens and stimulated consumption spending by them. A major chunk of this spending has been on health-care services. There is little doubt that the incentives in these programs have encouraged the rapid increase in the demands of older people for health care. These demands must bear part of the responsibility for the uncontrolled rise in the price of medical care. Moreover, these cost increases burden younger working citizens more than older citizens. And since the living standard of the retired elderly has risen by more than that of wage earners, is it any wonder that we see more serious conflicts between the generations?

• The financing of rising Social Security benefits by means of a payroll tax penalizes work and production, and rewards the consumption of leisure. Moreover, the payroll tax is a very regressive tax, burdening middle- and lower-income persons more than those with higher incomes. In sum, it penalizes

work, encourages the consumption of leisure, and increases the spread between the rich and the poor in our society.

• The exemption of fringe benefits from income taxation, in the case of health insurance, subsidizes its provision—in all likelihood, its overprovision—which in turn fosters the use of health-care services beyond the efficient level. In turn, the excess health-insurance coverage so stimulated by this provision increases business labor costs, thereby reducing employment, production, and productivity. Moreover, the exemption primarily benefits higher-income workers, again increasing the spread between the highest and lowest earners in the country.

• The neglect of infrastructure investment (highways, roads, sewers, parks, libraries, community public facilities), and the slowdown in public support for R&D contribute to torpid economic growth and sluggish gains in productivity in the same way that low levels of investment by private firms in plant and equipment inhibit output and growth. The government's neglect of these forms of public investment is part of the packet of policies that neglects investment and fosters consumption.

• The failure to maintain environmental quality has at least three major implications. It means that the prospect of our future enjoyment has been mitigated, that we have been overusing the environment in past production activities without paying its inevitable cost, and that future generations will have to foot the bill for improving the quality of the environment, if this basic aspect of life is to be sustained, let alone improved.

The failure to implement efficient environmental policies implies a public unwillingness to invest in our collective future well-being, to require production activities to bear the costs of the environmental degradation for which they are responsible, and to impose on ourselves—rather than our children—the costs of our own enjoyment.

• Federal tax policy has also contributed to our social and economic problems. I refer, in particular, to capital gains preferences, the subsidies of home ownership, the treatment of some forms of interest expense as a cost of doing business, the enormous reduction in tax rates on high-income people, and the preferential tax treatment of income earned by U.S. companies producing in Puerto Rico and overseas. These measures have fostered the rash of leveraged buyouts which has radically boosted the incomes of financial transactors in the 1980s, subsidized the housing purchases and other consumption of already wealthy citizens, and encouraged the relocation of production facilities to other countries, thereby costing numerous middle-income jobs.

In short, these tax provisions—many of recent vintage—have stimulated inefficient investment, encouraged excessive consumption expenditures, contributed to growing inequality in after-tax income, wage rates and earnings, and have led to serious problems of job loss and displacement in the nation.

• Retrenchment of federal support for urban areas— especially within the central city—is exemplified by the erosion of training programs, housing assistance, support for school facilities, improvements in teacher quality, and education program enrichment. Cutbacks in these areas have contributed to the plight of this nation's worst-off and most vulnerable. It has fostered what some commentators call the "two-tiered" society—rich "mainstream" families living in neighborhoods that are isolated from the abject poverty, homelessness, and destitution experienced largely by racial minorities.

The lapse of governmental investment in central cities—their schools, their workers, their homes— has fostered the growth of urban ghettos, has eroded social cohesion, and has reduced the economic potential of the next generation's work force of minority people.

What sort of policy strategy is now in order?

I have argued that the nation is afflicted with a set of economic ills that involve both serious inequalities and growth-constraining inefficiencies. The nation's inequality problems are draconian, pitting younger workers against older workers, high school dropouts against college graduates, and the 30-year-old unemployed or minimum-wage worker against the 30-year-old living in the suburbs and driving a new car.

The efficiency problems are no less in evidence— slow economic growth, productivity and wage stagnation, deteriorating public infrastructure, an educational system the performance of which is being increasingly questioned, and a work force that must compete in world markets with workers whose pay is but a fraction of its own. Given this constellation of problems, is it even possible to think about designing a single policy program—one package of policies, one set of resource shifts—that could simultaneously contribute to the solution of the nation's

inequity problems, and make the federal government an engine for investment and growth rather than consumption?

While I do not have the answer, I believe that devoting substantial thought to this broad question is a worthy activity. My hunch is that there is a package that would accomplish this, and that it would have as its components some of the items I suggest below. While each component in this package may not, itself, contribute to all the equity and growth goals, I am convinced that the entire package would secure for us both more efficiency and more equity, a more rapidly growing society, and a more cohesive one.

My candidates for inclusion in a national program for growth and equity include the following:

• Increased resources for improved education and skills for today's children, perhaps involving increased attention to apprenticeships and school-work transitions for the non-college bound, in order that we may increase the human capital and productivity of the next generation's workforce, and better match its skills to the jobs created by business.

• A refundable tax credit (or expanded Earned Income Tax Credit) serving as a safety net to those at the bottom of the nation's income distribution, in order that we may reduce the worst of the nation's poverty.

• Increased resources for central city improvements in the areas of crime, drugs, job training, housing, mass transit and health, in order that we may encourage a more even start for today's poor and disproportionately minority children and youths.

• A universal capital account for youths—a fund set up in the name of each child who turns 18 and who graduates from high school—from which withdrawals could be made for purchases of approved education, training, and health investment, in order that we may promote those human capital investments that youths would voluntarily choose if they had the resources.

• A wage-rate subsidy providing higher work-related income to today's youth and younger workers than their current real productivity may warrant, in order that we may give this cohort incentive to work and a cushion against the adversities with which they are saddled.

• An investment tax credit and encouragement to domestic R&D spending, in order that we may provide the incentive for private-sector enterprises to engage in those activities that will promote more rapid economic growth—the main hope of today's younger working-age people.

• Incentives directed at working-age people for increases in private saving, in order that we may finance the additional capital investment required by private businesses, and require working-age people to assume increased responsibility for their own well-being in retirement years.

• A radical revision of the Social Security retirement income program which would turn it into a universal poverty-line benefit program covering all citizens older than, say, 65, in order that we may free up monies to support these other initiatives and to encourage citizens to save while working and to support their own well-being during retirement.

• A carefully crafted estate and inheritance tax, in order that we may recoup for the purpose of these other initiatives some share of the enormous wealth holdings generated in the 1980s and now held by those who will be retiring over the next decades.

• A streamlined federal income tax that would eliminate most of the remaining special provisions, in order that we may encourage efficient private savings and investment decisions, redirect behavior from present-oriented activities toward future-oriented activities, and finance the other resource reallocations included in the package.

• And, if this does not generate enough revenue, a value-added tax of modest proportions.

Unless my perception is inaccurate, a package of this nature would yield the nation a greater degree of equality, increased economic growth, and an investment-oriented public sector. It would also require a larger and more efficient public sector. This last is, in my view, an essential element in working our way out of our current malaise, a prerequisite for securing a productive and equitable society over the next decades.

For some, a larger public sector may be a bitter pill to swallow. Nonetheless, I simply cannot envision a return to rapid economic growth and a taming of the unbridled market's apparent tendency to simultaneously create great wealth and abject poverty without a radically different vision of U.S. domestic policy.

Such a vision requires a public sector that serves as an engine for investment rather than consumption, a public sector that nurtures children and poor people rather than the elderly and the wealthy. It also implies a policy sea-change requiring national political leadership and the public resources to go with it. It requires that those in government again declare that the public sector has a responsibility to foster both growth and equity, and that it act on that declaration.

Cultural Pluralism: Race and Ethnic Relations

America has been referred to as the melting pot of the world because individuals from radically different cultural and ethnic backgrounds have been melded into "Americans." This means they have largely abandoned their histories, unique cultural heritages, and languages as they have acquired a common identity. Thus we have Irish Americans, Italian Americans, African Americans, and so on, with the focus being on their common identity as Americans, which has helped minimize cultural pluralism.

Some argue that this lack of cultural pluralism is what made America strong and that this lack of divisive ethnic, religious, and racial differences promoted unity. As a result, their argument goes, people were not restricted to specific geographic localities by race or ethnicity and could fit in any area. Even the American Civil War was not fought over cultural factors but over economic ones. The consequences of true cultural pluralism can clearly be seen in such locations as the former Soviet Union, South Africa, and North Africa.

Other individuals bemoan the fact that Americans expect new migrants to become both assimilated and acculturated. Newly arrived immigrants, they argue, should be able to retain most of their ethnic differences without becoming second-class citizens. Diversity, they claim, is the spice of life and ethnic tolerance the sign of social maturity.

"An American Melting Plot" supports the belief that ethnic and social class differences are divisive and should be actively discouraged. The author argues that volunteerism results in differing social camps, each with its own worldview and stereotypic perceptions of each other. Individuals with alternatives will gravitate toward those choices with the fewest risks and least negative consequences. Other individuals will be forced to fight the wars, do the dirty work, become guinea pigs for the novice physician, and so on. The author suggests ways in which ethnic and social class differences can be minimized. Rather than allowing people to volunteer for military service, attend schools of choice, or take part in community service projects, all citizens should be required to participate.

"America: Still A Melting Pot?" examines the impact that the existing immigration policies and immigrants have had and are currently having on the United States. With an economy that is slowing down, unemployment on the rise, overcrowded schools, increasing demand for taxes to support education, health care, and crime control, can the United States continue to function as the world safety valve? The emergence of racism, ethnic prejudice, and violence seem to be associated with fears that the new immigrants will take the few jobs that are available.

"Is White Racism the Problem?"—specifically, is it to blame for all the social ills of African Americans? The answer, according to Arch Puddington, is an emphatic "no." Focusing exclusively on racism as the source of all social problems for any minority not only is wrong, it is divisive and counterproductive.

Looking Ahead: Challenge Questions

Just what is meant by the concept "cultural pluralism"?

Should America still admit millions of foreign-born people fleeing poverty, racism, and war?

What implications do the existing U.S. immigration policies have for current citizens of the United States?

Is cultural pluralism a potentially divisive philosophy, a unifying situation, or an enriching phenomena?

What will be the implications for education when a majority of the residents of the United States do not trace their roots to western Europe? Should the educational curriculum of American schools be altered to reflect the unique makeup of specific communities?

Just what is meant by "white racism," and what are its origins within the United States?

To what degree is white racism responsible for the problems of African Americans? Explain.

In what unique ways would the three major theoretical perspectives defined in the Introduction tend to view the issue of cultural diversity?

What major issues, values, rights, obligations, and harms are the bases of race and ethnic issues?

An American Melting Plot

Why whine about our increasing

class segregation? Let's end it

Mickey Kaus

Mickey Kaus is a senior editor of The New Republic
and a contributing editor of The Washington Monthly.

What really bothers liberals about American society? Is it that William Gates, the 35-year-old founder of a computer software company, is worth $4 billion, and that some people drive Mercedeses and Acuras while others drive Hyundais and used K-cars? Is it that the wealthiest 40 percent of families receive 67.3 percent of the national income?

Or is it that the experience of confronting degraded beggars is now a daily occurrence for Americans who live or work in our major cities? Is it that a whole class of Americans—mainly poor, black Americans—has become largely isolated from the rest of society and is acquiring the status of a despised foreign presence? Is it that the wealthiest 20 or 30 percent of Americans are "seceding," as Harvard's Robert Reich puts it, into separate, often self-sufficient suburbs, where they rarely even meet members of non-wealthy classes, except in the latter's role as receptionists or repairmen? And is it the gnawing sense that, in their isolation, these richer Americans not only pass on their advantages to their children, but are coming to think that those advantages are deserved, that they and their children are essentially not just better off, but better?

If I'm right, distaste for this second sort of inequality—social inequality—is at the core of liberal discontent. Yet the primacy of this value is only occasionally made explicit in our ordinary political conversations. It is "subliminal" in the sense that it forms the unacknowledged motive of liberal policies that are justified on more familiar rhetorical grounds. Specifically, liberals tell themselves they are for "more equality" of income and wealth, when if they asked themselves, I think, they would probably discover they're actually after social equality—equality of dignity, of the way we treat each other in everyday life.

The point is that money equality isn't the only factor that determines social equality, and it may not be the crucial one. More important, perhaps, are the social attitudes and institutions that determine how much weight the money variable has. But if that's true, why spend all our energies trying to twiddle the dial that produces greater or lesser money inequality? An equally promising approach would focus on changing those attitudes and institutions that translate money differences, however large or small, into invidious social differences.

This is the Civic Liberal alternative. Confronted with vast disparities of wealth, it attempts, not to redistribute wealth "progressively," but to circumscribe wealth's power—to prevent money inequality from translating into social inequality. The primary way it does this is through social institutions that create a second, noneconomic sphere of life—a public, community sphere—where money doesn't "talk" where the principles of the marketplace (i.e., rich beats poor) are replaced by the principle of equality of citizenship. As the pre-1989 Eastern European champions of "civil society" tried to carve out a social space free of communist domination, so Civic Liberals would carve out a space free of capitalist domination, of domination by wealth.

The foundation of this community sphere is the United States is, of course, the political institution of democracy. There the marketplace stops, and the rule is not "one dollar, one vote" but "one citizen, one vote." The same principle applies to other important components of our community life, such as public schools, libraries, highways, parks, and the military draft. Each of these institutions attempts to treat all citizens, rich and poor, with equal dignity. They are especially valuable parts of the public sphere because, in contrast with the rather formal and abstract equality of voting, they require rich and poor to actually rub shoulders with each other as equals. So do many other, less obvious but important institutions such as museums and post offices, even parades and softball leagues.

Now, you can argue that money "talks" in our democracy, too, and that it talks even louder these days as politicians depend more and more upon rich donors to fund their increasingly expensive campaigns. Meanwhile, the affluent and the poor no longer rub shoulders in the public schools of even small cities, as the middle class flees to its suburban enclaves or else abandons public education entirely. In bigger cities, the everyday experience of public life in streets, parks, subways, and libraries has been ruined by crime, incivility, and neglect. The draft has been replaced by a volunteer army that the rich can simply avoid.

But these are precisely the sort of things with which Civic Liberalism concerns itself. Instead of worrying about distributing and redistributing income, it worries about rebuilding, preserving, and strengthening community institutions in which income is irrelevant, about preventing their corruption by the forces of the market. It tries to reduce the influence of money in politics, to revive the public schools as a common experience, to restore the draft. And it searches for new institutions that could enlarge the sphere of egalitarian community life.

Not all components of the public sphere have deteriorated in the late twentieth century. The jury system, for example, still brings disparate members of the community together, if only occasionally, in a way that often convinces those who serve that common sense isn't a function of income or race. More generally, the courts still treat a Michael Milken or Leona Helmsley with an inspiring lack of deference. But other institutions have not been so hardy. Let's start with the institution that has deteriorated most dramatically: the military.

There are perfectly good military reasons for replacing the current all-volunteer force (AVF). Some of these reasons are related to social equality. The Gulf war proved that the egalitarian objections to an AVF become loudest at the worst time, just as the prospect of combat and death looms. At the very moment we were trying to intimidate Saddam Hussein in the winter of 1990–91, our country was split by a debate over whether the rich would bear their fair share of the fighting. The only reason the controversy wasn't crippling may have been that the battle turned out to be short, with few casualties on our side.

There are other, more technical problems with the AVF that have less to do with egalitarianism, such as the fact that the pool of young men from which we must buy our volunteers is shrinking (from 8.6 million men aged 18 to 21 in 1981 to an estimated 6.6 million in 1995). But the main justification for a draft remains moral. Volunteer-army advocates rely on the logic of the private sphere, in which everything, even soldiers' lives, is convertible into cash. If some young Americans are freely willing to go into battle for $25,000 a year—well, it's a deal. ("You took the money, now shut up and die," as former Navy Secretary James Webb caricatured the argument during the Iraq crisis.) But it is one thing for society to pay people to pick up its garbage and drive buses. It's another to pay them to risk their necks in battle. If dying in combat isn't outside the economic sphere, what is? The draft is the most natural and—again, because it involves the risk of death—most potent, arena of democratic experience. It doesn't only break down class barriers for a couple of years; it breaks them down for life, in part by giving all who serve a network of military acquaintances that crosses class lines. Even Henry Kissinger used to hang out with his old Army buddies.

A democratic draft is hardly a bold, idealistic step into the future. It's something America has done before. To reinstate it, we don't need new taxes or new leaders—simply a new law.

True, thanks to communism's collapse, the military will only need about 11 percent of America's draft-age men by 1995. But, however modest the manpower needs of the military, a draft is the most socially egalitarian way of meeting them. Even if only 11 percent of men in the upper, middle, and lower classes served—and all the others had to think about serving—it would do more to promote social equality than all the "transfer payments" liberals might conceivably legislate.

Genuine draft

Yet it would be even more effective to involve more than 11 percent, and more than just men—to make the military part of a broader scheme of national service, including civilian service. Here is an idea that separates Civic Liberals from those with other priorities.

"At the age of 18, you should be focusing on your dreams and ambitions, not picking up cans in Yellowstone," sniffs Republican Jack Kemp. For social egalitarians, however, national service is valuable precisely because it would force Americans to pause in their disparate career trajectories and immerse themselves in a common, public enterprise. It is the draft in a weaker dose, more widely dispensed.

The notion of national service was revived in the eighties—to no apparent effect. Universal service was endorsed by Gary Hart, who predicted it "might be the biggest issue" of the decade. Senator Sam Nunn and Rep. Dave McCurdy introduced legislation that would have made federal student aid contingent on one or two years of service. (The Nunn-McCurdy bill went nowhere when the education establishment realized it would supplant existing loan programs.) William F. Buckley distinguished himself from most on the right by calling for a service scheme that would enroll 80 percent of America's youth by means of various "inducements" and "sanctions." Buckley's proposal, too, went nowhere.

For Civic Liberals the overriding goal, of course, is class-mixing. This helps clarify the sort of national service program we're talking about. For example, it excludes Job Corps-type programs designed to help salvage underclass kids through elaborate vocational training. The more national service "targets" the poor, the less it will be seen as a duty for all classes. Nor is the Civic Liberal test of success whether national service participants become less selfish. It's simply whether a large cross section of the population winds up serving together under conditions of equality.

Purely voluntary programs fail to meet this test; the ambitious sons and daughters of upper-class families simply don't sign up. Some national service advocates (like Buckley) nevertheless hope that "incentives" of various sorts might subtly induce participation by the rich. But such financial inducements can still be easily ignored by the wealthy. The only way to guarantee class-mixing is to make national service mandatory. That requires the threat of a penalty harsh enough to be coercive. It could be jail. It could also be a heavy monetary penalty that judges could tailor to fit the financial circumstances of any refuseniks—though it would have to be a potential fine of hundreds of thousands, perhaps even millions, of dollars if it were going to guarantee the participation of the truly wealthy.

A mandatory service scheme would enlist a lot of people—3 to 4 million a year, assuming the plan targeted young men and women of draft age. What would they be doing? Here again, it matters that social equality is the main goal. If we see national service mainly as an antidote to the "culture of selfishness," then the grungier the work, the better. Cleaning up mud slides is just the thing to teach incipient yuppies a thing or two. But the Civic Liberal imperative is to mix the classes, not to beat the selfishness out of them. National service jobs could be enjoyable, even career-enhancing. What's important is that they have a heterogeneous, communal aspect.

There are plenty of worthy tasks that fit this bill. Care for the infirm elderly is probably the most pressing need. Buckley notes that between 125,000 and 300,000 older Americans now living in nursing homes could move back into the "normal community" if there were enough workers to assist them with their daily chores. Those who are incapable of leaving nursing homes often lead lives of brutal loneliness—but the cost of professional attendants is simply too great for the vast majority of American families to bear by themselves.

In strict economic terms, national service is almost surely an inefficient way to help these lonely, old and ill Americans. It would be cheaper (once you count the "opportunity costs" of forgoing all the other things the servers could be doing with their time) to raise taxes to pay for a lot of nurses and hand-holders. But national service lets us do something in addition to providing services. It allows us to carve out a part of life where the market is negated, where common, nonmarket values that even conservatives like Buckley invoke—fellowship, solidarity, and social equality—can flourish.

There are other needs almost as critical: tutoring the illiterate and semiliterate, helping maintain or patrol public spaces, sorting library books, perhaps assisting in the care of preschool children in day care. As long as the tasks are class-mixing and valuable, a national service would be free to do whatever work the market, for one reason or another, cannot do—whether that work is grungy or exhilarating, and whether or not the government could do it more cheaply some other way.

Unfortunately, an emphasis on the most useful work puts national service on a collision course with public employee unions, which see young draftees as threats to their jobs (the same reason they also fear a WPA-style guaranteed jobs program). The more useful the work, the greater the chance some union member is already doing it.

One solution is to restrict national service to a few concrete tasks of proven utility and practicality. "There are four or five jobs we clearly know how to train kids to do," says Kathleen Kennedy Townsend, who runs a student service organization for the state of Maryland. Her list: teachers' aides, police aides, nurses' aides, a rural "conservation corps" to clean up the environment, plus a similar corps to repair and maintain urban public spaces. Put those together and you probably have enough jobs to keep several million young people usefully employed at a time.

The final question facing any mandatory national service scheme is how to integrate it with the military. That's trickier than you might think. The armed forces, as noted, need only a small fraction of those eligible to serve. What's more, they require stints of service lasting at least two years (otherwise training costs become too high). Requiring two years of civilian service seems a bit much. But one year of civilian service could hardly be treated as the equivalent of two years in the army.

Clearly, military service should count as the fulfillment of any service requirement. Beyond that, young Americans could be given a choice of military or civilian service—but the military's wages would have to be set much higher to compensate for the greater risks and longer tour of duty. Because the rich would be less tempted by such financial incentives than the nonrich, the result would probably be class division, with the military disproportionately poor and the affluent opting to avoid the perils of potential combat.

A better approach, for social egalitarians, would combine universal service with conscription. Teenagers would first be subject to a military draft, with no civilian alternative. If they escaped in the draft lottery, they'd have to do a year of civilian service. This hybrid draft/service setup might well be perceived as fairer than any attempt to allow more freedom of choice at the expense of universal exposure to military risks. Rich and poor teenagers would take their chances in the draft together. If chosen, they would serve together for two years. If they weren't chosen, they would still serve together as civilians for one year.

This sort of service scheme is the most intrusive Civic Liberal strategy; it would interrupt the lives of all Americans. But precisely because it is intrusive, it holds out the possibility of doing for everyone what Joseph Epstein, editor of *The American Scholar*, remembers the peacetime draft did for him: "[I]t jerked me free, if only for a few years, from the social class in which I have otherwise spent nearly all my days. It jerked everyone free. . . ."

Doctored results

Given the continuing threats to social equality, Civic Liberals can hardly be satisfied with restoring the public sphere where it has deteriorated. They need to seize on new possibilities to expand it. Of all the potential new egalitarian institutions on the horizon, the biggest involves the provision of health care.

Health isn't a good like other goods. If somebody can't afford a car, we're willing to say, well, he doesn't have a car. But if a man who can't afford medical care is bleeding on the sidewalk, we are going to provide him with it one way or another, at public expense if necessary. As with the draft, the issue is life or death.

Of course, saying health care should be available to everyone doesn't necessarily mean it must be available in equal measure, or that the experience of getting it will necessarily be one that mixes classes. But the goal of universal coverage offers a solid base for building a potent democratic institution. We know it cements social equality to have Americans attend the same schools and serve in the same army. What effect would it have if they used the same doctors? The experience might not be as intense as school or service, but it would be repeated throughout a person's life.

Certainly universal health insurance seems to play a major socially equalizing role in Western Europe, where every country has some sort of universal national health plan. In most of them, the plan's egalitarianism is a source of fierce national pride. When everyone uses the same system, it not only reinforces "solidarity," it also ensures the quality of care. Upper-middle-class Americans will not tolerate bad treatment for very long (just as they wouldn't have tolerated the Vietnam war if their sons had been drafted).

In the United States, we have a patchwork system that, rather than putting everyone in the same boat, puts different groups in different boats and lets some fall in between. At the bottom, Medicaid covers only about 42 percent of the poor, mainly those on welfare or other mothers with young children. At the top, the revenue code heavily subsidizes generous employer-paid health plans by not counting them as income (a $40 billion tax break). Falling between boats are those who are unemployed, self-employed, or whose employers don't have a company plan. They are left to fend for themselves, to buy private insurance (with after-tax dollars). Between 31 and 37 million people in this group aren't insured at all, and that number has been growing. But if Americans reach the magic age of 65, they can relax. They qualify for Medicare, which will cover most of their bills.

It's not necessarily true that the more "socialized" a system is, the better it satisfies the demands of social equality. The British, German, and Canadian systems all currently meet the goal. The "socialized" British system allows those with money to purchase private insurance, but that doesn't undermine class-mixing because most of the private insurance merely supplements the national health system, where the most advanced, high-tech medicine is still practiced. Only about 10 percent of the population uses the private system (though that percentage is growing).

Germany also manages to include about 90 percent of its population in a single system. The Germans do this by the simple expedient of requiring 75 percent of the population to join one of several "statutory sickness funds." Those with incomes above a certain threshold can opt out, but once they've done so, they can never opt back in. Not surprisingly, most remain with their assigned funds. The system's motto might be, "We have ways of making you stay." An even simpler, more effective strategy can be found in Canada, where it is flat-out illegal to buy basic private health insurance. Canadian waiting rooms mix virtually 100 percent of the population.

But less sweeping plans are less likely to achieve this objective. Senator Edward Kennedy's patchwork employer-based insurance scheme, in particular, looks like a loser for social equality. Medicaid and Medicare would still exist, probably with differential standards of care. Some employers would still provide lavish, fee-for-service insurance; some would consign their employees to spartan HMOs. Taxpayers (most of whom would already be covered, one way or another) probably wouldn't want to pay for much in the way of gap-filling last-resort insurance. We'd still have a system in which different classes report to different waiting rooms.

Even under the most promising plans, the crunch for Civic Liberalism will come when attempts to control the overall cost of health care force some method of rationing ever-more expensive medical procedures. What happens when affluent Americans—*increasingly* affluent Americans—are faced with this rationing? They will not calmly take their place in the queue for CAT scanners or proton-beam accelerators or artificial hearts. They will go outside the "universal" system and pay more money to get the expensive technology they want.

The temptation will be to let them, with the result of producing a two-tier health system of elaborate care for the affluent and basic care for everyone else.

A Civic Liberal strategy would require regulations, such as those in Germany, making it unappealing to opt out of the "universal" system. At the very least a heavy tax disincentive will be necessary. The goal would only be to make enough (say, 90 percent) of the populace use the public sphere's waiting rooms. It's one thing, Civic Liberals could argue, for the rich to be able to buy the nicest cars, or the houses with the nicest views. It's another thing to make it easy for money to buy life itself.

Kids or cash?

Health care isn't the only new public sphere possibility. Day care is another service with impressive potential for growth. The debate over day care has been between those (mainly Democrats) who want to encourage communal day care centers and those (like President Bush) who would simply give cash to parents with preschool kids and let the parents decide whether to use the money to buy day care. Civic Liberals would tend to favor communal centers. Indeed, day care is a public sphere institution offering a unique escape from the tyranny of suburban class-segregation. Unlike schools, day care centers can be conveniently located near places of work rather than near homes. And poor preschool children aren't nearly as threatening to upper-middle-class parents as, say, poor adolescents. Locate the day care centers near work, and let the toddlers of secretaries mix with the toddlers of bank presidents. Let their parents worry together and visit together.

A range of other government institutions—museums, post offices, libraries—at least potentially reinforce social equality by providing services to all citizens. There is an important distinction to be made here—one typically ignored by American admirers of European social democracies—between provision of such common services and the provision of cash. With "in-kind, universal" services, Robert Kuttner notes, people of all classes actually meet and interact with each other and with those doing the servicing. They wait together, flirt, swap sob stories and advice, save each other's place in line, keep an eye on each other's kids. The "middle class is . . . reminded that poor people are human," Kuttner writes. This is the stuff of social equality.

But none of these virtues is evident when all the government does is send out checks—even if, as liberals typically recommend, benefits go to the middle class and rich as well as the poor. Recipients receive their benefit checks in isolation. The cash is spent, and is intended to be spent, in the private, money sphere. No communal experience is involved. On the contrary, the recipient's attention is focused more intensely on the importance of money and what it can buy. How much solidarity is there in cashing a check? Rich and poor don't even cash them in the same places.

Out at third

Civic Liberalism would also recognize and protect the social-egalitarian power of class-mixing institutions that are technically in the "private sector." Particularly important are casual gathering places like taverns, coffee houses, and drug stores. Ray Oldenburg calls these "third places" because they offer an alternative to the other two main sites of our lives—home and work. One essential characteristic of a good third place is that it is accessible to people of all income levels; as Oldenburg puts it, "Worldly status claims must be checked at the door in order that all within remain equals." In the mid-seventeenth century, he points out, coffee houses were actually called "levelers" because they mixed the various classes in a way unheard of in the old feudal order.

It's easy to underestimate the significance of such unpretentious institutions. But they embody much of what Americans feel they've lost since the move from small towns—the general store, the pharmacy soda fountain of *It's a Wonderful Life*, the neighborhood bar romanticized on "Cheers."

The decline of those "private" democratic places is bound up in the process of suburbanization. Zoning changes that allow coffee shops, stores, and taverns to locate near residences, instead of in single-purpose commercial strips, would help. Still, it would be hard for even a nearby neighborhood tavern to mix classes in a neighborhood that is itself segregated by class. Fully restoring third places as class-mixing institutions will have to await the success of longer-term strategies to integrate the suburbs by income, as well as by race.

But some privately operated enterprises that are part of our public life don't rely on class-mixing at the neighborhood level. Organized professional sports are an obvious example. Going to a major league baseball game remains one of the few enjoyable experiences shared at the same time, in the same place, by people of various classes—one reason it's considered so precious. But even the democratic aspects of spectator sports are threatened by a number of recent developments. Attending a ball game has become a distinctly less egalitarian experience, for example, with the unfortunate invention of the tax-deductible corporate "skybox." Team owners now routinely demand stadium renovations that enable them to maximize the square-footage devoted to the rich. Another inegalitarian development is cable television, which allows broadcasters to restrict spectatorship to those who can afford to subscribe. In 1987, most New York Yankee home games were available only on cable. The result was a tremendous protest and a threat of congressional action, in part because large sections of New York—the poorer sections—weren't even wired for cable.

In general, the decline of network broadcasting (and the advent of demographically targeted "narrowcasting" on cable) should disturb social egalitarians. Network TV is often awful, but it once had the virtue of giving all Americans a common, classless set of cultural experiences. As the network audience share declines (it's fallen from 92 percent to 64 percent), that is increasingly no longer true. Instead of everybody watching Milton Berle, young professionals watch the Arts & Entertainment Network while the less cultured tune in to "Married with Children."

But once the egalitarian importance of these private institutions is acknowledged, Civic Liberals will be able to take steps to halt their deterioration. The tax deduction for stadium skyboxes and season tickets could be completely eliminated, for example—not on economic grounds, but on social-egalitarian grounds. Television coverage of sporting events could be regulated to keep it universal, preventing cable companies from buying the rights and then broadcasting only to the cable-ready affluent. If necessary, the sports franchises themselves could be regulated, purchased by municipalities, or even seized by eminent domain. If the TV networks collapse completely, the government could establish a BBC-style network, less snooty than the current Public Broadcasting System, with a preferred spot on the broadcast spectrum nationwide. These may seem like relatively small things, compared with the draft or national health care. But they matter.

The point isn't that the Civic Liberal reforms suggested above would ensure social equality. That will require something more. The point is that once we set out to rebuild the public sphere, we can make fairly large improvements fairly expeditiously. It requires nothing we haven't done ourselves in the past—or that we can't copy, with appropriate modifications, from other democratic capitalist nations. We can frame our obligations so that rich and poor Americans serve the nation together. We did that in World War II. We did it in the fifties. We can have a society in which the various classes use the same subways and drop off their kids at the same day care centers and run into each other at the post office. We don't have to equalize incomes or make incomes "more equal" or even stop incomes from getting more unequal to do these things. We just have to do them.

America: Still a Melting Pot?

Tom Morganthau

Few Americans remember Israel Zangwill, but he was a transatlantic celebrity in the years before World War I. Poet, novelist, dramatist and political activist, Zangwill was a founding father of the Zionist movement and an ardent suffragist. He knew Theodore Roosevelt, Oscar Wilde and George Bernard Shaw, and he was a prolific, if preachy, writer. Here is a bit of dialogue from Zangwill's greatest hit, a four-act melodrama that opened in Washington in 1908. The speaker is David, a young composer:

> *America is God's Crucible, the great Melting-Pot where all the races of Europe are melting and re-forming. . . . Germans and Frenchmen, Irishmen and Englishmen, Jews and Russians— into the Crucible with you all! God is making the American!*

The imagery comes from steelmaking, which was state-of-the-art technology then. The play is "The Melting-Pot," a phrase that has lived ever since. Zangwill, despondent at the eclipse of many of his political ideals, suffered a nervous breakdown and died in England in 1926. America had already turned its back on his optimism and, in an orgy of blatant racism, virtually cut off immigration. Two generations later, immigration is running full blast—and Americans once again are asking fundamental questions about the desirability of accepting so many newcomers and the very idea of the Melting Pot. They believe, with some justice, that the nation has lost control of its borders. They are frightened about the long-term prospects for the U.S. economy and worried about their jobs. They think, erroneously, that immigrants are flooding the welfare rolls and are heavily involved in crime. And

they are clearly *uncomfortable* with the fact that almost all the New Immigrants come from Latin America, the Caribbean and Asia.

The latest NEWSWEEK Poll reveals the public's sharply shifting attitudes. Fully 60 percent of all Americans see current levels of immigration as bad; 59 percent think immigration in the past was good. Fifty-nine percent also say "many" immigrants wind up on welfare, and only 20 percent think America is still a melting pot.

All this—an incendiary mixture of fact, fear and myth—is now making its way into politics. The trend is most obvious in California, where immigration is already a hot-button issue, and it is surfacing in Washington. Recent events like the World Trade Center bombing, the arrest of Sheik Omar Abdel-Rahman and the grounding of the

---

1600–1776
Seeking greater fortune and religious freedom, Europeans braved the Atlantic to settle in America before the Revolution

---

Golden Venture, an alien-smuggling ship crammed with nearly 300 Chinese emigrants, have revived the 10-year-old controversy about illegal immigration. "We must not—we will not—surrender our borders to those who wish to exploit our history of compassion and justice," Bill Clinton said last week, announcing a $172.5 million proposal to beef up the U.S. Border Patrol and crack down on

visa fraud and phony asylum claims. On Capitol Hill, the revival of an issue that many had thought dead is shaking both political parties, and Democrats such as Sen. Dianne Feinstein of California are scrambling to neutralize nativist backlash. "Some of the people who opposed me totally 10 years ago are now saying, 'What's happening to our country? We gotta do something!' " said Republican Sen. Alan Simpson of Wyoming, a perennial advocate of tougher immigration enforcement. "It's ironic beyond belief. Attitudes have shifted dramatically, and it's coming from the citizens."

This is not the 1920s—a time when most Americans regarded dark-skinned people as inherently inferior, when the Ku Klux Klan marched through Washington in a brazen display of bigotry and when the president of the United States could tell an Italian-American congressman, *in writing*, that Italians are "predominantly our murderers and bootleggers . . . foreign spawn [who] do not appreciate this country." (The president was Herbert Hoover and the congressman was Fiorello La Guardia.) The civil-rights revolution changed everything: it gradually made overt expressions of any ethnic prejudice into a cultural taboo. Almost accidentally, the moral awakening of the 1960s also gave the nation an immigration law that reopened the Golden Door. This law, passed in 1965 with the firm backing of Robert Kennedy, Edward Kennedy and Lyndon Johnson, has slowly led to a level of sustained immigration that is at least as large as that of 1900–1920. It inadvertently but totally reversed the bias in U.S. law toward immigration from Europe, and it created a policy so complicated that almost no one understands it. The policy, in fact, is a mess, whatever one thinks of the desperate Chinese on the

The Economic Cost of Immigration

IMMIGRATION HAS ranked with corn and cars as a mainstay of American economic growth. The traditional theory is simple: energetic workers increase the supply of goods and services with their labor, and increase the demand for other goods and services by spending their wages. A benign circle of growth uncurls as a widening variety of workers create rising riches for each other. Two hundred years of U.S. history seem to confirm this theory. Yet the perception today is that immigration is a drag on the economy, not a lift. In truth, it's both. "The short-term costs of immigration today are much higher," says Michael Boskin, formerly chief economist to George Bush, "but in the long run, immigrants are still great news for our economy."

The NEWSWEEK Poll shows that 62 percent of those surveyed worry that immigrants take jobs away from native-born workers. That can be true in times of high unemployment. In California, where the jobless rate is 9 percent, immigration is soaring and native-born Americans are actually leaving to find work in other states, some temporary displacement may be occurring. But in normal times, any job loss is more than offset by the creation of new jobs stemming from the immigrants' own work. The immigrants' new spending creates demand for housing, groceries and other necessities, and their employers invest their expanding profits in new machinery and jobs. "It is called competitive capitalism," says Tony Carnevale of the American Society for Training and Development, "and it works. It's how America got rich."

Two forces, however, have recently helped to undercut the benefits of immigration: the welfare state and the steep decline in the skill levels of immigrants since 1970. In the last great decade of immigration, 1900 to 1910, public education and a little public health were the only services provided to those migrating to New York and other Northeastern cities. One third of the new immigrants simply failed and moved back home. Today dozens of welfare programs—from food stamps to unemployment compensation—cushion failure and attract immigrants who might otherwise stay home. In California, children born to illegal parents now account for one in eight beneficiaries of one program alone, Aid to Families with Dependent Children (AFDC). The state-run Medicaid program provided $489 million in health care to more than 400,000 illegal aliens last year. Legal aliens got hundreds of millions more.

Donald Huddle, an immigration expert at Rice University, recently calculated that the 19.3 million legal, illegal and amnestied aliens accepted into the United States since 1970 utilized $50.8 billion worth of government services last year. They paid $20.2 billion in taxes. So the net burden on native-born taxpayers was $30.6 billion—a social-welfare cost per immigrant of $1,585. Huddle projects these immigrants will cost taxpayers another $50 billion a year on average over the next 10 years.

A decline in the skills of new immigrants helps to explain these numbers. Ninety percent of current immigrants arrive from Third World countries with income and social-service levels one tenth or even one twentieth those of the United States'. Their education levels relative to those of native-born Americans are steadily declining. So are their earnings. George Borjas of the University of California, San Diego, says that in 1970 the average immigrant actually earned 3 percent more than a native-born American but by 1990 was earning 16 percent less. "Each year the percentage is heading downward," says Borjas. What's more, welfare dependency has steadily climbed and is now above that of native-borns. In 1990, 7.7 percent of native Californians received

public assistance vs. 10.4 percent of new immigrants.

The welfare costs of immigration should dramatically decrease as the California and U.S. economies recover. The long-term benefits of immigrant labor and business enterprise will then be more apparent. But the age of innocence in the American immigration experience is over. The rise of the U.S. welfare state has placed a cushion under the immigrant experience—and diminished the benefits of immigration to the country at large.

RICH THOMAS *with* ANDREW MURR
in Los Angeles

Golden Venture or the young Latinos who scale the fence at Tijuana every night.

Bill Clinton's goal, like that of most defenders of continued large-scale immigration, is to drive home the distinction between legal immigration (good) and illegal immigration (very, very bad). Illegal immigration is undeniably out of control. Congress tried to stop it in 1986 with a law called IRCA, the Immigration Reform and Control Act, which was based on a two-pronged strategy. IRCA offered amnesty and eventual citizenship to an estimated 3.7 million illegal aliens and, at the same time, aimed at shutting down the U.S. job market by making it illegal for employers to hire undocumented aliens. The act has failed. Despite the amnesty, the estimated number of illegals has once again risen to between 2 million and 4 million people. "For the first two years there was a significant drop . . . because folks thought there was a real law here," says Lawrence H. Fuchs, acting chair of the U.S. Commission on Immigration Reform. "But the word got out" that IRCA had no teeth, Fuchs says, and the influx resumed. Fuchs concedes that as many as 500,000 illegals now enter this country each year, though he admits it is impossible to know for sure.

The concern over illegal immigration is fueled, in part, by two conflicting fears. Illegals are vulnerable to exploitation by employers and are often victimized—extorted, kidnapped, raped, tortured and sometimes killed—by crimi-

1820–1870
The potato famine of the mid-1840s sent the Irish scurrying to the promised land, while economic depression in Germany triggered an exodus

nals and smugglers. At the other extreme, in cities like Los Angeles, they flood the labor market and set off bitter competition with American workers and legal immigrants for jobs.

But the real problem is the subversion of U.S. law and policy, and that creates two dilemmas for the federal government. The first is what to do about the undocumented aliens who have made their way into this country since IRCA: another amnesty, obviously, would only encourage more illegal immigration. The second dilemma is worse. There is no particular reason to believe that the current influx of illegals cannot rise from 500,000 a year to 600,000 a year or even beyond. This is conjectural but not necessarily alarmist: as Fuchs says, the word is out. Looking around the world, "one can't find the natural forces that will bring down the flow," says Harvard University sociologist Nathan Glazer. "The first impact of prosperity will be to increase it. Look at China. These people don't come from the backward areas, they come from the progressive parts. As they learn how to run a business, they say to themselves, 'Why not go to the United States and do even better?' "

The same applies to Bangladesh, the Dominican Republic, Mexico or the Philippines. The dynamic, as Fuchs says, is rooted in powerful macroeconomic forces now at work all around the globe—rising birthrates and the conquest of disease, prosperity or the hope of prosperity, even modern telecommunications. (The glittery materialism of American TV shows is now being broadcast everywhere.) Much as Americans tend to regard the new immigrants as poor, uneducated and less skilled, the vast majority are surely enterprising. What they seek is opportunity—the opportunity to hold two jobs that no Americans want, to buy a television set and a beat-up car, to

start a family and invest in the next generation. Immigration is for the young: it takes courage, stamina and determination to pull up your roots, say goodbye to all that is dear and familiar, and hit the long and difficult trail to El Norte. Illegal immigration, with all its hazards, is for the truly daring: the Latino men who wait on Los Angeles street corners, hoping for daywork, have faced more risk than most Americans will ever know.

You can argue, then, that the distinction between legal and illegal immigration is nearly meaningless. Immigrants are immigrants: how they got here is a detail. And, in fact, the arcane system of regulation created by the 1965 law, together with its amendments and adjustments since, implicitly accepts this argument. The law recognizes three reasons to award immigrant visas—job skills, especially those that somehow match the needs of the U.S. economy; a demonstrable reason to seek refuge from war or political persecution, and kinship to an American citizen or a legal alien. This triad of goals replaced the national-origin quota system of 1924, which heavily favored immigrants from North-

America's Legal Immigrants:

The United States accepts more immigrants than all other industrialized nations combined. In fiscal 1991 the United States government granted 1,827,167 people legal permanent

CALIFORNIA

When Los Angeles erupted in rioting last year, tensions grew between the black community and immigrants; roughly 2,000 Korean-owned businesses were among those looted or damaged by fire.

IMMIGRANTS BY COUNTRY
Mexico 69%
Philippines 4%
El Salvador 3%
Vietnam 3%
China 2%
Others 19%

CALIFORNIA
735, 732
(40%)

By the Numbers: The Top Destinations
PERCENTAGES ARE OF TOTAL LEGAL 1991 U.S. IMMIGRANTS

TEXAS
212,600
(12%)

ARIZONA
40,624
(2%)

ARIZONA

Although many are just passing through in search of opportunities, Arizona's Mexican immigrants often feel at home amid the state's Hispanic heritage.

IMMIGRANTS BY COUNTRY
Mexico 86%
Vietnam 2%
Others 12%

TEXAS

Texas and Mexico share some 1,200 miles of porous border, along which the INS has apprehended about 380,000 illegal aliens so far this year.

IMMIGRANTS BY COUNTRY
Mexico 80%
El Salvador 4%
Vietnam 2%
Others 14%

ern and Western Europe and severely restricted immigration from everywhere else. It is a matter of lasting national shame that Congress, throughout the 1930s and even after World War II, refused to adjust the law to admit the victims of the Holocaust. That shabby record outraged Jews and had much to do with the passage of [the] act of 1965. So did the old law's bias against Slavs, Poles, Italians, the Chinese and the Japanese.

But all three of these goals have been steadily distorted—chipped at, twisted out of shape—by the realities of immigration since 1965. Kinship to U.S. citizens, known as the "family-reunification policy," has become the overwhelming

1880–1920
Persecution and poverty throughout Europe unleashed the greatest flock of immigrants ever; no fewer than 12 million sought refuge here

favorite of visa seekers and the primary reason the pattern of immigration has shifted so hugely to the Third World. It was never intended to be: given the fact

that most immigration to the United States had always been from Europe, those who voted for the act of 1965 generally assumed that family-reunification visas would be used by Europeans. They also assumed that there would be no large increase in immigration to the United States. "Our cities will not be flooded with a million immigrants annually," Sen. Edward Kennedy told a subcommittee hearing. "Under the proposed bill, the present level of immigration [about 300,000 a year] remains substantially the same. . . ."

That is not what happened. Immigration from Latin America, the Caribbean and Asia, a trickle in 1965, has steadily widened so that it now comprises about 90 percent of the total. Legal immigration from 1971 to 1990 was 10.5 million people—but if 3 million illegals are (conservatively) added in, the total is pretty much the same as 1900–1920, the peak years in American history. Owing partly to a further liberalization of the law in 1990 and partly to the IRCA amnesty, the United States now accepts more immigrants than all other industrialized nations *combined*. (Upwards of 80 percent are persons of color: so much for the myth that U.S. policy is racist.) Proponents of further immigration argue that the current influx is actually lower than the 1900–1920 peak when considered as a percentage of the U.S. population. They are right: it was 1 percent of the population then and about one third of 1 percent now. But it is still a lot of people.

Who They Are and Where They Go

residence. Seventy-nine percent of these legal immigrants, looking for everything from freedom to financial opportunity, chose the seven states below as their new homes.

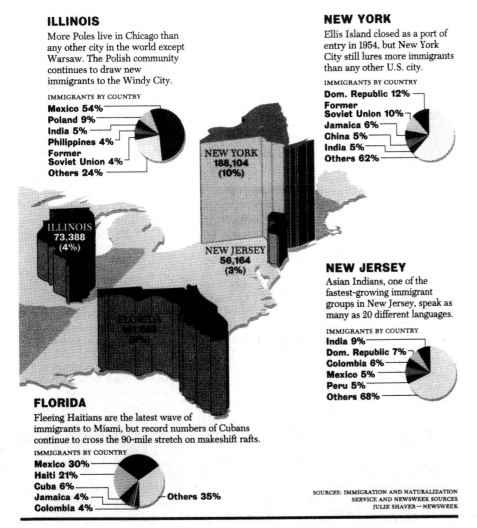

ILLINOIS
More Poles live in Chicago than any other city in the world except Warsaw. The Polish community continues to draw new immigrants to the Windy City.

IMMIGRANTS BY COUNTRY
Mexico 54%
Poland 9%
India 5%
Philippines 4%
Former Soviet Union 4%
Others 24%

ILLINOIS
73,388
(4%)

NEW YORK
188,104
(10%)

NEW JERSEY
56,164
(3%)

NEW YORK
Ellis Island closed as a port of entry in 1954, but New York City still lures more immigrants than any other U.S. city.

IMMIGRANTS BY COUNTRY
Dom. Republic 12%
Former Soviet Union 10%
Jamaica 6%
China 5%
India 5%
Others 62%

NEW JERSEY
Asian Indians, one of the fastest-growing immigrant groups in New Jersey, speak as many as 20 different languages.

IMMIGRANTS BY COUNTRY
India 9%
Dom. Republic 7%
Colombia 6%
Mexico 5%
Peru 5%
Others 68%

FLORIDA
Fleeing Haitians are the latest wave of immigrants to Miami, but record numbers of Cubans continue to cross the 90-mile stretch on makeshift rafts.

IMMIGRANTS BY COUNTRY
Mexico 30%
Haiti 21%
Cuba 6%
Jamaica 4%
Colombia 4%
Others 35%

SOURCES: IMMIGRATION AND NATURALIZATION
SERVICE AND NEWSWEEK SOURCES
JULIE SHAVER—NEWSWEEK

And the law is full of holes. A majority of those who get family-reunification visas (235,484 in 1992) come in with no numerical restriction at all: for them, at least, immigration is a form of entitlement program. Others game the system by forging documents, faking job histories and hiring smart American lawyers to get them eligible for resident visas and green cards. This is known in federal jargon as "adjusting status," and in most years it works for more than 200,000 immigrants. The asylum hustle is the newest wrinkle. By claiming political asylum, would-be immigrants circumvent the normal rules and, because the jails are full, are usually freed to stay and work. Many simply vanish into the underground economy. "We didn't [expect] the asylum problem," says Lawrence Fuchs. "We thought of it as the ballerina in the tutu saying, 'I defect, I defect'."

Immigration policy is simultaneously a statement of America's relationship with the rest of the world and a design for the national future: it is, and probably should be, a mixture of altruism and self-interest. Current U.S. policy contains elements of both—but it is a blurry, heavily brokered policy that has been cobbled together over the decades to reflect the changing fads and competing interests of domestic politics. A purely selfish policy would accept only immigrants who could contribute to economic or social progress. But this idea—awarding visas on the basis of talent or skill—

has always been opposed by organized labor and other groups, and it is a minor feature of today's law, totaling about 140,000 out of 810,000 visas annually. Conversely, providing a haven for refugees is in the best tradition of the American conscience, and the United States has taken a lot of refugees since 1970—1.5 million Vietnamese, Laotians, Cambodians, Cubans, Russians and other oppressed nationalities.

But the vast majority of those who get here are ordinary folks pursuing a better life—and although this, too, is part of the American tradition, the question can and should be asked: What's in it for *us*?

What does all this immigration do for America and Americans? Julian Simon, a University of Maryland economist, says he knows the answer: more immigration means more economic growth—more wealth and more progress for all Americans, period. Pat Buchanan, the talk-show host and erstwhile presidential candidate, has a different answer: more immigrants mean more social friction and the slow erosion of the English-speaking, hybrid European culture we call "American."

There is a third issue as well: how many people, really, can the territorial United States support? Immigration now

Immigrant Schools: The Wrong Lessons

UNION AVENUE ELEmentary school, a dusty sprawl of concrete, asphalt and chain-link fence just west of downtown Los Angeles, bears all the scars of the inner city. Yellow caution signs mark the perimeter: NARCOTICS ENFORCEMENT AREA. RESIDENTS ONLY. In the distance a police helicopter circles over a crime scene. After school, parents anxiously hook their fingers through the fence and wait for their kids to emerge. But because Union Avenue draws from a heavily immigrant neighborhood, its 2,000 students have even more to surmount than the grim realities of crime and poverty. They also face the enormous obstacles, educational and societal, that stand in the way of foreign-born newcomers.

The student body is more than 93 percent Latino. The second largest group is Filipino, at 2.9 percent. A third of the students were born outside the United States, and well over half are not proficient in English. As many as half may be children of illegal aliens. There are as few Anglos as there are Native Americans: six. In the school library there are books in Tagalog, Korean, Vietnamese, Spanish and English. But

not even a third of the faculty can speak Spanish. The others rely on bilingual teacher assistants to translate the lessons. This is an explosive subject here. Many claim that bilingual education has done more to divide teachers than to help Spanish speakers. Defenders see it as a multicultural keystone. The faculty has been Balkanized by bilingualism: at lunchtime the two sides segregate themselves by table.

Most of the newest immigrants come from Central America, and many bring with them the trauma of war. Asked whether he had witnessed much fighting in his hometown of San Rafael, El Salvador, which he left three years ago, fifth grader Angel Alfaro nods but doesn't want to talk about it. Asked about his school and what he would do to fix it, he perks up and says in unaccented English, "Nothing. It's perfect."

The Union Avenue kids' eagerness to please, and to learn, is irrepressible. Yet it is hard to be optimistic about their future. For all of its inadequacies, the school is a relatively calm way station. Most of the kids will go on to Virgil Middle School, where education competes with gangs, graffiti tag-

gers and drugs. Fifth grader Reggie Perez, whose parents are Guatemalan, says he is going to go to a school in North Hollywood "because at Virgil there are just too many gangs." Out of 15 students interviewed last week (the school is in session year round), all but one said their parents were trying to get them into a parochial school or bused to a school in a better neighborhood. Still, most of the fifth graders will end up at Virgil.

Schools like Union Avenue are making a valiant effort. But as a recent report from the Rand Corp. says, "School systems that are beset by debt, declining and unstable revenues, dilapidated buildings and inadequate instructional resources cannot improve simply by trying harder." The federal government has all but ignored the needs of states with large immigrant populations like California, New York, Texas, Florida and Illinois. The single federal program that targets immigrant students is funded at $30 million a year—or $42 per child. In California, where budget tightening has hit specialized programs especially hard, state officials estimate that they are short 8,000 bilingual teachers.

NEWSWEEK POLL

Do you agree or disagree: (percent saying agree)

62% Immigrants take the jobs of U.S. workers

78% Many immigrants work hard—often taking jobs that Americans don't want

59% Many immigrants wind up on welfare and raise taxes for Americans

THE NEWSWEEK POLL, JULY 29–30, 1993

Historically, a solid education has been the quickest road to assimilation. But today, during the greatest surge in immigration since the turn of the century, the schools are failing the 2 million children who have been part of the influx. Their education is isolating them from the mainstream, rather than helping them to join it, and exposing them to all of the pathologies of ghetto life. Meanwhile, as the NEWSWEEK Poll indicates, anti-immigrant sentiment is on the rise. Such a charged atmosphere "doesn't make the job any easier," said Lorraine M. McDonnell, coauthor of the Rand report. The kids, instead of getting the best that their new home has to offer, often get the worst.

STRYKER MCGUIRE *in Los Angeles*

produces about a third of U.S. population growth, and projections for the future range from a population of about 383 million in 2050 to 436 million by the year 2090. All of these projections are shaky—based on complex assumptions about birth and death rates as well as immigration policy. Some environmentalists (and many Californians) think the United States should immediately halt immigration to protect the ecosystem and the quality of life. Fuchs says his commission has consulted environmentalists and population experts. "They persuaded us that the population growth is terribly serious on a planetary scale, but not in the United States," he says. "So migration to the United States perhaps has a beneficial effect on the global environmental problem." Still, Congress took no notice of this question when it voted to increase immigration in 1990—and given the wide disparity of current views, picking the "right" number of future Americans is ultimately a combination of taste and guesswork.

1965–1993
The face of immigration has changed over the last few decades, adding non-European cultures, languages and religions to the melting pot

The further question is one that troubles Pat Buchanan and many others: can America absorb so many people with different languages, different cultures, different backgrounds? The answer, broadly, is yes—which does not mean there will be no ethnic friction and does not mean that assimilation is easy for anyone. Assimilation is a generational thing. The first generation—the immigrants themselves—are always strangers in the land. The second generation is halfway between or (kids will be kids) rejects the immigrant culture. The third generation is hyphenated-American, like everybody else, and begins the search for Roots. The tricky part, which worries Fuchs considerably, is that America's "civic culture" is unique in all the world. It is the belief, as embodied in the Constitution and our political tradition, "that it is individual rights, not group rights, that hold this country together." So here is the question for all of us, native-born and immigrant alike. At what point do policies like affirmative action and minority-voting rights stop being temporary remedies for past injustices and start being permanent features of the system? The whole concept of group rights, as Fuchs says, is tribalism—the road to Bosnia, not East L.A. And that, surely, is not what Israel Zangwill had in mind when he described America as the crucible of a new civilization.

With ADAM WOLFBERG and BOB COHN in Washington, ANDREW MURR in Los Angeles and bureau reports

Is White Racism the Problem?

Arch Puddington

ARCH PUDDINGTON, a former aide to the late civil-rights leader, Bayard Rustin, writes frequently on race relations. He works for Radio Free Europe-Radio Liberty in New York.

A CONSPICUOUS feature of the commentary on the recent Los Angeles riot was the many comparisons between racial conflict in America and the most murderous ethnic strife abroad. More than once, Los Angeles was likened to Yugoslavia, and frequent parallels were drawn between conditions here and in South Africa, with neighborhoods like South-Central Los Angeles identified as the American version of Soweto. Ethnic and religious hatred in the Middle East was also invoked. The British *Guardian* headlined one article, "Beirut in L.A."; inevitably, black neighborhoods were portrayed as similar to the West Bank, with blacks cast as America's Palestinians, and the riots characterized as a black *intifada.*

Some black political figures, particularly Jesse Jackson and Maxine Waters (who represents South-Central L.A. in Congress), referred to the riot as a rebellion, with the implication that the rioters should be regarded as the heroes of a struggle against despotism. Yet the black mobs who beat into senselessness white motorists who had strayed into the wrong neighborhoods were not participating in a rebellion; and most of the victims of the killing, burning, and looting were members of their own race. As for those engaged in the looting, it was difficult to believe that they were telling us anything other than that human beings will often yield to temptation if there appear to be no sanctions involved.

Of course, the commentators who drew comparisons between the Los Angeles disorders and conditions in other distressed corners of the globe had in mind the political similarities as well as the physical ones. But the view of an America plagued by a racial conflict as lethal as the struggle pitting Serbs against Croats or the Hezbollah against Maronite Christians cannot long be sustained.

To begin with, whites here are not killing blacks; less than 3 percent of wrongful deaths in 1990 involved white assailants and black victims, half the percentage of cases where blacks were the assailants and whites the victims.

Nor are American whites unmoved by cases of racial injustice. By overwhelming majorities whites expressed bewilderment and outrage over the not-guilty verdict rendered in the case of the four white Los Angeles police officers accused of beating a black man (Rodney King), the incident which triggered the riots in L.A. and several other cities. Whites might not have been ready to label the residents of Ventura County, where the trial was held, as reactionary white suburbanites (in the words of a black California politician, Willie Brown). But there was certainly a willingness to accept the proposition that blacks are treated less fairly than whites by the criminal-justice system, even though whites are aware of the high rates of black crime.

Nor is it accurate to accuse white Americans of complacency about the plight of the black poor. Many may believe that affirmative action has elevated blacks to the status of a preferred class, but most recognize that blacks are more likely than other groups to be afflicted by poverty, inadequate medical care, and a multitude of other such problems.

A more accurate statement is that Americans have suffered from a lack of leadership on racial matters, from both the Right and the Left. The Left's shortcomings were on display in black political leaders like Representative Ron Dellums and Jesse Jackson, who responded to the riots by demanding massive transfers from the military budget to the inner city, attacking foreign aid and free-trade policies, and issuing silly declarations about the bailout of the savings-and-loan industry. There was also the spectacle of Representative Waters assuring America that she did not condone violence and looting, and then, again and again, coming perilously close to doing just that.

Conservatives, on the other hand, were left with no credible response to the repeated references by liberals to "twelve years of neglect" under Presidents Reagan and Bush. For there was no denying that both of these administrations gave every sign of obliviousness to the racial problem and in the process reinforced the impression that conservatives simply do not care much whether blacks succeed or not.

From *Commentary,* July 1992, pp. 31-36. © 1992 by the American Jewish Committee. All rights reserved. Reprinted by permission.

For some commentators, finally, responsibility lay not with American leadership but with America itself. They were convinced, in other words, that America is a thoroughly racist society—that racism, and not the failure of this or that program, or the policies of this or that administration, is the source of the seemingly intractable problems of the inner-city black poor.

Charges of racism have, of course, been hurled about quite promiscuously in recent years, with the result that many Americans see it as one of those political terms which have been stripped of meaning through misuse by demagogues. Recognizing this, those who attributed the Los Angeles events to white racism usually refrained from the kind of generalized indictment of American society that was routinely voiced during the 1960's. Instead, they focused on specific institutions, such as the Los Angeles Police Department, the criminal-justice system, or the banks (for their reluctance to provide loans to inner-city businesses).

There was, however, at least one voice prepared to blame the riots on the bigotry of individual whites and the racism of American institutions: Andrew Hacker, the white political scientist whose controversial book, *Two Nations: Black and White, Separate, Hostile, and Unequal,* was published just a few weeks before the riots.* *Two Nations* was already on the best-seller lists when the Los Angeles riot broke out, and it climbed steadily in sales thanks to the consequent revival of concern over the country's racial troubles.

The thesis of *Two Nations* is set forth in the very first paragraph. Race, Hacker tells us, "has been an American obsession since the first Europeans sighted 'savages' on these shores." While the American Indians would eventually be "subdued" or "slaughtered," the importation of African slaves would ensure a permanent racial crisis for the new society. Today, the fact that America was once a slave-owning society "remains alive in the memory of both races and continues to separate them." "Black Americans," Hacker adds, "are Americans, yet they still subsist as aliens in the only land they know." Thus America is in reality "two separate nations," where blacks "must endure a segregation that is far from freely chosen."

These phrases resonate with the apocalyptic language used in 1968 by the National Advisory Commission on Civil Disorder in what became popularly known as the Kerner Report. In its most frequently quoted passage, the Kerner Report declared that America was becoming "two societies, one white, one black—separate and unequal," and placed the burden of responsibility for this development on "white racism."

The Kerner Report's long-term effect on social policy is debatable. Without doubt, however, the report had the unintended consequence of alienating many whites from the civil-rights agenda. These whites interpreted the more pointed Kerner formulations as blaming them for the rash of riots which had engulfed the nation's major cities, and they reacted with predictable indignation. Some black leaders also found the report unfortunate insofar as it focused attention on the psychology of individual whites rather than on the source of black economic inequality.

Yet Hacker is even more insistent than the Kerner Report was about the racism both of individual Americans and American institutions. He damns everything from the police to the schools to corporate executives to popular culture as complicit in a regime of racial subordination—a condition, he asserts, which exists because that is the way whites want it.

In addition, then, to echoing the Kerner Report, Hacker's analysis—for all the concise, matter-of-fact, dry prose in which it is couched—pulsates with the spirit of the radical 60's, when New Left and Black Power ideologues discovered systemic bias throughout American life. Hacker even betrays an attraction for the kind of theorizing which gained currency during the sourest period of racial radicalism and urban chaos. He is, for example, attracted to the young Eldridge Cleaver's ruminations about rape as an instrument of political revenge against white society, along with the late James Baldwin's proposition that whites "need the nigger"—that is, that whites have a stake in seeing blacks as inferior, in order to bolster their own illusion of racial superiority.

In general, Hacker uses racism the way Marxists use class oppression, as a ready-made explanation for all social phenomena, a sterile approach preordained to reach the gloomy, if sensationalistic, conclusion that racial progress will invariably be thwarted by a white majority living in constant dread of challenges to its supremacy.

Take Hacker's discussion of income inequality. He begins by noting that while whites have always earned considerably more than blacks on average, the income gap did narrow by a substantial amount in the three decades before 1970. The most pronounced improvement occurred in the years 1940-59—a period when Jim Crow prevailed in the South, where most blacks then lived, and when thousands of blacks were finding employment in the industrial centers of the North and Midwest. But since 1970, Hacker notes, the racial gap has narrowed hardly at all.

The trends emphasized by Hacker would seem to substantiate the conclusions of the sociologist, William Julius Wilson, that the failure of blacks to continue their march toward income parity stems primarily from their having been disproportionately hurt by the decline in industrial employ-

---

* Scribners, 258 pp., $24.95.

ment. But this theory clashes with Hacker's basic argument which traces inequality to racism and racism alone, and so he does not dwell on it. Likewise, he conveniently ignores the fact that working-class Americans of all races have suffered income stagnation during the past twenty years, another trend which challenges his book's main premise.

Nor is Hacker drawn to the idea that blacks should emulate the model of recent immigrant groups by seeking economic advancement through small businesses sustained by dawn-to-dusk hours and the mobilization of entire families. Hacker recognizes that during the period of legal segregation black-owned businesses often served black neighborhoods, but he seems to sympathize with the position now taken by many blacks that, having lived in America for generations, they should not have to make the sacrifices which newcomers are compelled to make. Hacker adds that whites themselves are less likely to engage in small business than such groups as Koreans, Japanese, and Cubans, and for this reason should refrain from passing judgment on blacks for their lack of entrepreneurial enthusiasm.

From just about every perspective, this is a thoroughly insidious argument, guaranteed to feed the flames of ghetto defeatism. Yes, there are whites who preach unappetizing sermons which counterpose the achievements of Asian immigrants to the failures of the black poor. Yet whites are still twice as likely as blacks to own their own businesses, and in any case whites are not confronted by the kind of economic crisis which now afflicts generation after generation of inner-city black poor.

Blacks, of course, do face certain hurdles to successful business ownership, and where government can assist in lowering these barriers, action should be aggressively taken. But part of the problem clearly involves the negative attitudes of young blacks not merely to business ownership but to the entire world of work.

To be sure, these attitudes are not shared by all or even most black males; we are, after all, familiar with the pictures of thousands of workers, mainly black, lining up to apply for a handful of positions at the post office or the assembly-line plant. There is, however, another image, one highlighted in an illuminating post-riot *MacNeil-Lehrer* segment, in which a group of young male Harlemites had no hesitation in telling an interviewer of their unwillingness to accept jobs advertised at a local placement office because the pay was too low.

Here, we were informed, was a graphic example of the dilemma confronting young black men whose employment opportunities were limited to "dead-end jobs." Yet it was not pointed out—it seldom is—that historically people without much education have very often started out at precisely such dead-end jobs, acquired a respect-

able work record, and then moved on to better-paying positions in other fields.

Even today, according to a recent study, 90 percent of those applying for new taxi-driver licenses in New York are foreign-born; and only a portion of the 10 percent who are native-born is black. Now, driving a taxi may not be the most lucrative job in the world, but it is not the kind of minimum-wage position which black men often deride; in many ways, it is an ideal transitional job for young men without a clear sense of what they want to do with their lives. Racial discrimination is not a problem, and hiring standards are far from stringent. Here, one would think, is an occupation ready-made for heavy black participation. That this is not the case inevitably raises questions about black male attitudes toward the world of work that Hacker, for one, does not even begin to deal with.

Yet this issue must be placed on the table, along with institutional racism, prejudice, and the changing nature of the economy, if the full and frank discussion about race advocated by Hacker and others is to be conducted.

One likely outcome of such a discussion might be the discovery that black attitudes are strongly conditioned by the repeated stress on the black community as the helpless victim of white society. Blacks like the writer Shelby Steele and the community activist Robert Woodson have argued persuasively that blacks cannot move forward as long as they see themselves in this way, since it leads to passivity, resentment, and demoralization. Hacker, by contrast, regards victimhood as the defining feature of American blacks, and in a self-defeating vicious circle dismisses any emphasis on personal responsibility and self-discipline as merely the latest weapon in white America's ongoing project of racial humiliation.

HACKER'S approach to the critical question of out-of-wedlock births is even more shocking than his treatment of employment. Thus, he makes much of the fact that over the past several decades there has been a proportionately higher increase in unmarried parents among whites than among blacks, the point being that whites have no standing to sermonize about the structure of the black family. Hacker may consider this an effective debater's point, but it is irrelevant, or worse, to any serious examination of the dynamics of black poverty, and is a piece of blatant evasion from a writer who takes pride in candor and plain speaking.

For one thing, there remains a huge difference in the proportion of single parents among blacks and whites. More to the point, a phenomenon which for whites represents a serious but containable problem is for blacks something truly catastrophic, as can be seen by reading the biographies of the teenagers who kill other teenagers over something so trivial as who was first in line at a fast-food restaurant. Almost always, the assailant is a black boy who knew his father fleetingly, if at all.

Hacker is just as bad on the question of education as a vehicle for racial progress. He suggests, correctly, that there is a genuine clash between the goal of employing more black teachers and the challenge of strengthening national educational standards. In states which have devised tests to measure teacher competence as part of a reform package, white teachers have consistently and by wide margins outperformed blacks. In a typical situation, 75 percent of a state's white teachers will pass competency tests, as compared with 45-50 percent of black teachers. In one state, Louisiana, the rate for whites was 78 percent; for blacks, it was a dismayingly low 15 percent—meaning that white teachers were five times as likely to achieve a passing mark.

Hacker's analysis of scores on the Scholastic Aptitude Test (SAT) also makes for disturbing reading. On this examination, so critical for college admission, blacks lag not only behind whites, but behind the sons and daughters of recent immigrants from Asia and Latin America. This is true even when the comparison is limited to low-income immigrants whose mastery of English is weak. In 1990, whites and Asians scored some 200 points higher than blacks on average, a huge difference. Hispanic students scored almost 70 points higher, even though their income levels were about equal to those of blacks, even though a similarly low percentage of their parents had attended college, and even though two-thirds of them described English as their second language.

It has, to be sure, been argued—and Hacker appears to agree—that the SAT is culturally biased against blacks. But he adds the intriguing observation that it is not so much "white" values which are reflected in standardized examinations as values which demonstrate a familiarity with the skills necessary to cope with the modern world generally. These modern skills and ideas may have had their origin in the United States and Europe, but through the globalization of the economy and the spread of mass communications they have by now filtered through to what was once known as the third world. It is this transnational flow of values, Hacker contends, which accounts for the impressive performance of recent immigrant children on American standardized tests.

The unsettling implication of this analysis is that within black America there is a generation of young people totally unprepared for modern economic competition. Is this, as Hacker insists, due to white racism? Or are there other causes—sensitive factors relating to the culture of inner-city life—which must eventually be addressed? How does Hacker's one-track explanation square with the fact that the earnings of black women have reached over 90 percent of average white female earnings? Or with the fact that college-educated black women earn *more* than comparably educated white women?

In times past, even during the pre-civil-rights period, urban blacks moved rather easily into the job market—the private job market, it should be stressed, since it has only been in recent times that blacks have been heavily represented in government employment. Clearly, the white racism invoked by Hacker—the de-facto segregation purposely set up by whites because they consider blacks a "degraded species of humanity"—cannot explain what is happening today. And it certainly cannot point us toward a way out.

IN THE aftermath of the riots of 1992, no institution of American life has been subjected to a scrutiny more intense, or angrier, than law enforcement. And indeed, the most frequent complaint of blacks is that they are systematically mistreated by the police. This complaint has been voiced by black corporate executives, physicians, actors, and university professors, as well as by the inner-city poor, with many black professionals recounting stories of abject humiliation at police hands.

On the surface, the King verdict would seem to reinforce Hacker's thesis of an inherently racist America, where whites automatically identify with state power even when the rights of blacks have clearly been violated. Yet the jury in the King case did not come across in press accounts as comprised of arrant bigots. Interviews with individual jurors reveal men weeping and women praying for divine guidance as a decision was reached, and of twelve average Americans agonizing over every detail of evidence. In other words, the jury was behaving much like juries in other lengthy, highly publicized trials of recent memory. Members of the jury took their mission with dead seriousness, and if, as seems likely, an error was made, it was committed by twelve people who were engaged in an earnest attempt to see that justice was done.

It is also possible that the jurors were motivated by an unconscious bias against blacks. Or, what is more likely, by a combination of attitudes, in which the police were seen as the last defense against society's predatory elements and Rodney King, a large man with a checkered, criminal past, as precisely the kind of person against whom society needs to be protected. If so, the reason can be found in the statistics assembled by Hacker himself, which point to the near-impossibility today of separating the issue of race from the issue of crime.

Drawing on arrest figures collected from local law-enforcement agencies by the Federal Bureau of Investigation, Hacker shows that in practically every category of violent crime, blacks are overrepresented by huge margins. Blacks comprise 61 percent of those arrested for robbery—

five times their proportion of the population (12 percent). The figure for murder is 55 percent; for rape, 43 percent; for weapons possession, nearly 40 percent; for aggravated assault, 38 percent.

To make matters worse, these statistics are nationwide in scope. They include the states (nearly half) in which blacks make up less than 5 percent of the population, and the many areas of industrialized states where the black presence is minuscule. Obviously, this means that in urban areas the proportion of blacks among the suspects in violent crimes is much, much higher even than the high numbers cited by Hacker.

Even if allowance is made for racial bias among police or for the ability of white criminals to elude arrest, these figures demonstrate, in stark terms, that to regard casually dressed young black men warily is a matter of prudence, not prejudice. The figures do show that in the murder and rape categories, black assailants choose black victims by overwhelming margins. On the other hand, the victims of robbery by blacks tend to be white.

A RELATED issue, from the perspective of the police, is the belief that black criminals are more likely to use violence in resisting arrest. Certainly blacks are better armed than in the past. By some measurements, the Los Angeles riot was less severe and less costly in terms of property loss than previous disorders, some of which raged for days and saw entire blocks destroyed. Yet more deaths occurred in Los Angeles in 1992 than in Newark, Detroit, or Watts in the 60's, and the reason almost certainly was the large number of sophisticated weapons among the rioters and the increased tendency of black criminals to shoot with deadly intent.

As one Los Angeles gang member told Ted Koppel of *Nightline*, the difference between Watts some 25 years ago and the most recent turbulence was the prevalence of Uzis and assault weapons among those participating in the two riots.

Given this lethal combination of skyrocketing violent crime, well-armed criminals, and a long history of hostility between blacks and police, one would expect fatal shootings of blacks by the police to be on the rise. Indeed, within the black community a whole mythology has emerged in which the victims of the police are regarded as heroes of racial struggle. Spike Lee dedicated his movie, *Do the Right Thing*, to blacks who died in controversial incidents at the hands of New York City police, and Hacker seems to feel that blacks are justified in looking upon the victims of police shooting as martyrs.

In reality, however, fatal shootings of blacks by the police have undergone a steady *decline* in recent years, amounting to 40 percent less than two decades ago. The same period has also seen a major increase in the number of blacks in big-city police departments. Nationwide, blacks comprise 40 percent of new police hires over the past two decades, and blacks are well represented on all major police forces, including the one in Los Angeles.

True, blacks are still three times more likely than whites to be killed by a policeman's bullet. But one simply cannot ascribe this to racism, since blacks are also three-to-five times more likely than whites to be arrested for crimes of violence. An interesting sidelight is that those blacks who die at the hands of the police are disproportionately the victims of black policemen. Hacker's comment, typically, is that "now there is a tendency to use blacks to control blacks" in the major cities.

F OR the past two decades, the strategy of America's black leadership has rested on two main pillars: securing jobs in the professions, skilled trades, and government service through affirmative-action programs, and gaining more and more political power, particularly local power in big cities. After Los Angeles, that strategy lies in ruins.

Affirmative action will continue: that was ensured by the passage of the most recent civil-rights act. But court decisions, the general political mood, and the wording of the new civil-rights law itself have combined to make it unlikely that racial-preference programs will expand beyond their current level. And as civil-rights leaders themselves acknowledge, policies of racial preference cannot deal with the problems of the urban underclass, the chief source of racial tension today.

Nor have the black poor derived much benefit from the impressive increase in black political power. Three of the cities hardest hit by the recent wave of disorders—Los Angeles, Atlanta, and Seattle—are led by black mayors, and Atlanta's political establishment is today predominantly black. Black political officials are not responsible for the persistence of poverty and the explosion of inner-city drugs and crime. Nevertheless, whether under white or black leadership, the problems of the black underclass persist. Meanwhile, immigrant groups which have eschewed serious political involvement while focusing single-mindedly on economic achievement continue their march toward integration and prosperity.

Despite the obvious failure of race-specific policies in meeting the needs of the underclass, we can be sure that the riots of 1992 will ignite new and ever more ambitious demands for racially balanced juries, police forces, and legislative bodies, along with renewed calls for multicultural education and an Afrocentric curriculum in urban schools. It would be highly unfortunate if such demands were acceded to: they represent an attempt to buy racial peace, similar to the Johnson administration's handing out of anti-poverty grants to youth gangs and posturing militants during the 60's, and they serve to reinforce the dangerous myth that the road to black economic integration will be significantly different from the road taken by all other groups.

On the positive side, the response to the riots has summoned forth a number of voices grounded in common sense and optimism. Of particular note have been the neighborhood activists, those involved in bringing business to black neighborhoods, working with the police to provide better street safety, trying to stimulate a more livable inner-city environment. Where national black leaders harp on the theme of white racism and call for urban Marshall Plans, many local leaders insist that measures be taken to ensure a level playing field for black businessmen and drive home the point that the solutions to the problems of black America will ultimately be found in the inner resources of black people themselves.

After Los Angeles, America has a clear choice in its approach to racial division. It could, on the one hand, follow Andrew Hacker and those, both white and black, who think as he does, into a soul-searching debate over white racism, much like the debate which followed the riots of the 60's. The result, this time, would be similar: bitterness, frustration, and little concrete action. Or we could begin paying heed to people, also both white and black, who have new thoughts about race, and especially new thoughts about reaching the underclass—thoughts based on the centrality of moral and spiritual factors like personal responsibility and initiative. It is this latter course, and only this latter course, that offers the possibility of new hope for blacks, and for all the rest of us as well.

Cities, Urban Growth, and the Quality of Life

Until 1965 the major problems facing cities were those associated with growth. People by the millions were abandoning rural areas and migrating to the cities. Because of a complexity of factors, this trend has been reversed. Since 1965 many U.S. cities have lost major industries—businesses as well as the people involved. These losses have produced a declining tax base and an aging infrastructure, both of which spawn a related host of social problems such as unemployment, underemployment, homelessness, crime, and gangs. But what is fascinating is that while many major cities are in trouble, others are thriving. *Annual Editions* has decided to create a new section for this edition of the book devoted specifically to cities and their struggles to survive and provide meaningful and safe environments for their residents.

Answering the question, "Can We Stop the Decline of Our Cities?" necessitates discovering the basic causes underlying the decline. The authors contrasted those cities in decline with those that are not and discovered that decline or growth is directly dependent on the costs of services provided by the city, the size of governmental bureaucracies, and the quality of services provided.

"Visions of Community in an Urban War Zone" describes innovative efforts of the Chicago Housing Authority to regain control of some of its 1,500 public housing complexes. After extensively remodeling specific high-rise complexes they filled them with a mix of welfare recipients and working families with the idea that the working families could be role models for the others. They then established tenant patrols in each project. These patrols were designed to function like a neighborhood watch, which, it was hoped, would create a sense of community. Where this "sense" developed, violent crime dropped by more than 33 percent.

"Cities of Violence" is one unanticipated consequence of democracy. With unprecedented freedoms come expectations that are often unrealized. In societal terms, the resulting manifestations are often anger, frustration, and violence. The author contrasts what is happening in the cities of Johannesburg, Rio de Janeiro, and Moscow with that of New York City and Washington, D.C.

The author of "Terminal Decline of a Nation" believes that Americans have been so busy worrying about all their problems that they have failed to notice that America is rapidly going bankrupt. In fact, the United States has gone from being the world's biggest creditor to the number-one debtor. What can be done, if anything, is not clear. But the author sees the solution as being the responsibility of the federal government.

Looking Ahead: Challenge Questions

What are the significant differences between those major cities that are thriving and those that are in decline?

In countering urban decline, how effective has the infusion of federal dollars into cities been? What are the primary reasons for this?

What are the advantages and disadvantages of tenant patrols?

What is meant by "community," and can it be artificially created?

Why does the emergence of a nation from a totalitarian state to a democracy seem to result in rampant crime, violence, and death?

What needs to be done to stay the terminal decline of the United States?

In what ways would researchers utilizing each of the three major theoretical perspectives defined in the Introduction differ in their approaches to the study of urban problems?

Can We Stop the Decline of Our CITIES

*Unless and until they start putting people first—
by cutting service costs and anti-growth tax rates—no amount of
Federal aid can reverse the trend.*

Stephen Moore and Dean Stansel

The authors are, respectively, director of fiscal policy studies and a research assistant, Cato Institute, Washington, D.C.

FOR MORE THAN a quarter-century, Americans have been voting with their feet against the economic policies and social conditions of the inner cities. Fifteen of the largest 25 U.S. cities have lost 4,000,000 people since 1965, while the total U.S. population has risen by 60,000,000. The exodus no longer is just "white flight"—minorities also are leaving the cities in record numbers.

In recent years, the departure of businesses, jobs, and middle-income families from the old central cities has begun to resemble a stampede. For example, since the late 1970s, more than 50 Fortune 500 company headquarters have fled New York City, representing a loss of over 500,000 jobs. Cleveland, Detroit, Philadelphia, St. Louis, and other major cities also are suffering from severe out-migration of capital and people. Those once-mighty industrial centers are becoming hollow cores of poverty and crime.

Ever since the Los Angeles riots and looting, urban lobbyists—including mayors, public employee unions, urban scholars, and many members of Congress—have been arguing that the inner cities were victims of Federal neglect under Presidents Ronald Reagan and George Bush. "There was, quite literally, a massive Federal disinvestment in the cities in the 1980s," according to Congressional delegate Eleanor Holmes Norton of Washington, D.C. To revive them, the U.S. Conference of Mayors is asking for $35,000,000,000 in new Federal funds—a "Marshall Plan for the cities."

The Federal government already has tried the equivalent of some 25 Marshall Plans to revive the cities. Since 1965, it has spent an estimated 2.5 trillion dollars on the War on Poverty and urban aid. (That figure includes welfare, Medicaid, housing, education, job training, and infrastructure and direct aid to cities.) Economist Walter Williams has calculated that this is enough money to purchase all the assets of the Fortune 500 companies *plus* all of the farmland in the U.S., but it has not spurred urban revival. In 1992 alone, Federal aid to states and cities rose to $150,000,000,000. Adjusted for inflation, that is the largest amount of Federal intergovernmental aid ever extended—hardly a massive disinvestment.

Central cities' budgets on the rise

The budgets of Cleveland, Detroit, Philadelphia, New York, St. Louis, and other large central cities have not been shrinking; they have been rapidly expanding for decades. In constant 1990 dollars, local governments spent, on average, $435 per resident in 1950, $571 in 1965, and $1,004 in 1990. The largest cities saw an even faster budget rise. In real dollars, New York's budget nearly tripled from $13,000,000,000 in 1965 to $37,000,000,000 in 1990. Philadelphia, another nearly bankrupt city, allowed its budget to rise by 125% between 1965 and 1990—from $1,600,000,000 to $3,500,000,000. During the same time period, the city lost 20% of its population. In short, 25 years of doubling and even tripling city budgets have not prevented urban bleeding.

Not all U.S. cities are in decline. Among the nation's largest urban areas, there are dozens—many on the West Coast, in the Sunbelt, and in the Southeast—that have been booming financially and economically for at least the past 20 years. Las Vegas, Nev.; Phoenix, Ariz.; Arlington and Austin, Tex.; Sacramento and San Diego, Calif.; Raleigh and Charlotte, N.C.; and Jacksonville, Fla., all have rapidly rising incomes, populations, and employment and low poverty and crime rates.

What do growth cities—Phoenix, Raleigh, and San Diego, for example—do differently from shrinking cities such as Buffalo, Cleveland, and Detroit? The answer is found, at least partially, in their fiscal policies. Bureau of the Census finance data from 1965, 1980, and 1990 for the 76 largest cities reveal significant and consistent patterns of higher spending and taxes in the low-growth cities than in the high-growth ones.

• For every dollar of per capita expenditures (excluding those spent on anti-poverty programs, education, and health care) in the highest-growth cities, the shrinking cities spend $1.71.
• In 1990, a typical family of four living in one of the shrinking cities paid $1,100 per year more in taxes than it would if it lived in one of the highest-growth cities.
• Shrinking cities' bureaucracies are twice as large as those of growth cities. In 1990, the latter had, on average, 99 city employees per 10,000 residents; the former, 235.
• Cities with high spending and taxes lost population in the 1980s; those with low spending and taxes gained. High spending and taxes are a cause, not just a consequence, of urban decline.

Expenditures are high and rising in large central cities primarily because their governments generally have above-average unit costs for educating children, collecting garbage, building roads, policing neighborhoods, and providing other basic services. In 1988, for example, the shrinking cities spent roughly $4,950 per pupil on education, whereas the high-growth cities spent $3,600. The $1,350 cost differential can not be explained by better schools in places such as Detroit and Newark.

The influence of municipal employee unions also contributes to higher costs in declining central cities. Compensation for unionized local employees tends to be roughly 30% above wages for comparably skilled private-sector workers. In New York, the average school janitor is paid $57,000 a year. In Philadelphia, the average municipal employee receives more than $50,000 a year in salary and benefits. According to the Census Bureau, cities with populations over 500,000 pay their mostly unionized workers more than 50% more than those with populations under 75,000, whose workforces are less likely to be unionized. In short, thriving cities are places where costs are lower, bureaucracies are smaller, and services are better.

Some city officials are beginning to recognize economic reality. Philadelphia Mayor Edward Rendell is challenging the entrenched municipal unions and other spending constituencies with a budget plan that calls for $1,100,000,000 in savings over five years. He has spurned more Federal aid as the poison that produced Philadelphia's near-insolvency in 1992. Chicago Mayor Richard M. Daley and Indianapolis Mayor Stephen Goldsmith have contracted out dozens of services to private providers and have slowed the growth of massive, bloated budgets to a crawl.

The decline of America's major cities is not inevitable. They can and should be saved. For generations, they have served as the nation's centers, not only of industrial might, but of culture, diversity, and intellect. Through an aggressive agenda of budget control, tax reduction, privatization, and deregulation, America's declining cities can rise again in prominence and prosperity.

The riots in Los Angeles in the spring of 1992 dramatized the social and economic deterioration of many central cities. At a rally held in Washington a month after the riots, then-New York Mayor David Dinkins aptly described the inner cities as places of "only grief and despair." Almost all quality-of-life indicators for many of the fastest shrinking cities confirm that gloomy assessment. Consider these examples:

• The 1990 census data reveal that 48% of all Detroit households are headed by a single female.
• Newark has a lower real per capita income today than it did in 1969.
• Cleveland had nearly 1,000,000 residents in the 1950s; now, it has fewer than 500,000.
• The Chicago area has averaged 10,000 manufacturing job losses annually for the past 15 years. A Feb. 14, 1992, *Chicago Tribune* headline said it all: "Factory Flight Hits Record Pace."
• St. Louis has lost more than two of every five jobs it had in 1965.
• Philadelphia has a four-year $1,000,000,000 budget deficit. Its bond rating sunk so low that it effectively is blocked from municipal capital markets and must borrow through a state oversight agency.
• Washington, D.C., has been dubbed the "murder capital of the world."
• In Baltimore, 56% of black males between the ages of 18 and 35 were in trouble with the law in 1991, according to a study by the National Center on Institutions and Alternatives.

The root cause of almost all the social, economic, and fiscal problems of America's depressed cities is the steady flight of businesses and middle- and upper-income families. In the past quarter-century, 15 major cities combined have lost 3,800,000 people and roughly the same number of jobs. No longer is the issue just white flight. The 1990 census data suggest that middle-income minorities are fleeing to the suburbs in record numbers.

The urban crisis is not shared by all cities. The declines in the most depressed are matched by impressive gains in the highest-growth cities. Raleigh, for instance, has seen its population almost double, jobs more than double, and real per capita income grow by better than 40% since the mid 1960s. The wide diversity in the economic performance of central cities suggests that the individual policies of each play an important role in explaining urban growth and decline.

In conventional analyses of the urban crisis, cities are portrayed primarily as victims of national trends, Federal mandates, and other conditions beyond their control. Factors blamed include the recession, Reagan budget cuts, suburbanization, decline in manufacturing, rise of the automobile, immigration, an aging infrastructure, racism, AIDS, homelessness, urban gangs, guns, and drugs. Each of these can place considerable strain on municipal budgets, yet city officials are impotent to combat them.

There is some truth to this. The last recession is painful evidence that no city is immune from the impact of national economic conditions and policies. For instance, from the 1950s through the 1980s, most California cities enjoyed spectacular rates of growth. The state widely was considered recession proof. Yet, the recession had a devastating impact on California localities—many of which are at the top of the list of growth cities. One-third of all job losses in the past two years has occurred in California. Another example is the impact that wide fluctuations in international oil prices in the 1970s and 1980s had on the economies and budgets of Texas cities.

Unquestionably, there are regional factors at play in determining relative rates of growth. Most of the declining cities are the once-mighty industrial centers in the Northeast and Midwest—the Rust Belt. Most of the growth cities are in the Sun Belt, on the West Coast, and in the Southeast. A related factor that usually correlates with the rate of economic growth is age—older cities tend to experience less economic growth, a phenomenon that often is attributed to their aging infrastructures.

Still, the fact that some cities have been flourishing for long periods of time as others have been deteriorating suggests that self-imposed policies play an important role in determining their economic fates. Regional factors can not explain fully the different growth rates of cities. Although the South has been a high-growth region, three of the fastest declining cities—Birmingham, Louisville, and New Orleans—are in that area.

Even within states, there are significant differences in the economic performance of cities. Why is Oakland declining, but Santa Ana growing? Why is Arlington doing so much better than Fort Worth, or Colorado Springs better than Denver? What explains the fact that the eighth fastest growing city, Lexington, and the ninth fastest declining city, Louisville, both are in Kentucky? An important factor is that their spending and taxing policies are very different. Growth cities have pro-growth fiscal policies; declining cities, anti-growth.

Taxes and spending. There are several potential problems in comparing spending and taxes by city. The major one is the division of responsibilities for program funding among state governments, counties, school districts, and cities differs from state to state. For example, in some, the responsibility for funding welfare assistance is delegated to the counties; in others, it is paid for by the state government; and in still others, the cities bear the cost. Another complication is that some cities are not part of independent counties, and so the city government funds all the activities of the county. By contrast, most cities are part of larger counties, which means that the costs of funding services such as hospitals and courts in the inner cities are spread to the suburbs. Finally, in some cities, school funding is handled by school districts or in large part by the state, not the city, government.

Another potential difficulty with comparing city growth rates over time is that borders change. Many cities, such as Portland, Ore., aggressively have annexed neighboring suburbs. In the case of Portland, annexation has been a major source of population growth. However, that annexation probably is as much a consequence of the city's economic success as it is an explanation. In many cases, localities have merged with central cities because it has been in their economic interests to do so. By the same token, more and more localities are attempting to secede from declining central cities because the latter's economic policies, such as tax rates and service costs, have grown too burdensome.

Population growth. The best indication of the livability of a city probably is whether people are moving to or out of it. Those that had large population losses from 1965 to 1990 spend, tax, and hire city workers at roughly twice the rates of the cities that had large population gains. For instance, the highest-growth cities (those with population gains of 100% or more) spend six percent of personal income, whereas the lowest-growth cities (those that lost at least 15% of their populations) expend 12% of personal income. The highest-growth cities had 107 employees per 10,000 residents vs. 217 in the lowest-growth cities. Those findings suggest that cities with high taxes and service costs are driving people away.

Job growth. Just as population changes are a measure of how people are voting with their feet, so are employment patterns. Firms and capital that create jobs tend to migrate to areas with pro-growth and pro-business climates. Per capita spending is roughly 50% higher in the lowest-growth cities than in those with the greatest increase in employment. The cities with the lowest growth in employment spend almost $1.40 for every $1.00 of municipal expenditures in the highest-growth cities. High taxes and spending are driving businesses and jobs away from shrinking cities.

Female-headed households. One indication of poverty and family disintegration in an area is the percentage of female-headed households. Fatherless homes are about eight times more likely to be poor than are intact families. Moreover, children who grow up in fatherless households are much more likely to commit crimes and engage in other socially unacceptable behavior of the type that plagues inner cities.

Between 1970 and 1990, the percentage of female-headed households rose at an alarming pace nationwide. The largest growth occurred in the inner cities, where Census Bureau data indicate an increase from about 15 to 35% in fatherless homes. Cities with the largest rise in female-headed households have spending and taxes at least 50% higher than those with small increases.

Per capita income growth is one of the best measures of the economic growth rate of a city and the standard of living of its residents. The cities with the lowest growth in income (less than 10%) are characterized by per capita spending and taxes that are about 10% higher than those of cities with the highest growth in income (more than 25%). As a share of personal income, spending and taxes are about 25% higher in cities with the lowest growth.

Where the money goes

The urban lobby and scholars invariably argue that low-growth cities spend more because their needs are greater. Poor cities have to meet increased demands for anti-poverty spending, subsidized child care, homeless assistance, drug abatement and rehabilitation, crime control, job training, etc. Because declining cities have less wealth and fewer workers and businesses to pay the cost of those programs, they have to impose higher tax burdens on their residents and businesses to raise the same amount of revenue wealthy and prospering cities do.

Education is a major budget item that should not cost much more on a per student basis in a low-growth city. If per student education costs were uniform across cities, one would expect to find higher per pupil expenditures in growing and affluent areas if only because the residents have more money to devote to the schools. Indeed, the education lobby successfully has argued before several state supreme courts that school financing is inequitable because wealthy areas spend more on schools than do poor areas.

The data show that, on average, per pupil expenditures on schools in the lowest job growth cities are approximately $1,800 higher than they are in the highest job growth cities. Yet, spending on schools and student performance appear to be wholly unrelated. For example, Washington, D.C., which spent almost $6,000 per student in 1988, has among the worst inner-city schools in the nation. Conversely, San Diego spent about $3,500 per child in 1988 for schools that are considered above average for cities its size.

Low-growth cities appear to provide education, one of the major items in local budgets, much less cost-efficiently than do high-growth cities. If declining central cities simply could lower their education costs to the national average for large cities, they could reduce their per family tax burden by hundreds of dollars.

City taxes and economic growth. A city's economic performance is influenced not only by its over-all tax burden, but by the composition of its taxes. In particular, income taxes have a consistently strong negative effect on city growth rates. Only one high-growth city—Lexington, Ky.— imposes a city income tax, whereas the low-growth cities have average per capita income taxes of approximately $100-200. The evidence suggests that imposition of a city income tax is a recipe for economic decline.

City property taxes also have a negative impact on economic growth, but not to the extent that income taxes do. Cities with high population and job growth, as well as those with low poverty rates, have substantially lower property taxes than cities in decline.

City sales taxes have no apparent positive or negative impact on economic growth. If anything, high-growth cities tend to rely heavily on sales taxes for revenue; declining cities, on income taxes.

Impact of state taxes. Workers and businesses are affected not only by local tax burdens, but by state taxes as well. High-growth cities tend to be located in states that have low combined city-state tax burdens. State and city taxes are about $360 per person higher in cities with population losses of 15% or more since 1965 than in those with population gains of 100% or more.

Even more dramatic is the destructive impact of high combined state and city income taxes on the economic performance of cities. Growth cities tend to have state and local income tax burdens that are, on average, about 60% of those of shrinking cities.

Federal aid. Cities have a multitude of problems, but too little money is not one of them. Real per capita spending escalated from $435 in 1950 to $571 in 1965 to $1,004 in 1990. At the start of that spending binge, America's largest cities were at the peak of prosperity—indeed, they had higher per capita incomes than the suburbs. Now, incomes are 50% lower than in the suburbs. A nearly 2.5-fold increase in outlays has not prevented urban bleeding; if anything, it has accelerated it.

Those figures understate the true extent of the budget buildup in cities. In the 1950s and early 1960s, cities had primary responsibility for funding welfare programs and indigent health care, whereas today the burden of funding anti-poverty programs is

borne mostly by the Federal government and the states. In fact, most cities spend a much smaller share of their budgets on health and welfare than they did 40 years ago.

The cities that are least underfunded are not the smaller, more affluent communities, but the largest ones (*i.e.*, those that would be the beneficiaries of more Federal aid). Cities with populations over 500,000 spend roughly $1,200 per resident (excluding health, education, and welfare), whereas communities with populations under 75,000 spend about $550. The primary reason the expenditures of large central cities are so excessive is not that they have more responsibilities; it is that they are increasingly inefficient in providing basic services. It costs New York, Chicago, Los Angeles, Philadelphia, and other big cities twice as much to educate a child, collect garbage, build a road, police a neighborhood, and provide other basic services as it does smaller communities.

From 1980 to 1990, direct Federal aid to cities was reduced by about 50%. That reduction was made up in various ways. A 1990 study in the *American Economic Review* reports that, for every dollar the cities lost in Federal aid, they received an additional 80 cents in state aid. Moreover, while direct Federal aid to cities was cut in the Reagan years, aid to poor people living in cities increased. Federal social welfare spending—on education, training, social services, employment, low-income assistance, community development, and transportation—rose from $255,000,000,000 to $285,000,000,000 from 1980 to 1992. Those figures exclude Social Security, Medicare, and Medicaid—programs that have mushroomed in cost and significantly benefit inner-city residents as well.

Since 1989, domestic spending across the board, including outlays on urban aid, has exploded. Federal domestic spending under George Bush rose by almost 25%, the fastest rate of growth of the domestic budget under any president in 30 years. In real terms, cities and states received more Federal money in 1992 than in any previous year.

Since the late 1960s, the Federal government has spent 2.5 trillion dollars on urban renewal and the War on Poverty, or the equivalent of 25 Marshall Plans. The reason the money has not caused an urban revival is that the programs, particularly those that were abolished in the 1980s, did not work. For example, Urban Development Action Grants, which finally were abolished in 1987, subsidized the construction of major chain hotels, such as Hyatts, and luxury housing developments with rooftop tennis courts, health spas, and indoor tennis courts in Detroit.

Despite Federal grants totaling more than $50,000,000,000 for urban transit since the mid 1960s, total ridership has declined. The Federal government spent over $2,000,000,000 to build Miami's Metrorail, which the local population calls Metrofail; today, it has less than 20% of predicted ridership and its operating subsidies are in the hundreds of millions of dollars a year. A Congressional Budget Office audit of Federal wastewater treatment grants to cities found that construction costs were 30% higher when plants were built with Federal funding than when local taxpayers footed the bill.

Even cities that have received huge infusions of direct Federal aid have not been able to leverage those funds to resuscitate their economies. For instance, Gary, Ind., got more than $150,000,000 from 1968 to 1972 for urban renewal—or about $1,000 per resident—yet the city's deterioration continued.

Cuts in urban aid can not account for the Los Angeles riots, the exodus from New York City, sky-high poverty in Detroit, and other woes of the central cities. The period of catastrophic decline of population, incomes, and jobs was the 1970s, when urban aid exploded. By every meaningful measure of social and economic progress, the 1970s were the worst decade for cities since at least the 1930s.

By contrast, the Reagan years were a period of economic gains for many big cities. "The 1980s was the best decade in this century for the old central business districts," maintains *Washington Post* reporter Joel Garreau in his 1992 book on urban America, *Edge City*. "From Boston to Philadelphia to Washington to Los Angeles to San Francisco to Seattle to Houston to Dallas to Atlanta, the business districts of the downtowns thrived." Adjusted for inflation, the tax base of America's inner cities expanded by 50% in the 1980s, compared to 20% in the 1970s. The entrepreneurial explosion unleashed by Reaganomics had a very positive effect on the finances of big cities.

Medium-sized areas fared even better. More than 150 thriving new suburban cities have grown up during the past decade, such as Fairfax, Va.; Mesa, Ariz.; and Irvine, Calif. They quickly have become centers of enterprise and job creation. Until the recent recession, the problem confronting those booming cities was too much development and business investment, not too little.

An agenda for urban renaissance

Reviving America's depressed cities will require implementation of a growth-oriented agenda on the part of the Federal government, states, and cities. The overriding goal of such a strategy must be to provide incentives for people, businesses, and capital to return to the inner cities.

Federal role. A proper adherence to the constitutional principles of federalism would dictate that the Federal government have almost no direct relationship with cities. All Federal programs that give direct aid to local governments and Federal regulations that mandate local spending should be abolished. Federal aid, to the extent that it continues, should be provided to the states. If cities and other jurisdictions of the states are in need of financial aid, it should be provided by the state legislatures.

If Congress feels compelled to assist areas that have deep pockets of poverty, money should be given directly to poor people, not city bureaucracies or service providers. There seems to be a bipartisan consensus emerging on such a strategy. A 1982 Brookings Institution report on urban decline emphasized that policymakers "should consider switching more federal aid from *empowering governments* to deliver services, to *empowering individuals and households* to purchase services or provide their own."

There are practical as well as philosophical objections to Federal grants to cities. As with Federal aid to foreign countries, little of the money ever gets filtered through the city bureaucracies. For example, according to the Wisconsin Policy Research Institute, Milwaukee spends about $1,100,000,000 in Federal, state, and local money annually on poverty abatement. That money flows through 68 programs that spend almost $30,000 per poor family, but only about 35 cents of every dollar ever gets to the poor. Most of the Federal money funds a massive welfare industry.

Probably the only effective Federal agenda for aiding the cities is the promotion of national economic growth. The lesson of the past three decades is that central cities' fiscal fortunes often turn with the national economy. In the slow-growth, high-inflation 1970s, cities rapidly deteriorated; in the prosperous 1980s, they partially revived; but in the recessionary 1990s, cities again are financially strapped. Reducing Federal deficit spending through expenditure control, growth-oriented reductions in payroll and capital gains taxes, a noninflationary monetary policy, and regulatory relief will have a very positive effect on cities. It would be best to provide the stimulus of tax cuts and regulatory relief to all areas nationwide, but, if politics precludes doing so, the enterprise zone concept is viable, as long as it means tax reduction and deregulation, not a new subsidy program.

States' role. State governments substantially increased their aid to cities in the 1980s, but during the 1990s, with budget problems in statehouses, aid to localities has declined. In general, such reduction is appropriate. States should not be in the business of paying for locally provided services or acting as the cities' tax collectors. Whenever possible, local services should be paid for with local taxes. State aid to localities is defensible only when it distributes funds exclusively to lower-income jurisdictions or pays for services that provide a direct benefit for the entire state.

The principal way state governments can promote the economic growth of their cities is to reduce the over-all state tax burden on individuals and businesses. States without an income tax—such as Florida and Texas—tend to have healthy and growing cities. Northeastern cities clearly have been harmed by the high state taxes in that region. For example, New York City has estimated that a $900,000,000 tax increase proposed by the state would cost the city some 300,000 jobs.

Cutting service costs

Cities' role. The key to restoring economic vitality and capital investment to declining cities is to reduce the costs of providing municipal services and then slash the heavy tax burdens that are required to pay for them. For no justifiable reason, unit service costs are substantially higher in large cities than in small ones—whether for education, public transportation, street cleaning, park maintenance, garbage collection, or police protection.

Labor costs appear to explain much of the inefficiency. Salaries of government workers in suburbs average $2,150 a month, compared to $2,700 a month in cities with populations over 500,000. If benefits are added, the disparities are even wider. Large cities also pay their employees substantially more than comparably skilled private-sector workers receive, and the gap is growing larger.

If cities had the political will to cut service costs and taxes, they could do so without sacrificing vital services. One way to begin is through competitive contracts. Smaller cities routinely contract out municipal services; large unionized cities seldom do. Indeed, some, such as La Mirada, Calif., contract out almost all their services and thus have tiny city bureaucracies. Several dozen studies verify that unit costs are reduced 20-50% by contracting out to the private sector. Moreover, the quality of contracted-out services is rated higher than that of services offered in-house.

However, public employee unions are so powerful in some large cities that not only is contracting out effectively prohibited, but any private-sector competition with the government monopoly service provider is forbidden by regulation. For instance, in New York City, private van and jitney services are providing fast, reliable transit for Manhattan commuters, yet the city transit agency has acted to shut such operators down. The action is contrary to the interests of residents and area workers. City provisions that prohibit private competition with the government should be ended.

Education is one of the largest items in city budgets. The declining cities tend to have much higher per-student costs, despite generally lower-quality public schools. In most large cities today, private schools provide a better education for half the cost of inner-city public schools. Central cities can cut costs significantly by recognizing that, when parents send their children to private schools, there are huge savings for the public school system. Even accounting for the fact that some school costs are fixed, if cities were to provide inner-city parents with incomes under $30,000 a voucher of, say, $2,500 per year to send each child to a private school, the public school systems significantly could reduce their operating costs and educational opportunities for children of low-income families would be improved.

There are diseconomies of scale in municipal services. Some cities, like New York, have such powerful special-interest lobbies and entrenched bureaucracies that it has become politically impossible to cut service costs, even in times of severe crisis. Large cities could reduce costs by splitting service responsibilities and conferring taxing authority on city districts, villages, or even homeowner associations. If the provision of services and the levying of service taxes were closer to homeowners and businesses, taxpayers would have greater influence on decisions about which services they need and which they do not, and they could place greater pressure on the government to reduce costs by diluting the influence of special-interest groups.

An even more radical idea is for cities to acknowledge that they have become unmanageable at their current size and to split up into separate smaller jurisdictions. It would make sense, for instance, for each borough of New York City to become a separate city, as Staten Island is attempting to do. Service responsibilities that can not be divided conveniently—poverty programs perhaps—then could be borne by the county government.

Finally, cities can lure businesses and people back by changing the composition of taxes. If all cities with income taxes were to replace them and other levies on industry with sales taxes, those cities substantially could improve the business climate within their borders. City income taxes are defended by local officials as fair because they fall primarily on upper-income individuals and big business. In practice, those taxes are paid by the working poor, the middle class, and small business owners, because the wealthy have fled most cities with income taxes or have received legislative exemptions from high taxes.

Urban advocates are right when they say that America's inner cities have been victims of destructive government policies, but not those of the Federal government. The wounds of the central cities largely are self-inflicted. A 1988 private audit of nearly bankrupt Scranton, Pa., stated that "the city government appears to exist for the benefit of its employees instead of the people." Those words could describe the operating principles and skewed priorities of too many ailing cities. Unless and until America's central cities start putting people first, cutting service costs and anti-growth tax rates, no amount of Federal aid can reverse the decline of urban America.

Visions of Community in an Urban War Zone

Creating life amid the wreckage of urban public housing.

ROB GURWITT

If Lake Parc Place were a few miles farther up, along the fashionable stretch of Lake Shore Drive north of Chicago's Gold Coast, its two neatly kept high rises would be unremarkable, one more pair of 15-story apartment buildings overlooking Lake Michigan, renting for $1,000 a month and more.

But situated where it is, 5 miles south of downtown on a desolate stretch of lakefront and near an oppressive expanse of public housing projects, it is striking in its incongruity. Seeing it is like stumbling on a rose garden in a red light district.

Lake Parc Place is in fact a creation of the Chicago Housing Authority, but it is unlike anything else in the city. It is the showplace project of the most interesting and controversial housing agency anywhere in America.

Half of the 282 units at Lake Parc are filled with public housing tenants, the other half with families that are poor but employed. The buildings are policed largely by a tenant patrol. To get inside, you have to be buzzed in by security. Since Lake Parc Place opened in 1991, there has not been a single crime reported within its gates.

"The first year was rough," says Carlos Roberts, an unemployed father who heads the seven-person tenant patrol. "We had graffiti and broken light bulbs, and there were fights. But that's all pretty much stopped now. Because the tenant patrol is out there, we catch the small things before they become big things."

Lake Parc Place is in the middle of a war zone in a city whose public housing units are lethally out of control. Last year, 66 people were murdered in the city's projects. More than 2,800 were assaulted, and an additional 218 sexually assaulted. There were 985 robberies, 1,168 burglaries, and 1,651 thefts. Innocent residents are gunned down in the crossfire of shoot-outs, teenagers—boys, really—carry weapons that rival anything the police can muster, and children learn to hit the floor at the first sound of gunfire. Those stories have come out of the projects so often that public housing there has become, in the popular mind, an irreclaimable wasteland of hopelessness.

Even among those who deal with public housing regularly, there remains an enormous amount of uncertainty over just how to get a handle on the problem. "Violence is the worst problem in public housing and no one is really sure yet what's effective and what's not," says Wayne Sherwood, director of research for the Council of Large Public Housing Authorities. "People are still fumbling in the dark."

So it might seem impossible that a place like Lake Parc should exist at all. Or that there should be, in Chicago and elsewhere, small but tangible signs of improvement. But the fact is there are.

In the past couple of years, a gathering of forces among city officials, public housing managers, police, private social service agencies and tenants has begun to make some headway toward checking both fear and violence. There have been dramatic turnarounds at individual projects and in solitary buildings. Public housing authorities have had varying success installing high-tech identification systems for residents, fencing off public housing developments, using police "sweeps" of buildings and creating more "defensible" layouts. Some housing authorities have begun developing community policing, encouraging organizing among tenants, toughening tenant screening and eviction procedures and breaking down bureaucratic walls to coordinate law enforcement and social service efforts focusing on particular projects.

In particular, public housing officials have begun to discern the outlines of a viable response to the violence, and to no one's surprise, beefed-up law enforcement is only a piece of it. The efforts that have shown the greatest payoff—in cities such as Chicago, Portland, Oregon, and Richmond, Virginia—have marshalled a broad range of initiatives that run the gamut from increased police activity to leadership training for public housing residents to a dramatic overhaul of management philosophy. What seems to be emerging is a consensus that ridding the projects of violence will mean a commitment to changing how we view public housing in the first place—in essence, stripping them of their image as warehouses for the poor and making them into neighborhoods.

"We have to start reviving public housing communities as communities," says David Cortiella, administrator of the Boston Housing Authority. "As integral, vibrant communities."

That is what Lake Parc Place is about. It is an ambitious attempt, in the midst of a public housing system gone wildly awry, to turn the tables in favor of community-building.

The project is the brainchild of Vince Lane, the chairman and executive director of the Chicago Housing Authority and possibly the best-known public housing official in America. In his five years at the CHA's helm, he has shaken up both its formerly complacent bureaucracy—replacing executives wholesale when he first took over—and Chicago's public housing community in general.

"My fundamental philosophy is that the system is broken," says Lane, who dealt with it as a private developer long before he was brought in to change it. "If there is to be any improvement, we're not going to make it happen by massaging it around the edges. There has to be radical change."

The results of that attitude have earned Lane local controversy as well as national attention, especially his pioneering use of massive shows of force to "sweep" troubled high rises for guns,

drugs and illegal residents, and his repeated lobbying to tear down parts of the notorious Cabrini-Green development on the city's North Side. The American Civil Liberties Union, which took the CHA and Lane to court over the sweeps, has been a constant voice of opposition, and some local housing experts contend that, while Lane has unquestionably brought a new sense of purpose to the CHA, some of his initiatives serve more to gain attention and applause than tangibly to improve the lives of residents.

But you will get no such arguments about Lane from the residents of Lake Parc Place. The two buildings were once known as Olander Homes, and they were as gang-infested and drug-ridden as any project in the city when the CHA closed them down in 1986. Five years and $18 million later, they reopened with 117 of their 282 former tenants moving back in and a list of 4,000 applicants for the 141 units made available to working families, which rent for anywhere from $315 a month for a one-bedroom apartment to $463 for a three-bedroom.

That mix of tenants, with families that depend on public assistance living next to families that get a weekly paycheck, is Lake Parc's essence. Lane argues that the CHA's biggest mistake (though it was certainly no accident) was to build such high concentrations of public housing in black neighborhoods that families living there encounter nothing but other public housing tenants and a vast stretch of bleak high rises on a plain of mud and broken concrete—a "concrete reservation," in the words of tenant activist Francine Washington. "When you limit kids' exposure from cradle 'til adulthood to all the negative things in life," Lane says, "you should not be surprised at what the outcome is."

To build Lake Parc, the CHA had to apply for a host of waivers from HUD. In particular, it had to bypass HUD's so-called "modest design standards," which essentially call for making public housing as spartan as possible. The apartments in Lake Parc have oak cabinets, ceiling fans, blinds—small details that are essential if they're to attract tenants who have a choice about where they live, even the limited choice given the working poor. Just as important, Lane insists, is the project's appeal to

public housing families. "Once poor people have something they know they couldn't get anywhere else," he says, "they're going to fight to protect it, whether it's against gangbangers or whoever."

That is certainly how Carlos Roberts and the tenant patrol see things. Though there are security guards posted at Lake Parc, they mostly stick to the lobby. Every day, and sometimes twice or three times, members of the tenant patrol walk through the hallways checking on lighting and door locks, listening for sounds of trouble, reporting gang graffiti and anything else amiss to development manager Ameshia Hardison. During the summer, they stand watch over the playgrounds and basketball courts, stopping the occasional fight, intervening when young men from nearby projects threaten Lake Parc residents and making sure that no drug dealing takes root on the project's perimeters. "We remember the past—the drugs, the gangs in the hallways, the shootings, how scared you were to get on the elevator," says Roberts. "Every time I walk these hallways, I remember what it was like, and I can't let it get back like it was."

To some degree, the deck is stacked in the tenant patrol's favor. In order to get an apartment at Lake Parc, a family—whether it's applying for public housing or one of the units for working tenants—has to undergo a credit check, a police background check, an inspection of current housing, checks of its members' social security numbers and its children's birth certificates and report cards, and a verification of its rent-paying history. Problem families, which account for an inordinate amount of the trouble in family public housing, don't have much chance to get in the doors at Lake Parc.

Still, there is no doubt that Lake Parc's tenant patrol members consider themselves to be on the front lines not only against violence, but against any signs of social decay. They cite children for running in the halls, they ask residents to turn down music when it's too loud, they report youngsters they find jumping the fence that surrounds the development. A few public housing residents, reports patrol member Marion Robinson, have found the rules too much to bear and moved out. Others call the patrol nosy. "But the majority," she says, "work with us. They want to live decent lives."

So, it's safe to say, do most of the CHA's estimated 150,000 residents, of whom only 86,000 are legally on their unit's lease. For many of them, however, it is a much more difficult proposition. Their hallways are marred by gang graffiti; drug dealers have taken over vacant apartments or, in some cases, occupied ones; lights, locks, doors and elevators are constantly being broken; even in some of the less dangerous buildings it is still routine to have to pass through gangs hanging out by the entrance; at Cabrini-Green and Robert Taylor Homes, snipers sometimes trade shots from the rooftops—and at Robert Taylor, which is the CHA's largest and most dangerous development, snipers a few months ago chased off work crews trying to child-proof upper-story windows. That incident took place even though the CHA police force is headquartered in one of the Robert Taylor buildings.

And yet Lake Parc is not the only bright spot in CHA's vast constellation of almost 1,500 buildings. Indeed, for the first time since the housing authority began collecting crime statistics in 1988, the overall level of crime in Chicago public housing dropped. It was down 7 percent last year; this year, if initial trends continue until year's end, it will drop again. The 66 murders in 1992 were 24 fewer than the number recorded in 1991. Sexual assaults, robberies and burglaries all dropped as well.

There is no question that tenant patrols had a great deal to do with this. Begun initially in one building at Cabrini-Green by a tenant leader named Cora Moore, they have reached 75 in number, all but one in high-rise buildings. Over 1,000 CHA residents are tenant patrol members. "You join," says Brenda Bolden, a tenant patrol leader at Ogden Courts, two slightly bedraggled mid-rises on the city's West Side, "because you're tired and you can't take it any more. And when you get worn down and feel like you can't go another step, someone does something—maybe people who don't live in the development come in and tell you they're going to take over—and you say, 'Who are they?' and you keep going."

The patrols have had some notable successes. Cora Moore's building is now considered one of the safest of those owned by the housing authority, although it's surrounded by some of the most dangerous. At Ida B. Wells Homes, a sprawling mix of low- and high-rise apartments just a few blocks from Lake Parc, gang violence and rumors of a rapist accosting children a few years ago led the residents of one building to start a patrol to safeguard their children on the way to and from school. These days, tenant patrol members, in blue nylon windbreakers and holding walkie-talkies, stand watch every afternoon along the desolate concrete field that separates the school from the rest of the development. They remain in place until their 500 young charges from throughout the development are inside.

The tenant patrols have become more than simply watchdogs that keep an eye on their buildings; they are the nucleus of tenant efforts to change the nature of life in public housing. At Lake Parc, Carlos Roberts is trying to raise money for a 4-H Club, and is starting a self-defense course for the project's youngsters to teach them discipline. Elsewhere, tenant patrols are building playgrounds, organizing scout troops and starting after-school programs. They have served to train tenants who want to start managing their own buildings as part of the CHA's tenant management program. Robert Bayas, a tenant patrol leader at Ida B. Wells, is hoping to organize a national conference of public housing tenant patrols, to share tactics and training. "There is a great hunger for that," he says, among tenants nationwide.

Without tenant involvement, there would be little the Chicago Housing Authority could do to change things—a point that CHA Police Chief Hosea Crossley is the first to recognize. "I don't think the police can ever make public housing safe," he says. "You can put in hundreds of police officers, and it won't do it. Resident involvement, though, can completely turn things around."

Still, there is a limit to what tenant patrols can accomplish, a fact no one knows better than their members. "Every development is different, and it's different from building to building,"

says Florine Miles, a tenant patrol leader at Stateway Gardens. "I can go to someone and talk about a drug problem, but you can't do that in Robert Taylor. At Lake Parc, they can even be assertive about following the rules. But if you did that at 4455 [one of the more notorious Robert Taylor buildings] you'd get shot."

Tenant patrol members are often treated with suspicion by other residents—their label, throughout CHA, is "snitch bitches," since most of them are women. Some have had their children beaten or threatened. Brenda Bolden has had her door smeared with feces and set on fire. And after eight years of trying to organize her project's tenants to improve their lives, she has occasional cause to wonder how much progress she has made: In the span of just a few days not long ago, she was called on to comfort the mother of a 14-year-old girl who had been shot in the head, go to the aid of a neighbor whose son had been shot eight times, and plead with the leader of the gang in her building to wait until the project's children were home from school before seeking revenge for the beating of one of his members.

Tenant activism alone, in other words, is not enough to rebuild communities that have been shattered by social dysfunction, crucial years of bureaucratic neglect, the spread of drugs and guns and the rest of the litany of ills besetting poor urban communities. What initiatives such as Lake Parc make clear is that success requires both tenant activism and an institutional framework that supports it. As Lane says, "The foundation of community is neighbors getting together to solve common problems. But when you've got random lawlessness, and a mentality that says you take care of yourself and forget everyone else, then you can forget it." If people are afraid to step forward, or are convinced that they will have no backing should they do so, they'll remain behind closed doors.

The first step toward bringing tenants out of the state of isolation is regaining a measure of physical control of a building or a project. In effect, that is what the CHA did by shutting down Olander Homes and then carefully screening the residents it

Physical security measures don't create community, but they make community possible.

allowed back into Lake Parc Place. But Lake Parc cost roughly $60,000 per unit to renovate. It is a model for what housing authorities and tenant activists can hope to accomplish, but it's only a model; it is too expensive to be a solution in itself on a large scale.

So the CHA launched "Operation Clean Sweep," which has since been adopted by other cities with troubled high rises. A sweep consists in part of a task force of police and CHA staff closing off a building and searching its units door-to-door. Under a court-ordered consent decree with the ACLU, authorities in Chicago can no longer search explicitly for weapons and drugs, but instead are limited to looking at physical conditions and for illegal tenants—"We believe the CHA should get out of the law enforcement business and back into the property management business," says the Chicago ACLU's public information director, Valerie Phillips.

Even so, the sweeps tend to turn up plenty of both guns and drugs. They also give the CHA a chance, sometimes its first in years, to start fixing up buildings and to reconfigure the ground floor by closing off any entrance except the one leading to the lobby; theoretically, that gives management a handle on who goes into the building, although residents complain that enforcement by private security guards can be lax.

Still, all a swept building provides is breathing room. Some cities, in which the legal system has proven more sympathetic to housing authorities' efforts at getting a handle on out-of-control projects, have been able to take the next step and toughen eviction procedures so that they can deal with residents who cause problems. "When you're face to face with troubled families, sometimes you realize there's nothing you can do to help them," says James Fuerst, a professor of social welfare policy at Loyola University, in

Chicago. "You have to get them out, or you'll never get at the root of the problem."

In Richmond, Virginia, for instance, the housing authority a few years ago developed a new lease for its residents forbidding any illegal drugs or alcohol, and making the head of the household responsible for family members and guests. "So if a teenage son is dealing, we evict the whole family," says Richard Gentry, Richmond's director of housing. "If a friend of the head of the household is coming in and dealing, the family goes," In the past four years, the authority has evicted 100 families.

Similarly, in Portland, Oregon, the housing authority prevailed on the state legislature to give it the right to evict families on 24 hours' notice in cases involving "extreme public safety." In practice, a case will move more slowly than that through the courts, but the authority has persisted in following eviction cases through to their conclusion. The result, says former director Don Clark, is that "word got around pretty fast that the housing authority is serious about evictions—we have people who won't even show up for the process, they just begin to move out once they get notice."

There is a contentious debate within the housing community over whether evicting a whole family is necessary; some advocates insist that putting an entire family on the street only moves the problem to the larger community, and believe that ejecting an individual offender is enough. In Chicago—and in other cities, such as New York—legal aid attorneys and the courts have made it difficult to get even that far. Lane is hoping to put together a meeting between local judges and residents—lots of them—so that, as he puts it, "the judges can understand that when somebody brings in a couple of little snotty-nosed kids who say, 'Well, where are we going to go?', the judges will be able to tell them, 'You've had your chance.' Until people know that there's a consequence to anti-social behavior, they will continue to be anti-social."

But no one involved in public housing believes that toughness alone, whether in the form of sweeps or evictions, is enough to help tenants rebuild their communities. It clears the space for a foundation; it doesn't build the foundation itself. In an insecure and

unmaintained project, community-building and social service efforts are a waste of time, if they are not utterly impossible. In a project that has been physically reclaimed, they have at least a chance to work.

Portland and Richmond have followed up on their security efforts by using both private social service providers and city agencies to beef up on-site health care, counsel young mothers, institute job training programs and in general strengthen the ties between public housing residents and the communities that surround them.

The results in the developments targeted by the two authorities have been encouraging. Richmond's Gilpin Safe Neighborhood Program was begun in the summer of 1990, and in the first year had little impact on crime. The following year, though, violent crime at Gilpin Court dropped 37 percent, compared with a citywide decrease of 8 percent; since then, it has remained level. At Portland's Columbia Villa, the number of gang incidents dropped from 153 in 1988 to 38 in 1991 and assaults from 252 to 193; citywide, gang incidents remained the same over that time period, and assaults increased by 13 percent.

The Chicago Housing Authority has launched a similar effort at Ida B. Wells. At one of the Wells high rises, referred to in CHA vernacular only by its street number, 706, tenants are sitting down with architects to help plan their building's rehabilitation, have put an end to trash and urination in their hallways, and have gotten a handle on much of the crime that once harried their lives in the building. "We screen prospective tenants," says Pat Perry, a tenant leader, "and tell them up front, 'We're nosy. If you're going to violate any parts of this lease, we will sing out.'" In all, Wells—one of the CHA's larger developments—saw a 29 percent drop in crime between 1991 and 1992, more than any other public housing project in the city.

In the coming months, more cities will get a chance to try out such programs. This year's federal budget included $300 million in so-called "urban revitalization grants," aimed at public housing in 10 cities—including $50 million for the Mission Hill project in Boston, which that city hopes to turn into a larger version of Lake Parc Place.

Another $800 million is in the pipeline for next year to help out other communities. HUD has been flexible in encouraging cities to think broadly about how they might use the money, but it is clear that initiatives like those at Columbia Villa, Gilpin Court and Ida B. Wells have attracted its notice.

"In the past, there have been people at all levels who have looked at public housing as a federal enclave, when it cannot succeed that way," says Mike Janis, a HUD deputy assistant secretary. "We realize that if you isolate public housing residents from the broader community, they cannot flourish. Public housing needs to be part of the community, and the community needs to be part of public housing."

As encouraging as such developments are, though, it is hard not to wonder whether they will be enough in the long run, at least for a city like Chicago, with its endless blocks of public housing high rises. "High rises aren't conducive to a community atmosphere," insists LeRoy Martin, the city's former police chief and now director of security for the CHA. "You can't even call those neighborhoods. If I was asked for my opinion, tearing them down would be my advice."

Vincent Lane does not have the option of tearing down Robert Taylor and Cabrini-Green overnight and starting again from scratch. He has 150,000 tenants who need a place to live. On the other hand, he does have a vision for what public housing in Chicago could become, and Lake Parc, he says, is its "first iteration." With a combination of new development on city-owned land and redevelopment of public housing—using tax breaks and low land costs to help write down the cost to developers—he is pushing for projects spread throughout the city and even the suburbs in which public housing families would never occupy more than a quarter of the units in a building, unless they were living in a duplex or a single-family home. In essence, he wants to rebuild community in public housing by completely redefining what constitutes public housing.

"If you go back 60 years, every community had some people who were very well off, most were working stiffs, and some were very poor. When we had those neighborhoods," Lane says, "they functioned. They might not have been glitzy, but they had family values, they had neighborhood values, they had a work ethic and they had religious underpinnings. Those are the critical elements that have to be present in any neighborhood in order for it to work."

Cities of Violence

Though the soaring number of murders and other violent crimes in Washington is in some ways a uniquely American problem, urban violence is exploding in countries around the world. In the rapidly growing cities of Latin America and Asia, in European capitals freeing themselves from years of Communist rule, and in societies in the throes of political and social change in Africa and the Middle East, millions of people have been frightened and angered by a seemingly boundless wave of bloodshed. As in the United States, criminals abroad are increasingly armed with sophisticated weapons and police are outmanned; increasingly too there is despair over the inability of political leaders to stop the killing.

[This article looks] at three cities whose crises are manifested in violent crime: Johannesburg, South Africa; Rio de Janeiro, Brazil; and Moscow, Russia. All are much larger than Washington, and so suffer from an even greater number of violent deaths. But only one—Johannesburg—has a higher murder rate compared with its population than the District of Columbia.

Johannesburg: Murder Knows No Color

Paul Taylor

Washington Post Foreign Service   JOHANNESBURG

Cross-national comparative crime statistics are notoriously unreliable, but for the past year Johannesburg has thought of itself as the murder capital of the world. "People here are under enormous stress," says criminologist Irma Labuschagne. According to figures published by the Johannesburg Star, the per capita murder rate here is nearly 100 times that of a typical European capital, 7.5 times that of New York City and 1.5 times that of Washington, D.C.

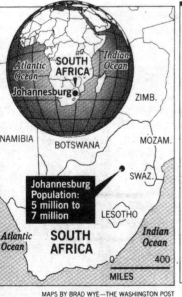

Johannesburg
Population:
5 million to
7 million

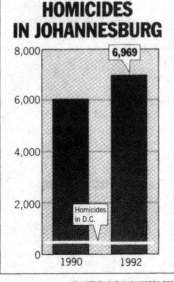

HOMICIDES IN JOHANNESBURG

MAPS BY BRAD WYE—THE WASHINGTON POST   CHARTS BY THE WASHINGTON POST

There were 6,969 murders and 27,420 armed robberies in the greater Johannesburg area last year, according to police. The area, which has an estimated population of 5 million to 7 million, includes Soweto and other black townships that surround the city.

South Africa differs from most violent societies in that there are two kinds of murder here—political and criminal. Sometimes the categories overlap. But as a rule, roughly 15 percent of the murders are political—the result of fighting among rival political, racial or ethnic groups, of economic warfare that has a political component, of conflict between citizens and security forces, and of random massacres by agents provocateurs bent on destabilizing the transition from the apartheid system of racial separation to democracy. These are the murders that make headlines here and abroad.

The rest of the killings are straightforward crimes of avarice or passion. All categories of crime have risen between 20 percent and 80 percent in the four years since South Africa's democratization process began, but the murder rate has grown most of all, nearly doubling.

Among white South Africans, the response to this crime wave may seem somewhat disproportionate to their exposure. Only 3 percent of South Africa's murder victims are white (the population is 13 percent white). On the other hand, the annual number of white victims has doubled in the past four years, coinciding with the near-doubling of the overall murder rate. All South Africans, regardless of skin color, are less safe than they used to be.

The response to this heightened risk has been to privatize law enforcement—although the phrase has different meanings in different South African communities. In white areas, police are seen as understaffed, underpaid, ineffectual and demoralized. No official figures are available, but the conviction rate on murder is thought to be in the 15 percent range. Private security companies, high walls and razor wires abound in the white suburbs.

The psychological climate among whites could be glimpsed at a recent dinner party in Johannesburg, as an elderly couple began strategizing The Trip Home.

He: "When should I tell them?"

She: "What is it, a five-minute drive? And first we must say our good-byes. Tell them 12 minutes."

Off he went—a retired lawyer with progressive views and buoyant hopes for the new South Africa—to his host's kitchen, to phone his private security company to have them dispatch a guard to meet him and his wife at their home. They want armed protection in case, during their evening out, an intruder scaled their walls, cut their razor wire, neutralized their guard dog, deactivated their alarm system and penetrated the house.

In black townships, the reputation of the police is far worse. They are seen as agents of a racist, repressive state, and as more likely to be involved in sowing violence than in solving it. Not a week goes by that one black politician or another does not call on police to leave the townships altogether.

In the absence of any legitimate mechanism of law enforcement in the townships, a private culture of street justice and people's courts has evolved. Most townships have criminal gangs, local warlords and self-defense units. All of this, of course, fuels cycles of vengeance killings.

"People feel endorsed and applauded for their violence—they feel like they are doing something for the community if they kill a criminal figure of a member of an opposition faction," says Lloyd Vogelman, director of the Center for the Study of Violence and Reconciliation at the University of Witwatersrand. "One way most societies maintain law and order is to morally isolate the perpetrators of violence. At the moment, we have largely lost that sanction in many communities in South Africa."

This growth in the culture of violence has come at a time of profound political and social transition—when the old order has lost its authority and the new one has not yet taken power. Most experts predict that once a democratic government is elected next year, it will have the legitimacy to take stern measures to crack down on political violence.

Rio de Janeiro: Carnage at Its Ugliest

Don Podesta

Washington Post Foreign Service

RIO DE JANEIRO

Wagner Ribeiro de Souza was asleep when two gunmen entered his house Oct. 31 about 3 a.m. Before he could make it out of bed, one of the men fired a bullet into his neck. Six hours later, his body was still in the bed. No ambulance had come; no police had been there to investigate. Ribeiro, 30, ran a small snack stand adjacent to his home in the working-class Rio neighborhood of Colegio, far from the glitzy hotels on the beaches of Copacabana and Ipanema. An uncle interviewed in the doorway of Ribeiro's home said that only Ribeiro's wife had seen the men, one of whom wore a ski mask. He said he had no idea why anyone would want to kill his nephew.

Ribeiro's slaying was just one of more than a dozen that took place that night. By Rio's standards, it was a pretty tame affair.

Rio has a worldwide reputation as a violent place, and it is no wonder: The city has registered more than 3,000 homicides a year since 1989. Nevertheless, as the worlds' 10th-largest city in population with 5.3 million people, the number of murders per capita is still lower than in Washington, D.C., which has a population of about 589,000.

What makes Rio stand out is not so much the amount of violence as its quality. This city—set amid a fantastically beautiful natural panorama—is also the scene of the worst form of human ugliness.

Every day, the front page of the city's crime newspaper, O Povo na Rua (the People in the Street), carries pictures of murder victims from the previous night. Often these are close-ups of headless bodies or disembodied heads. Sometimes the photos are of limbless trunks or bodies showing signs of torture. One sequence of front-page photos in September showed a man being burned in a bonfire by residents of the neighborhood after he was identified as the person who had torched a house, killing an infant. A tree limb had been inserted into his body.

The common term used by police, reporters and the general public for the bodies that are discovered daily is *presunto*, or ham.

One O Povo headline series on a recent story sums up the murder scene here: "20 DEAD. Explosion of Hate and Violence. Bodies Spread All Through the City. Poison, Robbery, Vengeance. No One Arrested."

Arrests for murder, let alone convictions, are rare. In nearby Duque de Caxias, an industrial suburb of Rio with a population about the size of the District of Columbia's, prosecutor Tania Maria Salles Moreira says her office handled more than 1,100 murder cases last year. Only 74 of them ever came to trial.

In 1990, there were 3,849 slayings in her jurisdiction, she says. In more than 85 percent of these killings, no suspects were ever identified.

One reason is that many of the slayings take place in Rio's notorious slums, called *favelas,* where gangs of drug traffickers hold sway, witnesses are afraid to talk and the police seldom enter. When they do, it is often to settle scores, and the police themselves engage in killing.

In August, 21 residents of a slum called Vigario Geral were killed by a squad of policemen bent on retaliating for the deaths of four comrades at the hands of suspected drug traffickers the previous night. A few weeks earlier, eight street children were shot to death as they slept.

In these two cases, some policemen have been detained, and state officials argue that this is a major step forward that other cities in Brazil are failing to take. In Sao Paulo, for instance, no one was charged following the massacre of 107 inmates when military police stormed a prison to put down a riot last year.

Rio's killings take place in what a report issued last month by the Institute for Research of Religion calls a "culture of fear." In the favelas, it seems more like a culture of war.

The weapons are not simple handguns. The gangs of drug traffickers who shoot it out with each other and with the police use rifles—including AR-15 semiautomatics—shotguns, hand grenades and even tripod-mounted .30-caliber machine guns.

"You could knock down a plane with one of those [machine guns]," says O Povo na Rua reporter Luiz Cerqueira Filho. He describes two adjacent favelas that have been the scene of gun battles for some time. In one of them, called Ramos, the drug gang named Comando Vermelho (Red Command) rules; the other, Roquete Pinto, is the territory of archrival Tercer Comando (the Third Command).

Last month, suspected drug traffickers from Roquete Pinto fired on a police barracks nearby, wounding one policeman in the stomach. For the next three days, police in camouflage uniforms and flak jackets swept the slum in an operation that more closely resembled a military raid than police work.

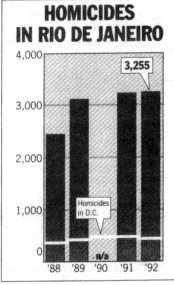

Much of the arsenal that enters Rio's favelas comes through these two slums, located near the sea. The guns are unloaded from ships and smuggled ashore in small boats. It is the army's job to enforce laws against possession of such weapons, but the army does not patrol the favelas.

Rio de Janeiro Gov. Leonel Brizola, whose state government came under criticism after the massacres, argues that there are two kinds of violence in the metropolitan Rio area: that from the bottom up and the top down. The latter, which he describes as institutionalized murder carried out by policemen or ex-policemen, is the most dangerous, he says.

In an interview at the governor's palace, he accuses elements in the city's business establishment of "seeking to create a culture of violence . . . using those who are charged with maintaining order. And it has a basis in discrimination—social and racial."

"This has created that second [kind of] violence," Brizola says, "the violence from the top down, repressive, discriminatory and that ended up organizing extermination groups to apply the death penalty summarily."

Brizola's government has cracked down on police violence and set up a telephone hot line to receive complaints from citizens, which police officials say are increasing.

Cerqueira, the O Povo reporter, says the arrests of policemen in the Vigario Geral and street children killings seem to have put a damper on the activities of the police-linked death squads, at least for the time being. Before, on a typical morning, a team of O Povo reporters and photographers would rush to the scene of eight or 10 killings, Cerqueira says. Since the arrests, there's much less action, sometimes only one or two bodies per team a day.

(continued)

Moscow: A Judicial System That Doesn't Work

Fred Hiatt

Washington Post Foreign Service

MOSCOW

When a gunman shot the cashier of a downtown jewelry store in 1977, all of Moscow seemed aghast. Crime was never as rare as Soviet propaganda pretended, but such acts of premeditated violence were uncommon.

Today, Vladimir Nenashev, a senior Moscow prosecutor, can leaf through his handwritten log of crimes and find dozens of such cases. In one 24-hour period two weeks ago, which Nenashev says was typical, police recorded 172 serious crimes—including six slayings and four assaults—and detained only 70 suspects.

Different experts off varying explanations for what Nenashev calls a "sharp and significant increase in crime." But all agree that ordinary Muscovites feel vulnerable and bewildered, unaccustomed not only to the lack of security but also to the sheer brazenness of the criminal world around them.

All agree, too, that most Muscovites feel abandoned and unprotected by police and other authorities. Underpaid, overworked and unprepared professionally for the new types of crime Russia is facing, the police and courts are almost universally viewed as either incapable or too corrupted to stem the criminal tide.

"The law enforcement system is choking on a flood of crime," says Azalia Dolgova, law professor and president of Russia's Association for Criminology. "Even honest businessmen would rather turn to racketeers than to policemen for protection."

For Russians and foreigners alike, swapping tales of true crime has become a consuming pastime. A musician who shot to death an intruder in his apartment was told by police that the burglar's gang would surely return for vengeance—and that the police could do nothing to protect him. The musician and his family went into hiding. Another Russian slept nightly in his new car to prevent its theft until he could find space in a lockable garage.

Statistics support the anecdotes. Moscow prosecutors report a 9 percent increase in crime in the first nine months of this year, compared with the same period in 1992, and a 45 percent increase in serious crimes such as murder, rape and assault.

Moscow officials reported 257 slayings in 1978 and only 239 in 1988. But through the following years, the numbers climbed steadily: 424 in 1989; 441 in 1990; 501 in 1991; 925 in 1992. The 1992 figure was topped during the first nine months of this year, when 968 people were slain.

But even those fairly dramatic numbers fail to portray the seriousness of the problem, Dolgova says. While pre-1989

crimes were underreported for political reasons—only solved cases were counted, she says—prosecutors these days may fail to open investigations in many instances simply because they are swamped for time.

For a city whose population is nearly 15 times that of Washington, D.C., but whose murder rate is only one-seventh that of the District, the number of slayings may not be startling. But for many Muscovites, it is the type of murders that is most unsettling.

In Soviet days, most slayings took place within families or among drinkers, says Vitaly Ryabov, another Moscow prosecutor. Now, many killings are premeditated, usually for economic motives, and gangland shootouts and contract hits are a matter of course.

"If a husband want his wife killed, it may cost half a million," says senior prosecutor Tatyana Kuznetsova. A half-million rubles is about $450. "But if it's the killing of a big businessman, then rubles aren't enough. It'll cost $3,000, maybe $6,000, maybe the cost of a new car."

Kuznetsova, a 23-year veteran of the Moscow prosecutors' staff, recently helped investigate what she says was a fairly typical case, the killing several months ago of Valentin and Valentina Alexandrov. According to the prosecutors' investiga-

HOMICIDES IN MOSCOW

tion, Valentin, a truck dealer in the provincial capital of Kazan, had a dispute with business colleagues here.

The colleagues kidnapped and threatened to kill him, Kuznetsova says. Alexandrov responded that his wife knew exactly where he was—whereupon the colleagues induced Valentina to come to Moscow and had them both killed.

"They hired a regular slaughterer, who killed them with one chop, cut them into pieces and buried them in the countryside," Kuznetsova says.

Arkady Murashov, a liberal politician and former Moscow police chief, says that such cases in part reflect the absence of a working judicial system in Russia. "If the state is unable to provide justice, economic subjects start to solve problems in other ways, using crime, guns, mafias and private guards," he says.

Not surprisingly, more conservative analysts blame the rise in crime on the reforms themselves. Dolgova says many youths are driven to crime by poverty, by resentment of the new rich and by the belief that many of Russia's new capitalists got their start in the criminal or quasi-criminal world.

Senior prosecutor Nenashev attributes the increase in crime to a loosening of all forms of societal control. In Soviet days, he notes, no one could live in Moscow without a special permit. Vagrants, drunkards and the unemployed were swept up and sent to prison camps. Convicted criminals were barred from living in the capital. Guns were extremely difficult to come by, whereas pistols that fire pellets of disabling gas now are sold at kiosks and more lethal weapons are available almost as openly.

"Maybe it was bad from the point of view of democracy, but all those control worked," Nenashev says. "Now they are lost."

Many experts say Russia's law enforcement institutions were poorly prepared for the combination of increasing crime and loss of totalitarian methods. Murashov says Russia has more law enforcement bureaucrats per capita than it needs, but because the system is so centralized, there are not enough policemen and investigators in the field.

In fact, investigators are solving a smaller proportion of crimes, experts say. Murashov estimates that fewer than half of all perpetrators now are caught. Nenashev says 20 to 25 murders each year used to remain unsolved. Of this year's 968 slayings, 284 already have been declared unsolved, meaning investigators have essentially given up.

Crime-solving has become more difficult in part because of an increased workload and also because so many more criminals are professional. "Our police always had good skills, but they didn't require the same level of skill, organization and mobility as now, when they may find three corpses lying on the street with no other evidence," Nenashev says. "Of course, we don't have the skills to investigate such cases, because we never had such cases before."

TERMINAL DECLINE OF A NATION

"America is being transformed from an industrial colossus to a tired, down-at-the-heels, post-industrial society."

Steve Slavin

Dr. Slavin is professor of economics, Union County College, Cranford, N.J., and New School for Social Research, New York.

AMERICANS have been so busy worrying about all their problems that very few noticed that the U.S. is going bankrupt. Ironically, it is those very problems that are driving the nation into bankruptcy. A partial list would include crime, drugs, poverty, a failing education system, a crumbling infrastructure, soaring health care costs, lagging productivity, a huge national debt, a large trade deficit, and an anemic rate of economic growth.

Can't America just muddle through, the way it always has? Not this time. The problems are so overwhelming that there are no easy solutions. Just take a look around.

All over the country, people are wearing signs that have not been seen since the Great Depression: "Will work for food." In Santa Fe, N.M., where several hundred homeless individuals have staked out places to sleep, there is a sign under a bridge proclaiming, "This is a home." In downtown Seattle, Wash., it is possible to see people with placards that say, "No Job, No Food, No Hope." They don't even bother to add, "No Home."

Former vice presidential candidate Geraldine Ferraro remembers a little girl she saw near a shut-down Pennsylvania steel mill, holding up a sign: "My daddy needs a job."

America is being transformed from an industrial colossus to a tired, down-at-the-heels, post-industrial society. It is becoming a nation of the rich and super-rich at the top, a mass of poor people on the bottom, and a powerless middle class squeezed in between.

More and more, the U.S. is taking on the trappings of Third-World poverty. The streets are filled with homeless people and beggars. Crime is rampant, and the drug epidemic continues to rage out of control. The contrast between poverty and affluence never has been sharper, except that now there seems to be a lot more poor people than ever before.

What really differentiates America from Mexico, Brazil, and Argentina? For years, many poor nations have come with tin cups and begged for loans and outright grants. The U.S. has gone from being the world's biggest creditor nation to the number-one debtor.

Mayors and governors go, hat in hand, to Japanese industrialists and beg them to set up factories in America. Often, they grant tax concessions and other costly inducements. When those factories are built, they provide thousands of jobs, but almost always semi-skilled, relatively low-paying, assembly line ones—and non-union as well.

What the U.S. has been doing these last 15 years is mortgaging the future for the present. Americans are indulging themselves in consumer goods—many supplied by foreigners—and incurring a huge national debt because they refuse to tax themselves for a growing proportion of what the Federal government spends. Americans are running up a huge tab and leaving it for future generations.

Since the early 1980s, Americans have been on a national shopping spree that has been subsidized by foreigners. What are these foreigners doing with all those dollars Americans spend? Not only have they been financing more than half the Federal budget deficit, they are purchasing huge chunks of U.S. real estate and corporate stock, often at bargain basement prices.

As foreigners buy up more and more of the U.S., the nation is beginning to lose its economic sovereignty. No longer are key decisions being made just in Washington, but in Tokyo, London, Frankfort, Amsterdam, and Toronto as well.

As a nation, Americans spend more than they earn, consume more than they produce, and go deeper and deeper into debt each year. They live for today, hoping tomorrow somehow will take care of itself. So far, their luck has held, but it can't last forever. As Joel Kurtzman observed in *The Decline and Crash of the American Economy*, the U.S. may "soon be seeing a Japanese or European economist appointed to oversee all major American economic decisions as prerequisite for more cash from abroad."

Any way it is measured, Americans' standard of living has not risen since the early 1970s. Average family incomes rose 111% between 1947 and 1973, but, over the next 19 years, increased just five percent. The only reason they grew at all is because so many housewives went out to work.

This is not to say all Americans fared poorly during this period. Between 1977 and 1990, compensation for top corporate executives rose by 220%. At the same time, their personal income taxes were cut dramatically. In 1960, the average pay for the chief executive officers of the nation's leading corporations, after taxes, was 12 times greater than the average wage for factory workers at their companies. By 1993, it was more than 100 times greater.

Another measure—median household income—was $36,000 in current dollars, $1,000 less than in 1973. Only 20% of the nation's households—those with incomes above $80,000—have gained ground on inflation since the early 1970s.

Democracy is based on some semblance of equal opportunity in the pursuit of affluence. A large and growing segment of the population virtually has given up hope of ever attaining any degree of affluence. These people include the predominately black and Hispanic permanent underclass, homeless, working poor, working class, laid-off blue- and white-collar workers, high school dropouts, and the functionally illiterate.

With the exception of the Depression years, every generation that came of age in any decade in the nation's history did better than its parents' generation—until the 1980s. Now, each new generation faces the prospect of having a lower standard of living. The implications are frightening. As *Newsweek* columnist Robert Samuelson has observed, "prosperity is what binds us together; if we don't all believe in a better tomorrow, America will become a progressively less civil, less cohesive and more contentious society."

The end of the American Dream

"America limps along, a superpower that, like a star high-school athlete grown middle-aged, ate too much but didn't exercise," is how *New York Times* columnist Anna Quindlen has described a nation well past its prime, as it struggles against the inexorable aging process. Is this decline inevitable, or are there still things that can be done to reverse the process?

In the years following World War II, the U.S. was the economic engine of the world, producing half its industrial goods. The nation also perfected its genius at distributing these goods at home and abroad. Nevertheless, it was inevitable that the American share of industrial production would decline as Western Europe and Japan rebuilt the factories that had been destroyed by the war.

By the 1980s, the U.S. had become increasingly dependent on foreign imports, while its exports had lost their cachet. Much of Americans' energy seems to have gone from production into distributing foreign goods among themselves. Advertising agencies, which bill close to $150,000,000,000 a year, bombard audiences with messages about the virtues of Toyotas, Nissans, and BMWs.

Much of our recent economic stimulus has been supplied by the computer industry and surging imports. However, most of this spending is concentrated on the East and West coasts. Everyone else in the country seems to be working for KFC, McDonald's, K-Mart, or 7-Eleven. Americans have been reduced to a nation of hamburger flippers, parking lot attendants, chambermaids, hair dressers, telemarketers, bedpan orderlies, gas pumpers, rent-a-car clerks, supermarket checkers, sales representatives, medical secretaries, and waiters and waitresses.

About the only good thing is that the majority of the population is employed. Sixty percent of the mothers with young children are working, as are teenagers. College students nearly all have part-time jobs. There are help wanted signs in shopping malls, supermarkets, and fast food restaurants. On the other hand, two or three people in every family have to work just to make ends meet. So more and more people are jumping into the employment pool and just treading water.

Although more Americans than ever hold jobs, the country's manufacturing base is disappearing. Employment in the auto and steel industries is down by more than 50% over the last two decades. The midwestern industrial heartland has become the Rust Belt. More Americans work in fast food restaurants than in all of the manufacturing industries combined.

Nearly everyone used to buy into the basic American dream of having a nice home, decent job, and better life for their children. For most, that dream is fading, while for many, it has become a nightmare. Farm foreclosures, evictions, corporate downsizing, plant closings, and long-term joblessness have robbed millions of their dreams. Fewer and fewer people are making it. Now, at long last, the nation is beginning to wake up to reality.

How did Americans manage to get themselves into such a fix? Why did the most prosperous nation in history fall so quickly from economic grace? The American standard of living, which long had been the highest in the world, has not increased in 20 years. The U.S. steadily is losing its manufacturing base, while hemorrhaging millions of well-paying blue-collar jobs. The educational system turns out 1,000,000 functional illiterates every year. One out of every 10 Americans is on public assistance, and there is a growing permanent underclass of hundreds of thousands of fourth- and fifth-generation welfare families. Even though there are more than 1,000,000 people in prison, the streets remain unsafe and drug dealers operate with near impunity.

The Federal government is part of the problem, not part of the solution. Escalating budget deficits are approaching $400,000,000,000. If it continues on its present fiscal course, the Federal government will go bankrupt soon after the turn of the century. Meanwhile, the problems have grown too massive for state and local governments to handle, and the "thousand points of light" that only Pres. George Bush was able to perceive have not been sufficient to stop the nation's social fabric from continuing to unravel.

Can the U.S. government actually go bankrupt? To even have asked that question a dozen years ago would have been absurd. Still, the national debt has more than quadrupled since 1981—to nearly $4.5 trillion—and the Federal budget deficit is nearly out of control. A growing number of economists finally are beginning to think about the once unthinkable.

This places the nation on the horns of a damned-if-we-do and damned-if-we-don't dilemma. If the government does nothing, the array of social and economic forces that is dragging the U.S. into bankruptcy will continue unabated. Even if the government does launch a massive program to reverse these forces, it will be extremely costly, adding well over $100,000,000,000 a year to the deficit, which well may tip the U.S. into bankruptcy even before the end of the century.

This dilemma easily is resolved, however. If the government does nothing, America goes bankrupt. If the government attempts to avert bankruptcy, it might succeed. So what do Americans have to lose?

Drug and Sexual Issues

One basic question facing society is, "How far should we go in attempting to regulate the private lives of our citizens?" We expect that when the actions of one person impact negatively on others, those others can demand and expect that the guilty party change or eliminate these behaviors. In such cases there is an identifiable victim who can seek redress. However, in many cases involving behaviors, the victim and the criminal/perpetrator are one and the same, so the legislating of morality becomes an issue. No one is "hurt" by these actions, but the potential for serious offense exists. These are known in the sociological literature as "victimless" crimes, because the so-called victim and the criminal are the same. The complainant is often a third party who is offended by the actions of the individual. One could always argue that there are no true victimless crimes because what a person does to himself or herself does indeed impact on significant others—that is, family, close friends, and children.

"Off Course" examines what is happening in many women's studies courses around the country. The author personally visited many campuses and discovered that "discussions run from the personal to the political and back again, with mere pit stops at the academic."

"Truth or Consequences: Teen Sex" explores the implications of earlier and earlier experiences of teen sexual activities. The "sexual revolution" is into its fourth decade, and the results are far from positive. The authors look at the social, medical, psychological, and economic costs and at what, if anything, can be done to reduce them.

"A Society of Suspects: The War on Drugs and Civil Liberties" reflects the paradoxes of trying to balance effective measures against crime with the upholding of civil rights. While trying to win the war on drugs, law enforcement personnel insist their hands are being tied.

But those constraints were established by the Founding Fathers to protect the rights of every American citizen to be free from unwarranted searches, entry into homes, and arrest. This author argues that constitutional rights are being systematically limited and redefined because of this "war."

"Separating the Sisters," reports the fact that many women feel that mainstream feminism has ignored their plight. Dominated by white, highly educated women, feminism has not adequately addressed issues facing the great numbers of women who fall outside of that classification—particularly women in "traditional" women's jobs, women who stay at home to raise children, elderly women, rural women, and poor women.

Looking Ahead: Challenge Questions

What should be the primary objective(s) of any academic program within a university setting? Why?

Just why are we so concerned, as a society, about drugs?

Distinguish between the harmful effects of societally approved drugs (alcohol, tobacco and, caffeine) and of those that are not (heroin, cocaine, marijuana).

What major ways can raising the fears of the members of a society impact on their rights as citizens?

Do the ends always justify the means used in a society to combat drug use/abuse?

To what degree does modern feminism reflect the concerns of all women?

Which of the three sociological theoretical positions do you think most clearly helps to understand the issues/problems covered in this unit?

What are the values, rights, obligations, and harms associated with each of the activities included in this unit?

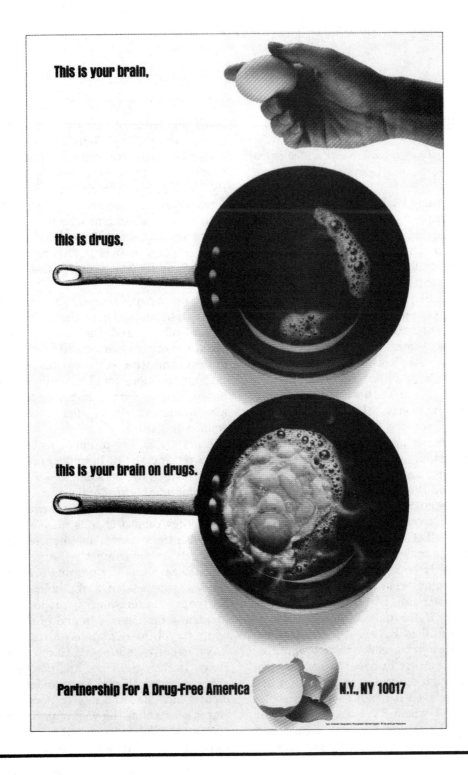

This is your brain,

this is drugs,

this is your brain on drugs.

Partnership For A Drug-Free America   N.Y., NY 10017

Off course

Women's studies has empowered women to speak up in class. The problem is what they're often talking about.

Karen Lehrman

Karen Lehrman is writing a book on postideological feminism.

It's eight o'clock on a balmy Wednesday morning at the University of California at Berkeley, and Women's Studies 39, "Literature and the Question of Pornography," is about to begin. The atmosphere of the small class is relaxed. The students call the youngish professor by her first name; the banter focuses on finding a man for her to date. She puts on the board: "Write 'grade' or 'no grade' on your paper before turning it in." Students—nine women and one man—amble in sporadically for the first twenty minutes.

Today's discussion involves a previous guest speaker, feminist-socialist porn star Nina Hartley. The professor asks what insights the students gained from Hartley's talk. They respond: "She's free with her sexuality. . . . I liked when she said, 'I like to . . . my friends.' . . . No body-image problems. . . . She's dependent in that relationship. . . ." The professor tries to move the discussion onto a more serious question: have traditional feminists, in their antiporn stance, defined women out of their sexuality? After a few minutes, though, the discussion fixes on orgasms—how they're not the be-all and end-all of sexual activity, how easy it is to fake one. The lone male stares intently at a spot on the floor; occasionally he squirms.

I never took a porn class when I went to college ten years ago. In fact, I never took a women's studies class and don't even know if the universities I attended offered any. Women's studies was about a decade old at the time, but it hadn't yet become institutionalized (there are now more than six hundred programs), nor gained notoriety through debates over the canon and multiculturalism. But even if I had been aware of a program, I'm certain I would have stayed far away from it. It's not that I wasn't a feminist: I fully supported equal rights and equal opportunities for women.

But I was feminist like I was Jewish—it was a part of my identity that didn't depend on external affirmation.

Perhaps more important, as a first-generation career-woman, I felt a constant need to prove my equality. I took as many "male" courses—economics, political science, intellectual history—as I could; I wanted to be seen as a good student who happened to be a woman. There were a couple of problems, though: I didn't learn much about women or the history of feminism, and like most of my female peers, I rarely spoke in class.

Last spring I toured the world of women's studies, visiting Berkeley, the University of Iowa, Smith College, and Dartmouth College. I sat in on about twenty classes, talked to students and professors at these and other schools, amassed syllabi, and waded through the more popular reading materials. I admit to having begun with a nagging skepticism. But I was also intrigued: rumor had it that in these classes, women talked.

And they do. The problem, as I see it, is what they're often talking about. In many classes discussions alternate between the personal and the political, with mere pit stops at the academic. Sometimes they are filled with unintelligible post-structuralist jargon; sometimes they consist of consciousness-raising psychobabble, with the students' feelings and experiences valued as much as anything the professor or texts have to offer. Regardless, the guiding principle of most of the classes is oppression, and problems are almost inevitably reduced to relationships of power. "Diversity" is the mantra of both students and professors, but it doesn't apply to political opinions.

Not every women's studies course suffers from these flaws. In fact, the rigor and perspective of individual programs and classes vary widely and feminist academics have debated nearly every aspect of the field. But it seems that the vast majority of women's studies professors rely to a greater or lesser extent, on a common set of feminist theories. Put into practice, these theories have the potential to undermine the goals not only of a liberal education, but of feminism itself.

This doesn't mean, as some critics have suggested, that these programs should simply be abolished. Women's studies has played a valuable role in forcing universities to include in the curriculum women other than "witches or Ethel Rosenberg," as Iowa's Linda K. Kerber puts it. The field has generated a considerable amount of first-rate scholarship on women, breaking the age-old practice of viewing male subjects and experience as the norm and the ideal. And it has produced interdisciplinary courses that creatively tie together research from several fields.

Whether all this could have been accomplished without the creation of women's studies programs separate from the traditional departments is a moot question, especially since these programs have become so well entrenched in the academy. The present challenge is to make women's studies as good as it can be. Although the problems are significant, they're not insurmountable. And perhaps more than anything else, women's studies prides itself on its capacity for self-examination and renewal.

Berkeley was the only stop on the tour with an actual women's studies department. It is one of the largest, most established and respected programs in the country. Overall, it impressed me the least. At the other extreme was Smith, where the classes tended to be more rigorous and substantive and there was a greater awareness of the pitfalls of the field. (The students were also far more articulate, though that may have little to do with women's studies.) I found the most thoughtful professors in Iowa's program, which doesn't even offer a major. The program at Dartmouth, perhaps compensating for the school's macho image, seemed the most prone to succumbing to the latest ideological fads.

Discussions run from the personal to the political and back again, with mere pit stops at the academic.

CLASSROOM THERAPY

"Women's studies" is something of a misnomer. Most of the courses are designed not merely to study women, but also to improve the lives of women, both the individual students (the vast majority of whom are female) and women in general. Since professors believe that women have been effectively silenced throughout history, they often consider a pedagogy that "nurtures voice" just as, if not more, important than the curriculum.

Women's studies professors tend to be overtly warm, encouraging, maternal. You want to tell these women your problems—and many students do. To foster a "safe environment" where women feel comfortable talking, many teachers try to divest the classroom of power relations. They abandon their role as experts, lecturing very little and sometimes allowing decisions to be made by the group and papers to be graded by other students. An overriding value is placed on student participation and collaboration: students make joint presentations, cowrite papers, and use group journals for "exploring ideas they can't say in class" and "fostering a sense of community" Because chairs are usually arranged in a circle, in a couple of classes taught by graduate students I couldn't figure out who the teacher was until the end.

Most of the women's studies students I met were quite bright, and many argued certain points very articulately.

To give women voice, many professors encourage all discourse—no matter how personal or trivial. Indeed, since it is widely believed that knowledge is constructed and most texts have been influenced by "the patriarchy" many in women's studies consider personal experience the only real source of truth. Some professors and texts even claim that women have a way of thinking that is different from the abstract rationality of men, one based on context, emotion, and intuition. Fully "validating" women, therefore, means celebrating subjectivity over objectivity feelings over facts, instinct over logic.

The day I sat in on Berkeley's "Contemporary Global Issues for Women" (all women except for one "occasional" male), we watched a film about women organizing in Ahmadabad, India. The film was tedious, but it seemed like grist for a good political/economic/sociological discussion about the problems of women in underdeveloped countries. After the film ended, though, the professor promptly asked the class: "How do you *feel* about the film? Do you find it more sad or courageous?" Students responded to her question until the end of class, at which point she suggested, "You might think about the film in terms of your own life and the life of your mother Women are not totally free in this culture. It just might come in more subtle ways."

A previous discussion was apparently not much better. "We had to read an enormous amount of interesting material on reproductive rights, which I was very excited to discuss," Pam Wilson, a women's studies sophomore, told me. "But all she did in class was ask each of us, 'What forms of birth control have you used, and what problems have you had?' We never got to the assigned readings."

Self-revelation is not uncommon to women's studies classes. Students discover that they're lesbian or bisexual, for example, and then share it with the class. In a group journal (titled "The Fleshgoddesses") from last year's porn class, B. wrote: "There is still something about a [man] eating a [woman] out ... that freaks me out! I guess I'm such a dyke that it seems abnormal." G. recalled that her father used to kiss her on the mouth "real hard" when she was eight or nine.

Of course, self-discovery and female bonding are important for young women, and so, one might argue, are group therapy and consciousness-raising. Indeed, I wish I had had some when I was that age; it might have given me the courage to talk in class and to deal with abusive bosses later in life. But does it belong in a university classroom?

Many of the professors I talked with (including the chair of Berkeley's women's studies department) viewed the more touchy-feely classes as just as problematic as I did. I saw a couple of teachers who were able to use personal experience, either of historical figures or students, to buttress the discussion, not as an end in itself. But even these classes were always on the verge of slipping into confession mode.

This pedagogy does get women talking. But they could do much of this type of talking in support groups at their schools' women's centers. Young women have many needs, and the college classroom can effectively address only one of them: building their intellects. As Ruth Rosen, who helped start the women's studies program at the University of California at Davis, puts it, "Students go to college to be academically challenged, not cared for."

But the problem with a therapeutic pedagogy is more than just allowing students to discuss their periods or sex lives in class. Using the emotional and subjective to "validate" women risks validating precisely the stereotypes that feminism was supposed to eviscerate: women are irrational, women must ground all knowledge in their own experiences, etc. A hundred years ago, women were fighting for the right to learn math, science, Latin—to be educated like men; today, many women are content to get their feelings heard, their personal problems aired, their instincts and intuition respected.

POLITICS, AS USUAL

"Don't worry. We've done nothing here since she forgot her notes a couple of weeks ago," Michael Williams reassures another male student. "We'll probably talk about Anita Hill again." We're waiting for Berkeley's "Gender Politics: Theory and Comparative Study" to begin. When the professor finally arrives and indicates

that, yes, we'll be talking about Anita Hill again, the second male student packs up and bolts. Williams tells me that during the first week or two, whenever a male student would comment on something, the professor would say, "What you really mean is ..." Most men stopped speaking and then dropped out. "Other classes I walk out with eight pages of notes," says Williams. "Here, everybody just says the same thing in a different way" (He stays, though, for the "easy credits.")

Most women's studies professors seem to adhere to the following principles in formulating classes: women were and are oppressed; oppression is endemic to our patriarchal social system; men, capitalism, and Western values are responsible for women's problems. The reading material is similarly bounded in political scope (Andrea Dworkin, Catharine MacKinnon, bell hooks, Adrienne Rich, and Audre Lorde turn up a lot), and opposing viewpoints are usually presented only through a feminist critique of them. *Feminist Frontiers III*, a book widely used in intro courses, purports to show readers "how gender has shaped your life," and invites them to join in the struggle "to reform the structure and culture of male dominance."

Says one student, "The way to get A's was to write papers full of guilt and angst about how I'd bought into society's definition of womanhood."

Although most of the classes I attended stopped short of outright advocacy of specific political positions, virtually all carried strong political undercurrents. Jill Harvey, a women's studies senior at Smith, recalls a feminist anthropology course in which she "quickly discovered that the way to get A's was to write papers full of guilt and angst about how I'd bought into society's definition of womanhood and now I'm enlightened and free."

Sometimes the politicization is more subtle. "I'm not into consciousness-raising," says Linda K. Kerber, a history professor at Iowa. "Students can feel I'm grading them on their competence and not on their politics." Yet in the final project of "Gender and Society in the United States," she asked students: "Reconsider a term paper you have written for another class. How would you revise it now to ensure that it offers an analysis sensitive to gender as well as to race and class?"

Politicization is also apparent in the meager amount of time the classes devote to women who have achieved anything of note in the public sphere. Instead, students scrutinize the diaries and letters of unremarkable women who are of interest primarily because the patriarchy victimized them in one way or another.

According to professors and students, studying "women worthies" doesn't teach you much about oppression. Moreover some added, these women succeeded by male, capitalist standards. It's time for women's traditional roles and forms of expression to be valued.

This may be true, but you don't need to elevate victimized women to the status of heroes to do that. It should also be noted that over the past twenty-five years feminists have been among those who have devalued women's traditional roles most vigorously. I bet not many women's studies majors would encourage a peer's decision to forgo a career in order to stay home and raise children. More important, examples of women who succeeded in the public sphere, possibly even while caring for a family, could be quite inspiring for young women. Instead, the classes implicitly downplay individual merit and focus on the systematic forces that are undermining everything women do.

In general, "core" women's studies courses are more overtly political and less academically rigorous than those cross-listed with a department. The syllabus of Iowa's "Introduction to Women's Studies" course declares: "As we make our collective and individual journeys during this course, we will consider how to integrate our theoretical knowledge with personal and practical action in the world." "Practicums," which typically entail working in a women's organization, are a key part of many courses, often requiring thirty or more hours of a student's time.

Volunteering in a battered-women's shelter or rape crisis center may be deeply significant for both students and society. But should this be part of an undergraduate education? Students have only four years to learn the things a liberal education can offer—and the rest of their lives to put that knowledge to use.

Courses on women don't have to be taught from an orthodox feminist perspective. Smith offers a biology course that's cross-listed with women's studies. It deals with women's bodies and medical issues; feminist theory is not included. Compare that to the course description of Berkeley's "Health and Sex in America": "From sterilization to AIDS; from incest to date rape; from anorexia to breast implants: who controls women's health?" Which course would you trust to be more objective?

Many women's studies professors acknowledge their field's bias, but point out that all disciplines are biased. Still, there's a huge difference between conceding that education has political elements and intentionally politicizing, between, as Women's Studies Professor Daphne Patai puts it, "recognizing and minimizing deep biases and proclaiming and endorsing them." Patai, whose unorthodox views got her in hot water at the University of Massachusetts, is now coauthoring a book on the contradictions of women's studies. "Do they really want fundamentalist studies, in which teachers are not just studying fundamentalism but supporting it?"

A still larger problem is the degree to which politics has infected women's studies scholarship. "Feminist theory guarantees that researchers will discover male bias and oppression in every civilization and time," says Mary Lefkowitz, a classics professor at Wellesley. "A distinction has to be made between historical interpretation of the past and political reinterpretation." And, I would add, between reading novels with an awareness of racism and sexism, and reducing them entirely to constructs of race and gender.

Apparently there has always been a tug of war within the women's studies community between those who most value scholarship and those who most value ideology. Some professors feel obligated to present the work of all women scholars who call themselves feminists, no matter how questionable their methodology or conclusions.

Unfortunately women's studies students may not be as well equipped to see through shoddy feminist scholarship as they are through patriarchal myths and constructs. One reason may be the interdisciplinary nature of the programs, which offers students minimal grounding in any of the traditional disciplines. According to Mary Lefkowitz, women's studies majors who take her class exhibit an inability to amass factual material or remember details; instead of using evidence to support an argument, they use it as a remedy for their personal problems.

But teaching students how to "think critically" is one of the primary goals of women's studies, and both students and professors say that women's studies courses are more challenging than those in other departments. "Women's studies gives us tools to analyze," says Torrey Shanks, a senior women's studies and political science major at Berkeley. "We learn theories about how to look at women and men; we don't just come away with facts."

Women's studies has generated first-rate scholarship on women, but professors often consider a pedagogy that "nurtures voice" just as, if not more, important than the curriculum.

Most of the women's studies students I met were quite bright, and many argued certain points very articulately. But they seemed to have learned to think critically through only one lens. When I asked some of the sharpest students about the most basic criticisms of women's studies, they appeared not to have thought about them or gave me some of the stock women's studies rap. It seemed that they couldn't fit these questions into their way of viewing the world.

For instance, when I expressed the view that an at-times explicit anticapitalist and anti-Western bias pervades the field, a couple of majors told me they thought that being anticapitalist was part of being a feminist. When I asked whether, in the final analysis, women weren't still most free in Western capitalist societies, the seemingly programmed responses ran from "I wouldn't feel free under a glass ceiling" to "Pressures on Iranian women to wear the veil are no different from pressures on women in this country to wear heels and miniskirts."

THE STUDENT PARTY LINE

Despite the womb-like atmosphere of the classrooms, I didn't see much student questioning of the professors or the texts. Although I rarely saw teachers present or solicit divergent points of view the students' reluctance to voice alternative opinions seemed to stem more from political intolerance and conformity on the part of fellow students.

In Smith's "Gender and Politics" class, several students spoke against the ban on gays in the military before Erin O'Connor, her voice shaking, ventured: "I think there is something to the argument of keeping gays out of the military because of how people feel about it."

After several students said things like, "The military should reflect society" O'Connor rebounded: "I'm sick and tired of feeling that if I have a moral problem with something, all of a sudden it's: 'You're homophobic, you're wrong, you're behind the times, go home.' There must be someone else in this classroom who believes as I do."

Professor: "No one is saying that support of the ban is homophobic."

"I would make that assertion," offered a student.

Professor: "But you can argue against the ban from a nonhomophobic perspective."

Another student: "It's homophobic."

When class ended, another woman approached O'Connor and said: "You're absolutely right, and I'm sure there are others who felt the same way but just didn't say anything. You went out on a limb."

No one used the word homophobic until O'Connor did. Still, students, especially in this ostensible "safe environment," shouldn't have to overcome a pounding heart to voice a dissident opinion. "Women's studies creates a safe space for p.c. individuals, but doesn't maintain any space for white Christians," says O'Connor, an English and government major and member of the College Republican Club.

In a study by the Association of American Colleges, 30 percent of students taking women's studies courses at Wellesley said they felt uneasy expressing unpopular opinions; only 14 percent of non-women's studies students felt that way.

Smith's Jill Harvey told me about a "Medical Anthropology" class filled with women's studies students. The professor presented an author's view that one difference between men and women when paralyzed is that men are rendered incapable of getting an erection. "The students jumped down his throat, believing he was insinuating that all women have to do is lie back and enjoy sex," says Harvey. "It was absurd, but I didn't feel like I could speak up. I sometimes feel the other students' attitude is: if you don't agree with me, you're too stupid to understand how oppressed you are."

The pressures on professors to toe the correct feminist line can be even stronger. History Professor Elizabeth Fox-Genovese says she stepped down as chair of Emory's women's studies program because of complaints from students and faculty that she wasn't radical enough. Political theorist Jean Bethke Elshtain left the University of Massachusetts after being attacked for including men on her reading list, allowing men in class, and presenting an array of different feminist positions. She now teaches at Vanderbilt. "Most teachers of women's studies presume that if you don't see yourself as a victim, you're in a state of false consciousness, you're 'male-identified? The professors here [at Vanderbilt] recognize that feminism is in part an argument."

Women's studies professors take little responsibility for turning female students into Angry Young Women. Yet the effect of these classes, one after another, can be quite intoxicating. (After just a few days, I found myself noticing that the sign on the women's bathroom door in the University of Iowa's library was smaller than the one on the men's room door.) The irony is not only that these students (who, at the schools I visited at least, were overwhelmingly white and upper-middle-class) probably have not come into contact with much oppression, but that they are the first generation of women who have grown up with so many options open to them.

POST-STRUCTURALISM AND MULTICULTURALISM

Perhaps the most troubling influence on women's studies in the past decade has been the collection of theories known as post-structuralism, which essentially implies that all texts are arbitrary all knowledge is biased, all standards are illegitimate, all morality is subjective. I talked to numerous women's studies professors who don't buy any of this (it's typically more popular in the humanities than in the social sciences), but nevertheless it has permeated women's studies to a significant extent, albeit in the most reductive, simplistic way.

According to Delo Mook, a Dartmouth physics professor who is part of a team teaching "Ways of Knowing: Physics, Literature, Feminism," "You can't filter other cultures through our stencil. Nothing is right or wrong."

What about cannibalism? Clitorectomies? "Nope. I can only say 'I believe it's wrong.'"

But post-structuralism is applied inconsistently in women's studies. I've yet to come across a feminist tract that "contextualizes" sexism in this country as it does in others, or acknowledges that feminism is itself a product of Western culture based on moral reasoning and the premise that some things are objectively wrong. Do feminist theorists really want the few young men who take these classes to formulate personal rationales for rape? There's a huge difference between questioning authority truth, and knowledge and saying none of these exist, a difference between rejecting male standards and rejecting the whole concept of standards.

Like post-structuralism, the concept of multiculturalism has had a deep influence on women's studies. Professors seem under a constant burden to prove that they are presenting the requisite number of books or articles by women of color or lesbians. Issues of race came up in nearly every class I sat through. I wasn't allowed to sit in on a seminar at Dartmouth on "Racism and Feminism" because of a contract made with the students that barred outside visitors.

Terms like sexism, racism, and homophobia have bloated beyond all recognition, and the more politicized the campus, the more frequently they're thrown around. I heard both professors and students call Berkeley's women's studies department homophobic and racist, despite the fact that courses dealing with homosexuality and multiculturalism fill the catalog and quite a number of women of color and lesbians are affiliated with the department.

Although many professors try to work against it, in the prevailing ethos of women's studies, historical figures, writers, and the students themselves are viewed foremost as women, as lesbians, as white or black or Hispanic, and those with the most "oppressed" identities are the most respected. Feminist theorists now generally admit that they can't speak for all women, but some still presume to speak for all black women or all Jewish women or all lesbians. There's still little acknowledgment not only of the individuality of each woman, but of the universal, gender-blind bond shared by all human beings.

THE ROAD NOT TAKEN

Women's studies programs have clearly succeeded with at least one of their goals: whether because of the mostly female classes, the nurturing professors, or the subject matter, they have gotten women students talking.

But getting women to speak doesn't help much if they're all saying the same thing. Women's studies students may make good polemicists, but do they really learn to think independently and critically?

Elizabeth Fox-Genovese says she had envisioned Emory's women's studies program as a mini-women's college: "I thought it should be a special environment that took women seriously and asked them to be the best that they could be by the standards of a good, liberal arts education." Young women—and men—would be steeped in sound scholarship on women, but they would also be offered a variety of theories and viewpoints, feminist and otherwise.

Unfortunately, this hasn't been the perspective of most women's studies professors. Women's studies was conceived with a political purpose—to be the intellectual arm of the women's movement—and its sense of purpose has only gotten stronger through the years. The result is that the field's narrow politics have constricted the audience for nonideological feminism instead of widening it, and have reinforced the sexist notion that there is a women's viewpoint. There's a legitimate reason why two-thirds of college women don't call themselves feminists. "When I got here I thought I was a feminist," Erin O'Connor from Smith told me. "I don't want to call myself that now."

Clearly the first step is for women's studies to reopen itself to internal and external criticism. The intimidation in the field is so great that I had trouble finding dissident voices willing to talk to me on the record. The women's movement has come a long way in the past twenty-five years-feminists should feel secure enough now to take any and all lumps.

Young women should also no longer feel it necessary to shun classes devoted to women, as my friends and I did. Women today still have to work for their equality, but they don't have to prove it every second. And as the status of women in this country evolves, so should the goals of women's studies. It's for its own sake that women's studies should stop treating women as an ensemble of victimized identities. Only when the mind of each woman is considered on its own unique terms will the minds of all women be respected.

Truth and Consequences
TEEN SEX

Douglas J. Besharov with Karen N. Gardiner

Douglas J. Besharov is a resident scholar at the American Enterprise Institute. Karen Gardiner is a research assistant at the American Enterprise Institute.

Ten million teenagers will engage in about 126 million acts of sexual intercourse this year. As a result, there will be about one million pregnancies, resulting in 406,000 abortions, 134,000 miscarriages, and 490,000 live births. Of the births, about 313,000, or 64 percent, will be out of wedlock. And about three million teenagers will suffer from a sexually transmitted disease such as chlamydia, syphilis, gonorrhea, pelvic inflammatory disease, and even AIDS.

This epidemic of teen pregnancy and infection has set off firestorms of debate in school systems from Boston to San Francisco. Last May, Washington, D.C. Mayor Sharon Pratt Kelly announced that health officials would distribute condoms to high school and junior high school students. Parents immediately protested, taking to the streets with placards and angry shouts. And the New York City Board of Education was virtually paralyzed for weeks by the controversy surrounding its plans for condom distribution.

Both sides have rallied around the issue of condom distribution as if it were a referendum on teen sexuality. Proponents argue that teenagers will have sex whether contraceptives are available or not, so public policy should aim to reduce the risk of pregnancy and the spread of sexually transmitted diseases by making condoms easily available. Opponents claim that such policies implicitly endorse teen sex and will only worsen the problem.

The causes of teen pregnancy and sexually transmitted diseases, however, run much deeper than the public rhetoric that either side suggests. Achieving real change in the sexual behavior of teenagers will require action on a broader front.

Thirty Years into the Sexual Revolution

Some things are not debatable: every year, more teenagers are having more sex, they are having it with increasing frequency, and they are starting at younger ages.

There are four principal sources of information about the sexual practices of teenagers: the National Survey of Family Growth (NSFG), a national in-person survey of women ages 15–44 conducted in 1982 and again in 1988; the National Survey of Adolescent Males (NSAM), a longitudinal survey of males ages 15–19 conducted in 1988 and 1991; the National Survey of Young Men (NSYM), a 1979 survey of 17- to 19-year-olds; and the Youth Risk Behavior Survey (YRBS), a 1990 questionnaire-based survey of 11,631 males and females in grades 9–12 conducted by the Centers for Disease Control (CDC). In addition, the Abortion Provider Survey, performed by the Alan Guttmacher Institute (AGI), collects information about abortions and those who provide them.

With minor variations caused by differences in methodology, each survey documents a sharp increase in the sexual activity of American teenagers. All these surveys, however, are based on the self-reports of young people and must be interpreted with care. For example, one should always take young males' reports about their sexual exploits with a grain of salt. In addition, the social acceptability of being a virgin may have decreased so much that this, more than any change in behavior, has led to the higher reported rates of sexual experience. The following statistics should therefore be viewed as indicative of trends rather than as precise and accurate measures of current behavior.

A cursory glance at Figure 1 shows that there was indeed a sexual revolution. The 1982 NSFG asked women ages 15–44 to recall their first premarital sexual experience. As the figure shows, teenagers in the early 1970s (that is, those born between 1953 and 1955) were twice as likely to have had sex as were teenagers in the early 1960s (that is those born 1944 to 1946).

The trend of increased sexual activity that started in the 1960s continued well into the late 1980s. According to the 1988 NSFG, rates of sexual experience increased about 45 percent between 1970 and 1980 and increased another 20 percent in just three years, from 1985–1988, but rates have now apparently plateaued. Today, over half of all unmarried teenage girls report that they have engaged in sexual intercourse at least once.

These aggregate statistics for all teenagers obscure the second remarkable aspect of this 30-year trend: sexual activity is starting at ever-younger ages. The 1988 NSFG found that the percentage of 18-year-olds who reported being sexually active increased about 75 percent between 1970 and 1988, from about 40 percent to about 70 percent. Even more startling is that the percentage of sexually experienced 15-year-old females multiplied more than fivefold in the same period, from less than 5 percent to almost 27 percent.

Moreover, the increase in sexual activity among young teens continued beyond 1988. In 1990, 32 percent of ninth-grade females (girls ages 14 and 15) reported ever having had sex, as did 49 percent of the males in the same grade. At the same time, the proportion of twelfth-grade females (ages 17 and 18) who reported ever engaging in sex remained at 1988 levels.

Teenagers are not only having sex earlier, they are also having sex with more partners. According to the NSAM, the average number of partners reported by males in the 12 months preceding the survey increased from 2.0 in 1988 to 2.6 in 1991. Almost 7 percent of ninth-grade females told the YRBS that they had had intercourse with four or more different partners, while 19 percent of males the same age reported having done so. By the twelfth grade, 17 percent of girls and 38 percent of boys reported having four or more sexual partners.

A major component of these increases has been the rise in sexual activity among middle-class teenagers. Between 1982 and 1988, the proportion of sexually active females in families with incomes equal to or greater than 200 percent of the poverty line increased from 39 percent to 50 percent. At the same time, the proportion of females from poorer families who had ever had sex remained stable at 56 percent.

Until recently, black teenagers had substantially higher rates of sexual activity than whites. Now, the differences between older teens of both races have narrowed. But once more, these aggregate figures obscure underlying age differentials. According to the 1988 NSAM, while 26 percent of white 15-year-old males reported engaging in sex compared to 67 percent of blacks, by age 18 the gap narrowed to 71 percent of whites and 83 percent of blacks. A similar trend appears among females. Twenty-four percent of white 15-year-old females have engaged in sex, compared to 33 percent

of their black counterparts, reports the 1988 NSFG. By age 16, the proportions increase to 39 percent and 54 percent, respectively. Even by age 17, fewer white females have started having sex (56 percent) than have blacks (67 percent). On the other hand, white teen males reported having had almost twice as many acts of intercourse in the 12 months preceding the 1988 NSAM than did black teen males (27 versus 15). The white males, however, had fewer partners in the same period (2 versus 2.5).

The Social Costs

Among the consequences of this steady rise in teen sexuality are mounting rates of abortion, out-of-wedlock births, welfare, and sexually transmitted diseases.

Abortion. About 40 percent of all teenage pregnancies now end in abortion. (Unmarried teens account for about 97 percent.) This means that of the 1.6 million abortions in 1988, over 400,000—or a quarter of the total—were performed on teenagers. In the 11 years between 1973 and 1984, the teenage abortion rate almost doubled, from about 24 to about 44 per 1,000 females ages 15–19. (Between 1984 and 1988, the rate stabilized.)

A study by AGI's Stanley Henshaw found that between 1973 and 1988, the abortion rate for girls ages 14 and under increased 56 percent (from 5.6 to 8.6 per 1,000), 62 percent for those ages 15–17 (from 18.7 to 30.3), and among older

FIGURE ONE: TRENDS IN PREMARITAL SEXUAL ACTIVITY FOR ALL FEMALE TEENAGERS

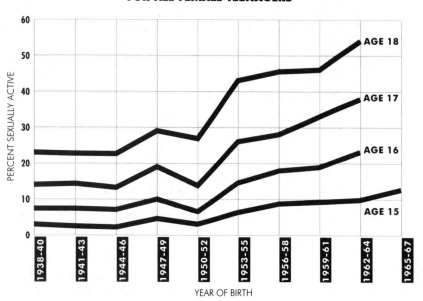

SOURCE: S. Hofferth, J. Kahn, and W. Baldwin, "Premarital Sexual Activity Among U.S. Women Over the Past Three Decades," *Family Planning Perspectives*, Vol. 19, No. 2, March/April 1987.

As Table 1 shows, welfare dependency is more a function of a mother's age and marital status than of her race. White and black unmarried adolescent mothers have about the same welfare rate one year after the birth of their first child. After five years, black unmarried mothers have a somewhat higher rate of welfare dependency than whites (84 percent versus 72 percent), but various demographic factors such as family income, educational attainment, and family structure account for this relatively small difference.

Disease. Over three million teenagers, or one out of six sexually experienced teens, become infected with sexually transmitted diseases each year, reports the Centers for Disease Control (CDC). One Philadelphia clinic administrator laments that she used to spend $3 on contraceptives for every $1 on disease screening and related health issues. Today, the ratio is reversed. Susan Davis, a contraception counselor at a Washington, D.C. area Planned Parenthood clinic, explains, "The risk of infection is greater than the risk of pregnancy for teens." These diseases can cause serious problems if left untreated. The CDC estimates that between 100,000 and 150,000 women become infertile every year because of sexually transmitted disease-related pelvic infections.

teens, almost 120 percent (from 29 to 63.5). In absolute numbers, the youngest group had about 13,000 abortions, the middle group had 158,000, and the oldest group had 234,000.

Out-of-Wedlock Births. Over 300,000 babies were born to unwed teenagers in 1988. That's three-fifths of all births to teenagers. Although the total number of births to teenagers declined between 1970 and 1988, the percentage born out of wedlock more than doubled (from 29 percent to 65 percent), and the teenage out-of-wedlock birth rate increased from about 22 per 1,000 to 37 per

1,000. Over 11,000 babies were born to children under 15 years old in 1988.

Welfare. Few teen mothers place their children up for adoption as was often done in the past. And yet most are not able to support themselves, let alone their children. Consequently, about 50 percent of all teen mothers are on welfare within one year of the birth of their first child; 77 percent are on within five years, according to the Congressional Budget Office. Nick Zill of Child Trends, Inc., calculates that 43 percent of long-term welfare recipients (on the rolls for ten years or more) started their families as unwed teens.

The recent explosion of these diseases is in large measure caused by the sexual activity of teenagers; sexually transmitted disease rates decline sharply with age. Take gonorrhea, for example. According to AGI, there were 24 cases per 1,000 sexually experienced females ages 15–19 in 1988. Among women ages 20–24, the rate declined to

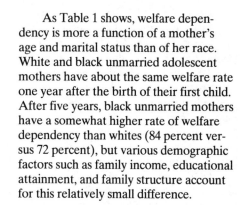

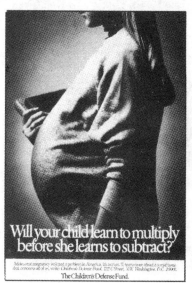

TABLE ONE: PERCENT OF ADOLESCENT MOTHERS ON AFDC

	BY FIRST BIRTH	WITHIN ONE YEAR OF BIRTH	WITHIN FIVE YEARS OF BIRTH
All	7%	28%	49%
Married	2	7	24
Unmarried	13	50	77
White	7	22	39
Black	9	44	76
White, Unmarried	17	53	72
Black, Unmarried	10	49	84

SOURCE: Congressional Budget Office, Sources of Support for Adolescent Mothers, Government Printing Office: Washington, D.C., 1990

15 and fell rapidly with age. For women ages 25–29, 30–34, and 35–39, the rates are 5, 2, and 1 per 1,000, respectively. Except for AIDS, most sexually transmitted diseases follow a similar pattern.

AIDS has not reached epidemic proportions in the teen population—yet. According to the Centers for Disease Control, fewer than 1,000 cases of AIDS are among teenagers. However, there are 9,200 cases among 20–24 year-olds and 37,200 cases among 25–29 year-olds. Given the long incubation period for the AIDS virus (8–12 years), many of these infections were probably contracted during adolescence.

According to Lawrence D'Angelo and his colleagues at the Children's National Medical Center in Washington, D.C., the rate of HIV (the virus that causes AIDS) infection among teenagers using the hospital increased rapidly between 1987 and 1991. For males, the rate increased almost sevenfold, from 2.47 per 1,000 in 1987 to 18.35 per 1,000 in 1991. The female rate more than doubled in the same period, from 4.9 to 11.05. These statistics only reflect the experience of one hospital serving a largely inner-city population, but they illuminate what is happening in many communities.

Use, Not Availability

Many people believe that there would be less teen pregnancy and sexually transmitted diseases if contraceptives were simply more available to teenagers, hence the call for sex education at younger ages, condoms in the schools, and expanded family planning programs in general. But an objective look at the data reveals that availability is not the prime factor determining contraceptive use.

Almost all young people have access to at least one form of contraception. In a national survey conducted in 1979 by Melvin Zelnik and Young Kim of the Johns Hopkins School of Hygiene and Public Health, over three-quarters of 15- to 19-year-olds reported having had a sex education course, and 75 percent of those who did remembered being told how to obtain contraception.

Condoms are freely distributed by family planning clinics and other public health services. They are often sitting in a basket in the waiting room. Edwin Delattre, acting dean of Boston University's School of Education and an opponent of condom distribution in public schools, found that free condoms were available at eight different locations within a 14-block radius of one urban high school.

And, of course, any boy or girl can walk into a drug store and purchase a condom, sponge, or spermicide. Price is not an inhibiting factor: condoms cost as little as 50¢. Although it might be a little embarrassing to purchase a condom—mumbling one's request to a pharmacist who invariably asks you to speak up used to be a rite of passage to adulthood—young people do not suffer the same stigma, scrutiny, or self-consciousness teenagers did 30 years ago.

Teenagers can also obtain contraceptives such as pills and diaphragms from family planning clinics free of charge or on a sliding fee scale. In 1992, over 4,000 federally funded clinics served 4.2 million women, some as young as 13. According to AGI, 60 percent of sexually active female teens use clinics to obtain contraceptive services, while only 20 percent of women over 30 do. In all states except Utah, teenagers can use clinic services without parental consent. To receive free services under the Medicaid program, however, a teenager must present the family's Medicaid card to prove eligibility.

In 1990, total public expenditures for family planning clinics amounted to $504 million. Adjusted for inflation, however, combined federal and state funding for clinics has declined by about one-third since 1980. But the impact of

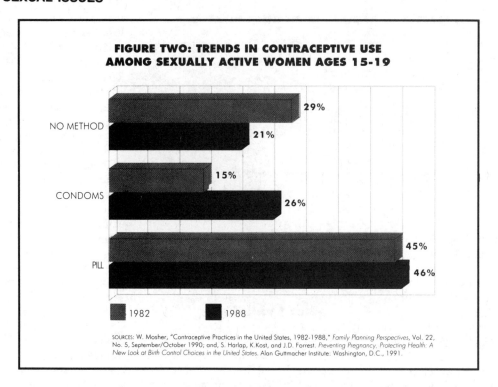

FIGURE TWO: TRENDS IN CONTRACEPTIVE USE AMONG SEXUALLY ACTIVE WOMEN AGES 15-19

NO METHOD — 29% / 21%

CONDOMS — 15% / 26%

PILL — 45% / 46%

■ 1982   ■ 1988

SOURCES: W. Mosher, "Contraceptive Practices in the United States, 1982-1988," *Family Planning Perspectives*, Vol. 22, No. 5, September/October 1990; and, S. Harlap, K.Kost, and J.D. Forrest. *Preventing Pregnancy, Protecting Health: A New Look at Birth Control Choices in the United States.* Alan Guttmacher Institute: Washington, D.C., 1991.

these cuts is unclear. On the one hand, the U.S. Department of Health and Human Services reports that the number of women using publicly funded clinics actually rose between 1980 and 1990, from 4.0 million to 4.2 million. When William Mosher of the National Center for Health Statistics analyzed the NSFG data, however, he found a slight decline between 1982 and 1988 in the proportion of respondents who had visited a clinic in the 12 months preceding the survey (37 percent versus 35 percent).

Whatever the effect of these cuts, the evidence suggests that as with condoms, teens know how to find a clinic when they want to. When they are younger, they do not feel the need to go to a clinic since condoms tend to be their initial form of contraception.

Susan Davis of Planned Parenthood explains, "The most common reason teenagers come is because they think they are pregnant. They get worried. Or they get vaginal infections. I had a whole slew of girls coming for their first pelvic exam and they all had chlamydia." The median time between a female teenager's first sexual experience and her first visit to a clinic is one year, according to a 1981 survey of 1,200 teenagers using 31 clinics in eight cities conducted by Laurie Zabin of the School of Hygiene and Public Health at the Johns Hopkins University in Baltimore.

The Conception Index

Two pieces of evidence further dispel the notion that lack of availability of contraception is the prime problem. First, reported contraceptive use has increased even more than rates of sexual activity. By 1988, the majority of sexually experienced female teens who were at risk to have an unintended pregnancy were using contraception: 79 percent. (This represents an increase from 71 percent in 1982.) When asked what method they use, 46 percent reported using the pill, 26 percent reported using condoms, and 2 percent reported using foam (see figure 2). In addition, the proportion of teen females who reported using a method of contraception at first intercourse increased from 48 percent in 1982 to 65 percent in 1988.

The second piece of evidence is that as they grow older, teenagers shift the forms of contraception they use. Younger teens tend to rely on condoms, whereas older teens use female-oriented methods, such as a sponge, spermicide, diaphragm, or the pill, reflecting the greater likelihood that an older female will be sexually active.

A major reason for this increase in contraceptive use is the growing number of middle-class youths who are sexually active. But it's more than this. Levels of unprotected first sex have decreased among all socioeconomic groups. Among

teens from wealthier families, the proportion who reported using no method at first sex decreased between 1982 and 1988 from 43 percent to 27 percent. During the same period, non-use among teens from poorer families also declined, from 60 percent to 42 percent.

Unprotected first sex also decreased among racial groups. Between 1982 and 1988, the proportion of white females who reported using a method of contraception at first intercourse increased from 55 percent to 69 percent. Among blacks, the increase was from 36 percent to 54 percent.

It's not just that teens are telling interviewers what they want to hear about contraception. Despite large increases in sexual activity, there has not been a corresponding increase in the number of conceptions. Between 1975 and 1988, when about 1.3 million more teen females reported engaging in sex (a 39 percent increase), the absolute number of pregnancies increased by less than 21 percent (see figure 3).

In fact, one could create a crude "teen conception index" to measure the changing rate of conception (composed of abortions, miscarriages, and births) among sexually active but unmarried teenagers. If we did so, the 1988 index would stand at .87, representing a decline of 13 percent from 1975 (down from 210 to 182 per 1,000 sexually active, unmarried teens). Most of this decline

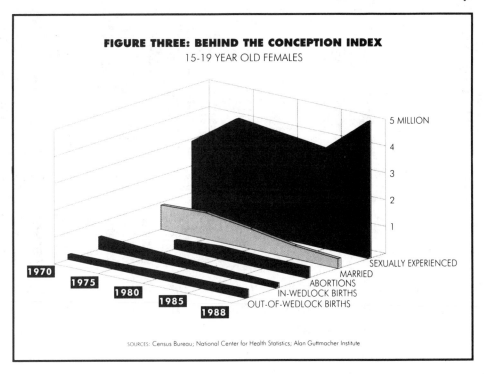

FIGURE THREE: BEHIND THE CONCEPTION INDEX
15-19 YEAR OLD FEMALES

SOURCES: Census Bureau; National Center for Health Statistics; Alan Guttmacher Institute

occurred between 1985 and 1988 as more middle-class teenagers had sex.

The Challenge

Although the conception index among teens is declining, the enormous increase in sexual activity has created a much larger base against which the rate is multiplied. Thus, as we have seen, there have been sharp increases in the rates of abortion, out-of-wedlock births, welfare dependency, and sexually transmitted diseases as measured within the whole teen population.

Teenage sexuality does not have to translate into pregnancy, abortion, out-of-wedlock births, or sexually transmitted diseases. Western Europe, with roughly equivalent rates of teen sexuality, has dramatically lower rates of unwanted pregnancy. According to a 1987 AGI study, the pregnancy rate among American teens (96 per 1,000 women) was twice as high as that in Canada (44), England and Wales (45), and France (43). It was almost three times higher than Sweden's (35) and more than six times higher than in the Netherlands (14). The answer, of course, is effective contraception.

The magnitude of the problem is illustrated by data about reported condom use. Between 1979 and 1988, the reported use of a condom at last intercourse for males ages 17–19 almost

tripled, from 21 percent to 58 percent. A decade of heightened concern about AIDS and other sexually transmitted diseases probably explains this tripling. According to Freya Sonenstein and her colleagues at the Urban Institute, over 90 percent of males in their sample knew how AIDS could be transmitted. Eighty-two percent disagreed "a lot" with the statement, "Even though AIDS is a fatal disease, it is so uncommon that it's not a big worry."

As impressive as this progress was, 40 percent did not use a condom at last intercourse. In fact, the 1991 NASM found that there has been no increase in condom use since 1988—even as the threat of AIDS has escalated.

The roots of too-early and too-often unprotected teen sex reach deeply into our society. Robin Williams reportedly asked a girlfriend, "You don't have anything I can take home to my wife, do you?" She said no, so he didn't use a condom. Now both Williams and the girlfriend have herpes, and she's suing him for infecting her. (She claims that he contracted herpes in high school.) When fabulously successful personalities behave this way, should we be surprised to hear about an inner-city youth who refuses his social worker's entreaties to wear a condom when having sex with his AIDS-infected girlfriend?

This is the challenge before us: How to change the behavior of these

young men as well as the one in five sexually active female teens who report using no method of contraception. First, all the programs in the world cannot deal with one vital aspect of the problem: many teenagers are simply not ready for sexual relationships. They do not have the requisite emotional and cognitive maturity. Adolescents who cannot remember to hang up their bath towels may be just as unlikely to remember to use contraceptives. Current policies and programs do not sufficiently recognize this fundamental truth.

At the same time, the clock cannot be turned all the way back to the innocent 1950s. Sexual mores have probably been permanently changed, especially for older teens—those who are out of high school, living on their own or off at college. For them, and ultimately all of us, the question is: How to limit the harm being done?

The challenge for public policy is to pursue two simultaneous goals: to lower the rate of sexual activity, especially among young teens, and to raise the level of contraceptive use. Other than abstinence, the best way to prevent pregnancy is to use a contraceptive, and the best way to prevent sexually transmitted diseases is to use a barrier form of contraception. Meeting this challenge will take moral clarity, social honesty, and political courage—three commodities in short supply these days.

A Society of Suspects:
THE WAR ON DRUGS AND CIVIL LIBERTIES

Property seized in drug raids, including large amounts of money, may be forfeited to the government without proof of the owner's guilt.

A decade after Pres. Reagan launched the War on Drugs, all we have to show for it are city streets ruled by gangs, a doubled prison population, and a substantial erosion of constitutional protections.

Steven Wisotsky

Mr. Wisotsky, professor of law, Nova University, Ft. Lauderdale, Fla., is a member of the advisory board of the Drug Policy Foundation, Washington, D.C., and author of Beyond the War on Drugs. *This article is based on a Cato Institute Policy Analysis.*

ON DEC. 15, 1991, America celebrated the 200th anniversary of the Bill of Rights. On Oct. 2, 1992, it marked the 10th anniversary of an antithetical undertaking—the War on Drugs, declared by Pres. Ronald Reagan in 1982 and aggressively escalated by Pres. George Bush in 1989. The nation's Founders would be disappointed with what has been done to their legacy of liberty. The War on Drugs, by its very nature, is a war on the Bill of Rights.

In their shortsighted zeal to create a drug-free America, political leaders—state and Federal, elected and appointed—have acted as though the end justifies the means. They have repudiated the heritage of limited government and individual freedoms while endowing the bureaucratic state with unprecedented powers.

That the danger to freedom is real and not just a case of crying wolf is confirmed by the warnings of a few judges, liberals and conservatives alike, who, insulated from elective politics, have the independence to be critical. Supreme Court Justice Antonin Scalia, for example, denounced compulsory urinalysis of Customs Service employees "in the front line" of the War on Drugs as an "invasion of their privacy and an affront to their dignity." In another case, Justice John Paul Stevens lamented that "this Court has become a loyal foot soldier" in the War on Drugs. The late Justice Thur-

good Marshall was moved to remind the Court that there is "no drug exception" to the Constitution.

In 1991, the Court of Appeals for the Ninth Circuit declared that "The drug crisis does not license the aggrandizement of governmental power in lieu of civil liberties. Despite the devastation wrought by drug trafficking in communities nationwide, we cannot suspend the precious rights guaranteed by the Constitution in an effort to fight the 'War on Drugs.' " In that observation, the court echoed a 1990 ringing dissent by the chief justice of the Florida Supreme Court: "If the zeal to eliminate drugs leads this state and nation to forsake its ancient heritage of constitutional liberty, then we will have suffered a far greater injury than drugs ever inflict upon us. Drugs injure some of us. The loss of liberty injures us all."

Those warnings are cries in the wilderness, however, unable to stop the relentless buildup of law enforcement authority at every level of government. In fact, the trend toward greater police powers has accelerated. One summary of the Supreme Court's 1990-91 term observed that its criminal law decisions "mark the beginning of significant change in the relationship between the citizens of this country and its police."

Despite such warnings, most Americans have yet to appreciate that the War on Drugs is a war on the rights of all of us. It could not be otherwise, for it is directed not against inanimate drugs, but against people—those who are suspected of using, dealing in, or otherwise being involved with illegal substances. Because the drug industry arises from the voluntary transactions of tens of millions of individuals—

all of whom try to keep their actions secret—the aggressive law enforcement schemes that constitute the war must aim at penetrating their private lives. Because nearly anyone may be a drug user or seller of drugs or an aider and abettor of the drug industry, virtually everyone has become a suspect. All must be observed, checked, screened, tested, and admonished—the guilty and innocent alike.

The tragic irony is that, while the War on Drugs has failed completely to halt the influx of cocaine and heroin—which are cheaper, purer, and more abundant than ever—the one success it can claim is in curtailing the liberty and privacy of the American people. In little over a decade, Americans have suffered a marked reduction in their freedoms in ways both obvious and subtle.

Among the grossest of indicators is that the war leads to the arrest of an estimated 1,200,000 suspected drug offenders each year, most for simple possession or petty sale. Because arrest and incarceration rates rose for drug offenders throughout the 1980s, the war has succeeded dramatically in increasing the full-time prison population. That has doubled since 1982 to more than 800,000, giving the U.S. the highest rate of incarceration in the industrialized world.

It has been established that law enforcement officials—joined by U.S. military forces—have the power, with few limits, to snoop, sniff, survey, and detain, without warrant or probable cause, in the war against drug trafficking. Property may be seized on slight evidence and forfeited to the state or Federal government without proof of the personal guilt of the owner.

Finally, to leverage its power, an increasingly imperial Federal government has applied intimidating pressures to shop owners and others in the private sector to help implement its drug policy.

Ironically, just as the winds of freedom are blowing throughout central and eastern Europe, most Americans and the nation's politicians maintain that the solution to the drug problem is more repression—and the Bill of Rights be damned. As Peter Rodino, former chairman of the House Judiciary Committee, said in expressing his anger at the excesses of the Anti-Drug Abuse Act of 1986, "We have been fighting the war on drugs, but now it seems to me the attack is on the Constitution of the United States."

In the beginning, the War on Drugs focused primarily on supplies and suppliers. Control at the source was the first thrust of anti-drug policy—destruction of coca and marijuana plants in South America, crop substitution programs, and aid to law enforcement agencies in Colombia, Peru, Bolivia, and Mexico.

Because this had no discernible, lasting success, a second initiative aimed to improve the efficiency of border interdiction of drug shipments that had escaped control at the source. There, too, success was elusive. Record numbers of drug seizures—up to 22 tons of cocaine in a single raid on a Los Angeles warehouse, for instance—seemed only to mirror a record volume of shipments to the U.S. By 1991, the amount of cocaine seized by Federal authorities had risen to 134 metric tons, with an additional amount estimated at between 263 and 443 tons escaping into the American market per year.

A reasonable search and seizure in the War on Drugs is interpreted very broadly and favors local police and Federal drug agents.

As source control and border interdiction proved futile, a third prong of the attack was undertaken: long-term, proactive conspiracy investigations targeted at suspected high-level drug traffickers and their adjuncts in the professional and financial worlds—lawyers, accountants, bankers, and currency exchange operators. This has involved repeated and systematic attacks by the Federal government on the criminal defense bar, raising dark implications for the integrity of the adversarial system of justice. Defense lawyers have been subjected to grand jury subpoenas, under threat of criminal contempt, to compel disclosures about their clients. Informants have been placed in the defense camp to obtain confidential information. In each instance, the effect has been to undermine the protections traditionally afforded by the attorney/client relationship. This demonstrates the anything-goes-in-the-War-on-Drugs attitude of the Department of Justice, which publicly defended using lawyers as informants as "a perfectly valid" law enforcement tool.

As these expanding efforts yielded only marginal results, the war was widened to the general populace. In effect, the government opened up a domestic front in the War on Drugs, invading the privacy of people through the use of investigative techniques such as urine testing, roadblocks, bus boardings, and helicopter overflights. Those are dragnet methods; to catch the guilty, everyone has to be watched and screened.

Invading privacy

Drug testing in the workplace. Perhaps the most widespread intrusion on privacy arises from pre- or post-employment drug screening, practiced by 80% of Fortune 500 companies and 43% of firms employing 1,000 people or more. Strictly speaking, drug testing by a private employer does not violate the Fourth Amendment, which protects only against government action. Nevertheless, much of the private drug testing has come about through government example and pressure. The 1988 Anti-Drug Abuse Act, for instance, prohibits the award of a Federal grant or contract to an employer who does not take specified steps to provide a drug-free workplace. As a result of these and other pressures, tens of millions of job applicants and employees are subjected to the indignities of urinating into a bottle, sometimes under the eyes of a monitor watching to ensure that clean urine is not smuggled surreptitiously into the toilet.

In the arena of public employment, where Fourth Amendment protections apply, the courts largely have rejected constitutional challenges to drug testing programs. In two cases to reach the U.S. Supreme Court, the testing programs substantially were upheld despite, as Justice Scalia wrote in dissent in one of them, a complete absence of "real evidence of a real problem that will be solved by urine testing of customs service employees." In that case, the Customs Service had implemented a drug testing program to screen all job applicants and employees engaged in drug interdiction activities, carrying firearms, or handling classified material. The Court held that the testing of such applicants and employees is "reasonable" even without probable cause or individualized suspicion against any particular person, the Fourth Amendment standard.

For Scalia, the testing of Customs Service employees was quite different from that of railroad employees involved in train accidents, which had been found constitutional. In that case, there was substantial evidence over the course of many years that the use of alcohol had been implicated in causing railroad accidents, including a 1979 study finding that 23% of the operating personnel were problem drinkers. Commenting on the Customs case, Scalia maintained that "What is absent in the government's justifications—notably absent, revealingly absent, and as far as I am concerned dispositively absent—is the recitation of even a single instance in which any of the speculated horribles actually occurred: an instance, that is, in which the cause of bribe-taking, or of poor aim, or of unsympathetic law enforcement, or of compromise of classified information, was drug use."

Searches and seizures. Other dragnet techniques that invade the privacy of the innocent as well as the guilty have been upheld by the Supreme Court. In the tug-of-war between the government's search and seizure powers and the privacy rights of individuals, the Court throughout the 1980s almost always upheld the government's assertion of the right of drug agents to use the airport drug courier profile to stop, detain, and question people without warrant or probable cause; subject a traveler's luggage to a sniffing examination by a drug-detecting dog without warrant or probable cause; search without warrant or probable cause the purse of a public school student; and search at will ships in inland waterways.

The right of privacy in the home seriously was curtailed in decisions permitting police to obtain a search warrant of a home based on an anonymous informant's tip; use illegally seized evidence under a "good faith exception" to the exclusionary rule (for searches of a home made pursuant to a defective warrant issued without probable cause); make a trespassory search, without a warrant, in "open fields" surrounded by fences and no trespassing signs and of a barn adjacent to a residence; and conduct a warrantless search of a motor home occupied as a residence, a home on the consent of an occasional visitor lacking legal authority over the premises, and the foreign residence of a person held for trial in the U.S. The Court also validated warrantless aerial surveillance over private property—by fixed-wing aircraft at an altitude of 1,000 feet and by helicopter at 400 feet.

Similarly, it significantly enlarged the powers of police to stop, question, and detain drivers of vehicles on the highways on suspicion with less than probable cause or with no suspicion at all at fixed checkpoints or roadblocks; make warrantless searches of automobiles and of closed containers therein; and conduct surveillance of suspects by placing transmitters or beepers on vehicles or in containers therein.

The foregoing list is by no means comprehensive, but it does indicate the sweeping expansions the Court has permitted in the investigative powers of government. Indeed, from 1982 through the end of the 1991 term, the Supreme Court upheld government search and seizure authority in approximately 90% of the cases. The message is unmistakable—the Fourth Amendment prohibits only "unreasonable" searches and seizures, and what is reasonable in the milieu of a War on Drugs is construed very broadly in favor of local police and Federal drug agents.

Surveillance of U.S. mail. Another casualty of the War on Drugs is the privacy of the mail. With the Anti-Drug Abuse Act of 1988, the Postal Service was given broad law enforcement authority. Using a profile, investigators identify what they deem to be suspicious packages and place them before drug-sniffing dogs. A dog alert is deemed probable cause to apply for a Federal search warrant. If an opened package does not contain drugs, it is resealed and sent to its destination with a copy of the search warrant. Since January, 1990, using this technique, the Postal Service has arrested more than 2,500 persons for sending drugs through the mail. The number of innocent packages opened has not been reported.

Wiretapping. As a result of the War on Drugs, Americans increasingly are being overheard. Although human monitors are supposed to minimize the interception of calls unrelated to the purpose of their investigation by listening only long enough to determine the relevance of the conversation, wiretaps open all conversations on the wiretapped line to scrutiny.

Court-authorized wiretaps doubtless are necessary in some criminal cases. In drug cases, though, they are made necessary because the "crimes" arise from voluntary transactions, in which there are no complainants to assist detection. The potential is great, therefore, for abuse and illegal overuse.

Stopping cars on public highways. It is commonplace for police patrols to stop "suspicious" vehicles on the highway in the hope that interrogation of the driver or passengers will turn up enough to escalate the initial detention into a full-blown search. Because the required "articulable suspicion" rarely can be achieved by observation on the road, police often rely on a minor traffic violation—a burned-out taillight, a tire touching the white line—to supply a pretext for the initial stop. In the Alice-in-Wonderland world of roving drug patrols, however, even lawful behavior can be used to justify a stop. The Florida Highway Patrol Drug Courier Profile, for example, cautioned troopers to be suspicious of "scrupulous obedience to traffic laws."

Another tactic sometimes used is the roadblock. Police set up a barrier, stop every vehicle at a given location, and check each driver's license and registration. While one checks the paperwork, another walks around the car with a trained drug-detector dog. The law does not regard the dog's sniffing as the equivalent of a search on the theory that there is no legitimate expectation of privacy in the odor of contraband, an exterior olfactory clue in the public domain. As a result, no right of privacy is invaded by the sniff, so the police do not need a search warrant or even probable cause to use the dog on a citizen. Moreover, if the dog "alerts," that supplies the cause requirement for further investigation of the driver or vehicle for drugs.

Monitoring and stigmatizing. In the world of anti-drug investigations, a large role is played by rumors, tips, and suspicions. The Drug Enforcement Administration (DEA) keeps computer files on U.S. Congressmen, entertainers, clergymen, industry leaders, and foreign dignitaries. Many persons named in the computerized Narcotics and Dangerous Drug Information System (NADDIS) are the subject of "unsubstantiated allegations of illegal activity." Of the 1,500,000 persons whose names have been added to NADDIS since 1974, less than five percent, or 7,500, are under investigation by DEA as suspected narcotic traffickers. Nevertheless, NADDIS maintains data from all such informants, surveillance, and intelligence reports compiled by DEA and other agencies.

The information on NADDIS is available to Federal drug enforcement officials in other agencies, such as the Federal Bureau of Investigation, the Customs Service, and the Internal Revenue Service. State law enforcement officials probably also can gain access on request. Obviously, this method of oversight has troubling implications for privacy and good reputation, especially for the 95% named who are not under active investigation.

Another creative enforcement tactic sought to bring about public embarrassment by publishing a list of people caught bringing small amounts of drugs into the U.S. The punish-by-publishing list, supplied to news organizations, included only small-scale smugglers who neither were arrested nor prosecuted for their alleged crimes.

Military surveillance. Further surveillance of the citizenry comes from the increasing militarization of drug law enforcement. The process began in 1981, when Congress relaxed the Civil War-era restrictions of the Posse Comitatus Act on the use of the armed forces as a police agency. The military "support" role for the Coast Guard, Customs Service, and other anti-drug agencies created by the 1981 amendments expanded throughout the 1980s to the point that the U.S. Navy was using large military vessels—including, in one case, a nuclear-powered aircraft carrier—to interdict suspected drug smuggling ships on the high seas.

By 1989, Congress designated the Department of Defense (DOD) as the single lead agency of the Federal government for the detection and monitoring of aerial and maritime smuggling into the U.S. DOD employs its vast radar network in an attempt to identify drug smugglers among the 300,000,000 people who enter the country each year in 94,000,000 vehicles and 600,000 aircraft. Joint task forces of military and civilian personnel were established and equipped with high-tech computer systems that provide instantaneous communication among all Federal agencies tracking or apprehending drug traffickers.

The enlarged anti-drug mission of the military sets a dangerous precedent. The point of the Posse Comitatus Act was to make clear that the military and police are very different institutions with distinct roles to play. The purpose of the military is to prevent or defend against attack by a foreign power and to wage war where necessary. The Constitution makes the president commander-in-chief, thus centralizing control of all the armed forces in one person. Police, by contrast, are supposed to enforce the law, primarily against domestic threats at the city, county, and state levels. They thus are subject to local control by the tens of thousands of communities throughout the nation.

Since the 1987 enactment of the Uniform Sentencing Guidelines, the penalties for drug crimes have become extreme and mandatory.

To the extent that the drug enforcement role of the armed forces is expanded, there is a direct increase in the concentration of political power in the president who commands them and the Congress that authorizes and funds their police activities. This arrangement is a severe injury to the Federal structure of our democratic institutions. Indeed, the deployment of national military forces as domestic police embarrasses the U.S. in the international arena by likening it to a Third World country, whose soldiers stand guard in city streets, rifles at the ready, for ordinary security purposes.

The dual military/policing role also is a danger to the liberties of all citizens. A likely military approach to the drug problem would be to set up roadblocks, checkpoints, and roving patrols on the highways, railroads, and coastal waters, and to carry out search-and-destroy missions of domestic drug agriculture or laboratory production. What could be more destructive to the people's sense of personal privacy and mobility than to see such deployments by Big Brother?

Excessive punishment

These are some of the many ways the War on Drugs has cut deeply—and threatens to cut deeper still—into Americans' privacy, eroding what Justice Louis D. Brandeis described as "the right to be let alone—the most comprehensive of rights and the right most valued by civilized men." Working hand-in-hand with the political branches, the courts have diminished constitutional restraints on the exercise of law enforcement power. In addition to expanded powers of surveillance, investigation, and prosecution, punishment has been loosed with a vengeance, against enemy and bystander alike.

Punishments have become draconian in part because of permission conferred by Justice William Rehnquist's 1981 circular dictum: "the question of what punishments are constitutionally permissible is not different from the question of what punishments the Legislative Branch intended to be imposed." The penalties have become so extreme, especially since the 1987 enactment of the Uniform Sentencing Guidelines, that many Federal judges have begun to recoil. U.S. district court Judge J. Lawrence Irving of San Diego, a Reagan appointee, announced his resignation in protest over the excessive mandatory penalties he was required to mete out to low-level offenders, most of them poor young minorities. Complaining of "unconscionable" sentences, the judge said that "Congress has dehumanized the sentencing process. I can't in good conscience sit on the bench and mete out sentences that are unfair."

Judge Harold Greene of the District of Columbia went so far as to refuse to impose the minimum guideline sentence of 17.5 years on a defendant convicted of the street sale of a single Dilaudid tablet, pointing to the "enormous disparity" between the crime and the penalty. In the judge's view, the minimum was "cruel and unusual" and "barbaric." Fourth circuit Judge William W. Wilkins objected to mandatory penalties because "they do not permit consideration of an offender's possibly limited peripheral role in the offense." Agreeing with that thinking, the judicial conferences of the District of Columbia, Second, Third, Seventh, Eighth, Ninth, and Tenth circuits have adopted resolutions opposing mandatory minimums.

As drug control policymakers came to realize that the drug dealers were, in an economic sense, merely entrepreneurs responding to market opportunities, they learned that attacks on dealers and their supplies never could succeed as long as there was demand for the products. Thus, they would have to focus on consumers as well as on suppliers. Pres. Reagan's 1986 Executive Order encouraging or requiring widespread urine testing marked a step in that direction. By 1988, Administration policy was being conducted under the rubric of "zero tolerance." In that spirit, Attorney General Edwin Meese sent a memorandum to all U.S. Attorneys on March 30, 1988, encouraging the selective prosecution of "middle and upper class users" in order to "send the message that there is no such thing as 'recreational' drug use. . . . "

Because of the volume of more serious trafficking cases, however, it was not remotely realistic, as the Attorney General must have known, to implement such a policy. Indeed, in the offices of many U.S. Attorneys, there were minimum weight or money-volume standards for prosecution, and the possession and small-scale drug cases routinely were shunted off to state authorities. In fact, in many districts, the crush of drug cases was so great that the adjudication of ordinary civil cases virtually had ceased. The courthouse doors were all but closed to civil litigants.

In the name of zero tolerance, Congress purposely began enacting legislation that did not have to meet the constitutional standard of proof beyond a reasonable doubt in criminal proceedings. In 1988, it authorized a system of fines of up to $10,000, imposed administratively under the authority of the Attorney General, without the necessity of a trial, although the individual may request an administrative hearing. To soften the blow to due process, judicial review of an adverse administrative finding is permitted, but the individual bears the burden of retaining counsel and paying court filing fees. For those unable to finance a court challenge, this system will amount to punishment without trial. Moreover, it has been augmented by a provision in the Anti-Drug Abuse Act of 1988 that may suspend for one year an offender's Federal benefits, contracts, grants, student loans, mortgage guarantees, and licenses upon conviction for a first offense.

Both sanctions are a form of legal piling on. The legislative intent is to punish the minor offender more severely than is authorized by the criminal law alone. Thus, the maximum penalty under Federal criminal law for a first offense of simple possession of a controlled substance is one year in prison and a $5,000 fine, with a minimum fine of $1,000. Fines up to $10,000 plus loss of Federal benefits obviously exceed those guidelines.

The most recent innovation of this kind is a form of greenmail, a law that cuts off highway funds to states that do not suspend the driver's licenses of those convicted of possession of illegal drugs. The potential loss of work for those so punished and the adverse consequences on their families are not considered. The suspension is mandatory.

Seizure and forfeiture

The War on Drugs not only punishes drug users, it also penalizes those who are innocent and others who are on the periphery of wrongdoing. The most notable example is the widespread and accelerating practice, Federal and state, of seizing and forfeiting cars, planes, boats, houses, money, or property of any other kind carrying even minute amounts of illegal drugs, used to facilitate a transaction in narcotics, or representing the proceeds of drugs. Forfeiture is authorized, and enforced, without regard to the personal guilt of the owner. It matters not whether a person is tried and acquitted; the owner need not even be arrested. The property nonetheless is forfeitable because of a centuries-old legal fiction that says the property itself is "guilty." Relying on it, in March, 1988, the Federal government initiated highly publicized zero tolerance seizures of property that included the following:

● On April 30, 1988, the Coast Guard boarded and seized the motor yacht *Ark Royal*, valued at $2,500,000, because 10 marijuana seeds and two stems were found on board. Public criticism prompted a return of the boat, but not before payment of $1,600 in fines and fees by the owner.

● The 52-foot *Mindy* was impounded for a week because cocaine dust in a rolled up dollar bill was found on board.

● The $80,000,000 oceanographic research ship *Atlantis II* was seized in San Diego when the Coast Guard found 0.01 ounce of marijuana in a crewman's shaving kit. The vessel eventually was returned.

● A Michigan couple returning from a Canadian vacation lost a 1987 Mercury Cougar when customs agents found two marijuana cigarettes in one of their pockets. No criminal charges were filed, but the car was kept by the government.

● In Key West, Fla., a shrimp fisherman lost his boat to the Coast Guard, which found three grams of cannabis seeds and stems on board. Under the law, the craft was forfeitable whether or not he had any responsibility for the drugs.

Not surprisingly, cases like the foregoing generated a public backlash—perhaps the only significant one since the War on Drugs was declared in 1982. It pressured Congress into creating what is known as the "innocent owner defense" to such *in rem* forfeitures, but even that gesture of reasonableness is largely illusory.

First, the defense does not redress the gross imbalance between the value of property forfeited and the personal culpability of the owner. For example, a Vermont man was found guilty of growing six marijuana plants. He received a suspended sentence, but he and his family lost their 49-acre farm. Similarly, a New York man forfeited his $145,000 condominium because he sold cocaine to an informant for $250. The law provides no limit to the value of property subject to forfeiture, even for very minor drug offenses.

Second, the innocent owner defense places the burden on the property claimant to demonstrate that he or she acted or failed to act without "knowledge, consent or willful blindness" of the drug activities of the offender. Thus, the Federal government instituted forfeiture proceedings in the Delray Beach, Fla., area against numerous properties containing convenience stores or other businesses where drug transactions took place, claiming that the owners "made insufficient efforts to prevent drug dealings."

Placing the burden on the claimant imposes expense and inconvenience because the claimant must hire a lawyer to mount a challenge to the seizure. Moreover, many cases involve the family house or car, and it often is difficult to prove that one family member had no knowledge of or did not consent to the illegal activities of another. For instance, a Florida court held that a claimant did not use reasonable care to prevent her husband from using her automobile in criminal activity; thus, she was not entitled to the innocent owner defense.

A particularly cruel application of this kind of vicarious responsibility for the wrongs of another is seen in the government's policy of evicting impoverished families from public housing because of the drug activities of one unruly child. The Anti-Drug Abuse Act of 1988 specifically states that a tenant's lease is a forfeitable property interest and that public housing agencies have the authority to hire investigators to determine whether drug laws are being broken. The act authorizes eviction if a tenant, member of his or her household, guest, or other person under his or her control is engaged in drug-related activity on or near public housing premises.

To carry out these provisions, the act funded a pilot enforcement program. In 1990, the Departments of Justice and Housing and Urban Development announced a Public Housing Asset Forfeiture Demonstration Project in 23 states. The project pursued lease forfeitures and generated considerable publicity.

In passing this law, it must have been obvious to Congress that many innocent family members would suffer along with the guilty. Perhaps it was thought vital, nonetheless, as a way of protecting other families from drugs in public housing projects. As experience proves, however, even evicted dealers continue to deal in and around the projects. It is hard to take public housing lease forfeitures very seriously, therefore, other than as a symbolic statement of the government's tough stand against illegal drugs.

Destructive consequences

A policy that destroys families, takes property from the innocent, and tramples the basic criminal law principles of personal responsibility, proportionality, and fairness has spillover effects into other public policy domains. One area in which the fanaticism of the drug warriors perhaps is most evident is public health. Drugs such as marijuana and heroin have well-known medical applications. Yet, so zealous are the anti-drug forces that even these therapeutic uses effectively have been banned.

Marijuana, for instance, has many applications as a safe and effective therapeutic agent. Among them are relief of the intraocular pressure caused by glaucoma and alleviating the nausea caused by chemotherapy. Some AIDS patients also have obtained relief from using cannabis.

Yet, marijuana is classified by the Attorney General of the U.S., not the Surgeon General, as a Schedule I drug—one having a high potential for abuse, no currently accepted medicinal use, and lack of accepted safety for utilization. It thereby is deemed beyond the scope of legitimate medical practice and thus is not generally available to medical practitioners.

The only exception was an extremely limited program of compassionate treatment of the terminally or seriously ill, but even that has been eliminated for political

The intensive pursuit of drug offenders has generated an enormous population of convicts held in prison for very long mandatory periods of time; so much so that violent criminals (murders, robbers, and rapists) often serve less time than the drug offenders.

reasons. Assistant Secretary James O. Mason of the Department of Health and Human Services announced in 1991 that the Public Health Service's provision of marijuana to patients seriously ill with AIDS would be discontinued because it would create a public perception that "this stuff can't be so bad." After a review caused by protests from AIDS activists, the Public Health Service decided in March, 1992, to stop supplying marijuana to any patients save the 13 then receiving it.

There also are beneficial uses for heroin. Terminal cancer patients suffering from intractable pain generally obtain quicker analgesic relief from heroin than from morphine. Many doctors believe that heroin should be an option in the pharmacopeia. Accordingly, in 1981, the American Medical Association House of Delegates adopted a resolution stating that "the management of pain relief in terminal cancer patients should be a medical decision and should take priority over concerns about drug dependence." Various bills to accomplish that goal were introduced in the 96th, 97th, and 98th Congresses. The Compassionate Pain Relief Act was brought to the House floor for a vote on Sept. 19, 1984, but was defeated by 355 to 55. Although there were some concerns voiced about thefts from hospital pharmacies, the overwhelming concern was political and symbolic—a heroin legalization bill could not be passed in an election year and, in any event, would send the public the "wrong message."

The final and perhaps most outrageous example in this catalog of wrongs against public health care is the nearly universal American refusal to permit established addicts to exchange used needles for sterile ones in order to prevent AIDS transmission among intravenous drug users. In 1991, the National Commission on AIDS recommended the removal of legal barriers to the purchase and possession of intravenous drug injection equipment. It found that 32% of all adult and adolescent AIDS cases were related to intravenous drug use and that 70% of mother-to-child AIDS infections resulted from intravenous drug use by the mother or her sexual partner. Moreover, the commission found no evidence that denial of access to sterile needles reduced drug abuse, but concluded that it did encourage the sharing of contaminated needles and the spread of the AIDS virus. Notwithstanding the commission's criticism of the government's "myopic criminal justice approach" to the drug situation, the prevailing view is that needle exchange programs encourage drug abuse by sending the wrong message.

Public safety is sacrificed when, nationwide, more than 18,000 local, sheriff's, and state police officers, in addition to thousands of Federal agents, are devoted full time to special drug units. As a result, countless hours and dollars are diverted from detecting and preventing more serious violent crimes. Thirty percent of an estimated 1,100,000 drug-related arrests made during 1990 were marijuana offenses, nearly four out of five for mere possession. Tax dollars would be spent better if the resources it took to make approximately 264,000 arrests for possession of marijuana were dedicated to protecting the general public from violent crime.

The intensive pursuit of drug offenders has generated an enormous population of convicts held in prison for very long periods of time as a result of excessive and / or mandatory jail terms. It is estimated that the operating cost of maintaining a prisoner ranges from $20,000 to $40,000 per year, depending upon the location and level of security at a particular prison. With more than 800,000 men and women in American correctional facilities today, the nationwide cost approaches $30,000,000,000 per year. This is a major diversion of scarce resources.

These financial burdens are only part of the price incurred as a result of the relentless drive to achieve higher and higher arrest records. More frightening and damaging are the injuries and losses caused by the early release of violent criminals owing to prison overcrowding. Commonly, court orders impose population caps, so prison authorities accelerate release of violent felons serving non-mandatory sentences in order to free up beds for non-violent drug offenders serving mandatory, non-parolable terms.

For example, to stay abreast of its rapidly growing inmate population, Florida launched one of the nation's most ambitious early release programs. However, prisoners serving mandatory terms—most of them drug offenders, who now comprise 36% of the total prison population—are ineligible. As a result, the average length of sentence declined dramatically for violent criminals, while it rose for drug offenders. Murderers, robbers, and rapists often serve less time than a "cocaine mule" carrying a kilo on a bus, who gets a mandatory 15-year term.

A Department of Justice survey showed that 43% of state felons on probation were rearrested for a crime within three years of sentencing. In short, violent criminals are released early to commit more crimes so that their beds can be occupied by non-violent drug offenders. Civil libertarians are not heard often defending a societal right to be secure from violent criminals, much less a right of victims to see just punishment meted out to offenders. In this they are as shortsighted as their law-and-order counterparts. The War on Drugs is a public safety disaster, making victims of us all.

However uncomfortable it may be to admit, the undeniable reality is that drugs always have been and always will be a presence in society. Americans have been paying too high a price for the government's War on Drugs. As Federal judge William Schwarzer has said, "It behooves us to think that it may profit us very little to win the war on drugs if in the process we lose our soul."

SEPARATING THE SISTERS

Many women feel mainstream feminism has ignored their plight

The feminist movement in America has made enormous progress toward ending discrimination against women in American schools, laws, governments and workplaces, but many American women don't think they've come such a long way, baby. "If you become a doctor, the feminists are right behind you," says certified nurse midwife LaVonne Wilenken of Antelope Valley, Calif., who holds a master's degree in health care administration. "They've done very little for the average woman."

Wilenken and other "separate sisters"—women in minority groups; women in "traditional" women's jobs; women who stay at home to raise children; elderly, rural, some poor and younger women—acknowledge their debt to feminism's early battles. But they charge that the feminist movement has failed to broaden its base and remains made up largely of white, highly educated women who have not adequately addressed the issues that matter to them: child care rather than lesbian and abortion rights, economic survival rather than political equality, the sticky floor rather than the glass ceiling.

Mainstream feminist groups have begun to acknowledge the need for a larger perspective. At a Women's Economic Summit in Leesburg, Va., in January, representatives from groups such as the American Association of University Women and the National Women's Political Caucus agreed that bread-and-butter issues must become a priority. Linda Tarr-Whelan, president of the Center for Policy Alternatives, which sponsored the summit, explains part of the reason for the change: "The feminist agenda up to now has been a reactive agenda," she says. "I don't think we would have wanted to spend 10 years defending a woman's right to choose if it hadn't been the Reagan and Bush administrations' agenda to remove it."

The progress women in America have made has been uneven. Women now fill some professional schools—40 percent of medical school students and almost half of law students are now women—and are advancing in many other fields as well. But like men, women without skills, training or advanced degrees are getting left behind in an increasingly knowledge-based economy. On top of that, many women workers are still crowded into traditional "women's occupations," including secretary, schoolteacher, cashier and nurse. In 1984, 21 percent of all women workers held jobs in six low-salaried fields; last year, the figure was 22 percent, according to U.S. Department of Labor statistics.

"One reason women earn so little money compared with men is that most women and men don't do the same job," says Ellen Bravo, executive director of 9 to 5, the National Association of Working Women. "And the jobs women do pay less, mainly because women do them. Unfortunately, not all women's groups have seen this as a women's issue."

The women's movement has made pay equity a priority for years, but the notion that those doing "women's work" should be compensated as well as those doing traditionally male jobs has been a hard sell in a sluggish economy. One consequence: Labor Department statistics show that women now earn 71 percent of what men do, compared with 64 percent in 1952.

Underpaid. Poverty also plagues women in much greater degree than it does men. Three out of 5 single mothers, whose ranks increased from 5.8 million in 1980 to 7.7 million in 1990, live in or near poverty, according to a study released last month by Washington, D.C.-based Women Work!, a training and advocacy organization for displaced homemakers and single mothers. Their median annual personal income: $9,353.

"The perception is that there's been dramatic change for women," says Women Work! Executive Director Jill Miller. "The troubling thing about the survey is that it shows it's not really that way."

Karen Leidy, a single mother of two in Palestine, Texas, says that "for women in small towns, there just aren't a whole lot of options" and that the concerns of big-city feminists aren't relevant to her. After her divorce three years ago, Leidy didn't want to leave Palestine, where relatives can help her care for her children, so she spent six months looking for work. Her choices ranged from a fast-food restaurant to a plastics factory.

Some women accuse feminist groups of a kind of elitism—or at best, benign ignorance. Lisa White, communications director of the Atlanta-based National Black Women's Health Project, which operates 150 self-help programs in 31 states, complains that other feminist groups tried to plan programs for black women with AIDS without seeking guidance from her organization. "We said, 'How can you possibly tailor programs for our needs if you're not even speaking with us directly or putting us on your steering committees?'" she recalls.

The twentysomething generation of women also complains of being ignored by its elders and has tried to create its own links. Young women in Washington, D.C., formed the Women's Information Network to bring young women who are just moving to Washington in contact with women who have been successful, says Leslie Watson Davis, an independent consultant and former student organizer. "The initiative to make this happen came from the young women, not the established feminists," she says.

Numerous organizations are trying to address the issues they feel have been ignored by most mainstream feminists. From El Paso, Texas—where La Mujer Obrera organizes Hispanic working women—to Washington, D.C., where the Older Women's League lobbies for 63 million women over 45, these groups claim they are the real women's movement. "The mainstream feminists can help shape the debate," says Leah Wise, executive director of Southerners for Economic Justice in North Carolina. "But I don't think they're going to start organizing working women."

Some issues, such as child care, may require a new approach. "It's no solution to come up with alternatives and institutions that require hiring low-paid women at impoverished wages to take care of high-paid women's children," says Ellen Carol DuBois, co-author of *Unequal Sisters: A Multicultural Reader in U.S. Women's History.* While economic necessity has forced many women to work outside the home, the United States still lags behind many other developed nations in providing child care and other assistance to working mothers.

Now the grass-roots women's groups hope to produce a "fourth wave" of the American feminist movement that would embrace everyone from Hillary Rodham Clinton to Annie Williams, 37, a former welfare mother in Atlanta who now holds a $20,000-a-year job at the Black Women's Wellness Center. Williams's daughter Natale is an honor-roll student in the 11th grade aiming for a career in medicine. Williams credits much of her family's progress to the Wellness Center, which helped her find education and child-care programs. "Most women think, 'What's the use even trying?' " she says. "Until I got in with this empowerment group, I didn't even know you could do such a thing."

BY MONIKA GUTTMAN IN LOS ANGELES WITH DAN McGRAW IN FORT WORTH AND JILL JORDAN SIEDER IN ATLANTA

Global Issues

- **Environmental (Articles 38 and 39)**
- **Cultural and Economic (Articles 40–42)**

Many of the social problems facing Americans today are shared by people worldwide, such as the environment, pollution, and inflation. Some problems facing the whole world are fueled by the consumerism of Americans, and some problems facing the United States are the product of other nations' improvements in production and their desire to improve their economic conditions. The world is no longer the exclusive marketplace for U.S. goods. What Americans do impacts on the world, and what happens around the world impacts on the United States.

"The Rape of the Oceans" focuses on the effects that technology, fishing policies, and international competition are having on marine life. The very attributes that made fishermen rugged individualists are the attributes that may destroy their occupations.

"The Mirage of Sustainable Development" refers to the belief that international governmental regulations or ownership is necessary if the world's environment is to be effectively protected. Through the use of data and examples, the author demonstrates that the world's environment is more effectively protected through private rather than public ownership.

"The West's Deepening Cultural Crisis" is reflected in its growing crime rate, increasing drug problems, rampant violence, and widespread depressive illnesses. The author argues that Western culture has failed to provide a sense of meaning, belonging, and purpose to life. Without these, individuals feel impotent, insecure, and vulnerable.

In "A Decade of Discontinuity" the author points out that humankind can no longer expect a future of ever-increasing productivity. World population growth is increasingly outstripping its food production and fossil fuel capacity. Scientists are concerned that the technological innovations that kept pace in the past may not be capable of doing so in the future.

"Crowded Out" examines the data underlying the optimistic views of economists and contrasts it with data underlying the pessimistic views of biologists as to the impact on developing world population trends. Are those who advocate population control in developing world countries racists or realists?

Looking Ahead: Challenge Questions

In what major ways will the abuse to which we have subjected our oceans eventually impact on us?

Why is international cooperation so vital if we are to save our oceans?

Which is most effective in protecting the world's environment, public or private ownership? Explain.

To what degree are the ideas of Thomas Malthus useful in studying or understanding world population growth?

Can the United States continue to be the police force or savior of the world?

Can technological innovation continue to meet the world's ever-increasing demand for food, fuel, and security?

What are the possible implications for world peace of increasing populations and shrinking resources?

In what significantly different ways would the three major sociological theoretical perspectives argue that we should study global issues?

What are the major values, rights, obligations, and harms associated with each of the issues covered in this unit?

THE RAPE OF THE OCEANS

■

*America's last frontier is seriously overfished, badly polluted, poorly managed
and in deepening trouble*

With Capt. Joe Testaverde at the helm, the trawler Nina T slips into its Gloucester, Mass., mooring at sunset. Joe's father, Salvatore Testaverde, and his Sicilian father before him were Gloucester fishermen, and the family has trawled Northeastern waters for close to 80 years. This night seems a comforting continuum as the fish are unloaded and the crew members josh with dockside onlookers, exaggerating the size of the catch. The scene in this snug New England harbor is as timeless and reassuring as the tides—and as deceptive as a roseate dawn.

In bygone years, Joe Testaverde's father and grandfather would return to port with their boats packed from bilge to gunwale with haddock and flounder, and with jumbo codfish weighing 50 pounds or better. Sal Testaverde recalls pulling up 5,000 pounds of cod in a one-hour tow. Today, if he can find them, son Joe might haul in 2,000 pounds of middling-sized cod in eight hours of hard trawling. And he won't even waste time searching for flounder and haddock. The Nina T, more than likely, will return with hake, whiting, spiny dogfish or skate—species despised in Sal Testaverde's day as "trash" fish. Shipped abroad or retailed in ethnic markets for about $1 a pound, they are the dominant and devalued currency of the Georges Bank, once the nation's richest fishing ground.

The precipitous, perhaps irreversible decline of New England's groundfish is one of the major casualties of an unrelenting assault on the nation's coastal oceans. The principal problems are overfishing, burgeoning seaside development, loss of coastal wetlands and pollution of bay and estuary fish breeding grounds. Compounding these pressures is the profligate waste of hundreds of millions of pounds of edible "bycatch" fish. And a political

---

About 1.5 million dolphins and other small whales are killed each year by tuna fishermen, by pollution or in targeted hunts.

---

consensus between fishing and federal bureaucrats to better manage the vast and valuable marine resources has yet to be reached. This looming disaster extends from the coastlines out to the 200-mile limit in the Atlantic and Pacific oceans, the Gulf of Mexico, the Gulf of Alaska and the Bering Sea. Together, they represent the country's last open frontier.

These 2.2 million square miles contain about one fifth of the world's harvestable seafood; enormous populations of marine birds and mammals, and spectacular undersea reefs, banks and gardens teeming with life forms

that have barely been studied. "We have two choices—conserve and develop a sustainable resource, or squander and destroy it," says Roger McManus, head of the Center for Marine Conservation, the only national environmental group devoted solely to the oceans' welfare. "Our record so far is abysmal."

Earth Summit. There is a growing belief among environmentalists that the world's overexploited and ailing oceans will replace tropical rain forests as the next global ecology concern. At the United Nations Earth Summit in Rio de Janeiro that wrapped up last week, participants pledged to try and control overfishing, pollution and coastal development. But the agreement contained no bold new initiatives and few specific goals or enforcement mechanisms. Not surprisingly, amid the rancorous parley that saw the United States excoriated for its independent stance on global warming, forest protection and biodiversity, marine issues drew scant attention from the media or from official delegates.

But elsewhere, the alarms are sounding—especially in America. Front-line U.S. environmental groups like Greenpeace, the National Audubon Society and the World Wildlife Fund are following the lead of the Center for Marine Conservation and turning their attention to ocean biodiversity. Until recently, they paid little attention to such unglamorous issues as fish. They favored instead emotional, hot-button topics like the killing of dolphins, harp seals and whales; birds and mammals dying in drift nets, or saving endangered species like manatees and sea turtles. "Marine fisheries are the nation's single most threatened resource," says Amos Eno of the nonprofit National Fish and Wildlife Foundation. "There has been weak involvement by major environmental groups and poor federal management."

Close to half of U.S. coastal finfish stocks are now overexploited—meaning that more are being caught than are replenished by natural reproduction. Scientists say 14 of the most valuable species—New England groundfish, red snapper, swordfish, striped bass and Atlantic bluefin tuna among them—are threatened with commercial extinction, meaning that too few would remain to justify the cost of catching them.

Only drastic conservation measures will restore these threatened stocks. However, a five-to-10-year fishing ban to allow rebuilding could spell economic disaster for segments of the fishing industry. Virtually all the remaining commercial finfish stocks—except in Alaskan waters—are now being harvested to their limits.

In 1990, Japanese drift netters dumped 39 million unwanted fish, 700,000 sharks, 270,000 sea birds and 26,000 mammals. Most were dead.

Further fishing pressure could put more species in jeopardy. Between 1986 and 1991, the finfish and shellfish catch off the lower 48 states declined by 500 million pounds, from 4.8 billion pounds to 4.3 billion. The harvest of menhaden—used to make poultry feed, fish oil and other products—dropped last year by 300 million pounds. "When Nature is at her best, you can fish with impunity and get away with it," says Lee Weddig, exec-

utive director of the National Fisheries Institute, a trade organization. "We can do that no longer."

Pollution's toll. The assault on the oceans begins at the shoreline. About half the U.S. population lives within 50 miles of the coastline, and the booming development is hard to control. The result: massive changes in coastal ecology that are destroying or damaging habitat for finfish and shellfish. Coastal wetlands are gobbled up: Louisiana, for example, loses about 50 square miles of piscatorial breeding ground annually. In California, only 9 percent of the state's original 3.5 million acres of coastal wetlands remain. These bays and estuaries are the breeding grounds and nurseries for fully 75 percent of commercial-seafood species. But they are being increasingly befouled by sewage, industrial waste water and runoff from cities and farms.

Half the fish in areas polluted by toxic chemicals fail to spawn and suffer from weakened immune systems. Chemical nutrients from smokestacks and sewers and from pesticides and fertilizers used on farms and front lawns stimulate explosive algae growth that blocks sunlight and eventually depletes the waters of oxygen, creating undersea dead zones. One acre of Narragansett Bay, R.I., or Delaware Bay, for example, now gets more nitrogen and phosphorus annually from urban and farm runoff than an average acre of cotton, soybeans or wheat grown in the United States.

At any given time, fully one third of the nation's oyster, clam and other shellfish beds are closed because of contamination. Some 27 marine mammals and birds in American coastal waters are now listed as threatened or endangered, and the rising phenomenon of mass die-offs of dolphins and seals is blamed on toxins like PCBs that are rapidly accumulating in the marine environment. And as every beachgoer knows, trash is piling up in ever increasing amounts. Some shorelines along the Gulf of Mexico are strewn with 2 tons of marine debris per mile.

This assault on the marine environ-

ment is being felt most keenly by the nation's commercial fisheries. Both the fiercely independent industry and the National Marine Fisheries Service, which tries hard to regulate it, are struggling over ways to control overfishing, reduce the number of boats, curb the waste of bycatch fish and find more efficient ways to manage and harvest the stocks. At present, fisheries are the least regulated of public resources. Enforcement of even the lax regulations is spotty, compliance is weak and there is simply no real incentive for individual fishermen to conserve.

The severely depleted finfish stocks in the lower 48 states, and the government's failure to manage effectively the coastal oceans for the commonweal, raise several questions. Should the seas up to the 200-mile limit be treated as a public resource—like federal lands—and administered like other natural assets? Industries pay the government to drill for offshore oil, cut national-forest timber and mine coal on public lands. Should fishermen pay to harvest seafood in federal waters? Before the Taylor Grazing Act of 1934, Western rangelands were nearly destroyed by cattle because ranchers had free access. Could this tragedy-of-the-commons be repeated in America's oceans?

Questions of control. The root cause of today's overfishing goes back to 1977, when the Magnuson Act extended U.S. coastal jurisdiction from 12 miles to 200 miles and the dominant foreign factory vessels were kicked out of American waters. Ironically, the nation managed to gain control of its coastal oceans but in so doing, simply traded overfishing by foreigners for unrestrained plunder by domestic fishermen.

Meanwhile, the rust-bucket American fleet was gradually replaced—thanks to more than $500 million in federal loan guarantees—with efficient, high-tech boats. And a $1.3 billion fleet of some 70 factory vessels, American-registered but mostly owned by Japanese, Scandinavian and Korean interests, now plies the Gulf of Alaska and the Bering Sea. From Gloucester,

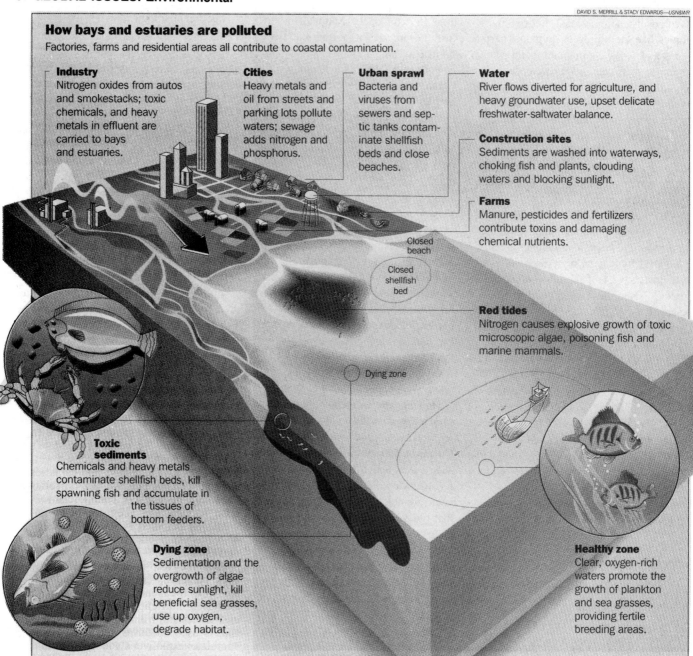

DAVID S. MERRILL & STACY EDWARDS—*USN&WR*

How bays and estuaries are polluted
Factories, farms and residential areas all contribute to coastal contamination.

Industry
Nitrogen oxides from autos and smokestacks; toxic chemicals, and heavy metals in effluent are carried to bays and estuaries.

Cities
Heavy metals and oil from streets and parking lots pollute waters; sewage adds nitrogen and phosphorus.

Urban sprawl
Bacteria and viruses from sewers and septic tanks contaminate shellfish beds and close beaches.

Water
River flows diverted for agriculture, and heavy groundwater use, upset delicate freshwater-saltwater balance.

Construction sites
Sediments are washed into waterways, choking fish and plants, clouding waters and blocking sunlight.

Farms
Manure, pesticides and fertilizers contribute toxins and damaging chemical nutrients.

Closed beach

Closed shellfish bed

Red tides
Nitrogen causes explosive growth of toxic microscopic algae, poisoning fish and marine mammals.

Dying zone

Toxic sediments
Chemicals and heavy metals contaminate shellfish beds, kill spawning fish and accumulate in the tissues of bottom feeders.

Dying zone
Sedimentation and the overgrowth of algae reduce sunlight, kill beneficial sea grasses, use up oxygen, degrade habitat.

Healthy zone
Clear, oxygen-rich waters promote the growth of plankton and sea grasses, providing fertile breeding areas.

Mass., to Cordova, Alaska, the industry has too many fishing boats—but there is no consensus on how to control this armada or limit access to the fisheries.

The fishing capacity of the new boats is staggering and, more than anything else, has exacerbated the destructive pressure on the fish stocks. Just a decade ago, many fishermen still used binoculars, shoreside landmarks and oilcan buoys to mark and relocate productive areas. Today, the smallest vessels employ sophisticated electronics that can pinpoint a single codfish at

100 fathoms or guide a captain to within 100 feet of a favorite hot spot. East Coast fishermen seeking increasingly scarce swordfish in the warm Gulf Stream waters, for example, once lowered thermometers over the side or scanned the surface for blue warm-water eddies. Now they can get ocean temperatures faxed to their boats via satellite.

To marine biologists, the decline of New England's prized cod, flounder and haddock stocks is a warning for all American fisheries. Many blame the mess on weak leadership by the

National Marine Fisheries Service and on the New England Fishery Management Council, one of eight regional groups set up nationwide by the NMFS to govern the industry. Critics contend that the councils are dominated by commercial-fishing interests that are less concerned with conservation than with maximizing profits. In 1981, for example, New England fishermen pressured their regional council to remove all catch quotas on cod, haddock and flounder. That led to the disastrous depletion of the most valuable commercial species. Short of a politically difficult multiyear fishing freeze, the NMFS wants to limit gradually the fishermen's days at sea, increase net-mesh sizes to reduce mortality of small, unwanted fish and ban new boats from entering the fishery. The alternative Darwinian solution is to let the fishermen fight for the dwindling supply.

David versus Goliath. Rooted in the colonial era and steeped in tradition, New England fisheries have long resisted regulation. Alaska's modern fisheries, developed in recent decades, more readily accept tight controls. But common problems are magnified in the Northern Pacific and they threaten the resource. Alaska's high-tech, industrial-strength fleet has too many boats, and there is enormous waste.

Some 70 factory ships are locked in fierce competition with thousands of small vessels in the Bering Sea and Gulf of Alaska. Together, the David and Goliath fleets have enough capacity to scoop up the entire annual Alaskan quota of about 4.8 billion pounds of groundfish in less than six months. With factory ships worth $75 million tied up in port and shoreside plants served by the small vessels periodically idled, with no fish to process, there is relentless lobbying by the rival fleets for a bigger share of the catch.

The very fecundity of the Alaskan waters, like that of other regions, encourages waste. Fishing everywhere produces bycatch that is thrown back—invariably dead or dying—because the fish are too small, too big, have lower market value than the target species, or because it is illegal to keep them. For every pound of shrimp hauled from the Atlantic Ocean and the Gulf of Mexico, for example, an estimated 9 pounds of red snapper, croaker, mackerel, sea trout, spot, drum and other species are brought up in the nets and tossed overboard. This annual shrimp-fishery bycatch alone is estimated by the NMFS at more than 1 billion pounds—a waste that equals 10 percent of the entire U.S. harvest.

"National scandal." In 1990, Alaskan trawlers fishing for pollock and cod jettisoned some 25 million pounds of halibut—worth about $30 million—plus vast quantities of salmon and king crab, because they were an incidental, prohibited bycatch. They also reported throwing away 550 million pounds of groundfish because they were the wrong size or to save space for more valuable species.

NMFS officials think the waste is actually higher than 550 million pounds because that total is largely reported by vessel captains and thus is unverifiable. Larry Cotter, a Juneau, Alaska, fisheries consultant and former bycatch chairman for the NMFS regional management council, calls the waste "a national scandal and an unconscionable disgrace."

Another pressing problem in Alaskan waters emanates from the traditional free-for-all culture that allows anyone with a boat to try his luck. So many fishermen compete for the valuable Pacific halibut that the entire year's quota—once harvested over a leisurely six-month season—is now taken in two frantic 24-hour periods.

Last year's derby for the giant flatfish was typical. At noon on September 3, some 6,000 vessels raced out of Alaskan ports in a maritime version of the Oklahoma land rush and began hauling in halibut like sharks in a feeding frenzy. At noon the next day, when the season ended, many vessels limped back to port dangerously overloaded. The Coast Guard handled 29 Mayday calls from sinking boats. There was no loss of life, but during the earlier one-day spring season, two crewmen had drowned. The September boats landed 23.7 million pounds but about 4 million pounds rotted because it couldn't be frozen quickly enough. And the massive glut hitting the market in one day meant no fresh halibut for most consumers.

To fix many of the problems on all three coasts, the National Marine Fisheries Service is eager to manage the nation's seafood stocks through a system of individual transferable quotas, called ITQs. Based on their previous fishing history, boat owners would be given a permit allowing them to harvest a fixed amount of finfish or shellfish each year. The permits could be leased, sold or passed on in a family. "We need to get fishermen to act more like farmers—give them an ownership privilege and a vested interest in the stocks," says NMFS conservation chief Richard Schaefer. "Fishermen don't own a fish until it's flopping around on the deck. If they own it before it is caught, they will manage it rationally."

The ITQ system is already being tested in two East Coast clam fisheries, and Alaskan halibut is one of several other species under consideration for ITQs. But while many fishermen favor temporary limits on the number of boats entering the industry, there is little enthusiasm for permits, quotas or other regulations. Their reluctance exemplifies the freewheeling, entrepreneurial independence that fishermen cling to—the right to get rich or go broke, unfettered or unprotected by Uncle Sam. "ITQs will destroy us," says Edward Lima, executive director of the Cape Ann Vessel Association in Gloucester. "Corporations will buy up permits and swallow us like corporate farms gobbling up family farmers." His friend Joe Testaverde agrees. And he objects on less tangible grounds, as well. "Quotas remove the lure and romance of fishing," he says. "Part of the thrill is to go out one day and catch nothing, then come home the next and beat out the other guy."

But dwindling stocks and the urgent need for conservation mean that fishermen will have to adapt and change—or risk destroying the very resource that sustains them. Like any good fisherman, Joe Testaverde is cheerfully optimistic. If the cod, haddock and flounder don't come back, he will fish for something else. "Yesterday, on the sonar screens, I saw tons and tons of small fish—whiting, mackerel, butterfish, squid and herring," he says. "If I didn't see that, I'd be scared of the future. We're the last surviving hunters and gatherers. I know I'm *always* gonna catch fish." Testaverde's attitude reflects much of what is right—and what is wrong—with the fishing industry. It is also the reason why America's oceans are in deepening trouble.

Michael Satchell

THE MIRAGE OF

SUSTAINABLE DEVELOPMENT

HOW DO WE ACHIEVE BOTH ECONOMIC GROWTH AND ENVIRONMENTAL PROTECTION? AN ECONOMIST ARGUES THAT PRIVATE-PROPERTY RIGHTS WILL WORK BETTER THAN INTERNATIONAL BUREAUCRACIES.

THOMAS J. DILORENZO

Thomas J. DiLorenzo is professor of economics in the Sellinger School of Business and Management, Loyola College, Baltimore, Maryland 21210. He has written and lectured extensively on public finance and public-policy-oriented issues and is an editorial referee for 15 academic journals.

A longer version of this article was published by The Center for the Study of American Business (CSAB), a nonpartisan research organization at Washington University in St. Louis. Copies of "The Mirage of Sustainable Development," Contemporary Issues Series 56 (January 1993), are available from CSAB, Washington University, Campus Box 1208, One Brookings Drive, St. Louis, Missouri 63130-4899, telephone 314/935-5630.

There is no precise definition of sustainable development. To some, it simply means balancing economic growth with environmental-protection goals, a relatively uncontroversial position. But to others, it means something different: dramatic reductions in economic growth in the industrialized countries coupled with massive international income redistribution.

According to advocates of the latter viewpoint, there are not enough resources left worldwide to sustain current economic growth rates, and these growth rates are also too damaging to the environment. Consequently, these advocates argue for government regulation of virtually all human behavior on a national and international scale and for governmental control of privately owned resources throughout the world. Such controls may be enforced by national governments or by international bureaucracies such as the United Nations. The "lesson" to be learned from the tragic failures of socialism, the sustainability advocates apparently believe, is that the world needs more socialism.

Such views would be dismissed as bizarre and irrational if they were not held by someone as influential as Norway's Prime Minister Gro Harlem Brundtland, who also chairs the United Nations World Commission on Environment and Development. This Commission published its views in a 1987 book, *Our Common Future*, which laid the groundwork for the June 1992 "Earth Summit" held in Rio de Janeiro.

But the policy proposals advocated by *Our Common Future* and the Earth Summit fail to recognize the many inherent flaws of governmental planning and regulation, and they ignore the important role of private-property rights, technology, and the market system in alleviating environmental problems.

What Role for Property Rights And Free Markets?

The final collapse of communism in 1989 revealed a dirty secret: that pollution in the communist world was far, far worse than virtually anywhere else on the planet. In theory, this should not have been the case, for it has long been held that the profit motive and the failure of unregulated markets to provide incentives to internalize external costs were the primary causes of pollution. Government regulation or ownership of resources was thought to be a necessary condition for environmental protection.

But that was just a theory. The reality is that, in those countries where profit seeking was outlawed for decades and where government claimed ownership of virtually all resources, pollution and other forms of environmental degradation were

COURTESY OF GERMAN INFORMATION CENTER

devastating. According to the United Nations' Global Environment Monitoring Program, pollution in central and eastern Europe "is among the worst on the Earth's surface."

In Poland, for example, acid rain has so corroded railroad tracks that trains are not allowed to exceed 24 miles an hour. Ninety-five percent of the water is unfit for human consumption, and most of it is even unfit for industrial use, so toxic that it will dissolve heavy metals. Industrial dust rains down on towns, depositing cadmium, lead, zinc, and iron. Half of Poland's cities do not even treat their wastes, and life expectancy for males is lower than it was 20 years ago.

The landscape is similar in other parts of central and eastern Europe, in the former Soviet Union, and in China. Eighty percent of the surface waters in former East Germany are classified unsuitable for fishing, sports, or drinking. One out of three lakes has been declared biologically dead because of decades of dumping untreated chemical waste. Some cities are so polluted that cars must use their headlights during the day. Bulgaria, Hungary, Romania, the former Yugoslavia, and the former

Czechoslovakia suffered similar environmental damage during the decades of communism.

These sad facts teach important lessons that the sustainable development theorists have not learned. The root cause of pollution in the former communist world, and worldwide, is not the profit motive and unregulated markets, but the absence of property rights and sound liability laws that hold polluters responsible for their actions. The environmental degradation of the former communist world is an example of one massive "tragedy of the commons," to borrow the phrase coined by biologist Garrett Hardin. Where property is communally or governmentally owned and treated as a free resource, resources will inevitably be overused with little regard for future consequences.

But when people have ownership rights in resources, there is a stronger incentive to protect the value of those resources. Furthermore, when individuals are not held liable for damages inflicted on others—including environmental damages—then there is little hope that responsible behavior will result. Needless to say, the state did not

Industrial effluents pour into river near Bitterfeld in eastern Germany. Decades of dumping untreated chemical wastes in the former East Germany have left one out of three lakes biologically dead and 80% of all surface waters unsuitable for human use.

hold itself responsible for the environmental damage it was causing in the former communist countries. Thus, far from being the answer to environmental problems, pervasive governmental control of natural resources was the cause.

Our Common Future's Misinterpretations

Our Common Future neglects the role of property rights, and, consequently, it grants entirely too much credence to the efficacy of greater governmental controls and regulations as solutions to environmental problems. Several examples stand out.

• **Deforestation.** International economic relationships "pose a particular problem for poor countries trying to manage their environments," says *Our Common Future*. For example, "the trade in tropical timber . . . is one factor underlying

223

tropical deforestation. Needs for foreign exchange encourage many developing countries to cut timber faster than forests can be regenerated."

But the need for foreign exchange is not unique to people in developing countries. All individuals prefer more to less, but they do not all cut down and sell all the trees in sight for economic gain. Deforestation was also a massive problem in the former communist countries, but the main reason was that the forests were communally owned. Consequently, anyone could cut them down, and there were virtually no incentives to replant because of the absence of property rights.

Deforestation has also taken place in democratic countries, primarily on government-owned land that is leased to timber companies who, since they do not own the land, have weak incentives to replant and protect its future value. Some of these same timber companies are very careful indeed not to overharvest or neglect replanting their own private forest preserves. They do so not so much out of a desire to protect the environment as to protect the value of their assets. Well-enforced property rights and the existence of a market for forest products will assure that forests are likely to be used wisely, not exploited.

• **Desertification.** The sustainable development theorists also misdiagnose the problem of desertification—

the process whereby "productive arid and semiarid land is rendered economically unproductive," as *Our Common Future* defines it. They blame capitalism for desertification, particularly "the pressures of subsistence food production, commercial crops, and meat production in arid and semiarid areas." Their "solution" is greater governmental controls on agriculture.

Desertification is undoubtedly a problem throughout the world—including parts of the United States. The primary cause is not commercial agriculture, however, but the tragedy of the commons.

A particularly telling example of the importance of private property to desertification was reported in *Science* magazine in a 1974 article on desertification in the Sahel area of Africa. At the time, this area was suffering from a five-year drought. NASA satellite photographs showed a curiously shaped green pentagon that was in sharp contrast to the rest of the African desert. Upon investigation, scientists discovered that the green blotch was a 25,000-acre ranch, fenced in with barbed wire, divided into five sectors, with the cattle allowed to graze only one sector a year. The ranch was started at the same time the drought began, but the protection afforded the land was enough to make the difference between pasture and desert.

• **Wildlife management.** The

Factory in Espenhain, eastern Germany, emits foul pollutants, darkening the sky. Some cities in the formerly communist half of the country are so polluted that cars must drive with their headlights on during the daytime, says author DiLorenzo.

Earth Summit advocated a "biodiversity treaty" whereby national governments would establish policies aimed at slowing the loss of plant and animal species. The type of policies most preferred by sustainable development theorists include prohibition of commercial uses of various plants and animals, such as the ban on ivory from African elephants, and the listing of more "endangered species," which may then be "protected" by governments on game preserves or elsewhere.

There is growing evidence, however, that the best way to save truly endangered species is not to socialize them, but to allow people to own them. As conservationist Ike Sugg has written:

[W]here governments allow individuals to reap the economic benefits of conserving and protecting their wildlife stocks—wildlife flourish. Where individuals are denied the opportunity to profit from wildlife legally, they do so illegally and without the sense of responsibility that comes with stewardship.

African elephants are protected by bans on ivory trade and other government measures. But there is growing evidence that private-property rights over wildlife may be more effective than "socialization" in protecting endangered species, according to DiLorenzo.

One particularly telling example that illustrates Sugg's point is the African elephant. Kenya outlawed elephant hunting in the 1970s; its elephant population quickly *dropped* from 140,000 in 1970 to an estimated 16,000 today as illegal poaching proliferated.

In contrast, Zimbabwe had only 30,000 elephants in 1979 but has over 65,000 today. The main reason for these differences, according to Sugg, is that in 1984 the government of Zimbabwe granted citizens ownership rights over elephants on communal lands—a large step in the direction of defining property rights. As expressed by one tribal chief who implicitly understood the value of property rights and the commercialization of elephants:

> For a long time the government told us that wildlife was their resource. But I see how live animals can be our resources. Our wealth. Our way to improve the standard of living without waiting for the government to decide things. A poacher is only stealing from us.

The preservation of endangered wildlife through private-property rights and free markets is also prevalent in parts of the United States in the form of game ranching, which typically involves "exotic" or non-native animals. Game rancher David Bamberger of Texas, for example, has preserved 29 of the 31 remaining bloodlines of the Scimitar-horned Oryx, a rare antelope that is virtually extinct in its native Africa. Despite such successes, several states have outlawed game ranching because the notion of privatizing wildlife is blasphemy to the "religion" of environmentalism (not to mention "animal rights"), which holds that markets and property rights decimate species.

The principle of using property rights and market incentives to protect global resources and the environment applies to a wide range of problems, including the exploitation of water resources in the American West, the mismanagement of government-owned forest lands, the over-fishing of public lakes and streams, and even the ocean commons: The Law of the Sea Treaty, which the United States has thus far refused to sign, would establish the oceans as the largest government-owned and regulated commons on Earth—and, inevitably, the largest tragedy of the commons.

This elementary principle, however, is not even acknowledged by the United Nations' sustainable development theorists. In answering the question, "How are individuals . . . to be persuaded or made to act in the common interest?," the Brundtland Commission answered with "education," undefined "law enforcement," and eliminating "disparities in economic and political power." No mention was made of the role of property rights in shaping incentives.

Sustainable Delusions

Sustainable development—as it is defined by the Brundtland Commission and the planners of the Earth Summit—can best be understood as a euphemism for environmental socialism—granting governments more and more control over the allocation of resources in the name of environmental protection. But if any lesson can be learned from the collapse of socialism in the former communist countries, it is that government ownership and control of resources is a recipe for economic collapse and environmental degradation. Socialism is no more effective in protecting the environment than it is in creating wealth.

Government ownership of natural resources inevitably leads to the tragedy of the commons, but that is all too often the "solution" offered by the Brundtland Commission. The Commission recommends government control of everything from outer space to energy, which is supposedly "too important for its development to continue in such a manner" as the free market allows.

Perhaps the top priority of sustainable development theorists is to expand the international welfare state by agitating for wealth transfers from "the rich" countries to the developing. But the whole history of development aid is government-to-government—most of it is typically used to finance the expansion of governmental bureaucracies in the recipient countries—which can be adverse to economic development. Even if most of the aid did make it into the hands of the citizens of the recipient countries, sustainable development theorists do not explain how that will translate into savings, investment, capital formation, and entrepreneurial activity—the ingredients of economic development.

THE SOVIET ENVIRONMENTAL LEGACY

Before its demise, the Soviet Union had the world's strictest, most detailed environmental regulations. But they were never enforced, says RAND researcher D. J. Peterson.

In his new book, *Troubled Lands*, Peterson points out that, in the late 1950s, once the Soviet economy began to decline and large-scale environmental degradation increased, the Communist Party passed a number of laws aimed at protecting land, water, air, and wildlife. But the regulations and codes met insurmountable obstacles in the Soviet bureaucracy itself, says Peterson. For one thing, responsibility for carrying out the government's efforts at environmental protection was divided among several ministries and state committees, all with other priorities besides protecting the environment. The regime's development imperative measured ministries' performance by how many tons of cement were produced, for instance, or how many hectares of land were irrigated.

Since environmental degradation—in the Soviets' mind—was associated with bourgeois development in the capitalist world, it took the Chernobyl disaster to wake the system up to reality. Peterson quotes one physicist: "Before the Chernobyl explosion, many important specialists and political figures believed that a nuclear reactor could not explode."

Peterson believes that environmental concern in the Soviet Union contributed to the forces that brought about the collapse of Communist control. "For Soviet society, the state of the environment, in physical terms, epitomized the state of the Union," he says. "Environmental destruction, added to social, economic, and political stresses, compounded the people's anger and ultimately undermined the Soviet regime. The Soviet Union can be relegated to history, but its *dostizheniya* (achievements), manifest in the legacy of widespread environ-mental destruction, cannot be easily erased. Will the emerging post-Soviet societies cope with the challenge?"

There is a danger that zealous new capitalists, both those within the former Soviet Union and those representing international investors, will overexploit the region's vast natural resources, creating a backlash of public sentiment away from cooperation with the global community, Peterson warns.

"The West bears responsibility, when possible, not to violate the good faith and hopes of the emerging societies in the region. . . . The scale of the post-Soviet environmental challenge, in terms of global interdependence, mandates cooperation to support the democratic alternative," he concludes.

Source: *Troubled Lands: The Legacy of Soviet Environmental Destruction* by D.J. Peterson. Westview Press, 5500 Central Avenue, Boulder, Colorado 80301. 1993. 276 pages. Paperback. $19.95.

Finally, the theory of sustainable development commits in grand fashion the mistake of what Nobel laureate Friedrich von Hayek called "the pretense of knowledge." The detailed and constantly changing "information of time and place" required to produce even the simplest of items efficiently is so immense and so widely dispersed that no one human mind or group of minds with the largest computer in existence could imitate to any degree the efficiency of a decentralized market system. This, after all, is the principal lesson to be learned from the world-wide collapse of socialism.

Moreover, the larger and more complex an economy becomes, the more remote the likelihood that governmental planning could be anything but guess work. As Hayek states in his 1988 book, *The Fatal Conceit,*

By following the spontaneously generated moral traditions underlying the competitive market order . . . we generate and garner greater knowledge and wealth than could ever be obtained or utilized in a centrally directed economy. . . . Thus socialist aims and programs are factually impossible to achieve or execute.

The theory of sustainable development calls for myriad varieties of *international* central planning of economic activity. If the "pretense of knowledge" is fatal to attempts at governmental planning at the national level, the belief that international or global planning could possibly succeed is untenable.

The Brundtland Commission's recommendation that every govern-ment agency in the world engage in economic planning and regulation in the name of environmental protection would lead to a massive bureaucratization of society and, consequently, a sharp drop in living standards. The image of millions of "green" bureaucrats interfering in every aspect of our social and economic lives is frightening.

The irony of it all is that the wealthier economies are typically healthier and cleaner than the poorer ones. By impoverishing the world economy, "sustainable development" would, in fact, also be harmful to the environment. Private property, free markets, and sound liability laws—anathemas to the theory of sustainable development—are essential for a clean environment and for economic growth.

The West's Deepening Cultural Crisis

Growing crime rates, increasing drug problems, rampant violence, and widespread depressive illness are all signs of Western culture's deepening crisis.

Richard Eckersley

Richard Eckersley is a science writer, social analyst, and policy consultant. He has written several major reports for the Australian Commission for the Future on youth, the future, science, technology, and society. His address is 23 Goble Street, Hughes ACT 2605, Australia.

A striking feature of Western civilization is that, for all our success in reducing the toll of lives taken by disease, we have failed to diminish that exacted by despair. According to the World Health Organization, suicide has steadily increased for both males and females in the developed world since the early 1950s.

What makes the trend particularly tragic is that the increase in suicide is occurring mainly among teenagers and young adults, especially males. In several countries, including the United States, Australia, and New Zealand, the suicide rate among young males has more than tripled since 1950.

We have also seen a dramatic deterioration in many indicators of the psychological well-being of youth over this period:

• Authorities and experts worldwide admit the war against illicit drugs is being lost, despite the expenditure of billions of dollars on law enforcement and education programs. Alcohol abuse among the young has become a major problem.

• There is a growing body of research suggesting that major depressive illness is becoming more widespread in Western societies, especially among teenagers and young adults.

• Obsessive dieting has become commonplace among teenage girls, and the incidence of eating disorders is rising. Recent U.S. research indicates that the incidence of anorexia nervosa among girls aged 10 to 19 has increased more than fivefold since the 1950s.

• Rates of crime, mainly an activity of teenage youths and young men, have risen sharply in most, if not all, Western societies since World War II, after a long decline from the high levels of the early 1800s.

The social reality reflected by these statistics is evident in any large Western city. One writer described a walk that he and his wife took through Sydney to "enjoy" the sights of the city:

We didn't. It was as if William Hogarth's *Gin Lane* stretched for blocks. The streets were littered with drunks, some vomiting where they stood. The footpaths outside the hotels were strewn with broken glass. People argued with and hurled abuse at one another. Others with vacant eyes stood mumbling soundlessly to themselves, arms whirling like aimless windmills. Through the streets surged packs of feral teenagers with brutish faces and foul, mindless mouths.

The reference to Hogarth's famous eighteenth-century engraving is apt: Then, the social upheaval and destruction of jobs during the Industrial Revolution, together with a booming population, produced soaring drunkenness, child abuse, and crime.

If the problems I have mentioned were limited to a small fraction of the population, while the vast majority of people were enjoying a richer and fuller life than ever before because of the changes that have taken place in recent decades—and I am not denying that there have been many positive changes—then we could conceivably argue that the problems are a price worth paying.

Yet, this is clearly not the case. Some of the problems, such as mental illness and eating disorders, are now affecting a significant proportion of the population of Western nations. The impact of increasing crime reaches far beyond the victims and perpetrators, tainting all our lives with fear and suspicion and limiting our freedom. Furthermore, surveys of public attitudes show these problems are just the tip of an iceberg of disillusion, discontent, and disaffection.

A Breakdown in Values

The modern scourges of Western civilization, such as youth suicide, drug abuse, and crime, are usually explained in personal, social, and economic terms: unemployment, poverty, child abuse, family breakdown, and so on. And yet my own and other research suggests the trends appear to be, at least to some extent, independent of such factors. They seem to reflect something more fundamental in the nature of Western societies.

I believe this "something" is a profound and growing failure of Western culture—a failure to provide a sense of meaning, belonging, and purpose in our lives, as well as a framework of values. People need to have something to believe in and live for, to feel they are part of a community and a valued member of society, and to have a sense of spiritual fulfillment—that is, a sense of relatedness and connectedness to the world and the universe in which they exist.

The young are most vulnerable to peculiar hazards of our times. They face the difficult metamorphosis from child into adult, deciding who they are and what they believe, and accepting responsibility for their own lives. Yet, modern Western culture offers no firm guidance, no coherent or consistent world view, and no clear moral structure to help them make this transition.

The cultural failing may be more apparent in the "new" Western societies such as the United States, Canada, Australia, and New Zealand than in other Western societies because they are young, heterogeneous nations, without a long, shared cultural heritage or a strong sense of identity, and hence something to anchor them in these turbulent times. Older societies may offer a sense of permanence and continuity that can be very reassuring.

Interestingly, youth suicide rates have not risen in countries such as Spain and Italy, where traditional family and religious ties remain strong. And in Japan, despite the persistent myth of high levels of youth suicide, the rates have plummeted since the 1960s to be among the lowest in the industrial world.

The United States, the pacesetter of the Western world, shows many signs of a society under immense strain, even falling apart. Recent reports and surveys reveal a nation that is confused, divided, and scared. America is said to be suffering its worst crisis of confidence in 30 years and to be coming unglued culturally—the once-successful ethnic melting pot that the United States represented now coagulating into a lumpy mix of minorities and other groups who share few if any common values and beliefs. Most Americans, one survey found, no longer know right from wrong, and most believe there are no national heroes.

Although the symptoms may not be as dramatic, Australians are suffering a similar malaise. Surveys suggest a people who, beneath a professed personal optimism, nonchalance, and hedonism, are fearful, pessimistic, bewildered, cynical, and insecure; who feel destabilized and powerless in the face of accelerating cultural, economic, and technological change; and who are deeply alienated from the country's major institutions, especially government.

Children's Views of the Future

The most chilling of such surveys, in their bleakness, are the studies of how children and adolescents in Western nations see the future of the world. To cite just one example, *The Sydney Morning Herald* in 1990 conducted a survey in which about 120 eleven-year-old Sydney schoolchildren were asked to write down their perceptions of Australia's future and how their country would fare in the new millennium. The idea was to publish a cheerful view of Australia's future. The newspaper chose bright, healthy youngsters, young enough to be untarnished by cynicism, yet this is what the *Herald* said of the results:

Yes, we expected a little economic pessimism, some gloom about the environment and job prospects and perhaps even a continuing fear of nuclear war. But nothing prepared us for the depth of the children's fear of the future, their despair about the state of our planet and their bleak predictions for their own nation, Australia.

In any other culture, at any other time, children this age would be having stories told to them that would help them to construct a world view, a cultural context, to define who they are and what they believe—a context that would give them a positive, confident outlook on life, or at least the fortitude to endure what life held in store for them.

Our children are not hearing these stories.

It may be, then, that the greatest wrong we are doing to our children is not the fractured families or the scarcity of jobs (damaging though these are), but the creation of a culture that gives them little more than themselves to believe in—and no cause for hope or optimism.

At the social level, this absence of faith grievously weakens community cohesion; at the level of the individual, it undermines our resilience, our capacity to cope with the more-personal difficulties and hardships of everyday life.

We can see clearly the consequences for indigenous people, such as American Indians, Innuits (Eskimos), and Australian Aborigines, when their culture is undermined by sustained contact with Western industrial society: the social apathy, the high incidence of suicide, crime, and drug abuse. We are seeing all these things increase among youth in Western societies. Other young people—the majority—may be coping and outwardly happy, but they often suggest a cynicism, hesitancy, and social passivity that reveal their uncertainty and confusion.

In making the individual the focus of Western culture, it seems we have only succeeded in making the individual feel more impotent and insecure. Not surprisingly, the more we feel diminished as individuals, the more insistently we stand up for our rights—producing, as commentators such as Robert Hughes have said of America, a nation of victims, a society pervaded by a culture of complaint.

The evidence strongly suggests that, robbed of a broader meaning to our lives, we have entered an era of often pathological self-preoccupation: with our looks, careers, sex lives, personal development, health and fitness, our children, and so on. Alternatively, the desperate search for meaning and belonging ends in the total subjugation of the self—in, for example, fanatical nationalism and religious fundamentalism. The suicidal deaths earlier this year of more than 80 followers of the Branch Davidian cult in the siege of its Waco, Texas, compound—like the Jonestown massacre in Guyana in 1978—have provided sad evidence of this social sickness.

The harm that modern Western culture is doing to our psychic well-being provides reason enough to forge a new system of values and beliefs. However, the need is made even more critical by the relationship between modern Western culture and the many other serious problems that Western societies face: the seemingly intractable economic difficulties, the widening social gulf, the worsening environmental degradation.

Fundamentally, these are problems of culture, of beliefs, and of moral priorities, not of economics. Furthermore, addressing these problems will require good management; good management requires clarity and strength of purpose and direction. How can we know what to do if we don't know what we believe in and where we want to go?

The Sources of Cultural Decay

There is a range of possible sources of the cultural decay of the West, all linked to the domination of our way of life by science.

The first source is the way science has changed the way we see ourselves and our place in the world through its objective, rational, analytical, quantitative, reductionist focus. Science, its critics say, has caused the crisis of meaning in Western culture by separating fact from value and destroying the "magic" and "enchantment" that gave a spiritual texture to our lives.

A second is the accelerating rate and nature of the changes driven by the growth in science and technology since World War II. These changes have torn us from our past and from the cultural heritage that provided the moral framework to our lives. Science undermined our faith in "God, King, and Country" by replacing it with faith in

"progress": the belief that the life of each individual would always continue to get better—wealthier, healthier, safer, more comfortable, more exciting.

A third source, then, is the collapse of this belief as the limits and costs of progress become ever more apparent: Economic, social, and environmental problems pile up around us; expectations are raised, but remain unmet. We are now failing even by the standard measure of progress: For the first time in many generations, today's youth cannot assume that their material standard of living will be higher than their parents'.

A fourth source of our cultural malaise is one specific set of products of our scientific and technological virtuosity—the mass media. The media have become the most-powerful determinants of our culture, yet we make little attempt to control or direct the media in our best long-term interests. Indeed, the style of public culture dictated by the popular media virtually guarantees that we will fail to address effectively the many serious problems we have.

For all their value and power as instruments of mass education and entertainment, the media:

• Fail to project a coherent and internally consistent world view.

• Divide rather than unite us, fashioning public debate into a battle waged between extremes—a delineation of conflict rather than a search for consensus.

• Heighten our anxieties and intimidate us by depicting the world outside our personal experience as one of turmoil, exploitation, and violence.

• Debase our values and fuel our dissatisfaction by promoting a superficial, materialistic, self-centered, and self-indulgent lifestyle—a way of life that is beyond the reach of a growing number of citizens.

• Erode our sense of self-worth and promote a sense of inadequacy by constantly confronting us with images of lives more powerful, more beautiful, more successful, more exciting.

Science and technology may not be the sole source of the cultural flaws that mar Western civilization. But they have certainly magnified cultural weaknesses to the point where they now threaten our culture—just as, for example, the October 1987 stock-market crash was

caused, in the words of one analyst, by "the emotions that drive a trader, magnified a millionfold by the technology at his disposal."

Creating a More Harmonious Society

If those who see science as intrinsically hostile to human psychic well-being are right, then we could be in for the mother of upheavals as Western civilization falls apart. But I believe that the problem rests more with our immaturity in using a cultural tool as powerful as science, and I remain hopeful that, with growing experience and wisdom, we can create a more benign and complete culture, and so a more equitable and harmonious society.

Aldous Huxley once said that if he had rewritten *Brave New World*—with its vision of a scientifically controlled society in which babies were grown in bottles, free will was abolished by methodical conditioning, and regular doses of chemically induced happiness made servitude tolerable—he would have included a sane alternative, a society in which "science and technology would be used as though, like the Sabbath, they had been made for man, not (as at present and still more so in the Brave New World) as though man were to be adapted and enslaved to them."

Paradoxically, given its role in creating the situation we are in, science can, I believe, provide the impetus for the changes that are required, both through the knowledge it is providing about the human predicament and also, perhaps, through its increasing compatibility with spiritual beliefs.

Having inspired the overemphasis on the individual and the material, science is now leading us back to a world view that pays closer attention to the communal and the spiritual by revealing the extent of our interrelationship and interdependence with the world around us. This is evident in the "spiritual" dimensions of current cosmology, with its suggestion that the emergence of consciousness or mind is written into the laws of nature; in the primary role science has played—through its discovery and elucidation of global warming, ozone depletion, and other global environmental problems—in the "greening" of public consciousness and political agendas in recent years; and in the part that scientists (such as David Suzuki and David Maybury-Lewis) are playing in validating to Westerners the holistic and spiritually rich world view of indigenous peoples.

But science, in effecting change, must itself be changed. While remaining intellectually rigorous, science must become intellectually less arrogant, culturally better integrated, and politically more influential. Science must become more tolerant of other views of reality, other ways of seeing the world. It must become more involved in the processes of public culture. And it must contribute more to setting political agendas.

Arguably, only science is powerful enough to persuade us to redirect its power—to convince us of the seriousness of our situation, to strengthen our resolve to do something about it, and to guide what we do. Science can be the main (but by no means the only) source of knowledge and understanding that we need to remake our culture.

So I am not pessimistic about our prospects, despite the grim trends. Nor do I underestimate the immensity of the challenge. I sometimes do feel, in contemplating what is happening, that we are in the grip of powerful historical currents whose origins go back centuries, perhaps millennia, and against which individuals and even governments can only struggle punily.

Yet, it is also true that people, collectively and individually, can stand against those currents—and even change their course.

A DECADE OF DISCONTINUITY

The 1980s may have been the last decade in which humankind could anticipate a future of ever-increasing productivity on all fronts. By one measure after another, the boom we have experienced since mid-century is coming to an end.

LESTER R. BROWN

When the history of the late 20th century is written, the 1990s will be seen as a decade of discontinuity—a time when familiar trends that had seemed likely to go on forever, like smooth straight roads climbing toward an ever-receding horizon, came to abrupt bends or junctures and began descending abruptly. The world's production of steel, for example, had risen almost as reliably each year as the sun rises in the morning. The amount of coal extracted had risen almost uninterruptedly ever since the Industrial Revolution began. Since the middle of this century, the harvest of grain had grown even faster than population, steadily increasing the amount available both for direct consumption and for conversion into livestock products. The oceanic fish catch, likewise, had more than quadrupled during this period, doubling the consumption of seafood per person.

These rising curves were seen as basic measures of human progress; we *expected* them to rise. But now, within just a few years, these trends have reversed—and with consequences we have yet to grasp. Meanwhile, other trends that were going nowhere, or at most rising slowly, are suddenly soaring.

That such basic agricultural and industrial outputs should begin to decline, while population continues to grow, has engendered disquieting doubts about the future. These reversals, and others likely to follow, are dwarfing the discontinuities that occurred during the 1970s in the wake of the 1973 rise in oil prices. At that time, an overnight tripling of oil prices boosted energy prices across the board, slowed the growth in automobile production, and spurred investment in energy-efficient technologies, creating a whole new industry.

The discontinuities of the 1990s are far more profound, originating not with a handful of national political leaders as with the OPEC ministers of the 1970s, but in the collision between expanding human numbers and needs on the one hand and the constraints of the earth's natural systems on the other. Among these constraints are the capacity of the oceans to yield seafood, of grasslands to produce beef and mutton, of the hydrological cycle to produce fresh water, of crops to use fertilizer, of the atmosphere to absorb CFCs, carbon dioxide, and other greenhouse gases, of people to breathe polluted air, and of forests to withstand acid rain.

Though we may not have noticed them,

these constraints drew dramatically closer between 1950 and 1990, as the global economy expanded nearly fivefold. Expansion on this scale inevitably put excessive pressure on the earth's natural systems, upsetting the natural balances that had lent some stability to historical economic trends. The trends were driven, in part by unprecedented population growth. Those of us born before 1950 have seen world population double. In 1950, 37 million people were added to the world's population. Last year, it was 91 million.

Against the Grain

The production of grain, perhaps the most basic economic measure of human well-being, increased 2.6 fold from 1950 to 1984. Expanding at nearly 3 percent per year, it outstripped population growth, raising per capita grain consumption by 40 percent over the 34-year period, improving nutrition and boosting consumption of livestock products—meat, milk, eggs, and cheese—throughout the world.

That period came to an end, ironically, around the time the United States withdrew its funding from the United Nations Population Fund. During the eight years since 1984, world grain output has expanded perhaps one percent per year. In per capita terms, this means grain production has shifted from its steady rise over the previous 34 years to a *decline* of one percent per year since then—a particularly troubling change both because grain is a basic source of human sustenance and because of the likely difficulty in reversing it (see Figure 1).

This faltering of basic foodstuffs was triggered by other, earlier discontinuities of growth—in the supply of cropland, irrigation water, and agricultural technologies. Cropland, measured in terms of grain harvested area, expanded more or less continuously from the beginning of agriculture until 1981. The spread of agriculture, initially from valley to valley and eventually from continent to continent, had come to a halt. Since 1981, it has not increased. Gains of cropland in some countries have been offset by losses in others, as land is converted to nonfarm uses and abandoned because of erosion.

Irrigation, which set the stage for the emergence of early civilization, expanded gradually over a span of at least 5,000 years. After the middle of this century, the growth in irrigated area accelerated, averaging

nearly 3 percent per year until 1978. Around that time, however, as the number of prime dam construction sites diminished and underground aquifers were depleted by overpumping, the growth of irrigated area fell behind that of population. Faced with a steady shrinkage of cropland area per person from mid-century onward, the world's farmers since 1978 have faced a shrinking irrigated area per person as well.

Although there was little new land to plow from mid-century onward, the world's farmers were able to achieve the largest expansion of food output in history by dramatically raising land productivity. The engine of growth was fertilizer use, which increased ninefold in three decades—from 14 million tons in 1950 to 126 million tons in 1984—before starting to slow (see Figure 2).

In 1990, the rise in fertilizer use—what had been one of the most predictable trends in the world economy—was abruptly reversed. It has fallen some 10 percent during the three years since the 1989 peak of 146 million tons. Economic reforms in the former Soviet Union, which removed heavy fertilizer subsidies, account for most of the decline. Letting fertilizer prices move up to world market levels, combined with weakened demand for farm products, dropped fertilizer use in the former Soviet Union by exactly half between 1988 and 1992. This was an anomalous decline, from which there should eventually be at least a partial recovery.

More broadly, however, growth in world fertilizer use has slowed simply because existing grain varieties in the United States, Western Europe, and Japan cannot economically use much more fertilizer. U.S. farmers, matching applications more precisely to crop needs, actually used nearly one-tenth less fertilizer from 1990 to 1992 than they did a decade earlier. Using more fertilizer in agriculturally advanced countries does not have much effect on production with available varieties.

The backlog of unused agricultural technology that began to expand rapidly in the mid-19th century now appears to be diminishing. In 1847, German agricultural chemist Justus von Leibig discovered that all the nutrients removed by plants could be returned to the soil in their pure form. A decade later, Gregor Mendel discovered the basic principles of genetics, setting the stage for the eventual development of high-yielding, fertilizer-responsive crop varieties.

Falling Capacities: *With human population growing by the equivalent of 12 New York Cities or 11 Somalias a year, the world's food-producing capacity has been seriously strained—and the amount per person now shows signs of reversing its historic growth.*

Figure 1. Grain, the basic staple of both direct human consumption and livestock feed, is now falling in per-person production after decades of growth.

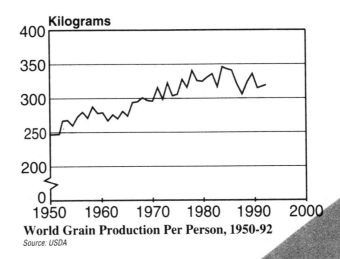

Kilograms

World Grain Production Per Person, 1950-92
Source: USDA

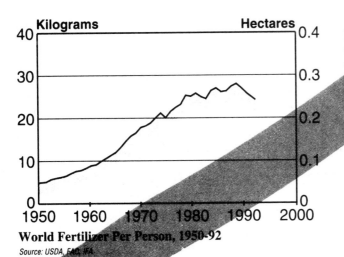

Kilograms   **Hectares**

World Fertilizer Per Person, 1950-92
Source: USDA, FAO, IFA

Figure 2. Fertilizer use, the engine that drove up farm productivity worldwide, is sputtering—and in per-capita terms, is falling.

Figure 3: Fish from the oceans, once thought virtually limitless in supply, may already have reached its global limit—launching a decline in the catch per person that will continue to worsen as long as human population grows.

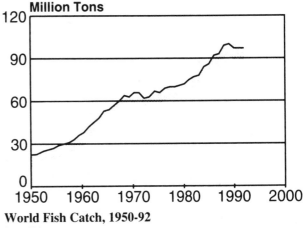

Million Tons

World Fish Catch, 1950-92
Source: FAO

As the geographic frontiers of agricultural expansion disappeared in the mid-20th century, the adoption of high-yielding varieties and rapid growth in fertilizer use boosted land productivity dramatically. In the 1960s, an array of advanced technologies for both wheat and rice producers was introduced into the Third World—giving rise to a growth in grain output that was more rapid than anything that had occurred earlier, even in the industrial countries.

Although it cannot be precisely charted, the backlog of unused agricultural technology must have peaked at least a decade ago. Most of the known means of raising food output are in wide use. The highest-yielding rice variety available to farmers in Asia in 1993 was released in 1966—more than a quarter-century ago. Today, the more progressive farmers are peering over the shoulders of agricultural scientists looking for new help in boosting production, only to find that not much is forthcoming. Agricultural scientists are worried that the rapid advance in technology characterizing the middle decades of this century may not be sustainable.

Less Meat *and* Less Fish
The growth in meat production, like that of grain, is slowing. Between 1950 and 1987, world meat production increased from 46 million tons to 161 million tons—boosting the amount per person from 18 kilograms in 1980 to 32 kilograms (about 70 pounds) in 1987. Since then, however, it has not increased at all. The one percent decline in per capita production in 1992 may be the beginning of a gradual world decline in per capita meat production, another major discontinuity.

Underlying this slowdown in overall meat production is a rather dramatic slowdown in the production of beef and mutton, resulting from the inability of grasslands to support more cattle and sheep. From 1950 to 1990, world beef output increased 2.5-fold. Now, with grasslands almost fully used—or overused—on every continent, this growth may be nearing an end. From 1990 to 1992, per capita beef production for the world fell 6 percent.

The supply of fish, like that of meat, no longer keeps pace with increases in human numbers. Here, too, there has been a reversal of the historic trend. Between 1950 and 1989, the global catch expanded from 22 million tons to 100 million tons. The per capita seafood supply increased from 9 to 19 kilograms during this period. Since 1989, the catch has actually declined slightly, totalling an estimated 97 million tons in 1992 (see Figure 3). United Nations marine biologists believe that the oceans have reached their limit and may not be able to sustain a yield of more than 100 million tons per year.

Throughout this century, it has been possible to increase the fish take by sending out more ships, using more sophisticated fishing technologies, and going, literally, to the farthest reaches of the ocean. That expansion has now come to an end. The world's ocean catch per capita declined 7 percent from 1989 until 1992, and is likely to continue declining as long as population continues to grow. As a result, seafood prices are rising steadily.

Getting more animal protein, whether it be in the form of beef or farm-raised fish, now depends on feeding grain and soybean meal. Those desiring to maintain animal protein intake now compete with those trying to consume more grain directly.

Table 1. Growth and Decline in Production of Fossil Fuels, 1950-92

Fossil Fuel	Growth Period		Decline Period	
	Years	Annual Rate (percent)	Years	Annual Rate (percent)
Oil	1950-79	+ 6.4	1979-92	- 0.5
Coal	1950-89	+ 2.2	1989-92	- 0.6
Natural Gas	1950-92	+ 6.2		

Fossil Fuels: The Beginning of the End
While biological constraints are forcing discontinuities in agriculture and oceanic fisheries, it is atmospheric constraints—the mounting risks associated with pollution and global warming—that are altering energy trends. Throughout the world energy economy, there are signs that a major restructuring is imminent. On the broadest level, this will entail a shifting of investment from fossil fuels and nuclear power toward **renewables—and toward greater energy efficiency in every human activity.**

We cannot yet see the end of the fossil fuel age, but we can see the beginning of its decline. World oil production peaked in 1979 (see Table 1). Output in 1992 was four percent below that historical high. World coal production dropped in 1990, in 1991, and again in 1992 (partly because of the recession), interrupting a growth trend that had spanned two centuries. If strong global warming policies are implemented, this could be the beginning of a long-term decline in coal dependence.

Of the three fossil fuels, only natural gas is expanding output rapidly and is assured of substantial future growth. Gas burns cleanly and produces less carbon dioxide than the others, and is therefore less likely to be constrained by stricter environmental policies. While oil production has fallen since 1979, gas production has risen by one-third.

With oil, it was the higher price that initially arrested growth. More recently, it has been the pall of automotive air pollution in cities like Los Angeles, Mexico City, and Rome that has slowed the once-unrestrained growth in motor vehicle use and, therefore, in oil use. With coal, it was neither supply nor price (the world has at least a few centuries of coal reserves left), but the effects of air pollution on human health, of acid rain on forests and crops, and of rising CO_2 concentrations on the earth's climate that have sent the industry into decline. Several industrial countries have committed themselves to reducing carbon emissions. Germany, for example, plans to cut carbon emissions 25 percent by 2005. Switzerland is shooting for a 10 percent cut by 2000, and Australia for 20 percent by 2005. Others, including the United States, may soon join them.

With the beginning of the end of the fossil fuel age in sight, what then will be used to power the world economy? Fifteen years ago, many would have said, with little hesitation, that nuclear power will. Once widely thought to be the energy source of the future, it has failed to live up to its promise (the problems of waste disposal and safety have proved expensive and intractable) and is being challenged on economic grounds in most of the countries where it is produced.

Nuclear generating capacity reached its historical peak in 1990. Though it has declined only slightly since then, it now seems unlikely that there will be much, if any, additional growth in nuclear generating capacity during this decade—and perhaps ever.

The Winds of Change

Even as the nuclear and fossil fuel industries have faltered, three new technologies that harness energy directly or indirectly from the sun to produce electricity—solar thermal power plants, photovoltaic cells, and wind generators—are surging. In wind power, particularly, breakthroughs in turbine technol-

ogy are setting the stage for rapid expansion in the years ahead. Wind electricity generated in California already produces enough electricity to satisfy the residential needs of San Francisco and Washington, D.C. Indeed, it now seems likely that during the 1990s, the growth in wind generating capacity will exceed that in nuclear generating capacity. Three countries—Denmark, the Netherlands, and Germany—have plans to develop a minimum of a thousand megawatts of wind

Table 2. World Economic Growth by Decade, 1950-93

Decade	Annual Growth of World Economy	Annual Growth Per Person
1950-60	4.9	3.1
1960-70	5.2	3.2
1970-80	3.4	1.6
1980-90	2.9	1.1
1990-93 (prel.)	0.9	−0.8

generating capacity by 2005. China aims to reach the same goal by 2000. Given the rapid advances in the efficiency of wind generating machines and the falling costs of wind generated electricity, the growth in wind power over the remainder of this decade could dwarf even current expectations.

The potential for wind power far exceeds that of hydropower, which currently supplies the world with one-fifth of its electricity. England and Scotland alone have enough wind generating potential to satisfy half of Europe's electricity needs. Two U.S. states— Montana and Texas—each have enough wind to satisfy the whole country's electricity needs. The upper Midwest (the Dakotas east through Ohio) could supply the country's electricity without siting any wind turbines in either densely populated or environmentally sensitive areas. And wind resource assessments by the government of China have documented 472,000 megawatts of wind generating potential, enough to raise China's electricity supply threefold.

For Third World villages not yet connected to a grid, a more practical source is photovoltaic arrays, which may already have a competitive advantage. With the World Bank beginning to support this technology, costs will fall fast, making photovoltaic cells even more competitive. Wind, photovoltaic cells, and solar thermal power plants all promise inexpensive electricity as the technologies continue to advance and as the economies of scale expand. Over the longer term, cheap solar electricity in various forms will permit the conversion of electricity into hydrogen, which will offer an efficient means of energy transportation and storage.

Technological advances that increase the *efficiency* of energy use are in some ways even more dramatic than the advances in harnessing solar and wind resources. Striking gains have been made in the energy efficiency of electric lighting, electric motors, the thermal efficiency of windows, and cogenerating technologies that produce both electricity and heat. One of the most dramatic, as recently noted in *World Watch* (May/June 1993), is the new compact fluorescent light bulb—which can supply the same amount of light as an incandescent bulb while using only one-fourth as much electricity. The 134 million compact fluorescent bulbs sold worldwide in 1992 saved enough electricity to close 10 large coal-fired power plants.

The discontinuities that have wreaked havoc with once-reliable trends are not random, but reflect an escalating awareness of the need to transform the global economy into one that is sustainable. They reflect the unavoidable reality that we have entered an era in which satisfying the needs of the 91 million people being added each year depends on reducing consumption among those already here. At this rate, by the year 2010, this growth will amount to a net addition equal to nearly 200 cities the size of New York, or 100 countries the size of Iraq—dramatically reducing the per capita availability of cropland and irrigation water. At some point, as people begin to grasp the implications of this new reality, population policy will become a central concern of national governments.

Economic Entropy

Whether in basic foodstuffs and fresh water, or in overall economic output, the decade of discontinuity has begun. Growth in the world economy reached its historical high at 5.2 percent per year during the 1960s (see Table 2). It then slowed to 3.4 percent per year in the 1970s, and 2.9 percent in the 1980s. Despite this slowdown, the per capita output of goods and services rose as overall economic growth stayed ahead of population growth. Now that, too, may be reversing.

From 1990 to 1992, the world economy expanded at 0.6 percent per year. If the International Monetary Fund's recent projection of 2.2 percent in world economic growth for 1993 materializes, we will find ourselves three years into this decade with an income per person nearly 2 percent lower than it was when the decade began. Even using an economic accounting system that overstates progress because it omits environmental degradation and the depletion of natural capital, living standards are falling.

Evidence is accumulating that the world economy is not growing as easily in the 1990s as it once did. The conventional economic wisdom concerning the recession of the early 1990s attributes it to economic mismanagement in the advanced industrial countries (particularly the United States, Germany, and Japan) and to the disruption associated with economic reform in the centrally planned economies. These are obviously the dominant forces slowing world economic growth, but they are not the only ones. As noted above, growth in the fishing industry, which supplies much of the world's animal protein, may have stopped. Growth in the production of beef, mutton, and other livestock products from the world's rangelands may also be close to an end. The world grain harvest shows little prospect of being able to keep pace with population, much less to eliminate hunger. And scarcities of fresh water are limiting economic expansion in many countries. With constraints emerging in these primary economic sectors—sectors on which much of the Third World depends—we may be moving into an era of slower economic growth overall.

The popular question of "growth or no growth" now seems largely irrelevant. A more fundamental question is how to satisfy the basic needs of the world's people without further disrupting or destroying the economy's support systems. The real challenge for the 1990s is that of deciding how the basic needs of all people can be satisfied without jeopardizing the prospects of future generations.

Of all the discontinuities that have become apparent in the past few years, however, it is an upward shift in the population growth trend itself that may be most disturbing. The progress in slowing human population growth so evident in the 1970s has stalled—with alarming implications for the long-term population trajectory. Throughout the 1960s and 1970s, declining fertility held out hope for getting the brakes on population growth before it began to undermine living standards. The 1980s, however, turned out to be a lost decade, one in which the United States not only abdicated its leadership role, but also withdrew all financial support from the U.N. Population Fund and the International Planned Parenthood Federation. This deprived millions of couples in the Third World of access to the family planning services needed to control the number or timing of their children.

The concern that population growth could undermine living standards has become a reality in this decade of discontinuity. There is now a distinct possibility that the grain supply per person will be lower at the end of this decade than at the beginning, that the amount of seafood per person will be substantially less, and that the amount of meat per person will also be far less than it is today.

The absence of any technology to reestablish the rapid growth in food production that existed from 1950 to 1984 is a matter of deepening concern. In early 1992, the U.S. National Academy of Sciences and the Royal Society of London together issued a report that warned: "If current predictions of population growth prove accurate and patterns of human activity on the planet remain unchanged, science and technology may not be able to prevent either irreversible degradation of the environment or continued poverty for much of the world."

Later in the year, the Union of Concerned Scientists issued a statement signed by nearly 1,600 of the world's leading scientists, including 96 Nobel Prize recipients, noting that the continuation of destructive human activities "may so alter the living world that it will be unable to sustain life in the manner that we know." The statement warned: "A great change in our stewardship of the earth and the life on it is required, if vast human misery is to be avoided and our global home on this planet is not to be irretrievably mutilated."

The discontinuities reshaping the global economy define the challenge facing humanity in the next few years. It is a challenge not to the survival of our species, but to civilization as we know it. The question we can no longer avoid asking is whether our social institutions are capable of quickly slowing and stabilizing population growth without infringing on human rights. Even as that effort gets underway, the same institutions face the complex issue of how to distribute those resources that are no longer expanding, among a population that is continuing to grow by record numbers each year.

This article is adapted from the overview chapter of Vital Signs 1993: The Trends That Are Shaping Our Future, *by Lester R. Brown, Hal Kane, and Ed Ayres, published by W.W. Norton and the Worldwatch Institute in July.*

Crowded out

Population-control advocates are often dismissed as racist and paranoid. But they increasingly have the facts on their side.

Will Nixon

Will Nixon is associate editor of E Magazine.

Americans always imagine that the disaster of overpopulation lies somewhere in the future, as in the 1973 science fiction movie *Soylent Green,* which envisioned a world so crowded that giant scoopers had to clear people like dirt from city squares. But we could just as easily look to the past. "Countryside hovels teemed with young children. . . . In the larger cities, a floating population of tens of thousands of unemployed slept on the ground overnight and poured into the streets the next day. Jails, pauper houses, foundling hospitals and lunatic asylums were packed with human casualties who had not yet arrived at their common grave," writes Yale historian Paul Kennedy in *Preparing for the Twenty-First Century.*

Kennedy is describing Europe in 1798, when the Caucasian population explosion was contributing to the social ferment of the French Revolution and inspiring Thomas Malthus to write *An Essay on the Principle of Population.* The Puritan professor was wrong about many things, such as failing to foresee the acceptance of contraception. But he was right to fear the potential gap between the exponential growth of human population and the linear growth of the food supply.

Malthus remains with us today mainly as an epithet cast at those who worry too publicly about the dangers of the world's rapidly growing population. Alexander Cockburn, in a series of columns in *The Nation* this year, has caricatured the new Malthusians as racist "overlords" eager to lock the gates against the world's poor and to promote sterilization as the cure for welfare. Cockburn writes in satirical

extremes, but many on the left still assume that "population" must be a code word for something sinister, masking the real issue of the distribution of wealth in the world. Once people in developing countries unshackle themselves from multinational capitalism and rise out of poverty, they will naturally have fewer children, or so the left claims. We should call for new economics, not new biology.

But the new Malthusians are hardly ogres—or even necessarily capitalists. In the debates over population, ideological lines are hardly so clear-cut; indeed, the most strident attacks on population control have come from Lyndon LaRouche. (In a recent full-page ad in the *Washington Post Weekly Edition,* LaRouche's Schiller Institute predicts "a new era of deliberate, global depopulation which will far surpass in savagery even Hitler's dreams.") Many on the right, only a little less stridently, dismiss concerns with population as disguised attempts to push an agenda of abortion and social control. Most capitalists, looking on people as potential customers, have no more interest in controlling population growth than Cockburn does.

The new Malthusians, often biologists by profession, simply do not share the common faith that humans are somehow exempt from the natural forces that lead other species to surge and collapse. At the least, they suggest that continued rapid population growth will add tremendous strains to the social problems we already have, from employment to ethnic strife to environmental degradation. The great spread of people is already causing the largest wave of extinctions since a meteor crash caused the death of the dinosaurs 65 million years ago. At the worst, the new Malthusians foresee a crash in the human population in the next century if we don't take steps right now

to change our reproductive behavior. It's this aura of apocalypse more than anything else, I think, that has made them pariahs. I don't care for the bleakness, either, especially if it comes tinged with misanthropy, but they are addressing one of the fundamental issues of our time.

The world today has 5.5 billion people, and the population grows by some 90 million each year. By the year 2000, the population of the world will likely top 6.2 billion. By the middle of the next century, according to United Nations estimates, population could reach 8 to 12 billion, depending on how quickly fertility rates drop. The International Conference on Population and Development, which is meeting in Cairo this month [Sept. 1994], has drafted a plan of action to steer us to the lower target. After 30 years of experience in the field, family planners believe we now know how to lower fertility rates. It doesn't require the redistribution of wealth so much as the empowerment of women—improved education for girls and women, better maternal health care, the freedom to choose the size of one's family. Only a decade ago, many feminists bristled at the concept of "population control"; now their ideas form the center of the debate. The major opposition to the conference now comes from the Vatican, which opposes abortion and birth control.

In the preparatory meetings for Cairo, the planners paid no attention to the neo-Malthusians. "The purpose of the conference is to bury Malthus, not to praise him," says Alex Marshall, who handles media for the United Nations Population Fund. The delegates have rejected the doomsday scenarios, dismissing "carrying capacity" and "optimum human populations" as fuzzy science at best, full of latent value judgments about how others should live. "In the Netherlands, people

From *In These Times,* September 5, 1994, pp. 14-18. © 1994 by the Institute for Public Affairs. Reprinted by permission of *In These Times,* a biweekly newsmagazine published in Chicago.

live comfortably with a density similar to that in Bangladesh," he says. And the population surge is not a spigot we can simply turn off because someone says the world would be a better place with 2 billion inhabitants. "No conceivable natural or human disaster is going to make much of a dent" in the growing wave toward 8 billion people, Marshall says, so conference delegates have focused on what the world can do to hold population growth to this level.

But the vital question that won't be debated at Cairo is whether the planet can even support 8 billion people. In the early '70s, Paul Ehrlich's book *The Population Bomb* galvanized the public by raising the specter of mass famine and impending scarcities of raw materials. His argument still thrives, albeit revised and refined, but the warning that struck a chord this year was Robert Kaplan's

"The Coming Anarchy" in the February *Atlantic Monthly*. Kaplan doesn't write about starvation or shortages; instead, he suggests that the environment will become "*the* national-security issue of the 21st century," because "surging populations, spreading disease, deforestation and soil erosion, water depletion [and] air pollution" will exacerbate the tensions between countries and between governments and their people. In West Africa, all too many people have egg-yolk eyes from repeated bouts of malaria, guards escort diners at restaurants across the sidewalk to their cars and bandits control the countryside. Kaplan foresees the same for much of the developing world. "We are entering a bifurcated world," he writes. "Part of the globe is inhabited by Hegel's and Fukuyama's Last Man, healthy, well fed and pampered by technology. The other,

larger, part is inhabited by Hobbes' First Man, condemned to a life that is 'nasty, brutish, and short.' Although both parts will be threatened by environmental stress, the Last Man will be able to master it; the First Man will not."

Overpopulation, Kaplan's article suggested, does not simply mean the starving children on UNICEF posters; it also means gun-wielding Somali teens dragging the bodies of their victims through the streets. "In the developing world," he writes, "environmental stress will present people with a choice that is increasingly among totalitarianism (as in Iraq), fascist-tending mini-states (as in Serb-held Bosnia) and road-warrior cultures (as in Somalia)." Two months after the article appeared, Rwanda, the most densely populated country in Africa, erupted in genocidal chaos, grisly coda to Kaplan's argument.

A sea change in U.S. policy

In what one leading advocate described as an "exceptionally important moment" in world population control, President Clinton recently announced a major shift in U.S. policy. At a State Department speech in July, the president declared that Washington—the world's leading contributor to population-control efforts—would no longer merely emphasize family planning.

Citing research showing that educated and empowered women have fewer babies, Clinton declared that "at the top of our agenda will be active support for the efforts to invest in the women of the world." He outlined a plan of action that called for equal education for girls, full rights of citizenship for women and the end of discrimination against women at home and in the workplace.

The speech didn't get Clinton much play in the American press; population control is generally considered too mushy for hard-nosed news editors. Nor did Clinton's bold new vision—endorsing prevention through universally available contraception and women's economic and social empowerment—endear him to powerful domestic lobbies, including the Roman Catholic Church, conservative Republicans and pro-life activists.

Much to their chagrin, Clinton expressed the hope that "new, high-quality, voluntary family planning and reproductive programs" would be available to

every person worldwide in just a few years. "Parents must have the right to decide freely and responsibly the number and spacing of their children," he claimed, endorsing the draft plan of action for this month's U.N. population conference in Cairo.

Many advocates in the field of sustainable development and population policy are pleased with the president's new policy. "I've been in this business 25 years, but in my entire career this was perhaps the most exceptionally important moment," says Adrienne Germain of the International Women's Health Coalition. "The president made clear the sea change in U.S. policy," "This field has never before dealt directly with the issues of sex and power relations."

But even some within the population community are concerned about Clinton's new approach, fearing that it strays too far afield from the concrete mechanics of family planning. They point out that the notion of full empowerment of women may seem abstract, even frivolous, when Third World women may be more concerned about feeding themselves and their families.

Still, Tim Wirth, a former Colorado senator who is now the State Department official in charge of formulating U.S. population-control policy, believes that empowerment of women is the necessary prerequisite to stabilizing population

growth. "In too many parts of the world, girls are fed less, given less medical care, withdrawn from school earlier and forced into hard labor sooner than boys," says Wirth. "And, although they perform an estimated 60 percent of the world's work, women own only 1 percent of the world's land and earn just 10 percent of the world's income."

The administration's makeover of U.S. population policy will have a ripple effect around the world. The United States is the single-largest contributor to population activities, earmarking $585 million in this year's budget for population stabilization. And the U.S. delegation to Cairo, led by Bella Abzug and comprised mostly of women, will loudly advocate the new themes of universally available contraception and the empowerment of women.

The developing world does want the United States' money. But lectures on stabilizing population irritate some leaders, who charge that the developed world's greedy consumption is more a threat to the Earth than Third World population booms. Notes another participant at the State Department event, Chief Bisi Ogunleye of Nigeria: "It is time for the rich to share their riches. If you don't, the poor will share their poverty."

—April Oliver (Sarah Colt contributed research to this article.)

Cockburn devoted two columns to calling Kaplan a racist, the U.N.'s Marshall wrote a letter to the *Atlantic* pointing out all the good that developing nations have accomplished, and many others read Kaplan as a dour traveller who looked upon all the countries he visited with a jaundiced eye. I'm not so sure. From Haiti to Somalia, from Chiapas to the Philippines, we see rural people in violent crises, with surging populations and declining natural resources. These people have been punished, too, by cruel politics and exploitative economics, but they still face the sheer crowding of the land. And, as Paul Kennedy has argued, these people don't really have the same options that Europeans had in Malthus' time: there's no undeveloped New World to which they can migrate.

The true pessimists in the debate are the naturalists watching the wild Earth vanish under the sprawl of people, who are consuming natural resources much faster than nature can possibly replenish them. "In the world where I spend my time—[among] thousands of people who are mostly scientists—there is no controversy," says Donella Meadows, who teaches environmental studies at Dartmouth College. "There is a hands-up-in-the-air helplessness. They expect a vast and terrible crash, and they can do nothing about it."

Meadows worked with the team that produced *The Limits to Growth* in 1972 and *Beyond the Limits* in 1992, two landmark studies that used computer models to predict future collisions over the next century between an economy geared to unlimited growth and a planet with limited resources. Since the industrial revolution, she notes, we have lost half of the world's wetlands and half of its tropical forests. Traditional economists have countered *Limits* by insisting that the market can handle the problems of environmental overuse: as resources grow scarce, the economists argue, they grow more expensive, spurring technological innovations that allow us new alternatives. But rising prices can just as easily set off a feeding frenzy—as capitalists and poachers chase after the last rhinos and tigers, virgin redwoods and tropical teak trees.

So far, society has survived the shortages and the environmental stresses, but computer scenarios suggest that eventually our luck will run out: the various crises will come to a head all at once. "[T]he world system does not run out of land or food or resources or pollution absorption capability," Meadows warns, *"it runs out of the ability to cope."* And so, like any other species that exceeds the carrying capacity of its ecosystem, we face the prospect of a catastrophic population collapse—unless we can stabilize the world population at 8 billion or so.

David Pimental, an agricultural expert at Cornell University, dismisses 8 billion as a virtual sentence of poverty. His studies suggest that an "optimum human population" of 2 billion could be reached by 2100. "And I'm the optimist," he insists. "I've heard of three other studies that project 500 to 600 million." Pimental sees land as the ultimate limit. Each person needs about 0.5 hectares of cropland to provide themselves a nutritious diet of plants and animals, he notes. While some countries—such as the United States—have more than enough land to feed their current inhabitants, the world average is only about half this amount, which partly explains why 1.2 to 2 billion people live in poverty. To keep up with 90 million new mouths to feed each year and to replace the farmland spoiled by erosion, desertification or acidification, we will need to clear about 15 million hectares of forests a year for new cropland. We can't do that forever.

But the real crunch will come after we've run out of fossil fuels. We'll have to rely on biomass fuels from plants and trees, as well as on photovoltaic panels that directly generate electricity. Both technologies take up a great deal of room. A city of 100,000 people would need some 200,000 hectares of forests for fuel or 2,700 hectares for solar panels. Pimental suggests that the world population would have to drop to 2 billion in order for the planet to support all of its citizens at the standard of living now enjoyed by present-day Europeans. But he doubts that the world will take such drastic steps to lower its birthrates.

Some people in the family planning field dismiss Meadows and Pimental as academics with too much faith in their computer models. It's hard to treat 100-year forecasts as anything but intriguing exercises. And Paul Ehrlich made doomsday predictions in the early '70s that sound like howlers today. But why look ahead 100 years? The world already suffers from social injustice and environmental abuse. In 1993, the global grain harvest fell by 5 percent. Nine of the 17 major ocean fisheries are in serious decline. We lose topsoil 20 to 40 times faster than nature replenishes it. And yet we assume that we can simply outgrow these problems.

The truly radical idea, Meadows suggests, would be to meet our crises without counting on growth as the only answer. "The moment you recognize limits the question of sharing becomes absolutely foremost in your mind," she says. Sharing our wealth, sharing our resources, sharing our knowledge. The new Malthusians don't ask us to close the door against the world's poor, but to begin respecting them as neighbors.

Credits/ Acknowledgments

Cover design by Charles Vitelli

Introduction

Facing overview—United Nations photo by John Isaac.

1. Social Problems

Facing overview—Dushkin Publishing Group/Brown & Benchmark Publishers photo.

2. Crime, Delinquency, and Violence

Facing overview—National Archives photo.

3. Aging, Health, and Health Care Issues

Facing overview—United Nations photo by Jeffrey J. Foxx.

4. Poverty and Inequality

Facing overview—United Nations photo by P. S. Sudhakaran.

5. Cultural Pluralism

Facing overview—United Nations photo by L. Solmssen.

6. Cities, Urban Growth, and the Quality of Life

Facing overview—EPA Documerica photo.

7. Drug and Sexual Issues

Facing overview—Partnership for a Drug-Free America photo.

8. Global Issues

Facing overview—United Nations photo.

ANNUAL EDITIONS ARTICLE REVIEW FORM

■ NAME: _____ DATE: _____

■ TITLE AND NUMBER OF ARTICLE: _____

■ BRIEFLY STATE THE MAIN IDEA OF THIS ARTICLE: _____

_____

_____

_____

_____

■ LIST THREE IMPORTANT FACTS THAT THE AUTHOR USES TO SUPPORT THE MAIN IDEA:

_____

_____

_____

_____

_____

_____

■ WHAT INFORMATION OR IDEAS DISCUSSED IN THIS ARTICLE ARE ALSO DISCUSSED IN YOUR
TEXTBOOK OR OTHER READING YOU HAVE DONE? LIST THE TEXTBOOK CHAPTERS AND PAGE
NUMBERS:

_____

_____

_____

_____

_____

_____

■ LIST ANY EXAMPLES OF BIAS OR FAULTY REASONING THAT YOU FOUND IN THE ARTICLE:

_____

_____

_____

_____

■ LIST ANY NEW TERMS/CONCEPTS THAT WERE DISCUSSED IN THE ARTICLE AND WRITE A
SHORT DEFINITION:

_____

_____

_____

_____

*Your instructor may require you to use this Annual Editions Article Review Form in any number of ways:
for articles that are assigned, for extra credit, as a tool to assist in developing assigned papers, or simply
for your own reference. Even if it is not required, we encourage you to photocopy and use this page;
you'll find that reflecting on the articles will greatly enhance the information from your text.

ANNUAL EDITIONS: SOCIAL PROBLEMS 95/96
Article Rating Form

Here is an opportunity for you to have direct input into the next revision of this volume. We would like you to rate each of the 42 articles listed below, using the following scale:

1. **Excellent: should definitely be retained**
2. **Above average: should probably be retained**
3. **Below average: should probably be deleted**
4. **Poor: should definitely be deleted**

Your ratings will play a vital part in the next revision. So please mail this prepaid form to us just as soon as you complete it.
Thanks for your help!

Annual Editions revisions depend on two major opinion sources: one is our Advisory Board, listed in the front of this volume, which works with us in scanning the thousands of articles published in the public press each year; the other is you—the person actually using the book. Please help us and the users of the next edition by completing the prepaid article rating form on this page and returning it to us. Thank you.

Rating	Article	Rating	Article
	1. Social Problems: Definitions, Theories, and Analysis		20. Mental Illness Is Still a Myth
	2. How Social Problems Are Born		21. Who's Protecting Bad Doctors?
	3. Fount of Virtue, Spring of Wealth: How the Strong Family Sustains a Prosperous Society		22. Old Traps, New Twists
			23. Does Welfare Bring More Babies?
			24. Going Private
	4. Endangered Family		25. No Exit
	5. The Disease Is Adolescence		26. When Problems Outrun Policy
	6. Why Leave Children with Bad Parents?		27. An American Melting Plot
	7. The New Outlaws: Cities Make Homelessness a Crime		28. America: Still a Melting Pot?
			29. Is White Racism the Problem?
	8. Getting Serious about Crime		30. Can We Stop the Decline of Our Cities?
	9. Ethics, Neurochemistry, and Violence Control		31. Visions of Community in an Urban War Zone
	10. Crime Takes on a Feminine Face		32. Cities of Violence
	11. Danger in the Safety Zone		33. Terminal Decline of a Nation
	12. Honey, I Warped the Kids		34. Off Course
	13. The Economics of Crime		35. Truth and Consequences: Teen Sex
	14. The Global Crime Wave and What We Can Do about It		36. A Society of Suspects: The War on Drugs and Civil Liberties
	15. Old Money		37. Separating the Sisters
	16. The New Face of Aging		38. The Rape of the Oceans
	17. Risky Business		39. The Mirage of Sustainable Development
	18. Deadly Migration		40. The West's Deepening Cultural Crisis
	19. Confronting the AIDS Pandemic		41. A Decade of Discontinuity
			42. Crowded Out

(Continued on next page)

ABOUT YOU

Name_____ Date_____

Are you a teacher? ☐   Or student? ☐

Your School Name _____

Department _____

Address _____

City _____ State _____ Zip _____

School Telephone # _____

YOUR COMMENTS ARE IMPORTANT TO US!

Please fill in the following information:

For which course did you use this book? _____

Did you use a text with this Annual Edition?   ☐ yes   ☐ no

The title of the text? _____

What are your general reactions to the Annual Editions concept?

Have you read any particular articles recently that you think should be included in the next edition?

Are there any articles you feel should be replaced in the next edition? Why?

Are there other areas that you feel would utilize an Annual Edition?

May we contact you for editorial input?

May we quote you from above?